MILTON MCC. GATCH is a member of the department of English at the University of Missouri, Columbia, Missouri. He is the author of *Death: Meaning and Mortality in Christian Thought and Contemporary Culture*, and *Loyalties and Traditions: Man and his World in Old English Literature*.

In *Preaching and Theology in Anglo-Saxon England*, Professor Gatch deals with two aspects of the writings of Ælfric and Wulfstan that have been hitherto ignored by scholars of the period.

First, he investigates the uses for which the two homilists prepared their sermons, analysing the homiliaries of the Carolingian church and its legislation concerning preaching and teaching, and showing that one should look not to the model of patristic preaching but to the development, in the place of exegetical preaching, of a vernacular catechetical office, the Prone. He also considers the evidence from England in the time of Ælfric and Wulfstan, distinguishing a number of uses which Ælfric intended for his homiletic materials, but questioning whether users of Ælfric's work (Wulfstan perhaps among them) understood or accepted the basic homiletic practices that the abbot had in mind.

Second, Gatch investigates the eschatological teaching of the homilists as specimen of the over-all content of their sermons and as indicator of their theological method. By throwing their work into relief against the background of the anonymous Old English homilists, he gives a more accurate picture than exists in textbook stereotypes of the beliefs of Ælfric and Wulfstan, and also of the general theological scene in England at the turn of the tenth and eleventh centuries.

The first complete edition of Ælfric's Latin epitome of Julian of Toledo's *Prognosticon futuri saeculi*, one of the most important of Ælfric's theological sources, is appended to the text.

This interdisciplinary study is an important addition to our knowledge of Anglo-Saxon culture and medieval church history, and a major contribution to the study of Old English homilies. For the uninitiated, it is an excellent introduction to Old English preaching; for the initiated, it opens a new field for investigation.

Frontispiece: Cambridge, Trinity College MS B.15.34, p. 1. Christ as Judge (The inscription on the breast reads IUSTUS IUDEX; on the knees REX REGUM; on the open book, *ego sum qui de morte surrexi; ego uiuo in eternum/ lux mundi; Ego uenio in die iudicii.*)

MILTON McC. GATCH

Preaching and Theology in Anglo-Saxon England: Ælfric and Wulfstan

UNIVERSITY OF TORONTO PRESS
Toronto and Buffalo

© University of Toronto Press 1977
Toronto and Buffalo
Printed in USA

Library of Congress Cataloging in Publication Data

Gatch, Milton McC
Preaching and theology in Anglo-Saxon England.

'Aelfric's excerpts from Julian of Toledo, Prognosticon futuri saeculi': p.
Bibliography: p.
Includes indexes.
1. Preaching – History – England. 2. Eschatology – History of doctrines – Middle
Ages, 600-1500. 3. Aelfric, Abbot of Eynsham. 4. Wulfstan II, Abp. of York, d. 1023.
I. Julianus, Saint, Bp. of Toledo, d. 690. Prognosticon futuri seculi. Selections. 1977.
II. Title.
BV4208.G7G37   251'.00942   77-3277
ISBN 0-8020-5347-5

This book has been published during the
Sesquicentennial year of the University of Toronto

DOROTHEAE BETHVRVM LOOMIS
et
IOANNI COLLINS POPE

discipulis erudentissimis Lupi Ælfricique
hic libellus ab auctore offertur

Acknowledgments

This volume has been more than a decade in the making; and I have incurred many debts in that time to teachers, colleagues, and friends whose wisdom and learning have helped to make this a better book, the residual shortcomings of which are entirely attributable to me. The greatest debts are inadequately acknowledged in the dedication of this volume to two scholars without whose published work and personal generosity this study could not have been written. Enid Raynes Edwards graciously relinquished her prior claim on the Latin text published in the appendix. Alan K. Brown most generously allowed me to report some of his unpublished findings on borrowings by Wulfstan from Abbo of St-Germain-des-Près. My last revisions were made in 1974–75 at Cambridge, where Michael Lapidge of Clare Hall both made me welcome in college and gave advice on matters pertaining to Anglo-Latin, Rosamund Pierce stimulated my thinking about Carolingian backgrounds of Anglo-Saxon preaching, and Dorothy Whitelock offered useful observations on Anglo-Saxon texts discussed in Part Two. Of others who have assisted me, I can name only a few: Roland H. Bainton, Jaroslav J. Pelikan, and Edward R. Hardy, among historical theologians; Rowland L. Collins and Paul Szarmach in Old English studies; and, above all, my colleague at the University of Missouri, George B. Pace. Several of my students, notably Mary Catherine Bodden, Cynthia E. Cornell, and Linda E. Voigts, have helped to prepare copy; Carey W. Kaltenbach assisted with the bibliography. The librarians at the University of Missouri, Harvard, and Yale, the British Museum, and the Bibliothèque publique at Boulogne-sur-Mer have been extremely helpful. My work has received generous support from the Research Council of the University of Missouri. Among other things, the council provided for the services of an expert typist, Jane McClure Bell. Rose McClure the administrative assistant of my department, ensured that the chairman could devote himself to scholarship from time to time. John Leyerle, Director of the

Centre for Medieval Studies of the University of Toronto, and Angus Cameron, also of the Centre, have been more than generous in offering assistance and advice; and members of the editorial staff of the University of Toronto Press have been unusually attentive and helpful.

Portions of editions issued by the Early English Text Society are quoted by courtesy of the Council of the Early English Text Society; and passages from *The Homilies of Wulfstan,* edited by Dorothy Bethurum, are reproduced by permission of the Oxford University Press, Oxford. The publisher and I are also indebted to the Conservateur of the Bibliothèque municipale at Boulogne-sur-Mer (Pas de Calais) for permission to print an edition of folios 1–10 of their MS 63 and to the Master and Fellows of Trinity College, Cambridge, for permission to reproduce the frontispiece.

Publication of this book has been made possible by grants from the University of Toronto Press using funds provided by the Andrew W. Mellon Foundation and from the Research Council of the Graduate School of the University of Missouri-Columbia.

M. MCC. G.
Columbia, Missouri
Epiphany, 1976

Contents

Abbreviations

Archiv	*Archiv für das Studium der neueren Sprachen und Literaturen*
ASE	*Anglo-Saxon England*, ed. Peter Clemoes (Cambridge, 1972 sqq.)
Assmann	Bruno Assmann, ed., *Angelsächsische Homilien und Heiligenleben*, Bibliothek der angelsächsischen Prosa, 3 (1889; rpt. with Suppl. Intro. by Peter Clemoes, Darmstadt, 1964)
Bede, *HE*	Bede, *Historia Ecclesiastica Gentis Anglorum*
Belfour	A.O. Belfour, ed., *Twelfth Century Homilies in MS Bodley 343*, I, E.E.T.S., O.S., 137 (London, 1909)
Bethurum	Dorothy Bethurum, ed., *The Homilies of Wulfstan* (Oxford, 1952) [cited by text-number and lines]
CCL	*Corpus Christianorum, Series Latina*
CH	Ælfric, *Catholic Homilies* (*Sermones Catholici*)
Clemoes, 'Chronology'	P.A.M. Clemoes, 'The Chronology of Ælfric's Works,' in *The Anglo-Saxons: Studies in Some Aspects of Their History and Culture Presented to Bruce Dickins*, ed. Peter Clemoes (London, 1959), pp. 212–47
Crawford, *Heptateuch*	S.J. Crawford, ed., *The Old English Version of the Heptateuch, Ælfric's Treatises on the Old and New Testament and His Preface to Genesis* ... E.E.T.S., O.S., 160 (London, 1922)
DACL	*Dictionnaire d'Archéologie Chrétienne et de Liturgie*
E.E.M.F.	Early English Manuscripts in Facsimile

E.E.T.S.	Early English Text Society
E.S.	Extra Series
O.S.	Original Series
EHR	*English Historical Review*
ES	*English Studies*
Fehr, *Hirtenbriefe*	Bernhard Fehr, ed., *Die Hirtenbriefe Ælfrics in alten-glischer und lateinischer Fassung*, Bibliothek der angel-sächsischen Prosa, 9 (1914; rpt. with Suppl. Intro. by Peter Clemoes, Darmstadt, 1966)
JEGP	*Journal of English and Germanic Philology*
Ker, *Catalogue*	N.R. Ker, *Catalogue of Manuscripts Containing Anglo-Saxon* (Oxford, 1957)
LS	Walter W. Skeat, ed., *Ælfric's Lives of Saints ...*, E.E.T.S., O.S., 76, 82, 94, 114 (1881–1900; rpt. London, 1966) [cited by volume, item-number, lines or pages]
MÆ	*Medium Ævum*
MGH	*Monumenta Germaniae Historica*
MLR	*Modern Language Review*
MP	*Modern Philology*
N&Q	*Notes and Queries*
Napier	Arthur Napier, ed., *Wulfstan: Sammlung der ihm zugeschriebenen Homilien ...* Sammlung englischer Denkmäler in kritischen Ausgaben, 4 (1883; rpt. with Suppl. by Klaus Ostheeren, Dublin, 1967)
NM	*Neuphilologische Mitteilungen*
PBA	*Proceedings of the British Academy*
PL	*Patrologia Latina, Cursus Completus*, ed. J.-P. Migne
Pope	John C. Pope, ed. *Homilies of Ælfric: A Supplementary Collection*, 2 vols., E.E.T.S. 259–60 (London, 1967–68) [consecutive pagination; cited by pages for editorial material; for texts, by text-number and lines]
PQ	*Philological Quarterly*
RB	*Revue Bénédictine*
RES	*Review of English Studies*
Thorpe	Benjamin Thorpe, ed., *The Homilies of the Anglo-Saxon Church: The First Part, Containing the Sermones Catholici or Homilies of Ælfric*, 2 vols. (London, 1844–46) [cited by volume, page and line]

TRHS	*Transactions of the Royal Historical Society*
SN	*Studia Neophilologica*
SP	*Studies in Philology*
ZHT	*Zeitschrift für die Historische Theologie*

N.B. Translations from Old English are my own except where facing translations appear in the editions (i.e., Thorpe and all the E.E.T.S. editions except Pope).

PREACHING AND THEOLOGY
IN ANGLO-SAXON ENGLAND:
ÆLFRIC AND WULFSTAN

PART ONE

ÆLFRIC AND WULFSTAN:
AN INTRODUCTION

ÆLFRIC AND WULFSTAN:
AN INTRODUCTION

The subjects of this book are an abbot and an archbishop who lived and worked in England in the last years of the first millennium and the first years of the second, almost a thousand years ago. They are universally recognized as the greatest prose stylists of the Old English period, but comparatively little attention has been given to their place in the history of Christian thought or in the history of preaching. In an effort to redress this situation at least partially, this study will address two topics. The first of these topics, the uses for which the Old English preaching materials were prepared, is one that has never before been pursued at length. The second, the theological method of the homilists, has been addressed a number of times; but I hope that, by restricting the present examination to the eschatological group of doctrines as exemplary of theology in general, I can shed some new light on the place of these Old English writings in the history of theology. An edition of a Latin text on eschatology, not hitherto printed in full, is appended to the volume. Before the chief subjects of this study can be considered, however, some general comments are needed on the ecclesiastical situation of England in the tenth century and on the careers and writings of our subjects, Abbot Ælfric of Eynsham and Archbishop Wulfstan II of York.

1

Theological Tradition and Monastic Reform

If a single word were to be chosen to characterize early medieval theology, it would probably have to be *conservative*. That is to say, theology was in no way a speculative or even metaphysical discipline in the Early Middle Ages as it was to become in the hands of pre-scholastic and scholastic theologians from the twelfth century to the end of the Middle Ages. To make this assertion is by no means to slip back into the old pattern of modern scholarship which dismissed our period as the 'Dark Ages,' nor is it to denigrate the intellectual achievements of the great scholars of the Carolingian era.[1] It is, simply, to accept the definition of intellectual work common to the age and to recognize that by some this work was carried out with remarkable skill and that by others it was done with comparative lack of discrimination. The task of the early medieval theologian was to hand on the traditional teaching of the church. Although the famous canon of Vincent of Lérins may have been unknown to the Anglo-Saxon theologians of the tenth century, its tests of ubiquity, antiquity, and universality (*quod ubique, quod semper, et quod ab omnibus*)[2] seem to have been applied intuitively by the Old English writers, as by most early medieval theologians. If a theological work appeared to be authoritative, its teaching was applied in appropriate situations. Only an attack upon its authenticity – that is, for example, an assertion that it was falsely attributed to an author of recognized authority – could undermine its value in the eyes of the theological writers or anthologizers of theological writing. Such accusations were only rarely made, however, so the modern reader has the general impression that authors adapted whatever materials were available in their libraries.

Because of the heavy reliance of writers upon their authorities, the study of the literary evidences of early medieval intellectual activity is first of all the analysis of sources.[3] To understand the work of a given author, it is first necessary to know whence he has borrowed his ideas, how he has adapted the phraseology of his sources to his own purposes, and whether there are passages which may be original contributions. But the matter is far more complex than it appears at first, for frequently when one has catalogued the possible sources of a literary item, he has the impression that its author had a far larger library than might have been expected. In fact, in such cases, the early medieval writer was often dependent upon some sort of anthology: the work of encyclopedists such as Isidore of Seville and Rabanus Maurus, a *florilegium* or commonplace book of striking passages on one topic or many collected over a period of time by himself or another reader, or (especially in the cases with which this book is concerned) a homiliary which gathered selected sermons of the Fathers for devotional reading or for reading in a liturgical setting on appropriate occasions. At other times, he may simply have recalled a suitable passage which he quoted or paraphrased from memory. The identification of sources like these is a complex and difficult matter, if only because the manuscripts have tended to be lost or ignored more often than codices containing a single work or the work of a single author. The study of homiliaries as sources for the Anglo-Saxon literature is, in particular, in its infancy; and one must be extremely careful about the kinds of assertions made as to the sources of Old English homilies.[4] But source study, after and in connection with textual criticism, is the most basic aspect of the examination of the ideas and methods of pre-Conquest English authors.

Such heavy reliance upon source documents to shape doctrinal, devotional, and hortatory writings can lead to logical inconsistency if the sources are not in agreement. Few early medieval theologians were critical of the writings from which they borrowed. It was apparently sufficient warrant of orthodoxy for many of these scholars that someone had troubled himself to copy his materials and that they seemed to be attributed to one of the Fathers of the church. Satisfied with the claim to orthodoxy, the early medieval collectors and re-writers of patristic texts did not bother themselves with harmony: for internal criticism was not one of their scholarly tools,[5] and it would not become a basic theological skill before the birth of the intellectual spirit which inspired the *Sic et non* of Abelard.

This methodological conservatism resulted, of course, in traditionalism of content. If there were occasional shifts of emphasis with far-reaching implications – the case history of the descent-into-hell motif is a good example[6] – those alterations were hardly intentional and came about almost imperceptibly.

The preceding characterization of early medieval theology is accurate, yet it is so baldly formulated that it is also a caricature of the received opinion of the intellectual life of the church in the tenth century.[7] The observation that the theology of the Early Middle Ages was conservative – that its writers lacked an innovative intellectual curiosity and sometimes even the ability to arrange ideas according to the dictates of basic logical precepts – has, not unnaturally, reinforced the general feeling that there is not much in the period to engage the attention of the historian of ideas. 'It is generally rightly assumed that Anglo-Saxon theology was mainly derivative in doctrine, pastoral in approach, and practical in the application of inherited teaching and in the devising of effective ecclesiastical administrations especially in the mission field,' wrote the late Professor C.L. Wrenn.[8] Aside from polemical exploitation, whether to justify the theological position of the Church of England or that of its detractors,[9] theological documents in Old English have rarely before recent times been examined with an eye to assessment of their content and of their place in the history of Christian thought and teaching. This situation is understandable. Old English is a language which has not been accessible to most trained theologians. The documents were apparently not influential in the subsequent development of doctrine. Textual, linguistic, stylistic, and source studies of the prose writings have only recently achieved sufficient maturity for analysis of content to be feasible. Interest in the thought, culture, and society of Western Europe in the Early Middle Ages has been a late development in academic circles. Perhaps the greatest deterrent of all to the theological analysis of Old English prose has been the belief that, because almost all of these writings were adapted from Latin sources, they were without originality and intrinsic interest.

Whatever the cause, it has been the fate of Ælfric and Wulfstan to be admired by modern scholars chiefly as stylists. That their works do have intrinsic interest in areas quite beyond matters of style, that they brought quite remarkable critical powers to bear on their treatment of their sources, and that they conceived bold and original practical uses for the writings they produced in English will be major theses of this study. Abbot Ælfric and Archbishop Wulfstan can, I believe, be compared favourably with the best theologians of the Early Middle Ages, the group associated with the court of Charlemagne.

Inherent interest aside, however, the writings of Ælfric and Wulfstan ought long ago to have attracted a wider scholarly audience if only because of their unique position as vernacular documents in the history of European culture. There is a large and important Irish vernacular literature, some of it homiletic in character. But this literature – 'characterized by an intense interest in the supernatural and the eschatological, and a constant delight in the wonderful and the bizarre'[10] – is a fairly special and isolated phenomenon; and, before the effects of the Cluniac movement were felt in Ireland in the twelfth century, medieval Irish literature was not part of the mainstream of European intellectual history. Interesting though it is in itself and intriguing though the possibilities of its occasional influence on Anglo-Saxon theological prose may be,[11] it does not present so good a case study as the Old English sermon texts of the dissemination at levels where the vernacular had to be used of the theological currents set in motion by the Carolingians and their successors. German vernacular prose would, of course, have been in this mainstream and, indeed, closer to its source than the English. But, aside from some translations of catechetical texts, fragmentary pieces, and a translation of a tract of Isidore dated about A.D. 800 and the writing of Notker Labeo (d. 1022), a contemporary of Ælfric and Wulfstan whose work is more pedagogic than pastoral in nature, little or no early German survives.[12] Clearly there was a prose tradition in German and other continental vernacular dialects, but most European vernacular preaching was apparently extemporaneous and, therefore, is lost forever. It is only in Old English that we are presented with a substantial body of writings which are not only reasonably close to the main intellectual developments of the tenth and eleventh centuries but also responsive to peculiar local traditions.

The importance of the achievement of Ælfric and Wulstan is, furthermore, enhanced by the fact that they were not the only writers of prose sermons in Old English. Two anonymous collections of sermons in Old English, the Blickling and Vercelli Books,[13] may be set against their writings as examples of vernacular theological writing of a slightly earlier period. To these books may be added a number of pieces scattered throughout various other codices.[14] I have analysed elsewhere the eschatological teaching of these earlier works[15] and have drawn two chief conclusions concerning their theological methodology. The first is that both individual homilies and the collections in which they survive were profoundly traditional. That is to say, their content is almost entirely derived from materials their authors found in Latin sources. The second is that, because the writers were uncritical of their sources, individual pieces and the homiliaries as anthologies contain a number of internal contradictions. In particular, within the perimeters of my study, contradictions are discernible in the treatment of the destiny of the soul between death and the Doomsday. The strength of the primitive tradition which stressed the apocalyptic expectation of the Last Times is surprising. There is also considerable attention to the fate of the soul – the convention of the address of the soul to the body and material based on the apocryphal and, in some respects, heterodox *Visio Pauli* are prominent, for example. But these materials are confused, and sometimes incompatible pictures are presented. I believe this is evidence that doctrines concerning immortality in the terms later made normative by the schoolmen had not been fully defined in the sources of the Anglo-Saxon homilists or by the homilists themselves and that they neither recognized this situation as a methodological problem nor needed to settle it. Neither of these conclusions is particularly surprising in the light of the general characteristics of Western theology in the Early Middle Ages.[16]

The homiletic matter collected in both the Blickling and Vercelli codices was probably written no later than the generation preceding the activity of Ælfric and Wulfstan. Palaeographically, Vercelli is dated at the turn of the tenth and elventh centuries and Blickling in the middle of the latter half of the tenth century.[17] Blickling contains an internal reference to the year 971,[18] and it is clear that both books draw on antecedent vernacular homiliaries which may have been in existence for some time.[19] Their relationship to the vernacular prose tradition, which it is now argued had pre-Alfredian roots in Mercia in the ninth century, is unclear; but it is believed by some that Vercelli, at least, may descend from ninth-century originals.[20] Since linguistic tests are impressionistic, final decision between a conservative dating of Blickling and Vercelli and one that would push the time of composition of at least some of these homilies back to the reign of Alfred or even beyond will ultimately depend on the results of comparative studies of homilies appearing in other manuscripts as well. Whatever the case, it seems fair to say that the homiletic materials of the Blickling and Vercelli books are at least a generation earlier than Ælfric's earliest publication of his work around 990.

It is reasonably, if not absolutely, clear that Ælfric had in mind the vernacular homiliaries when he remarked that he undertook to prepare the First Series of the *Catholic Homilies* 'forþan þe ic geseah and gehyrde mycel gedwyld on manegum Engliscum bocum, þe ungelærede menn þurh heora bilewitnysse to micclum wisdome tealdon.'[21] Whether or not the work of Ælfric (and, to a more limited extent, Wulfstan) was undertaken in reaction against what he regarded as the propensity to theological error (*gedwyld*) of the earlier homiletic writings in Old English is an issue that can not be resolved in the present study. If it can be taken as established that the Blickling and Vercelli homilies were products of at least a generation before Ælfric and Wulfstan, however, it must be that the educational and ecclesiastical movement in which Ælfric and Wulfstan had their training in some way shaped them as theologians.

The monastic revival of the tenth century[22] is, I believe, the theological watershed which lies between the work of the earlier, anonymous Old English homilists and that of Ælfric and Wulfstan. This movement was the local manifestation in England of a widespread phenomenon, often misleadingly called the Cluniac movement, in tenth-century Western European history. Its beginning is dated from the appointment of Dunstan to the abbacy of Glastonbury by King Edmund, ca. 940, since it was from this moment that the gathering desire for a revival of monasticism in England began to assume some form. More than a reform, the English movement was virtually a reintroduction of the regular life in a nation whose church had, in effect if not by intention, been secularized after the Danish raids. Although King Alfred had done much for the revival of learning, his reign had not been propitious for a monastic revival. But in the course of the tenth century, contacts with the new monasticism abroad and growing awareness of the scandalous lack of clerical discipline coalesced and resulted in a movement of major proportions which would profoundly affect all of church life in England.

Although Dunstan (d. 988) after his appointment to the episcopate probably assumed a secondary role in the strictly monastic movement, two of his close associates continued the monastic work under King Edgar and his successor, Edward the Martyr. Oswald (d. 992), nephew of Archbishop Odo of Canterbury, was ordained at the reformed monastery of Saint-Benoît-sur-Loire at Fleury, established many monasteries, and served as bishop of Worcester and archbishop of York. (The same sees were later held in plurality by Wulfstan.) Æthelwold (d. 984) was ordained with Dunstan and went from Glastonbury to the abbacy of Abingdon; he ended his career as bishop of Winchester. The long lives of these three leaders, coupled with their important posts in the hierarchy and at the court of the kings of Wessex, assured that the movement, firmly established and having overcome most of its opponents, could survive its founders.

The great document of the reform is the *Regularis Concordia*, a customary designed to standardize the usages of the monasteries old and new, which was promulgated by a 'synodal council'[23] meeting in Winchester at the behest of King Edgar about 973. The *Concordia* specifically mentions the presence of representatives of Fleury and St Peter's, Ghent, as advisers in the preparation of the customary,[24] which was to be supplementary to the *Rule* of St Benedict.

By the presence of these advisers at Winchester and by the other contacts of English monastic figures with Ghent and Fleury, the peculiar characteristics of the English reform can be explained. For two sub-types of the continental monastic reform came together in the English movement so as to give it a unique character. The first of these, stemming from Cluny via Fleury, was an effort to institute observance of the *Rule* of St Benedict in pure, albeit liturgically elaborated, form in monasteries freed from the fetters of obligations to local lords. The second, in Lorraine and emanating from the work of John of Gorze and Gerard of Brogne, was mediated by Ghent; it was more ascetic and was frankly reliant on the support of the local landowners; it placed more emphasis on the educational work of the monks.[25] Both rested their customs on the *capitula* of Aachen (817), 'running almost wholly upon the lines set down by Benedict of Aniane.'[26] Thus, in a sense, they are the fruition of the abortive Carolingian effort to standardize and reform monastic life.

From the marriage of these two types of reform, there emerged a monasticism emphasizing the liturgical work of its adherents, stressing the function of the monastic school and, at the same time, arguing for a strong dependence on the king but freedom from other secular persons. Thus the body of the *Regularis Concordia* is devoted to the regulation of the canonical hours and of life in general. But the boys of the school are often in mind, and the king is forever in the prayers of the community. In contrast to the Cluniacs, the monks of the English nation, which had always been grateful to St Gregory the Great – and hence to his successors in the papacy – for its conversion, mention their papal patron only in passing[27] and never allude to the Petrine see as the peculiar protector of monastic life. The spirit of the reform is symbolized by an eleventh-century illustration in which Dunstan and Æthelwold, the reformers, sit on either side of King Edgar, their royal patron, holding a scroll. Beneath them, a genuflecting monk binds himself with a scroll representing *Regularis Concordia*.[28]

The effects of the movement which is epitomized by the document were many but they can be subsumed under two headings. First, because of its ties to the kings of Wessex and because the episcopate was largely recruited from monastic ranks, the work of centralization of the state was furthered considerably by the reform, and the reform program was extended to the secular church. Second, a significant revival of learning and the arts was effected: architecture, illumination, copying, and literary work all flourished in service to the needs of the monasteries. In neither area did the results of this work cease to be felt after the Conquest of 1066.

Recent archaeological work has enhanced our appreciation of the grandeur of the achievements of the reformers and their royal allies. The style of illumination in the late Saxon period has long been given the name 'Winchester school.' (Actually, the term is a misnomer, for the style was national rather than local; many of its finest exemplars can be ascribed with certainty to scriptoria at Canterbury and elsewhere.) The significance of Winchester as a cultural centre has been demonstrated conclusively by excavations in the precincts of the present cathedral. They show that important and sophisticated building, rich in artistic detail, was undertaken from the time of Alfred's successor, Edward the Elder, on to the end of the Saxon age, and that no work was more important than the renovation of the Old Minster by Bishop Æthelwold.[29] Thus at Winchester, Canterbury, and elsewhere, the educational and religious work of the new monasticism was carried out in surroundings which rivalled those of its continental counterparts; and this cultural distinction both undergirds and confirms our sense of the intellectual distinction of the revived monastic centres.

From the monastic churches of Winchester, and particularly from the school of Æthelwold of Winchester, of which Ælfric so proudly claimed himself an *alumnus*, direction was given to the literary aspects of the reform. Whereas it used to be thought that the standardization of the West Saxon dialect of Old English might be traced to the efforts and prestige of King Alfred, Professor

Helmut Gneuss has recently offered convincing evidence that it was the school of Æthelwold, exercising a careful control over linguistic usage and vocabulary, which was responsible for the literary predominance of West Saxon from the episcopate of Æthelwold to the Conquest. Among the evidences of the deliberate efforts at standardization carried out in this school may be the fact that 'most scribes (from the tenth century onwards) carefully observe the distinction between two types of script – one for Old English and one for Latin.'[30] Wulfstan as a literary figure is curious in that, despite his ties with the Winchester movement, he ignored its dictates as to vocabulary. In Latin as well as English there was considerable literary activity at Winchester, and the Latin poetry of Wulfstan the Cantor, Lantfridus, and others is of considerable interest.[31]

It may, indeed, be that much late Old English prose falls into the homiletic genre because the milieu was that of the monastic reform. The literary monuments of the patristic age (which in this connection we may say ended with Bede's writings on the Bible) which most influenced the Early Middle Ages were the great exegetical studies that set the norms and methods of biblical interpretation. The tenth-century reform did not call forth new works of this kind, probably because its greatest creative efforts were devoted to the enhancement of the liturgy: its texts, its ritual, its architectural setting, and the utensils produced for liturgical use by craftsmen from the scribe to the goldsmith. Thus it is not surprising that, beginning with the Carolingian scholars whose work came to its fruition in the monastic-liturgical movement of the tenth century, the most original applications of the theory of multiple meanings were applications to the words and actions of the liturgy; and biblical explication appeared most often in homiletic form.[32] Explication, like the other theological disciplines and the arts, became a handmaid of the liturgy. In this sense, the occasion for the writing of the Blickling Homilies (but not so clearly the Vercelli) may have been essentially similar to that for the work of Ælfric. Both were part of 'a dramatic pause in the history of Bible studies,'[33] although Ælfric and Wulfstan, writing at the moment of the reform's maturity, were far more sophisticated, theologically and rhetorically, than the earlier homilists.

These factors are the immediate historical background of the work of Ælfric, monk and teacher, and Wulfstan, bishop and councillor. While the early moments of the reform may have inspired the transcription of the Blickling Homilies and of the Vercelli Book – and perhaps of a host of other books now lost – Ælfric and Wulfstan are the true products of the movement in its maturity.

2

Ælfric of Eynsham

Ælfric, abbot of Eynsham, was the greatest prose stylist of the Old English period and the most important theological figure of the late Anglo-Saxon church. Among writers of Old English, only Ælfric and King Alfred – the latter rather less revealingly – speak about the purposes and methods of their literary endeavour. These personal revelations, combined with what has been learned by inference about the man from his work, must be considered carefully before the achievement of the homilist can be appreciated. The biographical facts about Ælfric[1] are easily summarized. Born in the middle of the tenth century, he was educated at Æthelwold's monastery in Winchester and sent, in 987, to Cerne Abbas (Cernel) in Dorset, which had been founded by Æthelmær, son of ealdorman Æthelweard. These same noblemen are known to have been interested in the monk's literary work. At Cernel, where he was in charge of the school, Ælfric produced two sets of sermons, commonly known as the *Catholic Homilies*, the *Lives of Saints*, an English adaptation of Bede's *De temporibus anni*, a *Grammar* and a *Colloquy*, a translation of portions of Genesis and other Old Testament books, pastoral letters and replies to inquiries, and sermons supplemental to the series published earlier.[2] In 1005,[3] Ælfric apparently became abbot of Eynsham, a monastery newly founded near Oxford by Æthelmær who – without taking vows and having denied any intention of controlling the community – intended to live among the monks 'and enjoy the endowment as long as [his] life should last.'[4] At Eynsham, Ælfric wrote more pastorals for friends in the episcopate; a treatise, *On the Old and New Testaments*, for a layman named Sigeweard; a monastic customary based on the *Regularis Concordia* for his monks; a *Life of Æthelwold*; and additional sermons. He died after 1010.[5]

Although some of his writing was occasional, most of Ælfric's work seems to have been written in pursuance of a scheme which was almost encyclopedic in scope. He intended in his homilies to cover all the chief points of the 'universal history with Christ's redemption at its centre.'[6] The *De temporibus anni* and the grammatical writings are ancillary works, mastery of which would enable others to pursue the kind of study that supported his own homiletic *Summa*. The biblical translations and studies make available the original sources or explain the proper use of those sources. The pastorals were intended to disseminate a knowledge of canon law – the appropriation of the experience of the past in the ordering of the present – so that men might participate in the Christ-wrought redemption both in the present life of the church and in the eternal order. Clearly the homiletic work was central to the author's intention to provide material useful for the education of the clergy and the performance of the duties of their vocation.

Ælfric used terms to describe himself which, however conventional,[7] indicate his own conception of his role. He was, in the first place, *alumnus Æðelwoldi* or *Witoniensis alumnus*.[8] His alma mater was the great centre of the new monasticism at Winchester, his teacher Æthelwold the great reforming monastic bishop. His works, therefore, came highly recommended to those who did not otherwise know their author's reputation. More often, however, Ælfric styled himself more simply 'monk' or 'monk and masspriest'[9] and, later, 'abbot,'[10] again recommending himself as one with the authority of office and the learning to undertake the writing of the work in question.[11] By reference to his education and to his successive ecclesiastical offices, Ælfric showed that he was profoundly aware of the limitations placed on the several orders of Christian men and that he was anxious lest someone think he had overstepped the boundaries proper to his own station.

He was also scrupulously anxious that those for whom he wrote should not be given more knowledge than appertained to their rank. The preface to the *Lives of Saints* warned that certain knowledge was not suitable for the laity and hinted that Ælfric was dissatisfied with the role of translator and popularizer.[12] Æthelweard was clearly warned of the dangers of translation in the Preface to Genesis: in the case of the Old Testament, 'ic ondræde, gif sum dysig man þas boc ræt oððe rædan gehyrþ. þæt he wille wenan, þæt he mote lybban nu on þære niwan æ, swa swa þa ealdan fæderas leofodon þa on þære tide, ær þan þe seo ealde æ gesett wære, oþþe swa swa men leofodon under Moyses æ.'[13] Indeed, the problem so oppressed Ælfric that he said he would never again translate for Æthelweard: 'Ic cweðe nu ðæt ic ne dearr ne ic nelle nane boc æfter ðisre of Ledene on Englisc awendan; and ic bidde ðe leof ealdormann, ðæt ðu me ðæs no leng ne bidde, ði læs ðe ic beo ðe ungehyrsum, oððe leas gif ic do. God ðe sy milde a on ecnysse.'[14]

Ælfric was conscious of his style as well as of his personal qualifications and of the limitations of certain of his readers. The First Series of *Catholic Homilies* is written in a prose that for clarity of syntax and consistent elegance of statement is far superior to the homilies of the Blickling and Vercelli books and to the prose of the reign of Alfred.[15] Later, the homilist developed a remarkable style of his own which was never equalled for elegance and clarity by his contemporaries and has sometimes been regarded as having influenced Early Middle English prose.[16] There appeared first in the Second Series of *Catholic Homilies* and then in the *Lives of Saints*, later homilies, and in other types of writing, a rhythmical, alliterative prose made up of rhetorical units in which two elements of two stresses each were joined by alliteration. This style is thought by some to be imitative of late Latin rhymed prose;[17] but in general, efforts to find stylistic sources for Ælfric's work have failed to perceive its real genius: 'his rhythm was an English rhythm, arrived at in an English fashion and not in a Latin.'[18] Although the form of Ælfric's prose is also reminiscent of Old English verse form,[19] the looseness of the rhythmic structure, the disregard for the stricter conventions of alliteration observed by the poets, and the use of a prose vocabulary show that Ælfric intended only an elevated expository style. Professor Clemoes has argued that Ælfric's achievement is not merely stylistic, for he displays a remarkable ability to unify content and form and he often uses 'the rhythmical structure of his prose to express his sense of scheme in his subject matter.'[20]

Ælfric desired, above all, that the doctrine transmitted in his lucid English prose should be absolutely orthodox and firmly based in the theological tradition. Thus most of his work is translation or adaptation of the works of the most reputable ecclesiastical fathers. In the *Catholic Homilies*, he lists the homilists he has translated in his recommendation of the work to Archbishop Sigeric.[21] In shorter works, he sometimes comments on the author whose work is translated.[22] Very often where Ælfric does not cite sources, the source is easily discoverable or the reliance on patristic sources is evident from the content.[23] The traditionalism of the author is also to be observed in his request that Archbishop Sigeric purge the *Catholic Homilies* of any residual error.[24]

Furthermore, as I remarked in the preceding section, Ælfric was critical of the English vernacular literature in circulation in his own day. It is tempting to see in the Blickling and Vercelli collections at least one type of error to which Ælfric objected: the uncritical acceptance of pseudepigraphic literature. He specifically warned against the *Visio Pauli*,[25] fragments of which were available in both of the surviving homiliaries. Ironically, a translation of the *Paul* appears in a later manuscript which also contains work by Ælfric.[26] While visions from the hagiographic sources appear in his own homily directly after the attack on the pseudo-Pauline vision,[27] Ælfric generally avoided quoting knowingly from the apocryphal New Testament, and he was often critical of hagiographic sources. He had, in other words, what one often misses in the anonymous homilies: the ability to discriminate among his sources as to the relative weight of their authority. Recognizing the usefulness of a native homiletic literature, he sought to produce writings which were in accord with strict orthodoxy as it was understood in the reformed monastic schools.

Finally, several characteristic literary traits of Ælfric may be noted which, though they seem pedantic, were intended to keep his work free from association with heterodox writings and to avoid needless duplication of material. First, he appended notes to the scribes in the prefaces to the homilies, directing that, when these works were copied, care should be taken to protect their integrity as a whole.[28] While this direction was disregarded almost immediately,[29] it was an effort to keep pure a collection intended to be authoritative. Second, he put a note in the *Catholic Homilies* explaining that 'ecclesiastical customs' forbade preaching on Maundy Thursday, Good Friday, and Easter Even,[30] hoping to prevent accretions to the corpus and to combat a custom which he regarded as erroneous. Finally – and this testifies as well to the existence of a general scheme for the whole canon of his writing – Ælfric made some effort not to discuss the same subject extensively more than once, and he referred his readers, where necessary, to the work in which related subjects had already been discussed.[31] Where he found it necessary to treat the same subject again, he sometimes cancelled the first discussion.[32] There is also evidence to suggest that Ælfric exercised some care in establishing the system of punctuation for the *Catholic Homilies* so that those who read his work to the people would effectively communicate its true meaning to their hearers.[33] Indeed, recent study of the earliest extant copy of the First Series of *Catholic Homilies* has shown that Ælfric was constantly revising and improving his work and taking care that it be accurately reproduced.[34]

This self-conscious and traditionalist caution will be evident in the analysis of the sermons and in our consideration of his eschatological teaching. It now remains to describe the major bodies of homiletic work by Ælfric, the two series of *Catholic Homilies* and the *Lives of Saints*. The two series of *Catholic Homilies* were published separately shortly after 990.[35] Ælfric is thought to have composed the First Series in 989[36] 'to provide himself with the preaching material he needed as masspriest at Cerne.'[37] The composition of the Second Series had probably been begun by 990. The two volumes were sent to Archbishop Sigeric of Canterbury in 991 and 992, respectively.[38] Each contained forty items, most of which were assigned to occasions of the ecclesiastical year.[39] They were to be read in alternate years to avoid tediousness for those who faithfully heard each series through.[40] The homilies are of two types; expository sermons on the Gospel lection – the pericope – for a given occasion and lives of saints venerated by days of general obligation in the church. The Second Series also provides readings for the Common of Saints. For some of the Saints'-day sermons, of which there is an increased number in the Second Series, Ælfric used materials of the hagiographic tradition.[41] The exegetical sermons are usually adaptations of one or more of the homilies of the Fathers collected by Paul the Deacon at the request of Charlemagne[42] for monastic use.[43] Ælfric combined the sources with great ingenuity, producing sermons which are often far more than simple translation. He also employed the interpolated version of the ninth-century homiliary of Haymo of Auxerre for many shorter passages; he may have derived his method of combining patristic sermons from this earlier homiliarist, for it was Haymo's method to combine patristic sources so as to produce a single sermon for each liturgical occasion, whereas Paul characteristically collected several homilies by various Fathers for each occasion.[44] The Old English homilist can, however, by no means be considered merely a mechanical adapter of these standard homiliaries. Not only did he skilfully combine sermons he found in the collection of Paul the Deacon, occasionally adding notations from Haymo; but also he enriched his work with other pertinent material which he happened either to have at hand or to recall.[45] It is also clear that he went back to some of the *Catholic Homilies* and added materials which he felt would enhance his arguments so that the manuscripts give evidence of stages in the process of composition and revision.[46]

The homiletic works of Ælfric underwent development in other ways, too. *Catholic Homilies*, I, seems to be addressed directly to the laity as though 'to be read in order from the pulpit, presumably verbatim, in the course of a single year.' But the Second Series 'offers much more scope to the preacher for selection and arrangement' by providing more than one piece for several of the thirty-eight occasions treated and by addressing the user-clergyman in a number of notes.[47] The publication of the Second Series in 992 did not complete Ælfric's work on homilies for the Temporale. There is evidence, some of which will be surveyed in our study of the uses of Ælfric's work, of further stages of development of the two series; and Ælfric composed a number of additional homilies for the Temporale (which may or may not have been issued as definable series), the last of which have only recently been edited by Professor John C. Pope.[48]

The *Lives of Saints* is a more specialized collection of pieces (often erroneously called a third series of homilies) for days of the Sanctorale which were observed not by the church at large but by the monastic community. Written over a period of time, the *Lives* were collected and published before the death of ealdorman Æthelweard (ca. 1002), probably before the turn of the century.[49] The book translates portions of the monastic *Passionale*, 'The Passions of the Saints.'[50] Though thought to have been collected from several source books, it is probably not related closely to the martyrologies read daily at Chapter in the monasteries in which Ælfric had resided.[51] The book was probably intended for pious reading at any time (*quando volueris* is the term Ælfric used in other contexts), since the usual references in the text to the day of reading as the day of the saint are lacking.[52] Nevertheless, the pieces are arranged in the order in which the saints were commemorated in the liturgical year. The collection was, at any rate, written at the request of Æthelweard and Æthelmær, and it was evidently a more restricted book than they had requested, for Ælfric says that, 'ne forte despectui habeantur margarite christi,' he has translated a limited book.[53] He generally avoids the *Vitae Patrum*, a foundation-stone of medieval hagiography, 'in quo multa subtilia habentur quae non conueniunt aperiri laicis,' and which he admits he himself was unable entirely to fathom.[54] The *Lives of Saints* says nothing new, but it introduces laymen to materials heretofore chiefly available to monks for use in the Office.[55]

The preceding summary comments on Ælfric's works and methods are, I hope, sufficient to suggest the mind behind the writings. Ælfric was pedantic both by inclination and by virtue of the scholarly procedures which were universally accepted by his contemporaries. If his ideas were not original, the results of his efforts – his style in particular – were often unique. Above all, he was a patient and painstaking teacher who spared himself no labour in collecting soundly authoritative expositions of Christian teaching and in presenting his materials clearly, convincingly, and elegantly.

3

Wulfstan II of York

Neither the historical nor the literary and theological stature of the second of the great Anglo-Saxon homilists had been appreciated adequately before the present century. Thanks to recent scholarly labours, however, Archbishop Wulfstan II of York has now assumed a position of eminence, not merely as a homilist associated with Ælfric but also as an ecclesiastical statesman, legislator, and prose stylist of the first importance for the history of the late Anglo-Saxon period.[1] Like his cloistered contemporary, Wulfstan was motivated chiefly by the desire in the tradition of Dunstan, Æthelwold, and Oswald to reform and revitalize the church. But Ælfric and Wulfstan were 'as different as two devoted clergymen could well be, and complemented each other in talent and in performance.'[2]

Very little is known of the life of Wulfstan, who, like Ælfric, was not a candidate for sainthood – except for a rather localized cult at Ely and Peterborough – and had no biographer. Unlike Ælfric, he said very little about himself.[3] Indeed, much of the early historical recollection of Wulfstan is from the first years of the Norman period and is distinctly uncomplimentary. It is not known whence he came to the episcopate in London in 996, but his family seems to have been connected somehow with the Fenland area of the East Midlands, and it is universally assumed that in his training and earlier career he had been associated with the Benedictine reform, especially as the great majority of bishops in this period were recruited from monastic ranks. In London at a time of Danish harassment, he was known as a skilful orator and was active in civil affairs. He was already using the Latin pseudonym Lupus.[4] In 1002 Wulfstan became bishop of Worcester and archbishop of York.[5] He either resigned Worcester in 1016 or set up a suffragan for its administration. During the years of his archiepiscopate, Wulfstan drafted legislation for both Æthelred and his Danish successor Cnut,[6] wrote on the nature of the political order, and worked to reform clerical life and teaching. He had a remarkable knowledge of continental writing on canon law, made possible probably by the library at Worcester on which he drew in an effort 'to Romanize and modernize his church to cure its insularity and reform its practices by the best models he could find.'[7] His work in content and in effect was not unlike that of early eleventh-century statesmen-bishops on the continent. Wulfstan died on 28 May 1023 and was buried at Ely, where his bones remain today.

As a homilist, Wulfstan differed markedly from his contemporary and associate Ælfric. The corpus of sermons as it survives is small, and the preaching is largely topical and occasional, not exegetical and encyclopedic. To make the traditional distinction, his preacher's writings are in the main not homilies but sermons, not explications of the Gospel pericopes for selected occasions of the liturgical year but public discourses on religious topics. Although Wulfstan displayed, as must an archbishop almost perforce, a certain interest in liturgical administration, a number of his sermons may have been delivered on such occasions as meetings of the *witan*; and most of them cannot be associated with liturgical occasions.[8]

Wulfstan's sermons can be described as a series of variations on two or three themes which are made a homogeneous body of work by the appearance in each unit of one or more of the major motifs. The themes include the note of eschatological urgency, the necessity of living strictly in accordance with God's *lagu and lare*, 'law and teaching,' and (a variant of the second, but directed more to the clerical audience) the need of teaching the people forcefully and directly the content of divine law. The substance from which he worked in developing these variations was also fairly static: for theological concepts he turned to Ælfric and to Adso of Montier-en-Der, Abbo of St-Germain-des-Près, and Pirmin of Reichenau;[9] for moral and legal injunctions he relied on the Carolingian canonists and reformers;[10] for his exhortations to clerical teachers, he was indebted to the Old Testament prophets as interpreted in the patristic tradition.[11]

The analogy of musical variation can be applied to Wulfstan's actual method of composition as well as to the content of his sermons. Wulfstan frequently worked from a Latin draft or notes,[12] drawn usually from a number of sources. Like Ælfric, who used the same method at least once, he often returned to his sources and altered the Latin draft to suit his rhetorical and didactic purposes. More important, however, he used phrases, sentences, and even longer passages from his own earlier homilies and from the laws several times in his works and, most notably in the case of the *Sermo ad Anglos*, reworked whole homilies for subsequent use.[13] Reading Wulfstan's works, one continually discovers passages of prose which, like the great themes, he has encountered elsewhere.

Wulfstan was, like Ælfric, an unusually gifted rhetorician. He developed a style all his own which 'consists of a continuous series of two-stress phrases related in structure to the classical [Anglo-Saxon poetic] half-line, and severely restricted in somewhat the same fashion to certain rhythmical patterns.'[14] These two-stress units, often marked by alliteration or rhyme, give a greater sense of urgency than the more leisurely four-stress pattern of Ælfric. Heightened by other rhetorical devices,[15] the unique style makes Wulfstan's writing oratorically masterful. It was obviously intended for oral delivery and must be read aloud to be appreciated. At the same time, however, Wulfstan's rhetorical structure is so tight, his thoughts are so compressed, and he is so ruthless in the excision of detail and of development of the intellectual implications of his statements that one has sometimes the sense that his texts are more in the character of notes for a sermon than the discourse itself. This is particularly true of the earlier eschatological pieces. Only the care which the archbishop lavished on his style belies this conclusion; but the effect of the preaching on its auditors – almost breathless in its conciseness, imbued with a sense of radical urgency, its very rhythmic structure hammering home the message – must have been extraordinary.

It is not only style and methodology, however, which make it possible to distinguish Wulfstan's work from Ælfric's, even where he was directly indebted to the abbot of Eynsham. For Wulfstan made it a point to avoid theological subtlety, to drop exempla[16] and most traces of allegorical interpretation and, usually, to delete specific historical allusions. Thus, to take an example which has not been used before, he adapts the second half of Ælfric's *De Die Iudicii*, a homily which will be discussed at length in Part III, using as his text Mark xiii, whereas Ælfric had relied on Matthew xxiv, a parallel lection. At one point, however, he adapts a suggestion of Ælfric's on the interpretation of Matthew xxiv. 12: 'Quoniam abundabit iniquitas refrigescet caritas multorum:'

> Đæt is on Énglisc,
> forðam þe únriht wéaxeð
> éalles to wíde,
> sóð lufu cólað.
> Ne man Gód ne lúfað
> swa swa mán scólde,
> ne mánna getrýwða
> to áhte ne stándað,
> ac únriht rícsað
> wíde and síde,
> and téalte getrwýða
> sýndon mid mánnum,

and þǽt is gesýne
on mǽnigfealde wísan
gecnáwe se ðe cúnne.[17]

In Ælfric's homily (lines 326–7), the passage is an explication of the Dominical exhortation to pray that the Last Day not be in the winter:

Ne mænde he þone winter þe gewunelice cymð
on þæs geares ymbryne, ac swa swa he on oðre stowe cwæð,
Quia abundabit iniquitas, refrigescet caritas multorum.
Þæt is, on Engliscum gereorde, þæt on þam yfelan timan
arist seo unrihtwisnyss, and swiðe gemenigfylt,
and seo soðe lufu swiðe acolað,
na ealra manna, ac swiðe manegra,
þæt hy nateshwón ne lufiað þone lifigendan God,
ne hyra nyhstan, ne furðan hy sylfe;
for ðon se ðe God ne lufað, ne lufað he hyne sylfne.[18]

It is difficult to imagine that, had he not been following Ælfric, Wulfstan would have had recourse to this idea at this point in his sermon. But he completely alters his Ælfrician source, cutting the verbiage to achieve his urgent, rapid style, deleting reflective or theological words, omitting the allegorical and exegetical framework, introducing legal terminology to define what is meant by the cooling of love, and concluding with one of his favourite hortatory clauses.

Lest the reader be misled by the fact that Wulfstan characteristically deletes the niceties of biblical explication from his sources, it may be well to stress the fact that he does not reject the exegetical tradition. It is, simply, irrelevant to his parenetic, or hortatory, purposes, and its reflections are omitted lest they get in the way. Traces of the thought of the exegetes are to be discovered frequently; they are assimilated and incorporated, although the symbolic or typological framework is often sidestepped, as in the example quoted above. Other sermons betray more clearly Wulfstan's indebtedness to typology. *De Dedicatione Ecclesiae*, for instance, adheres closely to the basic notion that the temple of Solomon is the type of the church. In this piece, Wulfstan repeatedly uses the expression *getacnað* to point out such relationships as those between Solomon, the Temple, the congregation and Christ, the church, and Christians.[19] The differences between Wulfstan and his contemporaries in this regard are, in other words, differences of purpose and temperament and do not reflect basic intellectual disagreement.

Moral fervour, combined with legalistic and moralistic terminology and an impatience with detail and subtlety of idea, marks Wulfstan as preacher and theologian.[20] He came from the same theological milieu as Ælfric and worked closely with the abbot;[21] but, for all their personal and programmatic compatibility, the two were almost totally unlike as preachers. Perhaps their differences were, after all, differences arising from their stations in the church; but, if so, they have come after a millennium to seem to be primarily differences of temperament.

PART TWO

THE USES OF THE OLD ENGLISH SERMONS

THE USES OF THE OLD ENGLISH SERMONS

Although there are certainly a number of students who are aware that it is unclear in what settings and by whom the sermon literature of the Anglo-Saxon church was used, one can be fairly certain that a majority of those who are cognizant of the existence of an Old English homiletic corpus would, if queried, answer that the homilies – and especially those of Ælfric – were to be read by the clergy to the people on Sundays or Feasts in a liturgical setting, most probably at the Mass.[1] Some scholarly reviews of the place of preaching in the corpus of Old English writings, however, have avoided the issue, whether from circumspection or because the authors do not recognize the matter of the uses of sermons – or of their place in the history of preaching and of the liturgy – as a topic of literary history.[2] There is, however, a need for an examination of a number of facets of the history of preaching in the later-patristic and early-medieval periods in order to clarify the intentions of those who composed and collected sermons and homilies in England, if only because the apparent popular assumption does not accord with the evidence now available concerning the status of preaching elsewhere in Europe during the Saxon age.

The assumption that homilies were regularly preached on the Gospel pericope represents the post-Tridentine ideal[3] and the practice at certain moments both in the Later Middle Ages and the present. If one looks to the Carolingian church however, he finds contradictory situations. On the one hand, liturgical historians[4] agree that, in the process of adapting the Roman liturgy to the needs of the Gallican church, the reformers dropped references to the homily from service books for the Mass; but on the other hand, there was a concerted effort in the reigns of Charles the Great and his successors to revive the teaching and perhaps also the preaching office of the church. Furthermore, among the most frequently copied books of the Carolingian age were the homiliaries, collections of sermons and parts of commentaries by the Fathers; but this activity, scrutinized closely, seems more surely allied to the reform of monastic life or even to the pious practices of individuals than to the development of the secular or public liturgy.

These and other, more detailed, observations might lead one to doubt the accuracy of the received understanding of the purpose of Ælfric and others who wrote and collected vernacular homilies in England during the tenth and eleventh centuries; and, if so, we may often have misunderstood the nature and purpose of the confusing array of homiletic manuscripts which survive from the period. Recent work, such as Father Smetana's studies of Ælfric's dependence on Carolingian homiliaries and continental studies of the nature and composition of homiliaries[5] – not to mention the pressing need to edit and analyse the many late-Saxon homilies aside from those of Ælfric and Wulfstan and the Blickling and Vercelli books – has, however, brought us to a juncture at which questions can and must be asked and answered about the nature of homiliary-making and homily- and sermon-writing as ecclesiastical and literary activities in the tenth and eleventh centuries. The questions cannot all be answered definitively – indeed, the present examination of the matter is exploratory and selective – but some conclusions may be hazarded and areas for further study and argument defined.

Two aspects of the history of preaching in the Carolingian age must be surveyed before the problem of English sermon-materials can be raised. First, the nature and purposes of the homiliary-making movement, to which the Old English vernacular sermons are clearly related, must be considered. Second, the history of preaching in the Western church must be outlined with special attention to the nature of the Carolingian revival of preaching, to distinctions among kinds of preaching, to the dissemination of the preaching office among the ecclesiastical orders, and to the place of preaching in the liturgy. Only after such explorations can one turn directly to the Anglo-Saxon homilies and consider the place of Ælfric and Wulfstan within the larger history of preaching.

4

Carolingian Preaching

A / THE HOMILIARY

The study of the homiliary as a distinct and important genre of liturgical or devotional book was long neglected by liturgists except insofar as it reflected the development of the ecclesiastical calendar. Only recently has new light begun to be shed upon this difficult and complex subject;[6] and, independently, the importance of such study for the understanding of at least the sources of the Old English homilists has been demonstrated by the Reverend Cyril L. Smetana in several important articles.[7] Although the subject has hardly been opened, it is now possible to sketch provisionally the history of its development.

The first homiliaries appear to have been devotional books, designed to epitomize the doctrinal and moral teachings of the church. The existence of such collections is attested by a number of records from the mid-fifth and early-sixth centuries.[8] The principal of organizing homiliaries according to the liturgical calendar was adopted at an early date and was independent of their liturgical employment. This organizing principle was apparently introduced in imitation of sacramentaries arranged *per circulum anni*, which first appeared in the fifth century. Nevertheless, without losing their utility as more-or-less private manuals, the homiliaries were from an early date used as well to supply the readings prescribed (as in *Regula Sancti Benedicti*, cap. ix) for the Night Office from the 'expositiones earum quae a nominatis et orthodoxis catholicis Patribus factae sunt.'[9] The homilies of Caesarius of Arles (d. 542) were also arranged according to the liturgical calendar – and they stand out among the early collections as being intended for the use of parochial clergy.[10] But it is important to remember that the first homiliaries were intended for non-liturgical use and that the earliest liturgical homiliaries were probably written for use within a monastic setting. The wider circulation of homiliaries for the Office testifies both to the success of the monastic movement and to the gradual imposition upon all the clergy of the obligation to say the daily Offices.[11] The homiliaries for the Office supplied lections for a specific group of days: Sundays and a select group of feasts, notably Dominical, to which special Gospels were assigned and on which the Night Office was trebled in length by the addition of two extra 'Nocturns.'[12] Usually the homilies were devoted to exposition of the Gospel pericopes, the same pericope being read in the third Nocturn as at the principal Masses of the Sunday or holy day. Occasionally (as on Sundays in Lent when expositions of Genesis and Exodus were common) they looked to the Old Testament.

Among the most important of the early homiliaries from the great age of homiliary production is that of Alan of Farfa (d. 770), which is probably an elaboration, largely by means of conflation with materials assembled by Caesarius, of the sixth-century homiliary of St Peter's in Rome.[13] Its prologue[14] is conventional; indeed, it may have been taken from the introduction to an earlier homiliary, just as Alan's was later used by Egino of Verona (d. 802) at the head of his homiliary (which was in essence a fresh copy of Alan).[15] The prologue begins with an elaborate simile in which Christian literature is likened to a rich and ripe field which must be harvested for the nourishment of the Christian people (sec. 1). The author next pleads his own lack of ability to perform the task of selecting items for the homiliary with which his superiors have importuned him (2–3). But, he continues, he has made a choice designed to illuminate many facets of Scripture (4), and he has arranged his selections according to the calendar, beginning with the Vigil of Christmas (5). It should be noted that, although Alanus indicates his homiliary is calendrically arranged, he says nothing about its intended liturgical function, if any. By the same token, (employing the modesty topos) he identifies himself as a monastic scribe commanded by his abbot to undertake the task (3, 6), and he in no way indicates that the volume was intended for use in the secular church.

Alan of Farfa, whose collection was the parent of a number of homiliaries intended for use in the monastic office,[16] is second only to Paul the Deacon as a figure of importance in the history of the homiliary.[17] Paul's work, divided in parts for winter and summer, was commissioned by Charlemagne. The prefatory letter to the Homiliary of Paul the Deacon which the emperor supplied makes clear the uses for which it was intended and the situation which gave rise to its compilation:

Denique quia ad nocturnale officium compilatas quorundam casso labore, licet recto intuitu, minus tamen idonee repperimus lectiones, quippe quae et sine auctorum suorum vocabulis essent positae et infinitis vitiorum anfractibus scaterent, non summus passi nostris in diebus in divinis lectionibus inter sacra officia inconsonantes prestrepere soloecismos, atque earundem lectionum in melius reformare tramitem mentem intendimus. Idque opus Paulo diacono, familiari clientulo nostro, elimandum iniunximus, scilicet ut, studiose catholicorum patrum dicta percurrens, veluti e latissimis eorum pratis certos quosque flosculos legeret, ut in unum quaeque essent utilia quasi sertum aptaret.[18]

Paul's task was, so to speak, to clean up the homiliary; for, as in other areas, his ruler found that wide variation in local custom and the ignorance of copyists had rendered the homiletic lections of the Night Office largely unintelligible.[19] He was as much a textual editor as an anthologizer. Correct copies of homilies appropriate to the Night Office were needed, and their use was to be standardized by dissemination of Paul's volume.[20] Brief allusion will be made later to the contribution of Paul and other homiliarists to the development of the Breviary; but it should be remarked here that both Paul's presentation of a number of homilies for each occasion[21] and his division of his selections for the Night Office into a *pars hiemalis* (from the fifth Sunday before Christmas through Saturday in Holy Week) and a *pars aestavis* (from Easter to Advent) – to which is added a section for the common of saints (*commune sanctorum*) – reflect the fact that the schedule of Offices in summer varied from that of winter.

The homiliary of Paul the Deacon was devoted almost entirely to the Fathers' elucidations of the Gospel pericopes.[22] The need to explicate other lections, especially as a devotional act (the *lectio divina* of monastic *regulae*) gave rise to a new sort of homiliary which Henri Barré has called 'Carolingian' but which differs in several important respects from the 'official' homiliary Charlemagne commissioned Paul to make. Liturgical in arrangement, these homiletic collections were not destined for liturgical use. Rather than furnish lections for the Office, they provided meditational reading or materials for subsequent adaptation by preachers.[23] Both Barré and Grégoire, the most recent and expert students of these homiliaries, stress their devotional, as opposed to their preaching, uses. It is to this school that the practice of abbreviating and paraphrasing sources and even of constructing items from several sources is apparently to be traced. To this group of homiliaries are assigned, as transitional documents, the Mondsee homiliary, two collections of Rabanus Maurus, and the homiliary of Chartres. The 'Carolingian homiliaries,' properly so called, are distinguished by being devoted almost exclusively to explication of the lessons of the Office; they contain, in other words, exegetical homilies and not general or pastoral sermons.[24] But they contain, in addition to the sort of exegesis compiled in homiliaries for the Offices, commentaries on the Epistles (which were not ordinarily regarded as proper subjects for exegetical lections at Nocturns) and for such days as the feriae of Lent when the Nocturnal Office was not lengthened so as to make room for homiletic lections. The great monuments of this movement are the homiliaries of the school of St Germain of Auxerre. The work of the monk Haymo (ca. 850) was followed by that of his student Heric

(865–70); their work circulated as early as 870 in a combined version to which homilies on the Epistles were added. Between 873 and 876, Heric composed thirty-three homilies for the weekdays of Lent and these, too, were integrated in some homiliary manuscripts.[25] Among further versions of the work of the Auxerre homiliarists, one should mention the abridgement of Heric made by Remigius in the first decade of the tenth century.

The difficult and complex subject of the history of the homiliary cannot be pursued further here, but several points which have sometimes been overlooked need to be stressed. First, the complexity of the homiliary problem arises in large part from the fact that, despite Charlemagne's reasonably successful effort at standardization, these volumes were subject to alteration to meet local liturgical requirements or to satisfy the needs and desires of various kinds of readers. Jean Leclercq rightly speaks at the same time of a general unity of tradition and of a great diversity of contents.[26] One of the most difficult tasks of the student of later homiletic collections is to ascertain which collections lay behind them and for what purpose they were compiled. Second, the most important and influential homiliaries of which we know were made not so much for use at Mass or other public services of the secular churches as in connection with the monastic Office and in particular with the Night Office at which the reading of passages of the Fathers elucidating the appointed Gospel pericopes was enjoined on certain days. Even those homiliaries which were designed not for public reading but for private meditation (for the *lectio divinia*) were organized according to the dictates of the lectionary used in the community. Furthermore, it should be pointed out that the homiliary was one of the ancestors of the breviary, which was in the process of evolving from as early as the eleventh century, as is known from the appearance of various sorts of transitional compendia, notably the Portiforium (a portable compendium of materials for the Offices), the Capitulary, and the Collectar.[27] Homiliaries, then, form a complex genre of works strongly associated with the liturgical observances of the monastic movement or with the imposition of the requirement of daily observance of the Offices upon the secular clergy, They were intended either for use within the Night Office or for private meditation on the lections of the Office. That they may also have provided materials for public preaching seems to be an implication of the prefatory remarks in some homiliaries,[28] and this is an observation which leads us to the next topic for exploration.

B / THE PLACE OF PREACHING IN THE CAROLINGIAN CHURCH

In recent years, the history of preaching in the Early Middle ages has engaged the attention of only a few scholars working directly from the sources. Several notable attempts at the subject were made in Germany in the last century,[29] however, and there are a few recent studies which essentially restate the conclusions of the earlier students.[30] Study of the Carolingian capitularies and conciliar documents reveals that a new monograph based on re-examination of the sources is needed. Such a work ought to consider, in particular, the liturgical settings of sermons and the distinctions among such categories as missionary, catechetical, and liturgical-exegetical preaching. What follows involves several revisionary conclusions, which must be regarded as tentative until a more systematic study has appeared.

One fact of earlier ecclesiastical history which tends occasionally to be overlooked contributes to the difficulty of interpreting the history of preaching in the Early Middle Ages. The office of preaching and the sacerdotal function of celebrating the Eucharist were in early times reserved to the bishop. Sacerdotal duties devolved upon the presbyterate (in this connection, the term is more accurate than priesthood) only after the church had grown so large that not all its members could attend the bishop's celebration. But the preaching office apparently remained an episcopal preserve for some time. Thus the Latin homilies which survive even after the pontificate of Gregory the Great are almost all from the pens of bishops, and the tenth and eleventh centuries are known to the standard historians as an age of episcopal preaching.[31] Two forces seem to have been at work in the process by which the presbyter came to assume the function of preacher as well as celebrant.[32] The first was circumstantial. The teaching office could not be handled by the bishops alone; and, particularly north of the Alps, the missionary activities of the church required the assistance of persons other than bishops.[33] The second was doctrinal. As the sacerdotal duties came to be shared by the two orders, a curiously presbyterian doctrine, which has been maintained in Roman Catholic circles into modern times, achieved general acceptance in the Western church. It came to be agreed that there were seven orders of ministers: the standard list was priest (*sacerdos*), deacon, subdeacon, acolyte, exorcist, lector, and porter.[34] The episcopate and the presbyterate shared the sacerdotal order, in other words; and the bishop's special functions were simply additions to his basic ministerial order – a situation that reflected the fact that the bishop had become the ecclesiastical administrator rather than the usual liturgical president of the local church.[35] Given the doctrinal development, it is not surprising that, as one of the sacerdotal duties, the office of preaching should have come to be regarded as an adjunct of the presbyterate. It is perhaps more surprising that, as we shall see, there is very little record of presbyters as preachers; evidently there were forces at work which led to the retention in fact of a custom which had become doctrinally archaic.[36]

The most important early case of insistence by ecclesiastical authorities on the duty (let alone the right) of presbyters to preach is associated with one of the most difficult figures in the history of medieval preaching, Caesarius of Arles (470–543). His program of reform through preaching and teaching was undertaken in the face of the political and cultural crisis of the early sixth century, and it grew from the experiences of his episcopal visitations.[37] Most striking and, at the same time, puzzling were his statements in the famous *Admonitio ... vel suggestio humilis peccatoris generaliter omnibus sanctis vel omnibus sacerdotibus directa* and the canons of the Council of Vaison (529).[38] Caesarius both directed his presbyters in rural areas to open schools and firmly urged upon them the duty of preaching. In their absence or incapacity, the deacons were to read the homilies of the Fathers.[39] This radical tactic strikes one as being evoked by the historical situation in Gaul more than by precedent, and the few facts available concerning the practice of preaching in the following centuries lead one to doubt that, outside of southern France, the stance of Caesarius on the question of preaching came to be regarded as normative.[40] Nonetheless, the bishop of Arles' own sermons, which were themselves largely derived from the Fathers and, therefore, appropriate for use by deacons in case of necessity, were one of the great sources of the later homiliaries. Perhaps arranged in Caesarius' own time in the liturgical order which became normative, they differ from a number of the homiliaries surveyed in the preceding section in that many are general admonitory sermons (albeit attached to liturgical occasions) rather than exegetical homilies. However that may be, Caesarius' work was known primarily in later centuries of the first millennium as it was incorporated in the homiliaries of the offices, often attributed to other Fathers.[41]

In the later years of the Merovingian period, there seems to have been a reversion in many areas to the assumption that the preaching office appertained primarily to bishops. In one of the few references to preaching in conciliar canons of the era, the bishop is enjoined to preach to the people on Sundays and saints' days, 'ut gregem sibi comisso alimentis spiritalibus foveat.'[42] Nevertheless there were many attempts to encourage the clergy to teach on a wider scale in the pre-Carolingian legislation. One of the most striking is the canons of the English council held at Clovesho in 747, certainly at the instigation of Pope Zacharias and perhaps also in response to the remonstrations of Boniface to the pope and to Cuthbert, archbishop of Canterbury.[43] These canons, the importance of which in the present context arises from the fact that they were written during a period when Anglo-Saxon missionaries played a decisive role in the formulation of ecclesiastical policy on the continent, display the basic ambiguity of attitude towards the office of preaching which was to characterize canon law in the ninth century. References to teaching and preaching are scattered throughout the document. At the outset (canon iii) bishops are commanded to make annual visitations of their dioceses and to call the people together to hear the word. On the one hand, this canon seems to have in mind basic doctrinal or catechetical instruction of people in remote areas and, on the other, moral teaching. It may also have in mind missionary preaching, but it does not refer to liturgical preaching in the strict sense of regular, exegetical commentary on the Mass pericopes.[44] This directive is subsumed under the argument, very common in later Carolingian canons, that bishops are to teach both by the example of their own lives and by their learning and teaching (canon i).

Another series of the Clovesho canons pertains to the lesser clergy. In one of these (canon vi), bishops are commanded not to ordain monks or clerks to the presbyterate without examining their past and present moral character and their education in matters of doctrine to determine whether they are adequately prepared for preaching and teaching ('ratio aliis integram fidei preadicare, sermones [i.e., the word] scientificam conferre').[45] Canons ix and x throw doubt on the assumption that the framers of vi had preaching (in the strict liturgical sense) in mind. In the former, the 'office of apostolic preaching' is defined as 'baptizing, and teaching, and visiting,'[46] and in the latter the content of teaching is outlined: the priest must be able both to understand the liturgical words and actions he performs and to explain in the native tongue the services and the Creed and *Pater noster*. Finally, canon xiv is concerned with the observance of Sunday in monasteries and churches. Abbots and presbyters are to lay aside secular business:

... de sacrae Scripturae eloquiis subjectis famulis praedicando insinuent. Sed et hoc quoque decernitur quod eo die sive per alias festivitates majores, populus per sacerdotes Dei ad Ecclesiam saepius invitatus, ad audiendum verbum Dei conveniat, Missarumque sacramentis, ac doctrinae sermonibus frequentius adsit.[47]

Interpretation of this canon depends very largely upon a survey of later canons. One possible reading would make the celebration of the Mass and the preaching of the sermon separate or separable events.[48] For the present, it will suffice to conclude that the canons of Clovesho evince a strong interest in the catechetical or teaching office of the ministry but that it is unclear in what liturgical setting, if any, this office was intended to be fulfilled.

The conventional approach to Carolingian preaching is summarized in a sentence by Archbishop Brilioth: 'The Carolingian Renaissance gave new life to the sermon, but this new life remained basically reproductive.'[49] Such assertions refer, first, to the extraordinary attention given the matters of preaching and teaching under Charles the Great and, second, to the surviving homiliaries largely or exclusively drawn from patristic writing which, as the only surviving preachers' texts, have been assumed to have been assembled in pursuance of the directives of councils, bishops, and the emperor. It has already been argued that the homiliaries were compiled primarily for use in the Office or for private devotional reading and, therefore, have only a very severely limited relevance to the problem of public preaching. To examine the validity of the remainder of Brilioth's statement, we must turn to the official documents and ask what kind or kinds of preaching and instructions their authors had in mind.

The most important group of materials is the canons of a series of ecclesiastical councils convoked in 813.[50] Each contains a passage devoted to the preaching or teaching aspect of the episcopate. The Council of Tours (canons ii–iv), after specifying a minimal number of books the bishops ought to possess and know, ordains that they should teach by word and example. The group which met at Chalon, on the other hand, stressed the importance of the preaching of the bishop during his visitations (canon xiv). Rheims devoted two canons (xiv, xv) to the subject, the first of which is similar to those of Tours and the second of which reads, 'Ut episcopi sermones et omelias sanctorum patrum, prout omnes intellegere possent, secundum proprietatem linguae praedicare studeant.'[51] Mainz (canon xxv) recognizes the preaching office as episcopal but orders that, in the bishop's absence on Sundays and feasts, someone who can make the word intelligible should preach. Another canon (xiv) of the same synod treats of the catechetical teaching of the symbol and the Lord's Prayer by the 'sacerdotes.' (Canon xxxvii of Chalon treats the same subject in different terms.) The Tours synod (canon xvii) takes up the theme of Rheims xv, linking the bishop to the use of the homiliary:

Visum est unanimitati nostrae, ut quilibet episcopus habeat omelias continentes necessarias ammonitiones, quibus subiecti erudiantur, id est de fide catholica, prout capere possint, de perpetua retributione bonorum et aeterna damnatione malorum, de resurrectione quoque futura et ultimo iudicio et quibus operibus possit promereri beata vita quibusve excludi. Et ut easdem omelias quisque aperte transferre studeat in rusticam Romanam linguam aut Thiotiscam, quo facilius cuncti possint intellegere quae dicuntur.[52]

The homiliary mentioned must not be Paul the Deacon's Homiliary, for the addresses described are not exegetical but general or catechetical. The description is more reminiscent of the markedly pastoral homiliary made by Lantperthus of Mondsee for Hildebold, archbishop of Cologne (d. 819).[53]

Of the synods of 813, only that of Arles (canon x), echoing the language of the council held at Vaison by Caesarius in 529, ordains 'ut non solum in civitatibus, sed etiam in omnibus parroechiis presbyteri ad populum verbum faciant.'[54]

Clearly this canon reflects local traditions originating in the episcopate of Caesarius; and, except for the former see of Caesarius, preaching seems still to have been regarded primarily as an episcopal function which is distinguished from more general, or catechetical, teaching of the Creed and Prayer as rudiments of the faith.

The episcopal gathering (*Concordia Episcoporum*, canon x) which summarized the work of the local synods, however, cites Tours (canon xvii), broadening and changing its terms or at least, stressing the use of the homiliary by presbyters as opposed to its possession by bishops: 'De constituendis presbyteris et de eorum praedicatione et de habendis omeliis patrum et secundum eorum doctrinam ad praedicandum ita omnibus placuit, sicut in capitulare dominico et in conventu Turonensi statutum est.'[55] Perhaps Charlemagne and his advisers had expected that the preacher's duties would have been more widely enjoined. At any rate, the view that episcopate and presbyterate were in fact the same office makes the extension an easy one. With the possible exceptions of Rabanus' first homiliary (after 826) and the work of Abbo of St-Germain-des-Prés (ca. 900),[56] however, there is no record, so far as I know, of homiliaries or other manuals clearly designed to implement this section of the *Concordia Episcoporum*. Other collections of material for the use of preachers seem to have been produced only after 950 and, thus, coincide with the reappearance in Romano-Gallican *Ordines* of references to preaching at episcopal Masses.[57] It may well be that the Carolingian dictates on preaching and even catechetical instruction could not be implemented before the level of literacy of the lower clergy had been raised.

Other conciliar documents do not clarify the practices of the period. One is constantly faced with the ambiguity of *praedicatio* and *praedico*, which seem as often to mean enunciation of doctrine, or teaching, or even reading from the Fathers (as in Rheims, xv) as preaching. The capitularies[58] repeat much of the same material, and a number list the books which are needed both for monasteries and for secular churches.[59] The famous *Capitula* of Theodulf of Orleans (d. 818), translated at least twice into Old English,[60] are often taken as a significant manifesto of the revival of preaching. They do, indeed, stress the importance of catechetical teaching as a clerical duty, but there is only scant reference to a liturgical setting for the sermon and none to exegetical preaching.[61]

Part of the historical process, inseparable from the history of homiletic practice, is the regularization of the secular clergy, especially in the greater churches.[62] The most important of the rules, the *Regula Canonicorum* of Chrodegang of Metz (d. 766), in expanded versions, became an important document of Carolingian reform. The expanded *Rule* contains a moderate provision for public preaching on at least a fortnightly basis.[63]

Finally, passing reference must be made to Amalarius, the most famous liturgical scholar of the age; for it is surely indicative of the situation that Amalarius nowhere mentions the homily as a feature of the Mass. He does, however, refer in several places to the use of the Creed at Mass – a comparatively recent phenomenon – and he seems to imply that the Gospel itself stands in place of preaching and would make a homily a redundancy.[64] Even allowing for a tendency of liturgists to be disinterested in homiletics, this is a striking omission for the scholar who examined the symbolic and typological import of every word, instrument, and act of the liturgy. One of Amalarius' few sustained references to preaching is in a passage of this sort and implies the most general definition of the term. The bell of the church is the preacher, he says; its clapper his tongue, and so forth;[65] but preaching is not made an integral part of worship. For Amalarius, the reading of the Gospel is a re-enactment of the ministry of Christ and the preaching of the word. On the whole Amalarius' reticence on the subject of preaching must increase our scepticism that preaching in the strict sense was a feature of the Mass in areas under the influence of the Carolingian liturgists.

A few generalizations must now be offered by way of conclusion to the preceding considerations of the homiliary and of preaching in general. These subjects remain difficult ones about which firm conclusions are difficult or even impossible to reach. Our picture of Carolingian preaching practice is being changed and clarified by students of the homiliaries; but the meaning of the canonistic documents needs more careful reconsideration than it has hitherto been given, and it has only been possible here to suggest some of the kinds of reinterpretation which may emerge.

The practice of preaching at Mass seems to have fallen into disuse in the Carolingian age. This development may in part be due to the adaptation of Roman practice, for both the early Roman *Ordines* and the paucity of homiletic remains from Rome indicate that preaching was rare indeed in Rome after the time of Gregory I.[66] Although preaching has been somewhat more prominent in the Gallican rite,[67] the tendency (despite the efforts of Caesarius and others) to reserve preaching to the bishop and the Carolingian tendency towards Romanization seem to have intensified the divorce between exegetical interpretation of the pericopes and the Mass proper. Even the canons of Clovesho, which enjoin both preaching and the celebration of Mass on Sundays, seem not to regard the two acts as integral aspects of a single liturgical act. The Synods of 813 were in general inclined to allow the preaching office to remain an episcopal preserve and, in this, to judge from the *Concordia Episcoporum*, evidently ran counter to the desires of the emperor and his chief ecclesiastical advisers. But neither the canons of 813 nor the *Concordia* is clear as to the setting in which preaching, whether episcopal or presbyterial, was to occur.

If the canons seem unconcerned with exegetical preaching as an integral part of the Mass, however, they are deeply and consistently concerned with the church's teaching office. This is to say that the legislators seem to have in mind catechetical rather than exegetical preaching – *sermones* not *homiliae*, to make a terminological distinction which seems not to have been made by the framers of Carolingian legislation. By 'catechetical preaching' I mean general instruction on fundamentals of the faith which, like missionary preaching, need not have a liturgical setting. The directives of the canons on preaching put relatively little emphasis on biblical exposition but do stress precisely the subject matter of catechesis: the interpretation of the Creed and Lord's Prayer, morality and its eschatological sanctions, and explanation of the liturgy.[68] Such observations as these allow us to suggest a setting for the teaching so insistently required of the clergy and to account at the same time for another phenomenon – the use of the vernacular – the evidence for which there has not been space to examine in this argument

An office in the vernacular, called in later times the *Prone* was almost certainly coming into being in the Carolingian Age and may, in its nascent form, have provided the principal setting in which the sermons enjoined by the Carolinginan hierarchy were to be delivered.[69] In its fully developed form, it was separable from the Mass, but usually it occurred after the Gospel and consisted of a translation and brief explanation of the pericope, announcements of forthcoming liturgical events, catechetical instruction based on the Creed and Lord's Prayer, and biddings or prayers and other devotions. It is by no means certain that the Prone had assumed its full form in the Carolingian period. Linsenmayer, for instance, doubts that it included a translation of the pericope at this stage;[70] but Father Jungmann feels that the canons of 813, especially Tours (canon xvii, 'transferre ... in rusticam Romanum linguam aut Thiotiscam, quo facilius cuncti possint intellegere quae dicuntur'), point to adaptations and simplifications – rather than straightforward reading – of the patristic homilies.[71] The introduction of the Creed after the reading of the Gospel and the loss of the dismissal of the catechumens from the same place in the liturgy – both phenomena roughly contemporaneous with the developments of which we are speaking – must surely have influenced the shape assumed by the Prone at this early stage. It seems likely, in view of the language implying the separability of Mass and preaching, that the Prone was not regarded as integral to the Mass and that its elements may have been used *extra* as well as *intra Missam.*

The assumption that the Carolingian legislators usually had the framework of the Prone in mind when they spoke of teaching or preaching *ad populum* allows us, in the light of the other evidence, to understand the settings they had in mind for such addresses. It allows for preaching at Mass despite the silence of

Amalarius and the pre-Ottonian *Ordines*; yet it allows as well for the tendency to speak of Masses and sermons as different things done on Sundays. It comprehends the fact that the canons clearly have instructional or catechetical preaching in view more often than exegetical addresses and implies that we are dealing with addresses distinguishable from the exegetical Mass-homilies of the patristic era. It allows for the use of the vernacular and (in view of the relative lack of vernacular preaching texts) for extemporaneity. It makes more comprehensible the fact that few homiliaries were intended for reading at Mass or *coram populo*.

Exegetical preaching – the delivery of homilies in the strict sense – seems primarily to have been associated with the Night Office for Sundays and Feasts, and the evidence is very strong that it almost always consisted of the reading of the homilies of the Fathers from the homiliaries. To preach in many sources is, simply, to read a patristic exegetical passage.[72] It is unlikely that the laity were regularly present at Nocturns, and one doubts, therefore, that the laity often heard such expositions read in church. Homiliaries made for use in the liturgy were not, however, the only kinds available. There were also homiliaries apparently designed to be sources of preaching material and, most important, homiliaries for private, meditational reading on the lections of the Offices. This latter category is of great moment when we turn to an examination of Anglo-Saxon preaching materials.

Two kinds of uses of homiletic materials may be distinguished in the Carolingian church. The first, related to the homiliaries and the Offices, is primarily associated with monastic and canonical life. Homiliaries were provided for use in the Office or for *lectio divina* and rumination on Scripture as read in the office. The homiliaries may also have impinged on the devotions of the literate laity as their devotional use spread. The second kind of exploitation of sermon materials may broadly be denoted as catechetical, and in this class one would place the bishop's teaching, enjoined as a part of his annual visitation of the diocese, and that of local clergy, which seems very often to have been limited to explanation of the Creed and Lord's Prayer, basic fundamentals of Christian morality, and, less often, the liturgy itself. Such preaching seems to have been associated with the Prone, which is to say that in form and content it does not represent a strict continuity with the Mass-sermons of the Fathers of the church.

As in other areas, so also in the history of preaching the dictates of the early ninth century seem to have been implemented by the tenth-century reformers. Hence, references to preaching at Mass find their way into the *Ordines* of the early Ottonian period. Yet it should be understood that the nature of preaching changed radically after the eleventh century as the form of the sermon was transformed when exegetical, patristically based exposition of the Gospel gave way to the kinds of thematic, rhetorically elaborated preaching inculcated in the

Artes Praedicandi.[73] Nevertheless, when preaching – and particularly preaching in the people's language – had a setting in the Mass, the Prone was usually the frame within which it was delivered.

If one compares these tentative suggestions with those of earlier historians of these movements, he discovers that the present account is marked chiefly by uncertainty as to conclusions, by a more cautious or conservative reading of the documentary evidence, and by scepticism concerning the use of exegetical homilies at Mass. That there was important activity in the field of homiletics under Charles the Great and his successors goes without saying, but that we fully understand the forms this activity took or the settings in which preaching materials were used is less certain. It will be enough if these remarks should lead to a new examination of the matter and if they can assist us to look anew at the problem of preaching in England.

5

The Preaching Materials of
Ælfric of Eynsham

An inquiry into the uses to which churchmen put the vernacular homiletic materials produced in England at the end of the tenth century and the beginning of the eleventh must begin with some comment on the evidence of canonical and other documents. Here, as on the Continent, one is hampered by the paucity of material related to lesser, secular churches. Even if one makes allowances for this serious lacuna, however, the influence of the monastic reform movement on the homiletic literature is striking. One remembers, above all, that continental production of homiliaries was closely attached to the monastic tradition and that the most influential homiliaries were associated with the Offices.

In a number of ways, the monasteries of the Early Middle Ages kept alive the patristic tradition of exegetical preaching. The continental reformers of the regular life, continuing to incorporate homiletic lections from the Fathers in the third Nocturn of Sundays and feasts, nevertheless broadened the range of readings which touched on the homiletic; and the Capitularies of Aachen (817) of Benedict of Aniane[1] and the uses of such reformed centres as Cluny lie behind the prescriptions of the *Regularis Concordia*.[2] A chief feature of the *Regularis* was a quasi-Office, the daily meeting of the Chapter;[3] and it is to the Chapter that our attention must primarily be directed in connection with original preaching in English monastic centres, for homiletic exercises seem to have been concentrated there. As Dom Jean Leclercq has shown, most of the original preaching of the Benedictines, like the lections from the Fathers' preaching, was exegetical.[4] It took the form of commentary on the refectory and other readings, and it is in the direct line of descent from such exegetical conferences as the *Moralia in Job* of Gregory the Great rather than that of the non-expository conferences of Cassian. According to the *Regularis Concordia*, the capitular office took place after Morrow Mass and began with the reading of the Martyrology, collects, and versicles. Next 'legatur regula uel, si dies festus fuerit, euangelium ipsius diei, de qua lectione a priore prout Dominus dederit dicatur.'[5] An act of penance and prayers for the dead followed. Apparently in addition to the homiletic lections of the Night Office and perhaps also because the nocturnal lections had been abbreviated, a new place was found for additional homiletic exercises. That setting was very unlikely to have been available to the laity, and none of these sermons from our period have been preserved.[6] Nothing is said in the *Concordia* about preaching at Mass. Nor is anything said about the language in which the *lectiones* and the abbatial homilies were to be pronounced. One customarily assumes that the language of the monasteries was Latin; but, in fact, large numbers of monastic documents, liturgical and customary, were translated into English, and there is some evidence that in certain monasteries two schools – one in Latin, the other in English – were conducted.[7] Thus the reformed English monasteries may possibly have made liturgical use of the native tongue or have prepared vernacular texts to facilitate in some fashion the participation of members of the English school in the liturgical life of the community. The relationship of monastic liturgies to the rise of vernacular preaching materials may, then, have been underestimated.[8]

There is also ample evidence in other documents that the matter of preaching in the secular church received considerable attention in the late-Saxon period. Indeed, the evidence, which has not often been reviewed by literary historians, is such as to suggest a degree of concern similar to that of the Carolingian reformers at the beginning of the ninth century. First among these testimonies must stand the documents prepared for the instruction of the clergy by Ælfric and Wulfstan. Ælfric's pastorals[9] are all concerned primarily with the secular clergy.[10] Of the three letters relevant to this inquiry (i to Wulfsige; 2 and ii for Wulfstan), the earliest is dated shortly after the publication of *Catholic Homilies* ii in 992, and the later two belong to the middle of the following decade.[11] It will be suggested later that the letter to Wulfsige and the scheme of the *Catholic Homilies* may indicate that Ælfric was more greatly influenced in his homiletic expectations at the earlier stages of his career by rules for secular canons such as that of Chrodegang of Metz; but it will suffice here to treat these documents synoptically. All contain lists of the seven orders of clergy (i.29ff.; 2.115ff.; ii.99ff.; see also Fehr's Anhang v, which was probably written by Ælfric). All allude to the preaching function of the presbyterial office, which is shared by bishops and presbyters (i.42; 2.127; ii.113); but such expressions as *bodian* and *praedicare* are also used of the lector (i.31; Anhang v) and the deacon (i.42) in the letter to Wulfsige.[12] All the clergy are admonished to keep the Offices of the seven canonical hours (i.49; 2.62–4 and 136; ii.64–73 and 160).

When it comes to specific instruction regarding preaching, the letters of Ælfric display the same frustrating lack of precision that has been noted in the

Carolingian documents but seem, like the continental writings, to show a tendency towards the development of a Prone or teaching office after the reading of the Gospel. Thus one finds in the Wulfsige letter (1), among other instructions on the performance of the Mass, the following:

61. Se mæssepreost sceal secgan sunnandagum *and* mæssedagum þæs godspelles angyt on englisc þam folce.

62. *And* be þam pater nostre *and* be þam credan eac, swa he oftost mage, þam mannum to onbryrdnysse, þæt hi cunnon geleafan and heora cristendóm gehealdan.

63. Warnige se lareow wið þæt, þe se witega cwæð: *Canes muti non possunt latrare.* Þa dumban hundas ne magan beorcan.

64. We scelolon beorcan *and* bodigan þam læwedum, þe læs hy for larlyste losian sceoldan.[13]

Similarly 2.159 and 11.175 speak of the necessity 'dicere populo fidem catholicam *et* sensum euuangelii propria lingua' ('mannum bodian þone soþan geleafan *and* hym lár-spel secgan'); and the English version of the first Wulfstan letter acknowledges that since not all priests know Latin, 'Vs bisceopum gedafenað, þæt we þa bóclican lare þe ure cánon us tæcð *and* eac seo Cristes bóc, eow preostum geopenigan on engliscum gereorde.'[14]

Despite these clear statements that the clergy are expected to preach (or, more accurately, to teach) at celebrations of the Mass, homiliaries are apparently not among the books Ælfric expects priests to own when he lists the 'weapons' or liturgical books mass-priests must have for the fulfilment of their offices. Since the three lists of liturgical books Ælfric gives are not in absolute accord, they must be presented in parallel and compared with the list given in Ælfric's apparent source and another list, composed in English, of the late eleventh century.[15]

Fehr I.25	*Fehr 2.137*	*Fehr II.157*
saltere (1)	missalem (4)	mæsse-bóc (4)
pistolboc (2)	lectionarium quod vo-	pistel-bóc (2) [*MS D om*]
godspellboc (3)	cant epistolarium (2)	sang-bóc (5) [*MS D:* -bec]
mæsseboc (4)	psalterium (1)	ræding-bóc (10 or 3) [*MS D:* -bec]
sangbec (5)	nocturnalem (5 ?)	saltere (1)
handboc (6)	gradalem (5 ?)	handbóc (6)
gerím (7)	manualem (6)	penitentialem (9)
passionalem (8)	passionalem (8)	gerím (7)
penitentialem (9)	pœnitentialem (9)	
rædingboc (10)	Compotum (7)	
	librum cum lectionibus	
	ad nocturnas (10)	

Ecgbert[16]
psalterium (1)
lectionarium (2)
antefonarium (5)
missalem (4)
baptisterium (probably 6)
martyrologium (8)
in anno circuli ad praedica-
tionem cum bonis operibus
compotum et ciclo, hoc est jus
sacerdotum (7)
penitentialem (9)

Leofric Inventory[17]
Cristes-bec [*Eng. and Lat. versions*] (3)
mæsse-bec (4)
collectaneum (10 ?)
pistel-bec (2)
sang-bec [*perhaps* Antiph. diurnale] (5)
nicht-sang [Antiph. nocturnale] (5)
'ad te leuaui' [Antiph. missae; Graduale] (5)
tropere
salteras (1)
ymneras
sumer-ræding-boc (10)
winter-ræding-boc (10)
regula canonicorum
martyrologium (8)
canon on Leden 7 scrift-boc on Englisc (9)
spel-boc wintres 7 sumres

Fehr, in his edition of Ælfric's Pastorals,[18] takes great care to interpret these terms accurately. In general, his suggestions are acceptable, but the translation of *godspellboc* as *Homilienbuch* is open to serious question. Given Ælfric's customary use of the term *godspell* and his explication of it in one homily,[19] he must have had in mind for Fehr 1.52 either an Evangeliary or a complete copy of the Gospels.[20] It is conceivable that, in framing the Wulfsige letter in the early 990s, he had in mind an Epistolary containing all the subdeacon's lections and an Evangeliary, whereas by the time he wrote the Wulfstan letters he had come to think of a complete lectionary which, in the Latin version of the Wulf-stan letter, he calls *epistolarium*. In the homilies themselves, he uses *Cristes boc* to refer to an entire Gospel or to the four collectively; but *godspell*, although it may refer to the books, is also used of the liturgical pericopes. It may, then, be more likely that the list in the letter to Wulfsige refers to an Evangeliary than to a complete Gospel book.[21]

At any rate, it is striking that, except insofar as the *rædingbec* or books of lections for the nocturnal office may have contained *capitula* or lections from the homiliary, he does not include the homiliary *per circulum anni dominicis diebus et singulis festibitatibus aptae* (or what the Leofric list calls *spel-boc wintres 7 sumres*)[22] in his catalogue of priestly weapons. Apparently, it was not for Ælfric a necessary part of the secular clergyman's armory. Were it not for other and better-known evidence, one might wonder on the basis of the pastoral letters whether Ælfric knew of homiliaries at all or whether he thought them useful to the secular clergy. Insofar as the homiliary was needed for the recital of the Offices, the *ræding-bec* and other collections containing the lections of the Offices may have made it obsolete for clergymen bound by canonical Rules.

After these lists in the Latin letter for Wulfstan and in two manuscripts of the Letter to Wulfsige, there appears the declaration that these books are necessary possessions of priests ('nead-prin' [1.53]; 'necessitas ... non super-fluitas' [2.138]). The copy of the Wulfsige letter in a third manuscript (Bodleian, Junius 121, probably from Exeter) alters this requirement slightly in an 'un-authorised revision.'[23] The Old English letter for Wulfstan mentions the need of books (II.157) but without a list of indispensable volumes. Ælfric's stipulation that these liturgical books be owned by the clergy is, at any rate, deliberately omitted in a short piece by Wulfstan concerning the examination of ordinands and ordination.[24] Although Wulfstan relies here on the same *Capitula* of Haito of Basel which Fehr cites as a possible source for the list of necessary books in Ælfric's Latin Letter for Wulfstan (2), Wulfstan avoids any implication that an ordinand is to own books. One may assume he knew candidates were unlikely to possess books. The candidate was to be examined on his beliefs, his knowledge of how to teach others, his knowledge of what God has done and is expected to do (i.e., sacred history and eschatology), and his understanding of liturgics, canon law, and calendrical computation. The teaching function is quite clearly limited to catechesis rather than to explication and homiletics. If one is in-adequately trained ('samlæredne'), he ought to complete his education before taking orders unless there is extenuating need, in which case the ordination may take place on the condition that there is a firm intention on the part of the ordinand to continue his education. It is the clear implication of this and other mitigations of Ælfric's stipulations in Wulfstan's work that the archiepiscopal administrator found it necessary, owing to the level of clerical education (and also, perhaps, financial realities), to reduce the ideal requirements as to the training, possessions, and liturgical obligations of his clergy.[25]

Wulfstan's comments on ordination provide a context in which to consider his other comments on preaching and teaching. His scattered statements on the subject, closely related to Ælfric's and to the same sources, are even less helpful to the inquirer who asks in what setting and by whom the English vernacular homilies were used. In the *Institutes of Polity* phrases such as 'ge wel bodian ge wel bisnian' (I *Pol.* 67, 68, 70, compare 43; II *Pol.* 60, 103, 146, compare 42, 105) or 'læran and lædan' (I.66; II. 102, 176) are used of bishops, priests, and abbots.[26] Often such expressions echo commonplaces of the Carolingian canonists and are coupled with eschatological warnings which are also reminiscent of the earlier canonistic writings.[27] The necessity for pastors to exhort their flocks and to lead them by word and example is so frequent a theme in Wulfstan's writings that Professor Bethurum has called it 'Wulfstan's favourite subject.'[28] This judgment cannot, of course, be denied; but when one turns to the bishop and legislator for details concerning the practice of preaching, he is not greatly enlightened. In the *Canons of Edgar*, dated ca. 1005–1007, for example, the general canon dealing with the preaching office ('And we læraδ þæt preostas ælce sunnandæge folce bodigan and aa wel bisnian' [52])[28] is placed not among directions on the performance of the Mass and Offices but next to a canon (51) requiring priests to instruct the young so as to provide themselves with assistants. Furthermore, by linking *bodigan* with its alliterative partner *bisnian* in this context, Wulfstan actually weakens the force of his probable source: 'Ut omnibus festis et diebus Dominicis unusquisque sacerdos Evangelium Christi praedicet populo.'[30] He emphasizes the importance of teaching the laity the *Pater Noster* and Creed (17,22) and requires the clergy to read the daily offices in church at the correct times, but he omits Ælfric's list of the Offices.[31] He says priests are not to say Mass without a copy of the canon 'before their eyes' (32) and requires that priests have good copies of the requisite liturgical books (34), without listing the contents of a minimal library. The lack of precision in Wulfstan's canonistic writing confirms the impression given by his homilies themselves: that the archbishop was more concerned with the preaching office as a moral and instructional function than as a vehicle for systematic exposition of the Scriptures. Most of his preaching to the laity might have been set outside the liturgy, perhaps as a feature of his visitations and, on occasion, of meetings of the *witan*; if it came within a liturgical frame, it must often have been as part of the catechetical Prone.

Both Ælfric and Wulfstan seem to have known a fairly standard group of texts on which they based their occasional comments on the practice of preaching. The *Capitula* of Theodulf, the enlarged *Rule* of Chrodegang, the Ecgbert and pseudo-Egbert documents, and the like form a group of standard works which both clergymen kept to hand for reference in addition to such more exclusively monastic documents as the *Capitula* of Aachen (817) and the *Regularis Concordia*.[32] The picture we have both from these canonical writings and their reading and source lists is one very like that of the Carolingian situation in the first quarter of the ninth century. If they differ, it is, curiously, in that neither explicitly betrays an interest in the homiliaries. But the argument from silence clearly has little force here.

One might expect, in a search for evidence concerning the settings in which Anglo-Saxon preaching took place, to find some assistance from the hagiographers. But between the *vitae* of Dunstan, Oswald, and Æthelwold and the life of St Wulfstan of Worcester no English saints of the period were the subjects of hagiographers;[33] and only two of these four tenth- and eleventh-century lives are of interest here.[34] The first is the Life of St Dunstan by an Anglo-Saxon, of whose name we know only the initial, B.[35] B reports that on Ascension Day in 988, only two days before his death, the archbishop of Canterbury preached not once but thrice at a single Mass:

His ille alloquiis caeterisque praedicamentis salubribus ter sub una diei ipsius celebratione commissorum corda affatim permonuit; primo enim ut ecclesiasticus ordo post lectionis Evangelium jure insinuat [sic]; secundo post gratuitam collatae sibi potestatis benedictionem; tertio vero post piae pacis conferentiam quando communi carmine cecinimus, 'Agnus Dei . . . ,' tunc quidem et ipse commissos sibi agniculos, a peccatorum prius ponderibus leviatos, pio pastori, Agno videlicet Jesu Christo Qui mundi hujus crimina misertus tollere venit, sub pacis custodia servandos sine macula commendavit.[36]

The whole account is so framed as to emphasize the saint's anticipation of his death and his possession of peculiar sanctity, prophetic gifts, and charity as his life drew to a close. The second and third allocutions were clearly regarded as extraordinary. In content they seem to have been perhaps catechetical and certainly pastoral. They may simply have been rather moving commentaries on the pontifical blessing and the peace. There are textual problems with B's account of the place of the first sermon in the Ascension Day Mass, but B does give what purports to be a summary of Dunstan's Ascension Day teaching just above the passage quoted. Although he stresses its connection with the reading of the Gospel, the précis he gives does not seem to be exegetical; it is rather a summary of the work of Christ and of the Church's teaching concerning the nature of Christ, climaxed with an account of the Ascension.[37] The evidence is not sufficient to indicate whether we have here a bishop's exegetical homily in the patristic tradition or a more general address in the newer tradition of the Prone; but the witness of B seems to point towards the more modern approach to preaching. The sermon, in other words, was probably not an exegetical exercise but a vernacular explanation of the importance of the occasion, concluded, perhaps, with a paraphrase of the Gospel. The later biographers, including Adelard (who is almost contemporary with and in some ways independent of B), tend even more than B towards a miraculous interpretation of this event, which occurred after Dunstan had received a vision of his forthcoming death and at a moment when (as Gregory the Great argued in Dialogues, IV) the saints have a clearer view of things eternal.

The Vita of St Wulfstan of Worcester was written in English by Coleman and survives only in a Latin adaptation by William of Malmesbury.[38] It recounts several incidents of interest here. While he was yet prior at Worcester, St Wulfstan undertook not only to reform his monastery but also, by preaching, the pastoral care of the populace: 'omni dominica et maioribus sollempnitatibus in ecclesia infundebat ei monita salutis ... ex alto stationis.'[39] The indication of the place from which Wulfstan preached is interesting, if it is not an anachronism introduced by William of Malmesbury; and despite the reference to readings from the evangelists and prophets, the preaching sounds catechetical rather than exegetical. Most fascinating, however, is the fact that Wulfstan's preaching evoked a rebuke from a foreign monk, Winric, who believed that only bishops should preach and that monks should be both silent and cloistered. God punished Winric in a vision for this impudence; but one suspects he was honestly reflecting ecclesiastical laws and customs as he knew them. The author of the *vita* makes it clear that the inhabitants of Worcester were not accustomed to hearing sermons, whether by monks or by seculars.

In the context of St Wulfstan's seemingly futile efforts to inculcate Christian peaceableness within his diocese after his elevation to the episcopate, the *vita* recounts the delegation to Coleman of the preaching office: 'Colemanno predicationis delegabat officium' (cap. 16). There is no reference to a liturgical setting for this preaching, and it may be that Coleman's office was that of catechist and teacher or of missioner charged to reform the morals of St Wulfstan's subjects and not simply that of mass-preacher. The 'predicationis officium' here, in other words, evokes the kind of general moral admonition which is also associated with the bishop of Worcester's turn-of-the-century predecessor and namesake.[40] But we do know that Coleman read Ælfric in at least two manuscripts in which he made marginal notes and that in one of these he took issue with Ælfric's note to the effect that the three days before Easter are 'swig-dagum' or days on which there was to be no preaching.[41] It can be shown that Coleman had a fairly special knowledge of Ælfric's work and that in this instance he was thinking of catechetical preaching outside the Mass, not (as was Ælfric) of exegetical commentary on the propers.

The hagiographical evidence seems neither to confirm nor to contradict the conclusions reached from a study of the other external testimonies to the practice of preaching. Although I know of no explicit reference to the Prone from England as early as the lifetimes of Ælfric and Wulfstan,[42] the general evidence gives one a picture of a situation in which the Prone must almost necessarily have been the setting in which much of the preaching called for in the canonical writings and recalled in the *Lives* took place. If this is so, one would expect most of the vernacular preaching materials to be catechetical in thrust, not cut from the exegetical cloth of the patristic materials in most of the homiliaries.

B / THE INTERNAL EVIDENCE

Turning to the evidence of the homilies of Ælfric themselves and especially to the evidence of the manuscripts in which they survive, we may address ourselves first to the Prefaces of the *Catholic Homilies* – or *liber catholicorum sermonum anglicae in ecclesia per annum recitandi*, to quote the incipit of the only manuscript which contains the full set of Prefaces, Cambridge University Library MS Gg.3.28 (f. 3).[43] Although the Prefaces, like the incipit, stress the fact that the pieces which make up the two series are to be recited publicly in church, it needs to be observed, first, that Ælfric has other uses in mind for his work. The volume has been translated 'ob aedificationem simplicium ... sive legendo sive audiendo' (Thorpe 1.1/6–7), using simple language 'quo facilius possit ad cor pervenire legentium vel audientium ad utilitatem animarum suarum' (1/8–9). The Latin Preface of Series II does not repeat these expressions, but its English Preface states that the book is 'þam mannum to rædenne þa þæt Leden ne cunnon' (II.2/6–7).[44] These expressions suggest that, in addition to their primary use as books for public reading, Ælfric had it in mind that, like many of the Carolingian homiliaries Barré has studied, the *Sermones Catholici* could also be used for private, devotional reading. If one overlooks the incipit, the English Preface to the First Series contains no clear reference to public reading. Its concluding references to prophetic injunctions to preach could, if one read the Preface outside its context in MS Gg.3.28, refer to the act of writing the book as an act of preaching.[45] This prefatory item, elsewhere adapted as an independent homily,[46] might originally have been drafted as the opening to a devotional collection of sermons.

Further evidence that the *Sermones Catholici* may have devotional as well as liturgical uses is to be found in a Latin note to the scribe which was, happily, copied into the English Preface of Series I (8/16–18).[47] Aldorman Æthelweard – to whose son, Æthelmær, Ælfric has already made allusion (1.2/15) as the person responsible for his transfer from Winchester to Cernel – has asked for a copy containing forty-four *sententias*; he may have such a volume, but all others are to have forty items, as does the exemplar.[48] Æthelweard and Æthelmær are important figures in the literary history of Ælfric's period. Æthelweard probably translated the *Anglo-Saxon Chronicle* into Latin for his cousin Matilda, abbess of Essen;[49] the late Robin Flower sought to connect the family of Æthelweard with the early history of the Exeter book;[50] above all (as there has already been occasion to remark), they were patrons of Ælfric, whose interest in him extended from his early days at Winchester to his abbacy at Eynsham. Yet the role of these laymen in the formation of Ælfric's canon has been almost ignored in the most recent studies in favour of emphasis on the rationale of the abbots' life-work, the fact that 'the publication of his major works had the character of a consciously "literary" act'[51]

Æthelweard and Æthelmær are known to have commissioned the *Lives of Saints*, an augmented *Catholic Homilies* I, presumably also a version or copy of

Catholic Homilies II, and portions of Genesis.[52] Such a library – and one can be reasonably certain that these great lords had other books – would go a long way towards enabling Æthelweard and his son to follow in their own devotions the observances of monks.[53] Perhaps we see here – and elsewhere in the phenomena under discussion in this chapter – what Edmund Bishop, the liturgical historian, in a study of the influence of the *Regularis Concordia* on the much later *Prymer*, called 'a law' of liturgical history: 'the source of new forms of private devotion which becomes by and by popularized is in the religious order.'[54]

In support of this suggestion, which cannot be followed at length here, two observations may be made. The first is that Æthelmær's charter for Eynsham hints that, at least after the founding of Eynsham in 1005, he followed the devotions of the regulars: 'and ic me sylf wille mid þære geferrædene gemænelice libban. and þære are mid him notian þa hwile þe min lif bið.'[55] The second is that there is precedent for this kind of lay piety in the life of St Gerald of Aurillac (586–909) who, for Odo, second abbot of Cluny (d. 942), was the ideal layman: literate, inclined to the religious life but importuned by his bishop to remain a layman, leading the religious life in his own home as nearly as possible. Shaven and tonsured, Gerald read the Offices and heard readings at meals, sometimes explaining them to those at table rather as the abbot expounded lections to his community.[56] Ælfric, in presenting (*inter alia*) the *Sermones Catholici* to Æthelweard and Æthelmær as devotional manuals, may have been helping his patrons to imitate in the world some of the practices of the monks. His own patrons were not the only literate laymen contemporary with Ælfric who collected this sort of reading matter. Ælfwold, bishop of Crediton, willed a martyrology and a Hrabanus – both presumably in Latin – to one Ordulf, probably the ealdorman who founded Tavistock Abbey and was an uncle of Æthelred.[57]

A final observation on the Prefaces: they demonstrate (as also do the source studies of Father Smetana) that Ælfric knew how the usual homiliary for the Offices was put together and that he was quite consciously – at least in Thorpe's MS Gg.3.28 – making another kind of book. There is a strong tradition which goes back at least as far as Charlemagne's prefatory letter for the volume of Paul the Deacon, of describing a homiliary as a book of homilies for the Christian year; often, as in the Leofric Inventory, it is added that the collection is subdivided for the *horaria* of winter and summer. It has already been noted that Ælfric's sources for the Pastoral Letters contain such descriptions. So does the Latin Preface of the First Series: 'Alterum vero librum modo dictando habemus in manibus, qui illos tractatus vel passiones continet quos iste omisit; nec tamen omnia Evangelia tangimus *per circulum anni*, sed illa tantummodo quibus speramus sufficere posse simplicibus ad animarum emendationem ...'[58] Ælfric's concession that others might rearrange his Series I and II *per circulum anni* further stressed this point. The statements that his subject-matter is not restricted to the Gospel pericopes (I.1/18–20; II.2/14–15) are further signals that we are not dealing here with the homiliary as it was conceived by Paul the Deacon.

Further hints as to the sort of book Ælfric was intending to construct in Thorpe's exemplar, MS Gg.3.28,[59] are to be gained from an examination of its contents. First, Ælfric seems, in a rough way and in the First Series in particular, to be providing materials for roughly every other week except where a concatenation of events or a season of special importance seems to dictate otherwise. For example, Series I provides a sermon for Christmas, the three saints' days following, and the octave of Christmas; II reduces the selection to Christmas and St Stephen;[60] similarly the beginning and middle of Lent, Palm Sunday, Easter, and Rogationtide (that favourite season of Anglo-Saxon sermon writers) are treated in both series; the proximity of saints' days which seem to merit attention often disrupts the fortnightly scheme. In *CH* II, Easter is apparently provided with two sermons. The first is the non-exegetical *De Sacrificio in die Pascae*. The second is a composite sermon treating the pericopes for Monday and Wednesday in Easter week but for reading on Easter,[61] perhaps because it seems especially fitting to Ælfric to treat Scripture on the holiest of days and because the Sunday Gospel had already been explicated in the First Series. The second part of the composite piece, on the Wednesday lection, is clearly to be read on Sunday because 'We wenað þæt ge ealle on andwerdnysse her ne beon to ðam dæge þe we þæt godspel rædan sceolon.'[62] I would suggest that there is at work here – tempered in the extreme by Ælfric's sense of liturgical priorities – the principle of the expanded *Rule* of Chrodegang (cap. xliv; OE version, cap. xlii) that preaching should take place 'tuwa on monþe, þæt is ymbe feowertine niht.'[63] If one put the two Series together, he could come closer to the ideal of completeness advocated in Chrodegang's *Rule*; but it may be indicative of the state of affairs in England in the last decade of the millennium that Ælfric is content with a preaching schedule that is better than semimonthly. Even though he provides a bit less material on the pericopes for Sundays after Pentecost than for the great Dominical seasons, he has far more than is given in such homiliaries for use in the secular church as, say, that of Rabanus Maurus, which has only general sermons for use between Pentecost and Advent.

Second, there are aspects of the contents of the collection as exemplified by MS Gg.3.28 which lead one to feel rather strongly that the expression *liber sermonum catholicorum* in the incipits and the explicit[64] is not casual but deliberate. One would not be surprised to find such a nicety in Ælfric's writing, even though it is generally agreed that his contemporaries used *homilia* and *sermo* almost interchangeably.[65] The collection contains, in the first place, a number of items that are *sermones* in the strict sense: *De Initio Creature*, the initial item of Series I, with its rubric *quando volueris* is the most obvious example; and its hexaemeral subject matter is reminiscent of the great patristic catechetical orations. Next would come some of the Rogationtide items, especially the *De Dominica Oratione* and *De Fide Catholica* of Series I, which put one in mind of the frequently iterated injunction to explain the Symbol and *Pater Noster* and which appear in some manuscripts in contexts that make it clear they were also used *quando volueris*.[66] The same might be said of the Rogation Monday and Tuesday items in the Second Series. Indeed, if one examines as well the non-Ælfrician sermons *in letania maiore*, he has the impression that this season became in the late-Saxon church a conventional collecting-place for general catechetical and parenetic or hortatory sermons – a stress which is not, so far as I can discover, discernible in continental homiliaries.[67]

But perhaps it may also be said that the exegetical homilies are in fact *sermones*. They invariably begin with a translation,[68] which is reminiscent of the canonical injunctions to explain the pericope in the native tongue; and they proceed to abbreviate, paraphrase, and combine the *homiliae* of the Fathers in a way quite foreign to most of the homiliaries or to the breviaries. Perhaps as simple (and yet amazingly sophisticated) appropriations of the contents of the homiliary 'ob aedificationem simplicium' (I.1/5), Ælfric's conception of the *Sermones catholici* at the stage recorded by MS Gg.3.28 is more original than has been recognized. Although the method of composition by amalgamation of source homilies was probably derived from the school of Auxerre, the use of such writings for preaching to the people may well have been a new departure. Finally, one may note the occurrence in the *Sermones catholici* of passages that are essentially announcements to the congregation concerning the progress of the liturgical year. The note explaining the omission of the Alleluia and the Gloria from Septuagesima to Easter (Thorpe II.84) and the explanation of Pascha (II.282) are examples; there are, I think, others.[69] Another fairly unusual feature of the work is the inclusion in Series I of a homily for the First Sunday in Advent based on the Epistle. Max Förster saw some reason to connect it with Smaragdus,[70] which means that we may have to look for Ælfric's model among those Carolingian books into which the homilies on the Epistles had been interpolated. Such books, it should be remembered, tended to be devotional and not liturgical homiliaries.

If one considers these symptoms as a group, he may conclude that we see in Ælfric the tendency, which advances considerably beyond the practice of such predecessors as Rabanus, towards the development of the Prone or vernacular office in which the Gospel was explained, announcements were made about the season, the people were catechized, and prayers were bidden. If this is the case, we have in the *Sermones catholici* evidence of the kind of priestly office which was growing to replace the all-but-abandoned office of preaching as it had been practiced by the bishops of the early centuries of the Christian era. The Prone seems to have come into being under the aegis of the reformers alongside and under the influence of the Carolingian extension and development of the homiliary but not as an aspect of the work of the homiliarists.

The collection of materials appearing in MS Gg.3.28 after the explicit and *oratio* on folio 255 seems to confirm this conclusion. These pieces – *De Temporibus Anni*,[71] texts of creeds, the Lord's Prayer and other prayers in English, a piece on penitence in Lent; and the Pastoral for Wulfsige (Fehr I) – may, as Sisam argued,[72] have been added as they were prepared in a fairly casual manner; but they are copied into Gg.3.28 from an exemplar, and they seem to have been transcribed here because the scribe felt they completed the book and enhanced its usefulness. Since the manuscript is now thought to have been prepared at Ælfric's scriptorium,[73] the authority of these appendices must be greater than Sisam recognized. The utility of *De Temporibus Anni* as a companion to the *compotus* is clear. The Creeds and Prayers are semi-official translations on which the most essential elements of catechetical instruction could be based. The other prayers, which are both general and reminiscent of well-known Latin collects, would likewise have been useful for bidding at the end of a period of catechetical instruction. The passage on penitence, which also emphasizes the importance of knowing the *Pater Noster* and Creed (Thorpe II.604/15ff.) and contains what may have been a separate passage of general doctrinal instruction on the nature of the Trinity and the work of Christ,[74] begins with a bidding of repentance which expands on the note at the end of the Quinquagesima sermon in the First Series (Thorpe I.164). It contains a sentence which might serve both as a rationale for catechesis in general and the Prone in particular: 'Se láreow sceal secgan ðam læwedum mannum þæt andigit to ðam Pater nostre and to þam Credan, þæt hí witon hwæs hí biddon æt Gode, and hú hí sceolon on God gelyfan' (II.604/17–20).[75] Another note (II.608) stresses the requirements of abstinence by the laity in Lent and at other seasons of fasting. The manuscript concludes with an imperfect copy of Fehr's *Brief* I to Wulfsige, now usually dated 993–5. This letter, addressed to the secular or canonical clergy,[76] contains the instruction on preaching which has been discussed above. The reader need only be reminded that it enjoins explanation in English of the *angit* of the Gospel on Sundays and feasts and frequent catechizing on the *Pater Noster* and Creed.[77]

A recent study of the special qualities of the Second Series of the *Sermones catholici* as compared with the First supports the argument that Ælfric had in mind the needs of the preacher-catechist. Unlike the First Series, the later collection contains a number of composite homilies or items augmented 'with extra sections sometimes only remotely connected to the original conclusions or to provide linking passages.' Dr M.R. Godden argues that, whereas the first collection was to be read more or less as written to a congregation, the second is addressed rather to the preacher who would use it and not only allows him considerable choice of material but also on occasion retains learned comments or asides on Ælfric's rationale.[78] Thus the Second Series more nearly approaches the genre of the manual for preachers or catechists than the First.

At the stage represented by Cambridge University Library MS Gg.3.28, Ælfric seems to have conceived for the *liber catholicorum sermonum anglicae* two quite different uses. With some augmentation, it might be used by Æthelweard – and presumably also by others – as a manual of devotional readings. This clearly secondary use makes the book analogous to a large and important class of Carolingian homiliaries. Ælfric's books were to be used primarily for reading *ad populum*, however; and the intentions of the monk and mass-priest of Cerne Abbas appeared in this regard to be distinct from those of such homiliarists as Paul the Deacon, whose work provided lections for the third Nocturn *per circulum anni* and was arranged in parts for winter and summer.[79] Ælfric's arrangement, running from Christmas through Advent in two cycles of pieces for the Temporale and Sanctorale seems to be uncommon, if not unique. Furthermore, it looks as though he intended to make pieces better described as instruction for the laity in the Prone, a vernacular office which grew up *in medias missae* in place of the homily properly so called. The appendix of *Catholic Homilies* II, falling after the explicit but copied in the manuscript without evidence of having been added later, looks like a collection of materials useful to the clergy in the fulfilment of their catechetical and penitential functions. The appendix concludes with a summary of the canon law as it applies to the secular clergy. Though Ælfric worked from one or more homiliaries *per circulum anni* in preparing many of these *sermones*, his finished work was something quite different and intended for quite different uses.

Before turning to analysis of the later stages of the development of the Ælfrician corpus, we may allude briefly and speculatively to the stages which precede both MSS. Gg.3.28 and Royal 7C.xii – stages of which there is no record. It is generally assumed that Ælfric assembled and disseminated as the two series of *Sermones catholici* materials he had composed for preaching to the lay-folk as mass-priest at Cernel. This is, of course, possible – though there may have been a tendency to make *mæssepreost* mean too much.[80] His other work suggests that Ælfric was not simply the Cernel missioner or catechist, however, but the master of the school. If so, it is conceivable that originally his English sermons were for the monolingual of the school and community of Cernel or (earlier) of Winchester.[81] They may, thus, have been monastic rather than secular, and it is at least remotely conceivable that they had a place in the Night or the Capitular Office. Their use at meals or as *lectio divina* is more likely. If one of these possibilities were the case, the original uses of Ælfric's sermons would bring his work closer to the homiliaries than they were, according to the argument given above, at the stage represented by MS Gg.3.28. Even the Prefaces, which represent the later stage of development, might conceivably convey such an intention. *Simplices* ('ob aedificationem simplicium,' Thorpe 1.1/6,26) might be applied to monastic novices or members of the school as well as to the laity.[82]

My present strong feeling is that Gg.3.28 was intended primarily for use in instructing the laity at the Prone, although there are moments when it is tempting to put the *Sermones* into the monastic tradition from which they ultimately sprang and within which, in some ways, it would be easier to account for the existence of a collection so largely exegetical. Certainly the numerous introductory remarks in the First Series on the reading of the Gospel – in one case the deacon is specified as the lector (Thorpe 1.152/2–3), in others it is simply said to have been read (206/4; 238/13; 510/23; 548/7) – or of the Epistle (294/13; 314/1) argue strongly that the pieces were for use in the Prone. This possibility is fortified by the fact that these references are customarily associated with the reading of a vernacular paraphrase of the pericope. Twice the Mass is specifically mentioned (II.438/5–6; Pope XVII.19).[83] Thus, although the same Gospel was read at the Night Office as at the Mass of the same day, the evidence that Ælfric's *sermones* were for reading to the laity at Mass seems incontrovertible; that the setting of these readings was the catechetical Prone seems very likely.

There is evidence that in later years Ælfric came to conceive of his work in rather different terms from those discernible in Thorpe's manuscript. It is not possible here to outline all the stages of the development, for such a task requires minute analysis of each of the manuscripts;[84] but two stages – an intermediate and the final – may be mentioned briefly. The first involves the production of five homilies for the Fridays of Lent (Pope II, III, V, VI, and Assmann V), which were issued as a set, probably before the publication of the *Lives of Saints*.[85] Although Ælfric was by no means restricted to a given homiliary for sources or, indeed, for the chief materials which were used in developing these homilies, the interpolated homiliary of Haymo of Auxerre was almost certainly 'the starting-point for Ælfric's composition of the series.'[86] The evidence of reliance on Haymo here is not absolutely conclusive in Professor Pope's view, but the likelihood of such dependence is increased by the fact that there are few homilies on these weekday pericopes,[87] which came to be treated only as Carolingian homiliarists strove towards completeness in coverage of the pericopes and of the lections from the Epistles in order to provide devotional readings supplementary to the liturgical homilies for the Nocturns. Whether Ælfric expected the laity to be present on Fridays in Lent or planned to read these sermons on Sunday or designed them for devotional uses or for reading in a *familia* of canons or monks is not finally ascertainable.[88] Nevertheless it is interesting to observe that the monk of Cernel followed the Carolingian homiliarists beyond the earlier and standard practice of homiliaries for the Offices which provided items only for Sundays and Feasts.

Ælfric or a follower did finally issue a collection which conformed to the format of the 'official' homiliary of Paul the Deacon. The only surviving witness is Trinity College, Cambridge, MS B.15.34 (Ker 86), an incomplete codex of some elegance which seems to have been written at Canterbury in the middle of the eleventh century.[89] The manuscript is arranged as a homiliary, *pars aestiva*,[90] containing twenty-eight items for Easter through the eleventh Sunday after Pentecost.[91] Whether it conformed to the model of Paul and ran through October (plus *commune sanctorum?*) or, like *Sermones catholici* I and II included Advent, we cannot know; but, given the evidence of the growth of the Ælfrician canon to cover the entire Temporale, there surely was material available to assemble a homiliary of Ælfric's exegetical pieces on the pericopes for the Temporale, *partes hiemalis et aestiva*.[92] If we allow for the possibility, however, we have a new and more conventionally homiliarist organization of Ælfric's works for the Temporale which might have been intended for use in the Office by, say, seculars or canons who had inadequate Latin to follow the unenglished homilies of the Fathers or, more likely, for devotional reading.[93] This would not, of course, rule out the continued exploitation of this material *ad populum* in the context of the Prone.

One last note: Ælfric seems to have made an effort, at least at the earlier stages of his career, for which the manuscript evidence is clearest, to keep pieces related to the liturgy (and especially to the pericopes) separated from reading-pieces such as were collected in the *Lives of Saints*.[94] He seems to have regarded the two kinds of writing as generically incompatible. Some years ago, Professor Clemoes examined closely the issue whether Ælfric himself ever organized a set for the Sanctorale – especially since most manuscriptes we have containing *Lives* mix them with Sanctorale homilies from *CH* I and II' – and concluded 'there is no evidence that; he did.'[95] It does, however, seem unusual that, to go with the homiliary to which Trinity College MS B.15.34 testifies, nobody had the idea of constructing an Ælfrician passional.[96]

An equally interesting possibility is not that the *libri catholicorum sermonum* would have been intermixed with the *passiones vel vitae sanctorum* but that the two may have occurred as distinct parts of the same volume or in something like a matched set. Such a volume would almost certainly have been intended purely for devotional reading. Fragments from what may have been just such a volume have recently been published by Professors Clemoes and Rowland L. Collins.[97] It contained selections from *Sermones Catholici*, I, and, separated from these, a set (probably complete) of Lives. Not a product of Ælfric's scriptorium and therefore probably representing the notion of someone other than the author of how these writings might be used, the manuscript was, nevertheless, written 'very early in the eleventh century.'[98] This discovery underlines another theme which has been at or just beneath the surface of this discussion: namely, that Ælfric's homiletic effort, based on the monastic homiliary, was to a great degree inspired by the desire to share with the laity the devotional riches of the reformed monastic life. In this respect, it is useful to recall Beryl Smalley's remark that in the age of Ælfric exegesis had all but disappeared as a distinct intellectual discipline but continued to flourish as a devotional handmaiden of the liturgy, the enrichment of which was one of the chief aims and achievements of the flowering of Benedictinism,[99] and to recall once again Edmund Bishop's 'law' that 'the source of new forms of private devotion ... is in the religious orders.'[100]

One last glance may be taken at the use to which Ælfric's sermons were put at the cathedral of Worcester in the episcopate of St. Wulfstan (1062–95). A small number of manuscripts clearly belonging to Worcester and containing work of Ælfric survive.[101] At least two were used by Coleman to whom, according to William of Malmesbury, the bishop 'predicationis delegabat officium.'[102] Two kinds of preaching seemed to interest the church of Worcester. First, but less strongly attested, homilies for a limited portion of the Temporale – notably the Christmas-Epiphany complex and Lent to Pentecost – were collected, largely from Ælfric's sermons. Second, sometimes in connection with the work of Archbishop Wulfstan and others, Ælfrician homilies which were useful *quando volueris* were anthologized. There is evidence to suggest, though not conclusively, that the archbishop may have taken a hand in this appropriation of his associate's work; at very least he is responsible for certain emendations which were in later use.[103] At the time of the later Wulfstan, who alone among the members of the Saxon hierarchy retained the favour of the Normans and was famous for his qualities as a pastor, it seems likely that Ælfric's work was not known in Worcester either in the form of MS Gg.3.28 (the form in which we almost inevitably think of his *sermones*) or in the expanded recensions which, as I have argued, seem to betray a homiliarist reorganization of his sermons.[104]

The implication of these observations is that at Worcester exegetical preaching on the pericope was practiced only in the chief Dominical seasons and that most preaching there was catechetical; hence the emphasis on materials which are useful at will rather than seasonally. Even the strictures of Coleman, Wulfstan II of Worcester's official preacher, against Ælfric's effort to still the preacher at the week before Easter tend to confirm this situation, for Coleman's marginal jeremiad speaks primarily of the necessity for catechetical-penitential addresses and not concerning explication of the pericopes for these days.[105] By the time of

Coleman, Ælfric's scheme of using the Prone chiefly as an occasion for commentary on the Gospel seems to have been abandoned or forgotten for most of the year, although perhaps there had been reversion to the practice of extempore paraphrase of the text. The evidence of the surviving manuscripts is rather that the Prone (if, indeed, the Mass remained the locus of instruction) had become more pervasively catechetical and that Ælfric's work was prized insofar as it was adaptable to this scheme. Thus the example of Worcester is, in a sense, witness to the ephemeral results of the achievement of the abbot of Eynsham.

The strongest evidence of which I am aware that preaching in the church at Worcester took place in a catechetically oriented Prone is the opening paragraph of an Easter sermon in Bodleian, MS Junius 121: 'Nu we habbað eow gesæd anfealdlice þæt godspel ðe se diacon rædde nu ætforan us eallum, hu Crist on þysum dæge of deaðe aras. Nu wylle we eow gyt secgan hu he to helle astah and þone deofol geband and þanon gelædde ealle ða þe him her on life gecweme and gecorene wæron.'[106] These lines presuppose a classical definition of the Prone. The Gospel has been read by the deacon and simply explained by means of a translation or paraphrase. But the preacher, for one reason or another, elects not to dwell on explication of the Gospel; rather he will narrate the drama of the Harrowing of Hell – of events which fall between the crucifixion and the resurrection and were often regarded in the early medieval tradition as the pivotal incident in the drama of salvation. In this instance, even on the greatest feast of the year, the Prone as the framework for the sermon gives licence, after some explanation of the simplest signification of Scripture, for the preacher to move from the scriptural to the apocryphal, from explication to another sort of edification.

This is not the place to test at length the applicability of the conclusions of this study to the anonymous Old English homilies or to the work of Wulfstan, but a few comments are in order. The Vercelli Book with its unique combination of *sermones* and poems has already been characterized by Kenneth Sisam as a 'reading-book' and as an 'out-of-the-way collection.'[107] It is obviously related to several English and Latin sermon collections of the more usual sort;[108] but the book as we have it is essentially a florilegium for pious reading differing from the Carolingian homiliaries which were designed for the *lectio divina* in that it abandons (for the most part) the principle of calendar arrangement. One might compare it with collections *quando volueris*; but such collections are for public, catechetical reading, and such an employment seems unlikely to have been the chief aim for the Vercelli codex as it stands. Indeed, among the other survivors of the Anglo-Saxon age, the book is *sui generis*. When all the prose of the volume has been edited, perhaps more can be said.

As for the Blickling Homilies, one also looks for help from their new editor.

The organization of the manuscript clearly reflects and maintains the homiliarist tradition, and there may be some hints as to the strain of that tradition and as to the original scope of the collection to be gleaned from its rather unusual organization.[109] In the absence of prefatory matter, nothing can be said about the intended uses of these pieces. The Offices, however, seem less likely than the Prone or devotional reading: but none of these uses would necessarily exclude the others, and references to prior reading of the Gospel are by no means so clear as Ælfric's.[110] If conclusions are ever possible, they will probably be determined in large part by two considerations. Source study, to name the first, will help to strengthen our appreciation of the antecedent traditions. But the second matter, the dating of the codex and the earlier English collection or collections from which it may have been copied, will be especially important to those who wish to speak of the uses of the Blickling Homilies; for an early date at some remove from the internal reference to 971 and the palaeographical date of ca. 1000 might raise interesting but complex questions about preaching and devotional reading during a rather dark period of English ecclesiastical history.

My general conclusions about Wulfstan's uses of his sermons have already been stated above.[111] He is not an exegetical preacher, although he knows the Bible and uses it with sophistication. He sometimes preaches on liturgical functions but hardly ever[112] on events of the liturgical calendar. Much of his work is catechetical; all of it is hortatory. Although use in the setting of the Prone is both conceivable and possible, one thinks, too, of the canonical admonitions to bishops to teach in the course of their pastoral visitations. A great contributor to the liturgy and to the laws of the church, Wulfstan was not, on the strength of the documentary evidence, a contributor to the regular practice of liturgical preaching. A reader of Ælfric, he preached with different purpose and to different effects. Nevertheless, it would not be surprising if future source studies were to tie him far more closely with collections of pastoral materials and with pastoral homiliaries like that of Abbo of St-Germain-des-Prés, from which he had excerpts drawn for one of his florilegia.[113]

It is my hope that this chapter has demonstrated that we ought to speak more carefully and rather differently than has been our custom about the uses for which the Anglo-Saxon homilies were designed and to which they were put. It demonstrates also, I believe, that a very strict analysis of the source materials will increase our respect for the achievements of the English homilists. Given the paucity of the evidence from Germany and elsewhere on the continent, it is dangerous to make generalizations. Nevertheless, if the surviving documentation adequately represents practice and if vernacular preaching was not, in fact, customarily reduced to written form on the continent or in Ireland,[114] then the accomplishment of the Anglo-Saxons was truly audacious and original. If comparable bodies of material from the continent have been lost, the English achievement still demands our greatest respect. Ælfric, in particular, must impress all who know his work well with the broadness, variety, and originality of the purposes for which he destined his work. Whether the first English homilies were adapted from the Latin for the laity or not,[115] such adaptations ultimately appeared and were used for preaching to the people in the Prone. Drawing with considerable inventiveness of purpose from liturgical texts which had hitherto been in the province of the monks or of other pious readers who knew Latin, the English homilists – and especially Ælfric with his great and continuously evolving body of work – produced a monument the implications of which have not had their due.

PART THREE

THE ESCHATOLOGY OF ÆLFRIC AND WULFSTAN

THE ESCHATOLOGY OF ÆLFRIC
AND WULFSTAN

Having considered the place of Anglo-Saxon vernacular preaching in the history of the homiletic practices of Western Christendom, we turn now to an examination of one of the major themes of the sermons of Ælfric and Wulfstan. The singling out of the eschatological group[1] of doctrines is more than capricious, for these topics are prominent not only in the work of Ælfric and Wulfstan but also in the other Old English homilies and in Latin theology of the post-patristic period.

The reasons for the prominence of eschatology are fairly complex, but comprehensible. The Latin Fathers,[2] to whose work most teaching on the subject in the Early Middle Ages can be traced, themselves retained a strong eschatological strain in their writings. It might be said that the early Latin theologians revived the sense of eschatological urgency which pervades the New Testament writings, whereas the Greek Fathers, concerned more with process and with fitting Christian doctrine into the cosmological framework of late Hellenistic philosophy, had undercut biblical eschatology. The Latin Fathers who exercised the greatest influence on early medieval theologians, Augustine of Hippo and Gregory the Great, both exemplify the Western tendency to emphasize the eschatological. Early medieval theologians throughout Western Christendom continued to give a central place to the Last Things both because these subjects loomed so large in the traditions which they wanted to preserve and also because the apocalyptic picture of the great Judgment appealed to them as an appropriate extension of their own 'heroic' picture of man's social nature and destiny. For just as the ideal hero led his followers to actual or to moral victory, whatever the cost, so also Christ, the proper Lord of all mankind, led his faithful retainers to the most decisive and inevitable of victories.

The fact that eschatological reflection was prominent in Anglo-Saxon thought can be demonstrated by reference to Old English poetry.[3] One of the standard approaches to religious motifs in Old English poetry has been to subdivide its subject-matter as biblical (or Cædmonian) and hagiographic (or Cynewulfian). More recently, it has been recognized that such categorization does justice neither to the breadth of religious concern expressed by the poets nor to their subtlety. Although many critics now approach the poetry by means of analysis of the writers' reliance on the discipline of biblical exegesis and on the rhetorical commonplaces or *topoi* of the Christian literary tradition, it may be sufficient here simply to allude to several manners in which eschatological subject-matter is appropriated in the extant poetic corpus.

Most obvious, of course, are poems whose subject is explicitly eschatological. If one considers only the poems collected in the Exeter Book, he can cite Cynewulf's *Ascension* (*Christ II*), *The Last Judgment* (*Christ III*), *Soul and Body II*, *The Judgment Day I*, and *The Descent into Hell* as primarily eschatological poems. They are poetic depictions of aspects of the ultimate destiny of man. *The Last Judgment* (*Christ III*), for example, is what its modern title implies: a versified (but in tone and structure homiletic) depiction of the Judgment day, centring upon the division of the good and the evil for their appropriate rewards. Christ is a royal, heroic figure; and the scene in general reflects early medieval social order: the saved have been faithful to their Lord and have accumulated a treasury of gracious gifts.

The narrative religious poems, notably the biblical paraphrases (*Genesis*, *Exodus*, *Judith*, etc.) and the hagiographies (*Guthlac*, Cynewulf's *Juliana* and *Elene*, etc.) are designed to provide edification and examples for the poet's audience rather than doctrinal exposition. But, whether by means of depiction of great events of salvation history or of the lives of Christian heroes, the poems are all concerned to lead their readers or hearers to the kind of life which will win them acquittance at the great Doom. Thus, eschatology is at least implicit in all of these poems. In the *Elene*, to take but one example, there are occasional, conventional eschatological allusions which heighten the story of the recovery of the True Cross by St Helena, the mother of Constantine. The poem concludes (lines 1228b–35) with a prayer, not unlike the usual homiletic ascription, that heaven's gates and eternal joy may be opened for the poet and for all men who revere the cross.

More complex are the eschatological ramifications of the great Old English meditative poems or elegies, chief among which are the famous *Wanderer* and *Seafarer*. The latter, for instance, begins with reflection on the hardship of the involuntary exile or seafarer and proceeds, in what could be called a second movement, to reflect on life in the world as a kind of voluntary exile through which one seeks to return to his true or heavenly homeland by eschewing transitory, worldly values. The poem progresses in this manner by appropriating a number of commonplaces shared by the homiletic and poetic traditions from the lament of the exile in the world to the reflections on the Last Things of an exile from God. *The Wanderer* is remarkably free of explicit eschatological allusion; but concern with the Last Things is clearly implicit in the poet's use of the ruin *topos* and the *ubi sunt* device, both of which usually appear in eschatological contexts.

Finally, there are a number of important and perplexing eschatological allusions in the greatest of Old English poems, *Beowulf*, which is sometimes characterized as a heroic legend retold from a Christian perspective. The poet resorts frequently to the reflections that God controls the destiny of all men, whether or not they are Christians, and that, although life in the world is transitory and unpredictable, there is a future and stable existence for those who meet the standards of the Ruler. In particular, of course, there is the controversial and extended 'sermon' of Hrothgar (lines 1700–84), homiletic both in tone and in rhetorical structure, in which the hero is exhorted by the old king to use well the gifts of providence as long as he lives so that he may win a favourable judgment. In this passage and others, the poet incorporates his own concern for the Last Things in his narration of a tale set in the pagan past, so as to infuse his work with moral and religious reflections of relevance to his own historical and existential situation and to that of his audience.

These brief comments on some of the kinds of eschatological references that appear in Old English poetry gloss over the very great difficulties of the critical significance of the religious allusions in a poem like *Beowulf* and of their interpretation in the more explicitly religious verse. Those matters are beyond the present concern, which is simply to assert the predominance of eschatological ideas in the whole range of Anglo-Saxon thought. Whether in straightforward treatment of eschatological themes or in meditative allusions in which the Last Things are only implicit, the subject is never far from the poets' minds. And if this is the case with Old English verse, it is not surprising that it should also be true of the religious prose. To unearth the poets' sources is often more difficult than to determine what were the sources of the prose writers, but it is clear that the poets were appropriating traditional motifs in the same conservative manner.

A few comments on the methodology of this survey of the eschatological teaching of Ælfric and Wulfstan are in order. It adopts, first, a fairly broad and inclusive definition of eschatology. The term is taken to refer to the entire range of ideas dealing with the destiny of mankind: reflections on death and on man's destiny thereafter up to and including the events of the apocalypse and Last Judgment. This is approximately the definition implied by Ælfric in his most extensive consideration of eschatological matters, the sermon for the octave of Pentecost (Pope XI).

Second, although (as I pointed out in Part I) the theological thought of Ælfric and Wulfstan reproduces ideas found in the tradition and although source criticism is the usual approach to analysis of their writing, this study is essentially a description of their eschatology against the background of the related ideas of the anonymous Old English homilists. Our concern is not to demonstrate what is already known – that Ælfric and Wulfstan almost always adapted (however skilfully) the ideas of earlier writers – but to examine at a given moment a major aspect of the teaching of these two prominent figures in contrast with that of other writers of approximately the same date and geographical area who shared the same audience for theological literature.

It has not always been understood by those who have commented on Anglo-Saxon theology that, derivative though it may be, any body of thought is unique by virtue of the historical moment in which it was produced and by which it was conditioned. Augustine, to take as an example a figure who exercised a seminal influence in the history of the Christian thought of the West, has been a different man to different ages. Augustine worked out his later position on the problem of predestination in the context of theological controversy. Because the issues of the Pelagian controversy were no longer pressing and because of the compromise worked out by his followers at the second council of Orange in 529, the theologians of the Early Middle Ages were almost entirely ignorant of the whole problem of predestination. The Carolingian monk, Gottschalk, is virtually the only figure of the period who understood Augustine on this score and attempted to explain his thought; but Gottschalk – in part, perhaps, because he was so strident a controversialist – suffered for his aberrancy. Although such later medieval writers as Thomas Aquinas were aware of and made accommodation for this aspect of Augustine's thought, it remained for Calvin and other Reformed theologians, in a special manner determined by the intellectual context within which they worked, to reappropriate Augustine's notions of grace and predestination – not to mention Paul's, of which Augustine's views were themselves a special kind of reinterpretation.[4] To take an example closer to the world of Ælfric and Wulfstan, one may allude to the ninth-century eucharistic controversy between Paschasius Radbertus and Ratramnus of Corbie in which Ælfric was later tangentially involved by virtue of his adaptation of Ratramnus' tract on the subject in a sermon for Easter in *Catholic Homilies* II. Each of these Carolingian theologians believed he was presenting the traditional view of the nature of Christ's presence in the Mass; but Ratramnus argued, in the Ambrosian tradition, for a symbolic interpretation of the nature of the presence whereas Radbertus, in the Augustinian line, propounded the realistic interpretation which later would come to prevail as the doctrine of transubstantiation.[5] In both cases, one would do a grave injustice to the figures under scrutiny either to miss the fact that they were derivative thinkers or to concentrate his study on the sources to the exclusion of the historical context in which the documents under consideration were written. So, too, I hope to show, with Ælfric and Wulfstan in the history of eschatological thought.

A final methodological comment is needed. Beyond the intrinsic interest an analysis of the eschatology of Ælfric and Wulfstan may have for intellectual and literary historians, it can be a reference tool. Professor J.E. Cross has recently suggested that a motif-index of the homilies would be useful to source-searchers and students of the 'writing-methods and processes' of Ælfric in particular.[6] With this suggestion in mind, although it has not been possible to provide such an index, some care has been taken to make this survey of eschatological themes as inclusive as possible and to include ample quotation and reference. The notes draw attention to the placement of the homilies in the cycle of the liturgical year in order to assist those who want to compare Ælfric's emphases with those of the homiliarists and other Old English sermon-writers as more of their works become available.

The work of Ælfric is much more extensive than that of Wulfstan, thus it has been necessary to subdivide the treatment of his eschatology. The themes of the afterlife and the Last Judgment are the subjects of separate chapters, and a final chapter is devoted to three extensive eschatological writings which have not hitherto received close scrutiny.

6

Ælfric on the Afterlife[1]

Ælfric's understanding of the nature of the individual experience between death and Doomsday is set apart from the tradition of the anonymous homilists by his understanding that the historical church participates in the eternal order of the Kingdom of God. While hints of this doctrine are to be discerned in the anonymous homilies,[2] its eschatological implications were neither developed nor emphasized in those writings. Ælfric time and again speaks of the church as the Kingdom.[3] Not only do there exist two cities in eternal strife,[4] but the Kingdom of the parables is also to be interpreted as the church.[5] The church, which is tossed as a ship on the turbulent sea of the world,[6] is a mixed company, as was the Ark of Noah,[7] which will not be purified until Doomsday when the true Kingdom, composed of 'hosts of angels and of virtuous men' who will make up the number of the fallen angels, is to be assembled.[8] Nevertheless, through Baptism the gates of heaven are opened to men,[9] and they live thereafter as part of an earthly order to which Scripture refers as the Kingdom of Heaven.

Ælfric's occasional references to life as a period of exile in an alien land must be read in connection with this understanding of the church. In commenting on the story of the three Magi, for example, he dwells on the statement that they returned home from Bethlehem by another way; Paradise is man's true home; but we have lost it and must return to our homeland, 'for which we were created,' by another route.[10] Similarly, the fall of Jericho is an allegory of the fall of the world, for 'Jericho' means 'moon' and symbolizes the waxing and waning of life in this world.[11] The imagery of exile and the emphasis on transitoriness recall the *peregrinus* or stranger theme of *The Seafarer* and *The Wanderer*[12] and, like that theme, are based on the patristic and homiletical tradition of biblical exegesis. As a consequence of the fact that the church is to be identified with God's kingdom, man is placed in an order which, although it exists in the world, has the centre of its being outside the present historical context.

Perhaps partly because of the sophistication of these framing ideas, death was not so greatly to be feared for Ælfric as it was for the anonymous homilists. Indeed, since in Christ man participates in two kinds of life – the mortal and the immortal[13] – death is not fearful for the man who has been faithful in his earthly life; it is a salutary event which should be met with joy. For the martyr, in particular, to die is to change 'to wuldre of deaðe. swilce man lam sylle. and sylf nime gold.'[14] But the situation of the martyrs had been recognized from early times as exceptional. This ultimate sacrifice earned for that special class immediate communion with the Godhead.[15] For other Christians, the ultimate comfort is that, whatever the tribulations we suffer here, they cannot deprive us of everlasting life.[16] And death, insofar as it is to be feared, is dreaded because it ends one's struggle to win salvation. The condition of the unrighteous can be contrasted with that of the righteous in terms of their future rewards. The sinful man's death is 'yfel and earmlic, forðan ðe hí farað of ðisum scortan life to ecum pinungum,' but the death of the righteous is 'deorwyrðe' because he goes from 'ðis geswincfulle líf ... to ðam ecan life.'[17]

The common patristic definition of death as separation of body and soul is frequently cited in the Blickling and Vercelli homilies;[18] it is nowhere explicit but everywhere implicit in the *Catholic Homilies*. There is, however, greater emphasis than in the earlier English sermons on the nature of the soul. The soul is a gift from God endowed with immortality and happiness; happiness was lost in the fall, but immortality can never be lost.[19] Invisible, the soul is the life of the body,[20] and like the body, it had no existence before the birth of the human person.[21]

Furthermore, Ælfric on several occasions makes death a metaphor for the condition of the soul. Of particular interest in this connection are two homilies on the Gospel pericopes on the raising of the young man of Nain (Luke vii.11–16), and of Lazarus (John xi.1–45).[22] The latter, which is both later and more elaborate, can serve here as our example. After his customary translation of the Gospel, Ælfric declares that the work of creation is more difficult than the act of raising the dead – a work which, except for an example like that of Lazarus, is postponed until the end of the world.[23] But there is another kind of resurrection, typified by the raising of Lazarus, which Christ effects daily:

> þonne seo sawul arist of ðære synna deaðe,
> for ðam se ðe syngað, hys sawul ne leofað,
> buton heo þurh andetnysse eft acucige,
> and þurh dædbote hyre Drihten gladige.[24]

Unfortunately, few men fear this kind of death. The three miracles of raising recounted in the Gospels, Ælfric explains, signify types of death of the soul. That of the daughter of Jairus (Luke viii.41–56; Mark v.22–43), who lay secretly dead in her father's house, betokens inward or secret sinfulness; that of the boy at Nain, who was being carried to burial, a more open sinfulness which is known to the world by outward acts (the child's weeping mother is the type of the church); and the raising of Lazarus, buried and already decomposing in the grave, a more extreme instance of open and habitual sinfulness.[25] From this introduction, Ælfric proceeds to a consideration of the nature of sin and spiritual rebirth before completing his reflections on the Lazarus pericope.

The concepts of the true church as the Kingdom of God, of life as exile from one's true country, of death as a transition to glory, of the soul as immortal, and of death as a spiritual state establish a theological framework within which the homilist could easily proceed to elaborate a doctrine of the purgation or beatification of the soul before Doomsday. It is the kind of framework lacking in the anonymous homilies; and its absence was in some degree responsible for the ambiguities evident in the earlier pieces. Whether Ælfric took advantage of this framework can only be ascertained by analysis of three topics touching on the interim after death: Christ's release of those bound in hell at the time of his descent, visions of individual judgment and of the other world, and the doctrine of intercession.

There is no extended account of the *descensus ad infernum* in Ælfric's writings; but the common early medieval concept of atonement, which stresses the descent, undergirds his treatment of the work of Christ. It is summarized in Ælfric's survey of the history of salvation, *De Initio Creaturae*, which serves as an introduction to the First Series of *Catholic Homilies*:

he cóm to us þæt hé wolde for ús deað þrowian, and swa eal mancynn þa ðe gelyfað mid his agenum deaðe alysan fram helle-wite. Hé nolde geniman ús neadunge of deofles anwealde, buton he hit forwyrhte; þa hé hit forwyrhte genóh swiðe, þaða hé gehwette and tihte ðæra Iudeiscra manna heortan to Cristes slege. Crist ða geðafode þæt ða wælhreowan hine genámon and gebundon, and on róde hengene acwealdon. Hwæt ða twegen gelyfede men hine arwurðlice bebyrigdon, and Crist on ðære hwile to helle gewende, and þone deofol gewylde, and him of-anám Adám and Euan, and heora ofspring, þone dæl ðe him ǽr gecwemde, and gelædde hí to heora lichaman, and arás of deaðe mid þam micclum werede on þam þriddan dæge his þrowunge.[26]

This summary is remarkable, especially in contrast with those of the anonymous homilists,[27] for its clear statement that the souls of those released were reunited with their bodies. The obvious implication is that they participate now in the eternal order as mankind in general can do only after the general resurrection. Christ came to redeem man from the devil and 'hell-torment.'[28] Therefore his birth caused inhabitants of heaven, earth, and hell to rejoice.[29] Hell bowed to his powers at the descent,[30] and the holy men of the old dispensation were raised up to eternal life.[31] These passages do not speak directly to the issue of man's post-mortem existence; but Ælfric's source traditions, in contrast to those of his English predecessors, seem to infer that the faithful of the Old Law have been raised and participate presently in the Kingdom, and the significance of this teaching was apparently not lost on the homilist.

A number of visions of the afterlife are recounted in Ælfric's homiletic works.[32] These visionary passages can be divided into three classes: visions concerned with individual judgment, those revealing something of the life after death, and those intended to prove the efficacy of intercession. They must be studied in connection with expository statements on the same subjects.

Many of the visions imply that one undergoes an experience of judgment at the time of death which sets his destiny for the period before Doomsday. Thus an unbaptized man revived by St Martin of Tours says that before he was redeemed by the saint's intercession he was judged at the divine throne and cast into punishment.[33] Sometimes a vision is given as a warning at the hour of death. Such was the case of the fortieth of the martyr soldiers who, holding back at the moment of their martyrdom, saw a vision of thirty-nine crowns and was induced to rejoin his fellows.[34] At the time of a saint's death, other holy persons often have visions of the saint being escorted to heaven by angels or hear heavenly hymns.[35] In conjunction with these visions, one may also note statements that saints have been granted eternal life as a reward for their faithfulness.[36] The teaching implied by these visions is upheld in several expository statements. One important comment concerns the accosting of the dying soul by devils:

Þa deoflu æteowiað þære synfullan sawle ægðer ge hyre yfelan geðohtas, and ða derigendlican spræca, and ða mánfullan dæda, and hí mid mænigfealdum ðrea-tungum geangsumiað, þæt heo on ðam forðsiðe oncnáwe mid hwilcum feondum heo ymbset bið, and ðeah nán ut-fær ne gemet, hu heo ðam feondlicum gastum oðfleon mage.[37]

The statement is similar in its imagery to the apocalyptic traditions adapted by the Vercelli homilist; but it is clearly not drawn from such a tradition, and it is included to reinforce the idea that death is the beginning of eternal life. Not unlike this passage is the comment in another homily that, while bodies await the resurrection in the grave, pure souls await the end in glory with the saints but wicked souls in eternal torments.[38] Clearly, then, the soul's condition after death is, in Ælfric's writing, an active one, happy or unhappy according to the deserts of one's life.

A passage from the *Vitae Patrum* relating two visions concerning death and the judgment of the soul appears in one manuscript of the homily for the Sixteenth Sunday after Pentecost of the Second Series of *Catholic Homilies*. The passage, though written by Ælfric, was placed in its present context and supplied with non-Ælfrician transitions by a compiler.[39] It provides exempla to conclude an explication of Matthew v.24–34, which contrasts the transitory with the eternal. A penitential piece would have been a more suitable and characteristic setting for these *exempla*, both of which involve ascetics who were granted visions of the departure of souls. In one, a monk, having requested such a vision, was directed to a city. Outside the walls, he encountered a dying, sinful anchorite who was approached by a devil with a three-tined fork of glowing iron. The voice of God consigned this anchorite to the devil, who stabbed him in the heart repeatedly with the fork, until he finally gave up his soul. The visionary next went within the walls where he discovered a dying pilgrim to whom Gabriel and Michael came. But the soul did not want to leave the body, so Michael asked God's help. David and the heavenly choir were sent, and their music so charmed the soul that it relinquished the body and ascended in Michael's hands.[40] The second vision is that of an old and experienced contemplative who came into a city and sat at the gate of a dying rich man. A host of fearsome black riders on black horses arrived, dismounted, and entered the house, each carrying a fiery iron cudgel. The man cried to God for help, but he was told that it was too late, now 'þonne þin sunne þe is forsworcen mid ealle.'[41]

Two other visions, derived from Bede and concerned with individual judgment, are incorporated as concluding exempla in a penitential homily, *De Doctrina Apostolica*.[42] The first concerns a soldier of the saintly King Cenred of Mercia[43] who was negligent in the performance of his religious duties. Begged by the king to repent on his deathbed, the man declared that it was no use: he had seen a vision in which two angels showed him a very small book in which his good deeds were recorded and a host of devils, displaying a large volume recording his sins, had claimed his soul.[44] Clearly the vision was not intended to benefit the man himself but to warn those who heard of it, as also was the tale of the lax monk who saw in a vision the chair prepared for him in hell.[45] Urged to repent and to take the viaticum, he refused because he had seen his place in hell.[46] One who hopes for mercy on Doomsday ought to take care for his spiritual welfare now, Ælfric concludes. The latter of these examples of individual judgment is obviously as nearly classifiable with visionary materials having to do with the afterlife as with those that treat individual judgment.

The pair of visions from the *Vitae Patrum* and the pair from Bede are both added as exempla in the rhythmical prose style to homilies in Ælfric's earlier style, and both seem to have been connected with penitential doctrine. One might suspect a growing interest in the kinds of materials concerned with the judgment and destiny of the soul. Perhaps the homilist had rejected the similar materials of the *Visio Pauli* not so much because he found the document unorthodox as because he doubted its authenticity. At any rate, he was clearly not opposed to the use of this subject-matter when its sources were well documented. It is probably also important to point out that the context into which Ælfric customarily sets such visions of individual judgment is penitential: they exhort to amendment of life.

The second group of visions is concerned with the nature of life after death. In several shorter passages, families are assured by means of visions that the souls of their kin are in bliss with the angels.[47] The Dives and Lazarus parable is recounted with reference to the condition of departed souls.[48] Most important, however, are two visions used also by Bede which, in their Bedan setting,[49] have been considered classical loci of purgatorial teaching. Both find a place at Rogation Tuesday in the Second Series of *Catholic Homilies*. Ælfric introduces the first of these as a substitute for the *Visio Pauli*, which is patently false since Paul had said 'no earthly man can relate' his vision of the third heaven.[50] The visionary Fursey was, however, under no such restrictive injunction, and his experience, Ælfric thinks, can be regarded as true. Taken by angels at the time of death, he was returned to the body and lived another two days. Taken again by the same angels, he was protected from the onslaughts of devils who 'said that it was unjust that a man who had consented to evil should go to rest without punishment.' The angels sparred verbally and physically with the devils, finally overcoming them. Fursey was shown the earth being consumed by four fires, one of which approached without harming him. The devils again accosted the angels who confounded them. Looking up, Fursey beheld angels who drove off the devils; he recognized some of the angels from life. Told that he must again return to the world, Fursey asked about the end of the world and was informed that this event would occur in the future and would be preceded by hardships of which he should warn men. Fursey, returning through the fire, beheld a fellow townsman being tormented and was himself burned slightly. Telling him to warn men of their future punishments and to urge them to confess, the angels returned Fursey to his body. The rest of his life was spent preaching on the basis of this experience.

The vision of Drihthelm is 'of a certain man's resurrection.'[51] Drihthelm, a good man, died one evening and rose the next morning; he straightway divided his property and entered the monastery at Melrose. In the vision which inspired this conversion to monastic life, he was led by a monk to a great, burning valley filled with men's souls which suffered both hot and cold. Drihthelm thought this must be hell, but he was told it was not. He passed on to a worse black abyss where other souls suffered, but where he was protected from the devils. Thence he was led to a broad and pleasant field which he was told was not heaven. Finally, he was taken to a far brighter field. At last the angel explained the vision:

He me andwyrde, and cwæð, Seo micele byrnende dene, þe ðu ǽrest gesawe, is witnung-stow, on ðære beoð manna sawla gewitnode and geclænsode, þe noldon heora synna gerihtlæcan on gehálum þingum, hæfdon swa-ðeah behreowsunge æt heora endenextan dæge, and swa gewiton mid þære behreowsunge of worulde, and becumað on dómes dæge ealle to heofonan ríce. Eac hi sume, þurh freonda fultum, and ælmes-dædum, and swiðost þurh halige mæssan beoð alysede of ðam witum ǽr ðam micclum dóme. Witodlice seo swearte niwelnys ðe þu gesawe mid þam ormætum þeostrum and fúlum stence, seo is helle múð, and se ðe ǽne þæron befylð, ne wyrð hé næfre on ecnysse ðanon alysed. Þeos wynsume and ðeos blostmbære stow is ðæra sawla wunung ðe on gódum weorcum geendodon, and swa-ðeah næron swa fulfremede þæt hí ðærrihte moston into heofenan ríce, ac swa-þeah hí ealle becumað to Cristes gesihðe and myrhðe æfter ðam micclum dome. Witodlice ða ðe fulfremede beoð on geðohte, on worde, on weorce, swa hraðe swa hí of worulde gewitað, swa becumað hí to heofenan ríce; of ðam ðu gesawe þæt micele leoht mid ðam wynsumum bræðe, and þonon ðu gehyrdest ðone fægeran dream. Þu soðlice, nu ðu to lichaman gecyrst, gif ðu wylt ðine dæda and ðeawas gerihtlæcan, ðonne underfehst ðu æfter forðsiðe þas wynsuman wununge, þe ðu nú gesihst.[52]

There are, Ælfric concludes, many visions such as these, especially in the *Dialogues* of St Gregory, concerning men who have died, seen the condition of souls after death, and returned. We should beg God to be merciful both to ourselves and to those who suffer in torments.

The effect of the visions of Fursey and Drihthelm, from which Ælfric, like Bede and Gregory the Great, does not attempt to draw a systematic geographical picture of the cosmos, is hortatory. Both visionaries spent the rest of their lives communicating what they had seen and urging amendment of life; the homilist, the historian, and the theologian continue this work by passing on the warning that life in the world determines life in the future. In both the Fursey and the Drihthelm visions there is clearly an intermediate state before the consummation which ought to concern one almost as much as the Last Judgment itself. In both, the visionary picture is active, and the stories are told more to inspire repentance than to elaborate details of the future state. It is not necessary in the case of

Ælfric to base a doctrine of post-mortem punishments and rewards on the vision, however, for Ælfric's theological presuppositions about the church as the Kingdom and death as the beginning of eternity and his lucid statements about the state of the souls of the dead clearly depend upon belief in an active afterlife. The absence of such framing ideas from the anonymous homilies contributes to their lack of clarity.

Rather different from these visions but belonging to the category of visions of the afterlife is a very short passage probably translated by Ælfric from the *Liber de Visione et Obitu Wetini Monachi* by Haito which survives only as an introduction to a short piece on ordination by Wulfstan.[53] It describes the fate of priests and deacons who have not fulfilled the requirements of celibacy. They stand bound to stakes in hellfire up to their waists; facing them, their partners in sin are also bound in fire up to the navel. Their genitalia are regularly flogged by the devil. Although this vision wants Ælfric's usual delicacy, it seems stylistically to be his and, like his other visions of the afterlife, serves as a warning to the living. Its limited applicability suggests its original context may have been an admonition addressed to the clergy alone.

Finally, there are visionary and expository materials which, like those of the Blickling Book,[54] are related both to the afterlife and to the doctrine of intercession. It has already been shown that the Fursey and Drihthelm visions are retold to inspire fervent intercession. Associated with these visions under the Rogation Tuesday rubric is a miracle tale which in Thorpe's manuscript bears also the rubric 'Hortatorius Sermo de Efficacia Sanctae Missae.'[55] It concerns Ymma, a thane of Æthelred, King of Mercia, who was thought to have died in battle. His brother, a priest, took a body from the field and offered masses 'for his sawle alysednysse.' But the real Ymma was a captive of the Northumbrians, and whenever a mass was said for him, the bonds in which the Northumbrians placed him burst. 'Witodlice,' observed Ymma, 'gif ic nu on oðre worulde wære, þa wurde min sawul fram wítum alysed þurh da halgan mæssan.'[56] The Mercian thane was ultimately sold as a slave to a Frisian, who had no more luck than the Northumbrians in confining him, and subsequently released him. Ælfric concludes by observing that Gregory the Great's *Dialogues* – which is available in the Alfredian translation – contains similar evidence of the efficacy of the mass. Among shorter visionary tales of this type is one in the Homily on St Lucy. The saint's mother has been ill, and the daughter urges her to touch the tomb of St Agatha. Lucy falls asleep after their prolonged prayers and sees Agatha

> betwux engla werodum. ænlice gefretewode.
> and clypode hyre þus to. clypigende ufenne.
> Min swustor lucia. soð godes mæden

hwi bitst þu æt me þæs þe ðu miht sylf getiðian
þinre meder geheolp þin halga geleafa.
and efne heo is gehæled. halwendlice ðurh crist.[57]

Likewise St Maur is said to have revived a boy who has been saved by his
intercession from torments.[58] St Mary appears to a man praying to her and says
she has interceded for him with Christ.[59]

In his accounts of visions touching on individual or death-day judgment and
on the state of the soul before Doomsday, Gregory the Great persistently
warns against false dreams and visions. Ælfric, like Bede, regards Gregory as
the great authority on the subject of revelation by dream and vision, and there
are hints that Ælfric was aware of these caveats. Certain kinds of visions are
recounted only to illustrate certain kinds of moral observations. The illustrative
or metaphorical import of these materials was, apparently, more greatly valued
than their claims to reality or historical accuracy.[60] Ælfric commented on the
dangers of dream visions in a passage treating a posthumous healing performed
by St Swithun which involved the appearance of the saint to the sick man in a
dream. Not all dreams, he says, are from God:

> Þa swefna beoð wynsume þe gewurðaþ of gode.
> and þa beoð egefulle ðe of þam deofle cumað.
> and god sylf forbead þæt we swefnum ne folgion.
> þe læs ðe se deofol us bedydrian mæge.[61]

Ælfric's continuing concern lest his readers be misled is indicated in the fact
that he appended to the Swithun homily at least one and perhaps two monitory
exempla.[62] But it must be admitted that his warnings appear in a context
referring to visions connected with healing and divination, not eschatological
matters.[63] Perhaps this is because such visions, tempting the visionary to
blasphemous action, can cause immediate harm. At any rate, visions concerning
the afterlife are as often *egefulle* as *winsume*, whether they are designed (as only
rarely in Ælfric) to describe the nature of regions of the cosmos beyond those
man normally experiences or (as more customarily in Ælfric) to illustrate and
underline the importance of adherence to the moral teachings of the church.

Ælfric's beliefs concerning the value of the church's intercession are quite
explicit. In his translation of Maccabees, he dwells on the classic Old Testament
proof text, Judas's service of intercession for his slain companions:

> Iudas gegaderode ða godne dæl feos.
> þæt wæron twelf þusend scyllinga eall hwites seolfres.
> and sende to hierusalem for heora synnum to offrigenne

heora sawle to alysednysse þe ðær ofslagene wæron
æwfæstlice under-standende be ure ealre æriste.
buton hé gélyfde þæt hi æfter langum fyrste
of deaðe arísan sceoldon þe ðær ofslagene wæron.
elles he offrode on idel his lác.
ac he soðlice besceawode. þæt ða ðe mid soðre arfæstnysse
on deaþe ge-endiað. þæt hi mid drihtne habbað
þa selestan gife on þam soðan life.
Hit is halig geðoht. and halwende to gebiddenne
for ðam forð-farendum þæt hi fram synnum beon alysede.[64]

This passage looks primarily to the resurrection of the dead as the justification of intercession. Other comments address the benefit to churchmen of the intercessions of the saints and imply that martyrs and other heroes of the faith have achieved a present, beatified existence.[65] Ælfric most clearly implies a purgatorial state in such visionary exempla, though his emphasis on the efficacy of the saints' intercessions implies as well that this class of Christians achieves beatification before the day of Doom.

There is still in Ælfric's writing no firmly settled technical vocabulary for description of the state of souls between death and the Last Judgment. The terms used by the Vercelli and Blickling homilists, which can also refer to punishment and glory after Doomsday, are used for want of a better vocabulary.[66] But Ælfric's teaching in this area is far more consistent and more clearly on the side of the existence of a continued, conscious, and disembodied state for the soul between death and the reunion with the body on the Last Day than is that of either of the other collections. He makes explicit his understanding of the church as the present manifestation of the Kingdom and defines death in terms of continuation or new beginning, opening the way to a view of the cosmos – terrestrial and supra-terrestrial – as one great community. Thus it is likely that the soul while separated from the body will receive rewards and punishments according to the merits of its earthly life. The saints of both dispensations are in glory with God; and visionaries report knowledge of a post-mortem judgment and glimpses of souls in glory or in pain; the intercessions of saints for men and of men for their departed fellows are highly beneficial. Without painting a detailed cosmological picture and without committing himself to an extended discussion of these matters, Ælfric, following the exegetical-homiletic and the hagiographic traditions, has come far closer than his predecessors in the vernacular homiletic line to a consistent statement concerning the afterlife and its nature.

Despite Ælfric's care to avoid material of questionable authenticity, a good deal of exotic description of the afterlife has come into his writing via Bede's

History and the hagiographic tradition. Clearly then, the homilist's objections to apocryphal works like the *Visio Pauli* were (as he stated) based more on doubts of their authenticity than on scruples over their content. But Ælfric seems to have taken care to use visionary matter in contexts in which the primary aim was monitory. Indeed, it is striking that the passages cited in this chapter belong predominantly to two classes of writing: sermons for the penitential seasons – pre-Lent, and Rogationtide – and the saints' lives. The afterlife comes to the fore, in other words, in the context of moral teaching either in connection with penance and amendment of life or in connection with instruction by means of the examples of the saints.

7

Ælfric on the Last Times
and the Judgment

There is no sustained treatment in the *Catholic Homilies* or the *Lives of Saints* of the Last Times. As in the case of his treatment of materials concerning death and the interim after death, however, Ælfric touches on all the chief eschatological motifs and deals with these matters more consistently and with a better critical evaluation of his sources than did the anonymous homilists; and allusions to most of the eschatological topics can be found at all stages of the homilist's career. Thus one can assemble a synopsis of Ælfric's eschatology to be compared later with his more compendious statements on the subject.

Like the Fathers whose work he adapted in his sermons, Ælfric was sensitive to the pervasiveness of eschatology in the Gospels. In that there is a sense of present fulfillment, the church may be the Kingdom in the present world; but it is of equal (and frequently greater) concern that the world's harvest-time is approaching, that the final fulfillment is yet to be realized. Thus the Christian of the tenth century, like the Apostles who sowed the seed, must tend the crop, which is mixed with the weeds of vice. For the angels will be the reapers of the harvest, and they will burn the unacceptable portions of the crop.[1] One who wants to be gathered into the barn must be sensitive to the signs of the times.

In connection with the signs of the approaching end of the world, Ælfric shows far more interest than the earlier English homilists in the ages of history.[2] His chief treatment of the subject occurs in the Homily for the Second Sunday after the Epiphany of the Second Series, an adaptation of a homily of Bede from the Homiliary with a few touches drawn from Haymo of Auxerre.[3] The six water vessels of the marriage at Cana, says Ælfric, betoken the six ages of the world: from Adam to Noah, Noah to Abraham, Abraham to David, David to the Babylonian captivity, the captivity to the birth of Christ, and from the incarnation, 'mid ungewisre geendunge astreht oð Ante-Cristes to-cyme.'[4] The changing of water to wine in these vessels in lieu of creation of wine *de novo* symbolizes the fulfilling of the law and the prophets, the continuity of the two dispensations.[5] Ælfric outlines the events of each age, concluding that since his own advent Christ has poured out precious wine in the church and will continue to do so until the end of history.[6] This historical schema belongs, as the late Max Förster demonstrated, to the Augustinian-Vulgate tradition which was standard during much of the Middle Ages.[7] There are also incidental comments – notably the assertion in a variety of texts that the Incarnation inaugurated the sixth age[8] – which support the conviction that the six-ages scheme was basic to Ælfric's understanding of history.

In one homily, nevertheless, Ælfric adapts from Gregory, who also probably depended upon a well-established exegetical interpretation, a scheme in which there are only five ages of history: Adam to Noah, Noah to Abraham, Abraham to Moses, Moses to Christ, Christ to Doomsday. The passage is an allegorization of the significance of the hours at which the owner of the vineyard employed his laborers in the parable of Matthew xx.1–16, and it proceeds, tropologically, to identify these ages as well with stages in the life of the individual at which he may be brought into the vineyard.[9] Although this system is at variance with the more common six-age schema, the ultimate sanction of which was the hexaemeral creation story in Genesis,[10] Ælfric retained it as a useful and appropriate device for the interpretation of the biblical text. One may assume the writers were aware of the inconsistency but not troubled by it.

In the letter to Sigeweard, *De Vetere Testamento et de Novo*, Ælfric has some interesting remarks on the seventh age, the rest of the saints, which he says runs parallel to the others, encompassing the saints of all ages.[11] The ages of the saints of the old and the new laws runs separate from the historical epochs until the Last Day when the two orders will be joined in an eighth epoch:

and seo sixte yld þissere worulde stynt fram Criste astreht oþ domes dæg eallum mannum ungewiss, ac hit wat se Hælend. Seo seofoðe yld ys þe yrnð mid þisum sixum fram Abele þam rihtwisan oð þissere worulde ende, na on lybbendum mannum, ac on forðfarenum sawlum on þam oðrum life, þær þær hig blissiað andbidiende git þæs ecan lifes þonne hig arisað, swa swa we ealle sceolon, of deaðe gesunde urum Drihtene togeanes. Seo eahteoðe yld ys se an eca dæg æfter urum æriste, þonne we rixiað mid Gode on sawle and on lichaman on ecere sælþe, and ne biþ nan ende þ[æ]s anes dæges, þonne þa halgan scinað swa swa seo sunne deð nu.[12]

It is now usually thought that there was no widespread alarm in Europe around the millennial year in anticipation of the coming of Antichrist and the end of the world.[13] The end of the millennium did bring bad times, however.

The Scandinavian invasions were suddenly and violently renewed and the political order, in England and on the continent, appeared to be crumbling. It is not surprising that Christian writers expressed concern as to these portents. But it was probably no more than coincidence that the time was almost *anno Domini* 1000, the end – if one took the round number literally – of the sixth millennial age. Ælfric like many of his contemporaries saw evidence of the last times in current events and often warned his readers to gird themselves against the coming dénouement. Not infrequently, he reflects the common sentiment that one sign of the approaching end of the world is its state of deterioration, which can be expected to become progressively worse as the end draws even nearer.[14]

Among the most interesting of the allusions to the impending end of the world is one that occurs in the adaptation of a homily of Gregory the Great. Concluding the homily, which is concerned with the signs of the end, Ælfric says,

Mine gebroðra, settað þises dæges gemynd ætforan eowrum eagum, and swa hwæt swa bið nu héfigtyme geðuht, eal hit bið on his wiðmetennysse geliðegod. Gerihtlæcað eower líf, and awendað eowre ðeawas, witniað mid wope eowre yfelan dæda, wiðstandað deofles costnungum; bugað fram yfele, and doð gód, and ge beoð swa micclum orsorgran on to-cyme þæs ecan Déman, swa micclum swa ge nu his strecnysse mid ege forhrádiað. Se witega cwæð, þæt se miccla Godes dæg is swiðe gehende, and þearle swyft. Þeah ðe gyt wære oðer þusend geara to ðam dæge, nære hit langsum; forðan swa hwæt swa geendað, þæt bið sceort and hræd, and bið swilce hit næfre ne gewurde, þonne hit geendod bið. Hwæt þeah hit langsum wære to ðam dæge, swa hit nis, þeah ne bið ure tíma langsum, and on úre geen-dunge us bið gedémed, hwæðer we on reste oþþe on wite ðone gemænelican dóm anbidan sceolon. Uton forði brucan þæs fyrstes ðe us God forgeaf, and geearnian þæt ece líf mid him seðe leofað and rixað in ealra worulda woruld. Amen.[15]

Comparison with Gregory's remarks show that Ælfric has expanded his comments considerably:

Unde et considerare necesse est quia ab illa tribulatione ultima tantum sunt, istae tribulationes dissimiles quantum a potentia judicis persona praeconis distat. Illum ergo diem, fratres charissimi, tota intentione cogitate, vitam corrigite, mores mutate, mala tenentia resistendo vincite, perpetrata autem fletibus punite. Adventum namque aeterni judicis tanto securiores quandoque videbitis, quanto nunc districtionem illius timendo praevenitis.[16]

Although Gregory continually evoked eschatological sanctions for his exhortations[17] and believed quite as strongly as Ælfric that his own age was the last of history, Ælfric saw fit to heighten Gregory's sense of impending doom. He added comments on the shortness of the existence of all things temporal and on the state in which souls await Doomsday, thus making his exhortation even more awe-inspiring.

The pastoral concern which motivates such remarks is evident in passages in which he argues that the laity need sound learning in time of crisis as protection against the wiles of the devil.[18] Ælfric also struck this note in the English preface to the First Series of *Catholic Homilies*: 'and eac forðam þe menn behofiað godre lare swiðost on þisum timan þe is geendung þyssere worulde, and beoð fela frecednyssa on mancynne ærðan þe se ende becume ...'[19] This thought brings to mind Matthew xxiv,[20] which speaks of false Christs who will deceive mankind in the last times and of the Antichrist.

Thus Ælfric approaches the subject of Antichrist, about which the authors of the Blickling and Vercelli homilies knew little and were confused; and he displays far greater knowledge of the subject than the anonymous homilists.[21] As Christ is God incarnate, so Antichrist is the devil incarnate:

se bið mennisc mann and soð deofol, swa swa ure Hæland is soðlice mann and God on anum hade. And se gesewenlica deofol þonne wyrcð ungerima wundra, and cwyð þæt he sylf God beo, and wile neadian mancynn to his gedwylde; ac his tima ne bið na langsum; forþan þe Godes grama hine fordeð, and þeos weoruld bið siððan geendod. Crist ure Drihten gehælde untrume and adlige, and þes deofol þe is gehaten Antecrist, þæt is gereht, ðwyrlic Crist, aleuað and geuntrumað ða halan, and nænne ne gehælð fram untrumnyssum, buton þam anum þe he sylf ær awyrde.[22]

His disciples will assist him in injuring men. They will compel men to turn from God's faith to his lies, and God will permit him to do miracles and signs for three and one-half years. Many will be martyred, others lost. He will cause fire to come down from heaven, but that is not its source. I have said these things, Ælfric concludes, because, as Ezekiel said, the preacher who does not warn of God's wrath is himself culpable, but the preacher who warns is justified though his words are not heard.[23] A short passage added to late manuscripts of the homily for the Common of Virgins in the Second Series[24] cites II Thessalonians ii.7–8 and Jerome's comment on that passage in *Epistula* cxxi, *ad Algasiam*, as support for the notion that the Antichrist will not come so long as Ceasar rules in Rome. After Caesar, Antichrist will come, and he will be slain when Christ arrives, 'swa swa þeostru fordwinað on þære sunnan tocyme.'[25]

Taken together, Ælfric's interest in the ages of history, his remarks on the tribulations of his own period, and his interest in the Antichrist show that, though he was hardly an alarmist,[26] he was more convinced than some of his predecessors that the last days were at hand. This conviction, indeed, is the sanction for his work as a teacher and preacher. But his views were all derived from the Latin theological tradition. The content of his sources seems to depart from that of the sources of the Blickling and Vercelli homilists. Although Ælfric introduces what may be a personal note of genuine concern over the tribulations of his own days, he departs in no significant way from his authorities.

The Homily for the Second Sunday in Advent, based on St Gregory, deals primarily with the signs of the last times as they are described in the apocalypses of Luke and Matthew. Following Gregory,[27] Ælfric holds that the rising of nation against nation is worse now than in the accounts of the historians, and that the earthquakes, pestilences, and hunger of the last times are known. But the astronomical signs, by which the Lord did not simply mean eclipses and the like, are yet to come. When the sun and moon are darkened and Christ's cross appears, earthly powers will mourn and the heavenly powers – the angels and archangels and others of the heavenly host – will be agitated. Christ will appear in might and majesty with these powers. When these things come to pass, we should lift up our heads – that is, our minds – to the joys of the heavenly country.[28] Not only does the New Testament foretell these events: they are anticipated by the prophets and the Sibyls as well.[29] Unlike the earlier English homilists who turned to the Apocalypse of Thomas for clarification of the signs, Ælfric contented himself with the account of the Gospels and the explanations and amplifications in the Latin exegetical tradition.[30]

On Doomsday at the sound of the trumpet,[31] all will die in the purging fire; the dead will be raised and the fire will purge those who have not yet atoned for all their sins; but the conflagration will leave the pure unharmed.[32]

The resurrection of the body is a concept which Ælfric makes an effort to clarify for his audience. Everlasting life is not natural to man, but a gift of God.[33] Nevertheless, it is possible, as St Gregory has said, to discover analogies which help to elucidate the miraculous event in which man will be endowed with incorruptibility:

We sprecað embe ærist. Nu sind sume men þe habbað twynunge be æriste, and ðonne hi geseoð deadra manna bán, þonne cweðað hí, Hu magon ðas bán beon ge-edcucode? Swilce hí wíslice sprecon! Ac we cweðað þær-togeanes, þæt God is Ælmihtig, and mæg eal þæt he wile. He geworhte heofonas and eorðan and ealle gesceafta butan antimbre. Nu is geðuht þæt him sy sumera ðinga eaðelicor to aræenne ðone deadan of ðam duste, þonne him wære to wyrcenne ealle gesceafta of nahte: ac soðlice him sind ealle ðing gelice eaðe, and nán ðing earfoðe. He worhte Adam of láme. Nu ne mage we asmeagan hú hé of ðám láme flæsc worhte, and blod bán and fell, fex and næglas. Men geseoð oft þæt of anum lytlum cyrnele cymð micel treow, ac we ne magon geseon on þam cyrnele naðor ne wyrtruman, ne rinde, ne bógas, ne leaf: ac se God þe forðtihð of ðam cyrnele treow, and wæstmas, and leaf, se ylca mæg of duste aræran flæsc and bán, sina and fex, swa swa he cwæð on his godspelle, 'Ne sceal eow beon forloren an hær of eowrum heafde.'[34]

Ælfric later returned to this passage and amplified it in an addition to be studied below. The awakening of the Seven Sleepers of Ephesus and the undecayed body of St Edmund the Martyr betoken the power of God to raise the dead.[35] This raising will be a third rebirth: following natural birth and baptismal regeneration, men's bodies will be renewed as incorruptible bodies.[36] The very body which rots to dust while awaiting the resurrection is the same which will be raised.[37] No matter how a man died, God can raise him up; no matter what infirmities he bore on earth, he will be whole and sound; no matter what his age at the time of death, he will be raised in the same body which he now bears as it was – or would have been – at thirty-three, the age of Christ at his crucifixion.[38] It will be a physical body with eyes and teeth, one which can truly suffer if that is the individual's lot;[39] but it will be clothed in heavenly garments instead of those in which it was buried.[40] Resurrection, which can be compared with healing,[41] could easily be effected by God at any time if it were his will, but he has reserved this work until the end of the world.[42] Not only will human physical nature be restored at the time of the general resurrection but also the nature of the cosmos. At the time of the creation, the sun was seven times brighter than after the fall, and the moon was as bright as the sun now is; both will be restored to their original radiance, and the moon will cease to wane.[43] However much attention Ælfric paid in his homilies to the condition of the soul between death and the resurrection on Doomsday, he clearly found in his tradition much information about the resurrection, and he was at pains to clarify this difficult tenet of the faith for those who would hear or read his sermons.

With the exception of two summary passages which are credal in tone and structure,[44] Ælfric's accounts of the judgment scene itself generally follow the account of the Synoptic Apocalypse and the exegetical tradition. Christ, who sits at the right hand of the Father,[45] will appear mild to the righteous and awful to the sinful.[46] About him will sit the Apostles on twelve thrones,[47] having led to Judgment the nations they converted.[48] The Judge, who knows all, will require no witnesses; and, although he extends mercy to those who repent during their lives, it will be too late for men to repent at the Doom.[49] One will have to account strictly according to his deserts.[50] Christ will divide men, calling to himself the elect and dismissing the condemned,[51] handing over the Kingdom to the Father.[52] As he ascended alone after his resurrection, so he will ascend alone again, for all will be one in Christ.[53]

Two notes in Ælfric's treatment of Doomsday deserve further notice. First, he specifically condemned one notion expounded in Vercelli Homily xv.[54] Heretics, who do not want to earn their eternal reward, claim 'þæt seo halige Maria, Cristes modor, and sume oðre halgan, sceolon hergian, æfter ðam dome, ða synfullan of ðam deofle, ælc his dæl.' But this is a vain delusion: 'Nele seo eadige Maria ne nán oðer halga lædan ða fulan, and þa mánfullan, and ða árleasan, þe æfre on synnum þurhwunodon, and on synnum geendodon, into ðam clænan húse heofenan ríces myrhðe; ac hí beoð deoflum gelíce ...'[55] There is no easy way around the requirements for justification on the Last Day.

Second, Ælfric introduces in the St Paul homily of the First Series an idea which, at least in this elaborate form, is new to the English vernacular tradition:

Þær beoð feower werod æt ðam dome, twa gecorenra manna, and twa wiðercorenra. Þæt forme werod bið þæra apostola and heora efenlæcendra, þa ðe ealle woruld-ðing for Godes naman forleton: hí beoð ða demeras, and him ne bið nan dóm gedemed. Oðer endebyrdnys bið geleaffulra woruld-manna: him bið dóm gesett, swa þæt hi beoð asyndrede fram gemanan ðære wiðercorenra, þus cweðendum Drihtne, 'Cumað to me, ge gebletsode ...' An endebyrdnys bið þæra wiðercorenra, þa þe ciððe hæfdon to Gode, ac hí ne beeodon heora geleafan mid Godes bebodum: ðas beoð fordemede. Oðer endebyrdnys bið þæra hæðenra manna, þe nane cyððe to Gode næfdon: þisum bið gelæst se apostolica cwyde, 'Ða ðe butan Godes æ syngodon, hí eac losiað butan ælcere æ.' To ðisum twam endebyrdnyssum cweð þonne se rihtwisa Dema, 'Gewitað fram me, ge awyrigedan, into ðam ecum fyre ...'[56]

He quotes the favourite monastic text about the renunciation of the world for Christ (Matthew xix.28–9) and proceeds to state that monks – save those who, like Judas, are faithless – are to be classed in the first, apostolic, group who judge and will not be judged.[57] Monks should take heed of wicked examples like Judas, Ananias and Sapphira, and Gehazi, 'and geefenlæcan þam apostolum, þæt hí, mid him and mid Gode, þæt éce líf habban moton.'[58] Thus Ælfric divides mankind according to present merits and says that these divisions will be reflected in the grouping of men about the throne on the Last Day.

The way to heaven is narrow, and the way to hell wide,[59] so toiling like the martyrs, one should accumulate heavenly wealth on earth.[60] In heaven, faith and hope will have been fulfilled; but love, which for this reason is the greatest of the three, will never cease.[61] There we will not need food or the sacrament, and there will be no temptation and no need for repentance.[62] There the humble will be in places of greatest dignity.[63] The elect will shine brightly and will be amply rewarded for their faithfulness.[64] Hell, in contrast, will be a place of suffering in the eternal fire from which there is no release.[65] The fire burns and causes pain but does not consume.[66] Classes of sinners – adulterers, murderers, robbers – will be segregated so that they must suffer together:

Þær bið wóp and toða gebitt, forðan ðe ða eagan tyrað on ðam micclum bryne, and ða teð cwaciað eft on swiðlicum cyle. Gif hwam twynige be ðam gemænelicum æriste, þonne understande he þisne drihtenlican cwyde, Þæt þær bið soð ærist, ðær ðær beoð wepende eagan and cearcigende teð.[67]

As was the case in Ælfric's treatment of the interim after death, so also his treatment of the approaching end of the world and the Last Judgment is more consistent than are the discussions of the anonymous homilists. Following sources which eschew the apocryphal in favour of the biblical and patristic traditions, he tries conscientiously and quite successfully to communicate clearly and according to the best available authorities the teachings of the church, taking special pains with such difficult topics as the resurrection of the body. Many of the passages cited in this chapter are fairly incidental statements found in the midst of general homilies or saints' lives; others derive from typological treatments of the parables. But the most important passages are associated with Dominical seasons, notably Advent, Easter, and the Ascension. In Ælfric's tradition, therefore, the topic of the Last Times and the apocalypse has to do with Christ's work of salvation, whereas the topics associated with the disembodied afterlife of the soul have to do with penance and ecclesiastical discipline.

8

Three Extended Eschatological Pieces
by Ælfric

For several reasons, it seemed advisable in the preceding, synoptic survey of Ælfric's eschatological teachings to exclude the three items under consideration here. In the first place, these texts have not been known to many students of Ælfric's homiletic work, for two are sermons first published by Professor John C. Pope in 1967 and 1968, and the third, an addition to the First Series of *Catholic Homilies*, remains at this moment unpublished. These pieces are also all probably to be dated a bit later than most of the work already surveyed – all have been identified as work of the period 1002–1005[1] – and are thus Ælfric's most mature comments on eschatology. Most important, however, is the fact that they are the most extensive statements of Ælfric on these aspects of Christian doctrine. The unpublished fragment amplifies a point taken up in an earlier exegetical homily; the Judgment-Day homily, albeit exegetical, is liturgically unattached;[2] and the encyclopedic sermon for the octave of Pentecost (Trinity Sunday) is not exegetical. Thus one may posit that, looking over his work on the pericopes for the Temporale, Ælfric found a basic category of Christian teaching inadequately treated and provided these items to fill the gap.

As in the two preceding chapters, my primary concern here is to summarize the content of Ælfric's teaching. But, by their very nature, the three documents to be considered also open topics which for methodological reasons could not be addressed in the foregoing chapters. The first shows Ælfric as teacher and pastor, concerned to make difficult matters clear to the simple. The second, though not liturgical, is a superb specimen of his exegetical method. The last is a comprehensive treatment of eschatological matters which allows one to assess the relative importance to Ælfric of the fate of the soul after death and the destiny of man at the Last Judgment.

'HWÆR BEOÐ WYRTA BLOSTMAN?'

In six of the eleven surviving manuscripts of the sermon for the First Sunday after Easter of the First Series of the *Catholic Homilies*,[3] there appears a seventy-eight line passage in the rhythmic style which was added to the original homily by Ælfric in the period 1002–1005.[4] In the supplementary addition Ælfric elaborates Gregory the Great's proof of the resurrection of the body by adding further examples.

The opening lines of the fragment were probably suggested by the paragraph from Gregory's homily which Ælfric had previously abridged:

Cuncta ergo in semine simul latent, quae tamen non simul ex semine prodeunt. Ex semine quippe producitur radix, ex radice prodit virgultum, ex virgulto oritur fructus, in fructu etiam producitur semen. Addamus ergo quia et semen latet in semine. Quid igitur mirum, si ossa, nervos, carnem, capillosque reducat ex pulvere, qui lignum, fructus, folia, in magna mole arboris ex parvo quotidie semine restaurat?[5]

Adapting Gregory's rhetorical question to the *ubi sunt?* topos in an original, even bold, fashion,[6] Ælfric adduces examples from nature:

> Hwær beoð wyrta blostman on winterlicre tide?
> Hwær beoð ealle ofǽtu of eallum treowcynne?
> Hwær beoð hi gesewene on winterlicum cyle
> on ænigum beame, þe ealle eft cuciað,
> on wyrtum and on treowum, þurh þone écan wyrhtan,
> se ðe ða deadan bán of þam duste arærð
> eal swa eaðelice swa hé hí ær geworhte?[7]

Similarly, he continues, where are the flies and birds in the winter, and the hibernating animals which sleep all winter and rise sound in the spring?

More unusual, but not without precedent in Christian literature, is the next example: the silkworms.[8] They, make silk 'with wondrous skill' in the summer and then dry up like dust. The dust particles, placed in pokes, are hung on the wall through the winter until spring and pleasant weather return. Then the dust is placed in lead dishes in the sun and is raised again as worms. They are entirely white 'as we have often seen' (line 23); fed by men, they again make silk and return to dust.[9] The exemplum is concluded with a specific application to the problem of the resurrection of the body:

> Nu is full swutol bysen on ðisum syllicum wurmum,
> þe of ðam duste acuciað: þæt ure drihten mæg

of deaðe us aræran of þam duste to lífe;
we ðe beoð þonne éce æfter urum æriste
þonne hé þa wácan wurmas ðe wurðað eft to duste
swa eaðelice geedcucað to þam ænlican cræfte.[10]

Another example of God's power is the phoenix, an incomparable Arabian bird which lives five hundred years and then dies in his nest. But a worm grows from his flesh, becomes a bird just like the old phoenix, and lives quite as long.[11] Like the silkworm, the phoenix is a sign that on the Last Day God will raise us to eternal life in eternal bodies.[12] Finally, the Seven Sleepers of Ephesus provide an example from human experience. Ælfric had previously referred to these saints in a short homily.[13] He had pointed out there, as here, that their case demonstrated the reality of the doctrine of the resurrection of the body to the emperor Theodosius II:

Wylle wé, nelle we, we wuniað æfre cuce
æfter urum æriste be urum gewyrhtum,
oððe wel oððe yfele be þam ðe we geworhton ǽr.[14]

Thus Ælfric introduces the application of his demonstration of the resurrection of the dead. The concluding passage, which states that one must consider where he will dwell eternally and prepare his place, shifts from the first person plural to the singular, and thus the urgency and applicability of the preceding passage are enhanced:

and ic beo sylf unwís gif ic nelle me gewyrcan
þa ecan wununge þa hwile ðe ic [mæg] and mót,
þonne ic nelle furðon nu faran ofer land,
oððe to hirede geridan, butan ic hæbbe beðoht
hwær ic wunian mæge and [gewiss] inn hæbe
to ðam lytlan fyrste þæs hwilwendlican færeldes.[15]

Tenth-century travel had some of the problems of twentieth-century tourism, and therein lay a moral related to man's journey to his heavenly homeland. Although the concept of the world as an inn is probably conventional, Ælfric's concern with advance reservations appears to be his own extension of the theme.[16]

The addition to the homily for the First Sunday after Easter shows Ælfric seeking to make clear the orthodox teaching on a difficult subject. Though his demonstrations may seem quaint to the modern reader, they represent an honest attempt by reference to natural science and hagiography to elucidate one of the most puzzling mysteries of the faith so as to make it easily understandable to a lay congregation. Such congeries as this of natural analogies to or proofs of the resurrection of the body are not uncommon in patristic literature.[17] But I can find no collection exactly analogous to Ælfric's. Since the piece probably had no single source, it may well be one of the most personal passages in the Ælfrician corpus. It draws from nature to expand the traditional Pauline image of the seed as a symbol of resurrection. The silkworm is elaborated as a further natural allegory for the resurrection which was both conventional and, for Englishmen in the early eleventh century, exotic. The phoenix is a well-known type of the same order. Finally, there is the famous matter of the Seven Sleepers of Ephesus. And all is concluded by a reference to life as a journey through the transitory world during which one prepares his lodgings in the intransient world. Although the conclusion is localized in terms of a trip from one monastery to another, the passage is reminiscent of the basic peregrinus imagery of *The Seafarer*. To expand on Gregory's proofs of the resurrection, Ælfric constructed a passage describing other proofs and types of resurrection. But in developing his text he seems to have relied on memory, report, and experience rather than a literary model. As a result the piece is at once traditional and highly personal, and in method and tone it is as close as Ælfric ever ventured to the modes of Old English poetry.

SERMO DE DIE IUDICII

Two manuscripts contain a homily in Ælfric's rhythmical prose which is not designated rubrically for an occasion of the liturgical year but, like a number of anonymous homilies and many Latin sermons as well, is entitled *Sermo de Die Iudicii*. Unlike the similarly rubricated Homilies II and xv of the Vercelli Book,[18] however, Ælfric's sermon on the Day of Judgment is an exegetical one. It may be supposed, then, that Ælfric's purposes in preparing the piece were twofold. He wanted to treat the subject with reference to the Scriptural tradition in order to combat the popularity of treatments indebted to the apocryphal and apocalyptic traditions. And he wanted to consider at length an important topic – and one on which some Carolingian canons had instructed preachers to touch – for which the liturgical pericopes and the Latin homiliary tradition provided no suitable opening.

No homiletic source has been discovered for the work, although it bears a general resemblance to known exegetical writings.[19] In view of what is known of Ælfric's preference for adaptation of source materials in the preparation of his homilies, one might suppose that the piece relies on one or more homilies on Luke xvii.20–37 and Matthew xxiv.15–31, for the homily is an exegetical treatment in that order of those two lections. But, on the basis of the evidence now in hand, it must be concluded that in the main, *De Die Iudicii* is an original exercise in exegesis,[20] and as such, it is a good index of the homilist's method.

De Die Iudicii is reminiscent of the work of Bede, whose sermons tended also to be exegetical exercises.[21] It adheres very closely, as had many of the *Catholic Homilies*, to the task of expounding its texts. The Gospel passages are translated, and sections of the readings are repeated as the preacher comes to explain their 'spiritual' or allegorical meaning. This is, of course, the method of 'continuous gloss,'[22] which more often than not gave rise to writing that was disjunctive and, to modern taste, uninteresting. But as used by Ælfric, the repetitions of continuous gloss are so handled as to give the piece a fine rhetorical flavour and balance which make it an excellent composition. Although it is so constructed as almost to make two separable homilies, there is an intended contrast between Jesus' answers to the Pharisees concerning the coming of Judgment and his private teaching to the disciples on the same subject.

The Lucan half of the homily (lines 1–221) is an explication of the interview of Jesus with the Pharisees in which he is asked about the coming of Doomsday. Jesus, it will be remembered, answered that no man knows when the end will come but that its advent will be sudden as was Noah's flood and as was the destruction of Sodom. Those who are at work will not have time to rescue anything: two men will be together in bed and two women at a mill grinding and two men in a field ploughing, and of each group one will be taken and one left behind. Asked where they would be taken, Jesus replied cryptically, 'Where the carcass is, there gather the eagles' (line 39). For the homilist, the three pairs typify the common classification of the three orders of men – monks, laymen, and clergy. Each class is mixed, and so its members are subject to different kinds of judgments.

Ælfric opens with a commentary on the observation that nobody knows the hour of the end:

> ac we gelyfað swapeah þæt us alogen ne bið
> þæt he cymð soðlice mid hys scínendum englum
> on þisse're' worulde geendunge
> us to demanne, ælcum be hys geearnungum;
> and he þonne forgifð þam þe hym gehyrsumedan,
> and þam þe hine gegladodan mid góódum weorcum æfre,
> þa écan myrhðe and þa écan (mid)wununge
> mid eallum his halgum on heofonan rice.[23]

Sinners will then be damned. He who does not believe this has no faith.

The story of Noah and the use of the flood as a type of the Judgment are well enough known that Ælfric feels the matter can be passed over. The story of the saving of Lot and the destruction of the Sodomites, however, requires explanation. Like the flood of Noah, the sudden coming of the fire on Sodom is a figure of the Doomsday fire, for it, too, will come quickly and consume everything in its path. No man will be able to escape the fire, which will purify and renew the earth:

> and heo ne bið na forburnen, ac bið geclænsod
> fram eallum þam fylþum þe hyre fram frymðe becomon,
> and heo swa on ecnysse eall scinende þurhwunað.[24]

Ælfric proceeds to the verse concerning two men who in that night will be in a single bed. 'Night' signifies the ignorance and persecution of the age of Antichrist. As for the two in one bed:

> Ða beoð þonne on bedde þe beoð on stillnysse,
> and fram eallum woruldcarum æmtige þonne beoð,
> and Godes þeowdóm begað mid góódum inngehyde;
> ac hi ne beoð na twegen, ac on twá todælede.
> Oþre beoð gecorene and Gode gecwéme,
> oðre beoð mid híwunge on his þeowdóme afundene.[25]

Those in the monastic order who have rejected the world and are faithful in their service will go to heaven, but not those who are hypocritical and guilty of false adulation. One is taken, the other left behind. Next the Gospel speaks of two women at the mill, only one of whom is to be taken. These are secular men whose wordly cares are symbolized by the mill:

> Be þysum he cwæð twá, and nolde cweðan twegen,
> for þam þe hi soðlice ne beoð on swylcere fullfremednysse
> þæt hi sylfe magon hy[m] sylfum wissian,
> ac hy sceolan lybban be heora lareowa wissunge.[26]

The laity are depicted as female in a stroke of traditional, post-Pauline anti-feminism because, like women, they are dependent on spiritually stronger men. Bishops and priests must instruct and shrive them and direct their almsgiving. Thus they cannot be like those who follow the counsel of perfection. These men are of two kinds: some elect, others condemned; and they, too, will be rewarded accordingly. Two men will be ploughing in one field, but only one of them will be elect. The clergy, like the monks, are described so as to indicate their separation from the world: they labour in God's field, the church. Bishops and priests are teachers of men and must seek to gain many souls for the Saviour. Fulfilment of this work brings great glory and eternal lordship over the souls acquired. But, Ælfric reflects in a moralistic digression, few teachers do this work now. Like the prophet's hounds which were dumb and could not bark, they are slack in their duties and unrighteousness abounds. The situation is in marked contrast with that of the age of the Apostles and the martyrs; whereas they lived among heathens and persecutors and gave their lives for the faith, Anglo-Saxon preachers are afraid to preach God's commandments and his will to Christian kings and Christian folk. Some teachers are zealous, some negligent; they will be rewarded accordingly. The three symbolic orders of the Gospel passage betoken the whole of mankind.

Finally, Ælfric continues, Jesus' statement about eagles gathering where bodies are to be found must be explained. It is a response to the Pharisees' question about the destiny of good and evil men in which Jesus ignores the evil, attending only to the good. The eagles are the saints, and they will assemble about the throne of the Saviour who will rule, true man and true God, with Father and Spirit. Those who are left behind will dwell eternally with devils.

Ælfric's treatment of these Lucan sayings is remarkable in several respects. In the first place, it puts great emphasis on the point which Ælfric makes in two other places:[27] those who have renounced the world by taking the monastic vows will be honoured in the same manner as the Apostles, who were called to make a similar profession. As the three classes symbolized by the three sayings of Jesus collectively symbolize all of mankind (line 200), the privilege apparently does not include those bishops and priests who are only secular clergy. Ælfric placed great store in the monastic profession, even to the extent of believing that, if a monk were scrupulously faithful to it, it offered him preferential treatment on Doomsday. Second, despite its seeming excessiveness to modern eyes, the exegetical procedure of Ælfric in this sermon is entirely faithful to the task of speaking about the approach of the end only in terms of the scriptural texts as interpreted by the exegetes. Perhaps apocryphal sources would not have produced more fanciful results, but the only authority that is reliable is the tradition of Scripture and the Fathers.

The second half of the sermon (lines 227–439) moves from observations about the suddenness of the coming of Doomsday and the need to be morally prepared to teaching about the Last Days. It deals with the Matthaean passage, but occasionally the readings are based on the parallel passages of Mark xiii; portions of Matthew not also included in Mark are omitted from consideration.[28]

Its Latin introduction[29] is not a biblical text but a free composition based on Matthew xxiv.3 which introduces the lection. The device is of the sort which Latin homilists sometimes used in the course of exegetical passages, and it was sometimes used to provide contextual introductions for the liturgical pericopes. Ælfric also alters Matthew's 'secreto' to *endemys* 'with one accord' (line 231), evidently feeling that he could thus best emphasize his desire to contrast the teaching to the disciples with that to the Pharisees. These little touches are representative of the attention to detail so characteristic of the work of Ælfric.

Jesus tells the disciples that when they see the *onscuniendlic deofolgild* or 'abominable image of the devil' (line 234) they must understand that the end will come without warning. Since these will be times of great distress, one ought to pray that they will not come in winter or on the Sabbath when one is not occupied. If God in his mercy did not intend to shorten the days of tribulation for the benefit of the elect, no one could escape perdition. There will be false Christs working wonders and signs in the sun and moon and stars. And then the Son of Man will come in glory to gather the elect. The abominable devil image of Daniel will be set up in the days of the Antichrist. Idol worship has been proscribed since the coming of Christ, but Antichrist, by God's leave, will test men in the last times. Antichrist, as the symbol of the devil image signifies, will count himself God and seek men's worship. Those who are pregnant and giving suck symbolize false Christians, 'þe beoð mid leahtrum afyllede, swa swa gefearhsugu.'[30] We should pray that the reign of Antichrist will not come in winter, for winter symbolizes the cooling of true love so that one is unable to love God, his neighbour, or himself. One should pray that Antichrist not come on the Sabbath which betokens idleness. When Christ speaks of persecutions such as have never been before and will never be again, he refers to the age of the martyrs and the age of Antichrist, the latter of which is by far the more perilous. God's shortening of the days refers to the end of the reign of Antichrist after three and one-half years. False Christs are to be avoided. The Christian knows that

> Ure Hælend Crist ne cymð na to mancynne
> openlice æteowed on þissere weorolde
> ær þam micclan dæge þonne he mancynne demð;
> ac þa leasan Cristas and þa leasan witegan
> þonne cumað on Antecristes timan.[31]

Those who persevere in Christ's faith will be protected. We should give up our lives rather than deny him.

Finally, there are the astronomical signs. Sun and moon will be darkened and eclipsed; stars will fall and heavenly powers will be stirred up. Then Antichrist will be slain, and the Lord will come. For Christ himself is the Son of Man who will come in clouds and glory to gather his elect, raised at the sound of the trumpet with all men of all ages, to rule with him. The evil will be separated out and sent to the fire.

Again Ælfric follows closely the text at hand. He had treated much of the material concerning Antichrist in the English Preface of *Catholic Homilies* I and had considered the signs of the Last Times in the Homily for the Second Sunday in Advent of the same volume. Although the explication offered here differs in detail, the passages are similar in spirit. Because he is concerned in both halves of the homily with the Last Times – the suddenness of their coming, the need to be ready, the signs of the age of Antichrist, and the end of Antichrist's time – it is not necessary for him to give a full treatment of the Judgment itself. The rubrical title might, then, be regarded as misleading; for the subject is not the Day itself but its advent. *De Die Iudicii* is not important for departures from the English homilist's previous position. It reaffirms Ælfric's earlier teaching, makes it more specific in several respects, and reveals continued loyalty to his strict methodological principles.

The matter of method, however, requires some comment. All students of medieval literature are now acquainted with the theory of the three- or four-fold signification of Scripture and the so-called allegorical method of exegesis. In point of fact, the method is often difficult to discern in early medieval writings, although statements of the theory are common enough. Bede, as Professor Bolton remarks, often states the theory but rarely, if ever, fulfils in practice the expectations he raises in his modern readers.[32] One explanation of this phenomenon is the fact that, although theoretical statements often speak of four levels of meaning (literal, typological, tropological, anagogical), the practitioners who most deeply influenced early medieval exegetes and homilists – notably Gregory the Great and Bede – followed the more ancient three-level theory (literal, tropological, typological).[33] It was also common almost to ignore the literal or historical.[34]

There has been only one study of Ælfric's exegetical theory and practice.[35] Its conclusions are approximately what one would expect in the light of the situation just outlined. In the homilies, comparatively little attention is given to the literal interpretation. Typological significance receives a great deal of attention, as does the tropological – the latter often introduced with the formula *æfter þeawlicum andgite*.[36] The anagogical sense, however, is almost entirely lacking. There are a few rather general statements of theory.[37]

One good example of Ælfric's procedure when he is adapting a basic source to his own homiletic ends is the Septuagesima homily of *Catholic Homilies* II, on the parable of the vineyard (Matthew xx.1–16).[38] The outline of the work is dictated in part by the method of continuous gloss; and, within that frame, it is further determined by the dictates of the exegetical method. First, there is the translation of the pericope. After a brief statement in which Ælfric says his sermon is in the main a simplification of Gregory's Homily XIX, he undertakes an explanation of the basic allegorical structure and its typological references: the five hours of hiring are five ages of Old and New Testament history (lines 37–87). There follows a tropological application of the fivefold structure to the five ages of man and to the condition of men in the congregation (lines 88–118). The conclusion of the parable is explained (lines 119–80) as an allegory of the Judgment. In this passage, moral admonition is freely mixed with typological explanation. Although the subject is the matter of anagogy, the method is that of typology. The difficult last sentence of the pericope ('Many are called and few are chosen') is treated separately (lines 181–202). Finally, there is a concluding admonition (lines 203–30) which replaces Gregory's exemplum, probably because Ælfric had used it elsewhere and avoided repetition of material whenever possible.[39] A closer reading of the homily than can be afforded here would show that Ælfric clearly understands the method being followed by Gregory, that he brings in other sources wherever they serve to clarify Gregory, and that the result is a sermon more suitable to his audience than a mere translation of Gregory would have been, yet basically faithful to the original. Both authors balance three requirements: the needs and limitations of the audience, the need for sequential explication of the text, and the need to expound the spiritual significations of the text.

In *De Die Iudicii*, the appropriation of the early medieval theory of biblical interpretation can be discerned in a situation where, because the homily is as close to original explication as anything we have from his pen, Ælfric seems to be free of two constraints: the liturgical, which would have confined him to a single pericope and to emphases of the liturgical season, and the constraint imposed by following a single source or the sources assembled in the homiliaries for a liturgical occasion. It ought to be clear from what has already been said about the homily that Ælfric displays a mastery of the method as he and his usual exemplars understood it and that he is able to work within the methodological confines of the continuous gloss without loss of coherence, clarity, or elegance of expression. Indeed, despite the difficulty of achieving unity with the glossator's method and the additional roadblock created by the use of two texts, Ælfric's piece achieves both rhetorical unity and homiletic tone. His primary concern is with the spiritual meaning of notoriously cryptic passages of the Synoptic Apocalypse, but he also displays a desire to apply the unravelled mysteries tropologically to the situation of the late-Saxon church.

The two passages of *De Die Iudicii* in which Ælfric comments on his method seem to be in accord with these conclusions. After the repetition of Matthew xxiv.16–18, he says,

> We moton eow secgan swa swa ge magon understandan,
> hwilum anfealdlice be eowrum andgite,
> hwilum eow geopenian þa inran digolynsse,
> for þam þe eaðe ne magon hit eall understandan.[40]

In fact, he does not expound Matthew xxiv.16–18, and he seems to mean that those verses are self-explanatory: at the last hour men will be variously occupied and will not have time to make last-minute arrangements. But the lamentation in verse 19 over those 'who are pregnant and giving suck' requires exposition: the Gospel speaks of false Christians. Thus the passage quoted is an aside to explain why one group of verses of the text can stand without more than literal translation while another verse requires attention since, read literally, it is meaningless. The other note occurs at lines 40–2. It introduces the interpretation of the *digolstan* ('most obscure') passages of the lection from Luke, and it is at this point that Ælfric begins his exposition, with assistance from Bede's commentary on Luke. It seems to imply that the homilist need only attend to those portions of his text which need clarification if their significance is not to be lost. These passages seem to me to imply both an awareness of the traditional method and a desire to allow the text to stand on its own where it can do so without confusing or misleading the congregation. It may be that Ælfric takes the literal more seriously than has been thought and that, working from Latin to English, he regards the translation of the text into clear, idiomatic English prose as fulfilling, in a number of instances, the requirement for commentary on the literal or historical or grammatical meaning. At any rate, *De Die Iudicii* is an effective presentation of materials not covered adequately by the homilies of the Temporale and Sanctorale. With considerable freedom and skill Ælfric presents a traditional reading of the metaphors of the texts he had selected for exposition within the twin constraints of the framework of continuous gloss and his own understanding, which he had acquired from his study of Gregory and Bede, of the nature of the expositor's task.

SERMO AD POPULUM IN OCTAVIS PENTECOSTEN DICENDUS

Among the sermons for the Temporale which Ælfric wrote after the publication of the Second Series of the *Catholic Homilies* is one for the octave of Pentecost which is preserved complete in six manuscripts.[41] Written in the earlier years of the period 1002–1005,[42] the homily is entirely in his mature, rhythmical style.

The liturgical development of the day for which it was written was, in Ælfric's period, not complete. The Sunday after Pentecost had originally been a vacant Sunday, not supplied with propers because it was in the octave of Pentecost. The feast of the Trinity was a tenth-century innovation which was not accorded universal acceptance until several centuries later, although by the end of the tenth century it was observed in some places north of the Alps, where the propers of a votive mass for the Trinity were appropriated to it.[43] The octave of Pentecost was regarded by Ælfric as stressing the Trinity but not as a distinct feast, for he states in the introductory portion of the *Sermo* that the church has been observing the gift of the Holy Spirit during the past week,

> and nu todæg wé heriað þá hálgan Þrynnysse
> mid úrum ðeowdome, and on ðyssere wucan
> oð Sunnanæfn wé singað be þam.[44]

At about the time of the writing of the *Sermo*, Ælfric also provided a homily for the pericope of the octave of Pentecost.[45] Thus the *In Octavis Pentecosten* is a discourse on matters the homilist felt required coverage and wanted to assign to this day. The term *sermo* in rubrics (as opposed to the general title of his two great series) seems to be reserved by Ælfric for discourses not based on the appointed pericopes.[46] That he did not feel constrained to discuss the Trinity may be due either to the novelty of the observance, of which the homilist might be expected to have been dubious, or to his feeling that he had treated the matter adequately elsewhere.[47]

The *Sermo* begins with a summary of the sequence of observances of the Temporale

> þæt ge sum andgit þæron tocnawan magon,
> hú eall ðæs geares ymbegang Gode Ælmihtigum deowað.[48]

This passage, which occupies ninety-four of the five hundred and seventy-four lines in the piece, is rounded off with another reference to the service offered God by the annual liturgical cycle and the statement that the author intends now to turn to other matters.

The long sermon that follows is based on a tract, the *Prognosticon Futuri Saeculi* by Julian, bishop of Toledo (680–90),[49] which gathers in its three books patristic commentary on the subjects of death, the state of souls before the Second Coming, and the Day of Judgment. Julian's was the most compendious treatment of these subjects available in the Early Middle Ages, and, for that reason, it circulated widely. In composing his work Ælfric drew from a homiletic epitome of Julian's treatise. This document, written in Latin, must have been prepared by Ælfric himself, for in the *Sermo* he shows an intimate knowledge of the original, and at the same time, he adapts features peculiar to the excerpts.[50] He seems occasionally to have used both sources in a similar way in preparing several of the *Catholic Homilies*.[51]

The homiletic adaptation of Julian's *Prognosticon* falls, like the original, into three parts. The first of these (lines 94–215) is concerned with death and the merits of intercession. After sketching the story of the fall, by which death was introduced through the devil's malice, Ælfric lists three types of death:

> Mors acerba, mors inmátura, mors naturalis.
> Ðæt is on Englisc, sé bitera deað
> sé ungeripode deað, and se gecyndelica.
> Sé bitera deað is gecweden þe bið on cildum,
> and se ungeripoda deað, on geongun mannum,
> and se gecyndelica, þe becymð þam éaldum.[52]

Men commonly fear the death of the body, which is mortal, and neglect the immortal soul. But for those who have cared for the soul, physical death is not an evil. So one should not consider how he will die, but how his soul will fare after death. There are two deaths, that of the body and that of the soul. The former happens to all men, but the latter only to the wicked whose soul is eternally lost:

> and ne swelt ðeah næfre on ðære hellican susle,
> ac bið æfre geedniwed to þam ecum witum. [53]

Obedience to the Lord's will is the only way to escape the second fate. One should strive, therefore, to please God and to earn the eternal dwelling place for which we dare hope only because Christ came of his own kindness to redeem mankind,

> ægðer ge weras ge wíf, and ðá unwittigan cíld,
> and ða gehádodan menn þe healdað heora clænnysse,
> and wið déofles costnunge dæghwamlice campiað.[54]

In heaven our friends await our coming and are anxious for our safety. We need their prayers against the machinations of the devil. The prayers of men in orders are of special value: witness the case of a person who at the point of being carried off by the dragon was rescued by monks' prayers, atoned for his sins, and died peacefully.[55] The sacrament should be admnistered to the sick while they can still eat it.

When good men die God sends his angels to lead their souls to Christ, who will reward them according to their merits.[56] Those who had not entirely purged themselves will be punished,

> oððæt hí wurðon clæne,
> and þurh ðingrædene ðanon alysde.[57]

The wicked are immediately doomed; but, if one intended to confess, he will be pardoned so that there is hope for him at the Last Judgment. Death is not always painful, but sometimes forgiveness comes through the pains of last illness. Some men, on the other hand, rejoice in death because they see that they are going to rest. Masses and alms help only those who are not utterly condemned.

Like the first section of *In Octavis Pentecosten*, the second (lines 216–72) epitomizes much material also found in Ælfric's earlier homilies and clarifies what was only allusive in the other works. This dissertation on the fate of the soul after death begins with the assertion that, though deprived of the body, the soul is not deprived of the capacity for suffering:

> Seo sawul hæfð soðlice, swa swa ús secgað béc,
> þæs lichman gelicnysse on eallum hyre limum,
> and heo gefret softnysse oððe sarnysse,
> swa hwæðer swa héo on bið, be þam ðe heo geearnode ær.[58]

Although serious sins cannot be atoned for by the soul, lesser ones can be. The purgatorial fire, inflicting worse torture than any human king could devise, punishes remediable sins for as long as is necessary, given the gravity of the misdeeds and the interposition of intercessory prayers. Those in heaven pray for those being punished as well as for those on earth, and living men, especially through masses, can join this work. The holy ones in eternal bliss are anxious for the double joy which will be theirs at the resurrection of the Last Day, but they must await the perfection of the number of the elect. Meanwhile, they enjoy the blessing of God's splendour. They can see all in heaven, earth, and hell and thank God that they have been saved from punishment. The wicked in torment, by contrast, have no such vision, and their solicitude for men on earth profits no one.

The third and longest section of *In Octavis Pentecosten* (lines 273–574) celebrates the Day of Judgment, the time of which is unknown to the living and the dead. Life on earth will continue until the day of the Lord's coming with his angels who will bear the cross. Their glory will be so great as to cut off the light of sun and moon. Fire will overrun the earth, killing those who are still in the world; and at the sound of the last trumpet, all men will rise with living bodies. The glorified, or raised, body will be as man would have been or was at the same age as Christ at his passion; for, as God created and redeemed soul and body, male and female, he will raise them up in the same way, but without licentiousness. The body will be made whole, but the appearance of those who will be in black fire throughout eternity is an indifferent question. Shrouds will be replaced with spiritual apparel. All of mankind will be gathered about the throne of Christ. He will seem gracious to the good and harsh to the sinful who, unlike the good, will be unable to see the Godhead. About him will sit the twelve on Judgment-seats,

> and ealle ða hálgen weras ðe ðas woruld forleton,
> and woruldlice æhta mid ealle forsawon,
> sittað on dómstlum soðlice mid him,
> and hí mid þam Hælende mancynne þonne demað.[59]

The four groups of men about the throne are enumerated: those who join in judging and are immune from judgment; those whose faithfulness and good deeds have won them a heavenly dwelling; those who, though they knew the faith, sinned and must be condemned; the heathen who had no knowledge of the faith and, having lived without the law, must perish eternally without the law among the false Christians. At the Judgment, there will be no secrets, for all unatoned sins will be revealed to the entire company. All will be equal, no matter what their former social stations.

In describing the actual Judgment (lines 405–50), Ælfric quotes more extensively than Julian of Toledo from Matthew xxv. He relates in the case of the redeemed and damned the sentence of the Lord, their query, 'When did we see thee hungering?' and his explanation of the sentence:

> Sóð ic eow secge, þæt ge me sylfum dydon
> þas foresædon ðing, swá oft swa ge hí dydon
> anum of ðisum lyttlum minra gebroðra . . .
> Sod ic eow secge, me sylfum ge his forwyr[n]don
> swa oft swa ge his forwyrndon ánum of þisum lytlum.[60]

Immediately the wicked depart into eternal punishment with the devil. Hell is described, as in Apocalypse xx.14, as 'the broad lake of crackling fire' (line 462):

> On ánum fýre hí byrnað on þam byrnendan mere,
> dá earman menniscan menn, and ðá modigan déoflu;

þæt fyr bið ðonne écé, and hi écelice byrnað,
ac héora lichaman ne magon næfre forbyrnan,
for ðan ðe hí beoð éce æfter þam æriste.[61]

If anyone should ask how devils, which are spirits and have no bodies, can feel the fire's burning, Ælfric, following Julian and Augustine,[62] points to the soul of man which suffers 'for better or worse' in the body:

> Eall swa eaðelice mæg sé ælmihtiga God
> belúcan ðá déofla on þam deorcan fyre,
> þæt hí ðǽron cwylmion, and ofcuman ne magon;
> and sé ðe þá halgan englas on heofonum gegladað,
> sé mæg éác gedreccan [þa] déoflu on þam fyre,
> ðeah ðe hí gastas syndon, forscyldegode ealle.[63]

In hell as in the temporary punishments, suffering will be differentiated according to merit, the lightest penalties being reserved for unbaptized children who are guilty only of original sin. Those in the fire will be unable to see the joy of the redeemed. Meanwhile, in other quarters, earth and heaven will be renewed and the sun and moon seven times brighter. The elect will dwell in their light; and Christ will entrust the Kingdom to his Father, fulfilling the prayer of his incarnate life. The elect will no longer see as in a mirror, but face to face. The great band will live in peace and glory, and will be without want. In joy with Christ

> hine lufigende buton toforlætennysse,
> and hine herigende butan werignysse,[64]

they will live forever, shining as brightly as the sun.

The *Sermo ad Populum in Octavis Pentecosten Dicendus* is Ælfric's most complete eschatological statement. In its systematic treatment of death, the destiny of the soul, and Judgment, it clarifies much that Ælfric had said in the *Sermones Catholicae*. Because the task of preaching on given texts and commenting on the lives of given saints in the two series of addresses gave Ælfric no opportunity to make so complete a statement as in the *Sermo*, this homily contains far more explicit teaching about punishment and reward for souls between death and Judgment. It reinforces his prior statements about the benefit of intercessions for those in punishment and gives a complete account of his understanding of the New Testament tradition concerning the Last Day and its approach.

Since *In Octavis Pentecosten* is Ælfric's most complete outline of his eschatological belief, it is important to notice that, although he has a developed understanding of purgatory, the individual judgment and its consequences have not usurped the primacy of the Last Judgment in his theology. The moving and extended picture of the great Doom at the end of this homily is cast in the heroic mould and is clearly the development that consummates the whole and not simply an extension or consequence of the events of the post mortem interim, as one often feels treatments of the Last Judgment to be in scholastic writings. Rhetorically, the *Sermo* builds to its conclusion; and it is the Judgment, as both the length of his treatment and its eloquence demonstrate, which Ælfric clearly feels is the most important aspect of the Christian eschatological tradition. One must, therefore, conclude that, although Ælfric assembled and used all the materials for the treatment of the destiny of the soul between death and the Judgment, he is not a precursor of scholasticism. The heroic emphases of the Early Middle Ages remain predominant in his approach to eschatology.

The source of this homily, the excerpts in MS Boulogne-sur-Mer 63 of Julian's *Prognosticon Futuri Saeculi*, has been shown to have been used by Ælfric in preparation of short portions of the First Series of *Catholic Homilies*. Thus the Boulogne excerpts can be said to be the earliest datable work of Ælfric,[65] and it can now be assumed that it was with this understanding of eschatology that Ælfric approached the task of adapting in English the exegetical homilies and hagiographic materials. Ælfric had from the first an orderly understanding of punishments and rewards for the soul after death and of the value of intercession by men and saints for the souls of the redeemable dead; and his understanding of the Last Judgment was based almost exclusively on the Matthaean apocalypse as it was interpreted in the patristic exegetical and theological tradition.

9

Some General Reflections on Ælfric's Eschatology

If one compares the work of the anonymous homilists and of Ælfric, he has the impression that two different theological traditions underlie their work. The former is picturesque, confused, disorderly. But the abbot of Eynsham was cautious and orderly almost to a fault.[1] These surface distinctions do not, however, define accurately enough the differences between the two. When one compares their sources, he discovers that only in one area does their material overlap extensively: both the anonymous writers and Ælfric drew extensively from the lives of saints and the legends about the apostles. But in this area of agreement, there is not much material directly concerned with eschatology.

By contrast, the liturgical and doctrinal homilies had almost entirely different sources. In the Blickling and Vercelli homilies,[2] Gregory the Great is only sparingly drawn upon; and he is the only significant authority also used by Ælfric. Many of the sources of the anonymous homilists – now identified with pseudo-Augustine, Caesarius of Arles, and Peter Chrysologus – seem to have been associated in a common, homiliarist textual tradition which descended to the modern period (and thus to the editors of the *Patrologia Latina*) – as supposedly Augustinian preaching.[3] Further, the anonymous writers drew on visionary and apocryphal materials such as the Thomas Apocalypse, the *Visio Pauli*, and apocrypha derived from the pseudo-Pauline *Visio*. The Vercelli homilist had a limited acquaintance with Alcuin and Isidore. Ælfric, however used authentic Augustinian items and made even more extensive use of both Gregory the Great and Bede. All these he knew, as I have already reported, from the authoritative homiliary of Paul the Deacon, which he augmented by reference to the later Carolingian homiliaries of Haymo, Smaragdus, and others. His visionary materials came from his homiletic sources and from saints' lives, and he explicitly condemned the apocrypha used by the anonymous authors. Although he used Caesarius and some of the other authors who were important in the line of homiliaries related to Alan of Farfa, he seems to have done so sparingly.[4] Thus while Ælfric and the editors of the Blickling and Vercelli codices were all traditionalist theologians, their traditions were almost entirely disparate.

The Blickling Homiliary is incomplete and the Vercelli Homilies are not calendrically designated with any consistency, so there is not enough evidence to determine whether or not they are based on calendars or lectionaries markedly different from those of Ælfric. Although Ælfric's use of eschatological material in Lent, Eastertide, Ascensiontide, and Rogationtide agrees well enough with Blickling's use, he also uses eschatological materials for Epiphany, on the octave of Pentecost, and in Advent – seasons in which the Blickling Book is silent. The Vercelli Codex is a curious book – 'an out-of-the-way collection,' as Kenneth Sisam said.[5] It reminds one of the traditions of the *florilegium* or commonplace anthology[6] or of the very earliest stages of the development of the tradition of the homiliary during which sermon anthologies were made not for liturgical use but for spiritual edification: *ad utilitatem legentium*, to quote one early testimony.[7] Its compiler clearly drew upon liturgical homiliaries, but his own purposes were, as clearly, non-liturgical.

The difference between Ælfric, his predecessors, and (as I shall argue in Part IV) his followers, however, apparently lies not so much in the liturgical tradition as in the sources used and in the methodological principles Ælfric brought to his work. He required of himself consistency, clarity, and strict orthodoxy as opposed to the confusion and heterodoxy he found in the older English writers. He was proud of his credentials as a representative of the new monasticism which had done so much to revitalize Christianity in England and recommended himself as a representative of that tradition. By appropriating the intellectual fruits of the work of the continental monastic reformers – and they were largely products which were related in some way to the liturgical program of the reform movement – he was able to produce a very different kind of homiletic corpus. As the work of Father Smetana clearly establishes, he relied for sources chiefly upon the semi-official Carolingian liturgical homiliary of Paul the Deacon and on Haymo.[8] Yet, as I have argued in Part II, he had uses in mind for his writings which can be distinguished from those of Paul and other Carolingian homiliarists. The Ælfrician corpus is, understandably, more unlike than like the anonymous homilies, although it shares with them a reverential attitude towards the traditions of the Fathers and the early-medieval or heroic point of view. It is based for the most part on the appointed pericopes for the calendar; and except for their occasional exempla, the majority of the homilies are exegetical.

Ælfric presents a consistent doctrine of rewards and punishments for the souls of the dead which, though vague at points in the *Catholic Homilies*, is clear in the *Sermo ad Populum in Octavis Pentecosten Dicendus*. In the latter work, which is (as its rubric was probably intended to indicate) more like a tract, he also clarifies his belief that intercession avails for those who are being purged after death of culpability for sins, a belief that was evident as well in the visionary materials of his earlier works. These views are made plausible in Ælfric by his belief that life in the world is a period of exile from one's heavenly homeland, his understanding of death as the progression of the immortal soul from the present state of alienation to one of glory, and his description of the church as the Kingdom of God.

Ælfric was more concerned than his predecessors with the implications of his belief that his own period was the end of the sixth age of history and that the signs of the last times were to be seen in current history. Thus there is a revived interest in those signs and in the reign of Antichrist, but his comments on these subjects are almost invariably based on Scripture as interpreted in the orthodox tradition. He was deeply desirous of explaining clearly the doctrine of the resurrection of the body, and he often used Matthew xxiv-xxv as the basis for description of the Judgment scene.

Perhaps the most characteristic note of Ælfric's teaching on the Last Day is his vision of monks as honoured even above bishops for following the counsel of perfection. He sought a different kind of perfection in his literary work, but one related to the monastic perfection of renunciation of the world, for complete loyalty to Christ required complete and diligent submission of oneself to the othodox tradition. To say that Ælfric was a product of the monastic revival, then, is far more then to say he was a monk: in everything that he did his obedience to the Rule was implicit, and he worked as he did with a view to obtaining the reward promised those who renounced the world entirely and followed Christ with utmost faithfulness.

10

Wulfstan's Variations and Developments
of the Antichrist Theme

The topic of eschatology is, as I have already mentioned in introducing the archbishop, one of the main motifs of the homiletic work of Wulfstan. It was chiefly developed by means of variation upon a given theme, the age of Antichrist, which the homilist employed again and again. Indeed, he uses the motif so often that it can be called the theological preoccupation of Wulfstan at the beginning of his career, though at the end of his period of homiletic productivity he had shifted his theme somewhat.[1]

As the sermons of Wulfstan other than the *Sermo Lupi ad Anglos* are read so infrequently, it may be well to begin by presenting the full text of a representative eschatological homily in order to give the reader an idea of the basic methodology and central concepts of Wulfstan on which an analysis of his variations can be based. For this purpose the homily *De Anticsristo*[2] serves well. Not the earliest of Wulfstan's eschatological homilies,[3] it is nevertheless one of the earlier works and the first full development of the Antichrist motif. The homily was adapted from the homilist's own Latin text, which he both modified and elaborated in the English version. Like many of Wulfstan's sermons it is addressed to the clergy.

DE ANTICRISTO

Leofan men, understandað swyðe georne þæt ge rihtlice and
wærlice þæt healdan þæt eow mæst þearf is to gehealdenne,
5 þæt is, rihtne cristendom. Forðam ælc þæra þe ongean þæt
to swyðe deð oððon oðerne ongean þæt læreð þe his cristendome
to gebyreð, ælc þæra bið Antecrist genamod. Anticristus is on
Læden *contrarius Cristo*, þæt is on Englisc, Godes wiðersaca.
Se bið Godes wiðersaca þe Godes lage and lare forlæt, and ðurh
10 deofles lare of ðam deð ðe his cristendome to gebyreð, and on

synnum hine sylfne to swyðe befyleð oððon oðerne man
on synna belædeð. And ðeath þæt sy þæt fela manna Antecrist
sylfne næfre his eagum ne geseo, to fela is þeah his lima þe man
wide nu geseon and ðurh heora yfel gecnawan mæg, ealswa hit
15 on þam godspelle geræd is: *Surgent enim pseudocristi, et reliqua.*
Wide hit gewyrð þæt up arisað lease leogeras and beoð swæslice
swicole, and ða mænigne man amyrrað and on gedwylde gebringað.
And swa mycel earfoðnes gewyrð on mænige wisan gyt wide
on worulde, þæs þe bec secgað, þurh deofles bearn þe uriht
20 dreogað, swa naefre ær on worulde ne gewearð; forðam þæt
mæste yfel cymð to mannum þonne Antecrist sylf cymð, þe
næfre ær on worulde ne gewearð. And us þincð þæt hit sy þam
timan swyðe gehende, forðam þeos woruld is fram dæge to
dæge a swa leng swa wyrse.
25   Nu is mycel neod eac eallum Godes bydelum þæt hy Godes
folc warnian gelome wið þone egesan þe mannum is towerd, þe
læs þe hy unwære wurðan aredode and ðonne to hrædlice ðurh
deofol beswicene. Ac do sacerda gehwylc on his
scriftscire þæt hit man gehyre oft and gelome, þe læs ðe hit
30 geweorðe þæt þurh larleste Godes folc losie; and ðeah þæt
geweorðe þæt ure ænig þe nu leofað þonne ne libbe, þeah we
agan þearfe þæt we godcunde heorda warnian nu georne hu
hy þam deofle Antecriste sylfan wærlicast magan þonne
wiðstandan, þonne he his wodscinn widdast tobrædeð. And
35 utan warnian us eac swa wið his unlara nu swyðe georne and God
ælmihtigne georne biddan þæt he us gescylde wið þæne
þeodscaðan. God us gescylde wið þæne egesan, and he us geryme
to ðære ecan myrhðe þe þam is gegearwod þe his willan
gewyrcað. Ðær is ece blis and æfre byð in ealra worulda woruld
40 a butan ende, amen.[4]

This short, topical homily sets the main theme of eschatology as it was to be developed in Wulfstan's writing. One must maintain his orthodoxy against the time of Antichrist, who is God's adversary. There are even now adversaries of God abroad, the ministers of Antichrist or the false Christs, who attempt to seduce men with their amicable treachery. In the end there will be greater hardships, especially when Antichrist himself comes; and the hour of his coming seems to be very near. Therefore, let the preacher preach to prepare his people, even though he may be dead by the time of the advent of Antichrist. Wulfstan has drawn from his sources a basic outline of the age of the Opponent, omitting most of the details of the history of the age of the Antichrist as they had been outlined by Adso.[5] He says he thinks his own days are surely just before the last time, and he uses this belief as the touchstone for an exhortation to the clergy to teach diligently.

The manner in which Wulfstan adapted his own Latin composition in preparing this piece requires a few comments, for it is paradigmatic of his methodology; both the amplifications and the deletions are significant. The Latin text of *De Anticristo* fills fifty-five lines of print compared with the forty lines of the Old English version. It consists of a collection of biblical and patristic references to the age of Antichrist and an admonition to preachers to warn the people against the approaching danger. Its brevity is such that Professor Bethurum suggests it may have been only a set of notes from which Wulfstan preached,[6] although the combination of even greater brevity and rhetorical mannerism in the English version may, as has already been suggested (p. 20), militate against this possibility for the Latin as well.

Notwithstanding its brevity, the English version of *De Anticristo* is introduced by a hortatory sentence not found in the Latin version, which opens with the characteristic address, *Leofan men,*[7] and contains echoes of legal codes with which Wulfstan has been connected[8] concerning the importance of scrupulous pursuit of true Christian faith. In the next two sentences, the English runs parallel to the Latin in its definition of the term Antichrist. It is worth noting that Wulfstan replaces Ælfric's Englishing of 'Antichrist,' *þwyrlic crist,*[9] which he surely knew, with *Godes wiðersaca*, an expression that better suits his hortatory and rhetorical strategies but is less close to his own Latin expression, *contrarius Cristo.*[10] Lines 9–12 of the Old English text, which have no parallel in the Latin, recapitulate and expand the first three sentences and introduce legalistic terminology typical of Wulfstan's work. The following sentence adapts the source document, repeating its quotation of Matthew xxiv.24; but in the English, Wulfstan simplifies the biblical passage to fit it into his alliterative and metrical scheme by deleting such terms as *pseudocristi et pseudoprophete* and the reference to the elect. The latter omission necessitates the omission also of the following sentences of the Latin, an admirable but sophisticated adaptation of a play on the biblical words, *si fieri potest*, based perhaps on several passages in the exegetical writings of Gregory the Great.[11] But the Old English version follows the Latin in adopting Matthew xxiv.21, neglecting, however, to translate verse 22. The dogmatic or expository paragraph ends with a passage in lines 20–4 which are without precedent in the Latin but are typical of Wulfstan both for their urgent suggestion that the time of Antichrist is at hand and for their characteristic form of expression. This passage eloquently and very definitely closes the paragraph, for Wulfstan had clearly concluded that lines 20–9 of the Latin version, a pastiche of passages from canonical apocalyptic writings with some exegetical reflections, was not to be adapted in the Old English *De Antichristo*.

The second, concluding paragraph of the English version similarly compresses twenty-six lines of Latin into sixteen of the vernacular, mostly by excluding scriptural quotations; but there is room at the end for a stronger parenetic close and doxology. Because this paragraph is largely moral rather than doctrinal, it is not necessary to trace it closely here. Wulfstan's principles for composition in English are, furthermore, clear enough from the first half of the homily. Quite certainly being guided by the Latin, he nevertheless reinforces its moralistic and legalistic implications and omits all biblical quotations except two verses of Matthew xxiv. These alterations are accompanied by other changes to accommodate the archbishop's highly personal style. And minimal though the doctrinal content of the Latin might seem to readers steeped in biblical and expository treatments of apocalyptic materials (let alone the kind of *vita Anticristi* which preoccupied Adso), Wulfstan radically restricts the Old English to exclude confusing concepts, loan words, speculation, and niceties of theological argument. He is left with bare bones, but these he invests with a sense of urgency of moral or legal rigorism in a time of great danger.

Two earlier sermons approach the subject of the imminent dénouement by means of commentary upon two of the versions of the Synoptic Apocalypse. One, *Secundum Matheum*,[12] begins with a long quotation and translation from Matthew's Gospel. The passage selected, Matthew xxiv.1–14, 36, and 42, deletes the more exotic apocalyptic elements of the chapter and the verses quoted in the later *De Anticristo*;[13] and it is conceivable that Wulfstan was avoiding multiple commentary as well as eschewing the mysterious in favour of the moral. The archbishop follows the Gospel lection fairly closely, but with his characteristic freedom underlines legalistic and moralistic aspects and omits the reference to the Mount of Olives, which (like the opening allusion of the Temple) would have required explanation for an English lay audience. Also sidestepped is verse 12 (*refrigescet caritas multorum*), to which Wulfstan later addressed himself in Homily v, *Secundum Marcum*, with assistance from Ælfric.[14]

The content of the piece can be summarized as follows: Christ predicts the destruction of the Temple, and the disciples ask when this event will be and when the end will come. No one knows, he replies. There will be many false Christs and persecutions. The time was not yet, for he also predicted great strife which would come before Antichrist's age. Then there will be great hardship and sorrow for Christians. The end, the time of which neither angels nor men know, will be sudden. At the Judgment, Wulfstan continues, having completed his adaptation of the text, the Lord will display his wounds and the cross, and will examine the faithfulness of men. So men must love God and do his will. At the time of writing on the commentary, Wulfstan apparently did not know the Antichrist texts or was not yet preoccupied with them, but the germ of his later treatment of the Last Times is present. At the end, he alludes to Doomsday itself as a means of introducing the closing exhortation, but there is no effort to treat more than one detail of the Judgment scenes.

The second of the earlier texts, *Secundam Lucam*,[15] has for its text Luke xxi.25ff. (*Erunt signa in sole et luna, et stellis* ...) This pericope is parallel to Matthew xxiv.29ff., removed from consideration in Wulfstan's Matthaean homily but quoted here. The same Lucan text was also treated by Ælfric in the *Catholic Homilies*.[16] Ælfric, who based his work primarily on a homily of Gregory which is included in the Homiliary of Paul the Deacon, had recourse to the aging cosmos topos in explaining verses 29–30, in which Jesus likens the leafing out of the fig tree and the coming of summer to the advent of the Kingdom. Wulfstan, who probably relied in this homily on a yet unpublished piece from the homiliary of Abbo of St-Germain-des-Près, follows his source in passing over the rather difficult passage on the fig tree,[17] although the pericope for the second Sunday in Advent (on which Abbo, at least, was preaching) runs to verse 32. Indeed, both Abbo and Wulfstan concentrate on verse 25, turning to Matthew xxiv for amplification. Before the discovery of the source of this piece, one would have said Wulfstan excluded the parable of the fig tree in order to avoid a long and distracting exposition. Now it must be said only that his source dictated this particular choice of material. Even so, Wulfstan cuts Abbo ruthlessly and for the characteristic reasons.

Secundum Lucam begins with a general statement on the signs of the end and then departs from its source to allude to Luke xvii.26 by comparing the destruction of Doomsday fire with that of the Noachian flood. Perhaps Wulfstan was under the guidance here of the Ælfrician interpretation in *De Die Iudicii* of the flood and the burning of Sodom. But, characteristically, the historical references are deleted:

And witodlice ealswa flod com hwilum ær for synnum, swa cymð eac for synnum fyr ofer mancynn, and ðærto hit nealæcð nu swyðe georne.[18]

When evil has greatly increased in the world, Antichrist will come. Man's sin has soiled the once-clean world; hence there is discord and turmoil in the cosmos. At the end, Wulfstan declares, returning to Abbo's sermon, there will be conflict in the heavens. The darkening of the sun signifies the darkness of the age of Antichrist; that of the moon betokens the inability of the saints to work wonders in that era. The falling of the stars means

þæt licceteras and leaslice cristene hrædlice hreosað of rihtan geleafan and to Antecriste geornlice bugað and weorþaþ his gefylstan eallum heora mihtum.[19]

The worst terror of all times will arise. But soon thereafter heavenly powers will be stirred and men raised. Woe to those who earned hell's punishments, eternal burning and oppression; it were better that they had never been born. So we must guard against the terror which will come when we least expect, loving God and doing his will. Wulfstan stays close to his text and develops the theme of the Last Times and the reign of Antichrist as a warning to his hearers.

The allegory employed in *Secundum Lucam* to explain the cosmic signs is probably based on Abbo. It is, however, characteristic that, indulging himself in a figure he normally eschewed, Wulfstan took pains to underline clearly his moral point and to introduce the Antichrist at an earlier point in his sermon than Abbo had done. If Professor Bethurum's chronology is correct, Antichrist makes his earliest appearance in Wulfstan's writing at this point. Another remarkable feature of this homily is the chilling picture of hell, introduced after the reference to the general resurrection in lines 61–3. Wulfstan did not soften it with a correlative description of heaven, as Abbo had done, for he did not want his audience to relax before he launched his concluding exhortation on rigorous moral scrupulousness and the necessity of loving God. He cut from his sermon some of Abbo's more exotic passages, particularly those dealing with the Apocalyptic book, all references to the punishment of the Jews, and other passages which might have tended to undermine the stern moral tone for which he was striving. Thus even when – as here, at the present stage of our knowledge of his use of sources – he is more closely following a single model than in any other homily, Wulfstan still displays those very special traits for which he is well known.

A fourth homily, probably written after *De Anticristo*, was more topical. This piece, *De Temporibus Anticristi*, is a troublesome one, for in several respects it is unlike Wulfstan's other work.[20] Wulfstan begins with a warning to beware of the future, terrible time which will be more awful than we can imagine. Antichrist is the incarnation of the devil from whom all evil comes. If the days of his age were not to be shortened, all men would perish.[21] God will allow Antichrist his reign for two reasons: the first is to try men, the second to purge quickly those who will be martyred, for all must be purged. Those who turn to Antichrist will be doomed eternally to hell. To win men, Antichrist will work wonders and claim to be God, sorely deceiving men. He will heal only those whom he has first deceived and bring down fire as though from heaven, as he did against Job. But those who turn to him will burn. Antichrist, 'the same devil who is in hell,' will greatly beset mankind, so we must be prepared for his coming, praying for help, for the days grow progressively worse. Based largely on the English Preface to *Catholic Homilies* I, this homily is a more complete statement than Wulfstan's earlier homilies concerning the reign of Antichrist, as its title promises. He displays an unusual biographical interest as he dwells on the contrast between Christ and the incarnation of evil and speaks of the necessity to purge oneself of guilt for sins as the justification of the divine license for his reign. As in the other homilies, these remarks are all intended to prepare for the parenetic conclusion. The homily adds detail to its immediate predecessor, *De Anticristo*, but differs from its three forerunners in that it is not exegetical – even in the sense of Wulfstan's severely limited customary practice of exegesis – and in its unusually measured, non-rhetorical tone.

The final homily of the eschatological group, *Secundum Marcum*,[22] is one that has already been noticed briefly (pp. 20–1) by way of emphasizing the contrast between Ælfric and Wulfstan as stylists and theologians. The homily depends on two works of Ælfric, the English preface to *Catholic Homilies* I and *De Die Iudicii*;[23] and, the latter text not having been available to Professor Bethurum at the time of the publication of her edition of *The Homilies of Wulfstan*, it is necessary to go through the homily carefully in order to appreciate adequately Wulfstan's methodology and the content of his most extensive eschatological writing.

Wulfstan begins his homily by quoting in Latin the same Latin tag which Ælfric adapts from Matthew xxiv.3 (Mark xiii.4) to introduce Mark xiii.14, 17, 19, parallels to verses 15, 19, 21 of Ælfric's text, Matthew xxiv.15–25.[24] Wulfstan had treated the last of these texts in all the earlier eschatological homilies except *Secundum Matheum*.[25] As Professor Pope pointed out in his note on line 227 of *De Die*, the coincidence is hardly fortuitous, for resemblances persist throughout *Secundum Marcum*. The archbishop proceeds to translate the Latin tag and verses 19 and 17 of Mark xiii (in that order), but he omits verse 14, which in its parallel (Matthew xxiv.15) contains one of the sorts of allusions to the apocalyptic writers – here to Daniel and the *abominationem desolationis* – which he excised in the process of Englishing his Latin *De Anticristo*.[26] He proceeds in an improvised sentence to state that things are going to become far worse because of men's sins, for now is the time of which Paul spoke[27] in II Timothy iii.1–5, a passage that he translates with elaborate attention to the rhetorical possibilities of the Vulgate text. Exhorting his audience to recognize in their own times the signs of the Last Days outlined by Paul, he then quotes Matthew xxiv.12, following Ælfric's lead as I have already attempted to demonstrate in Part I.3, but interpreting the verse with characteristic legalistic terminology and imbuing it rhetorically with a greater sense of urgency. For virtuous men, he continues in a movingly eloquent passage, Christ brought bliss and a great reward; but now all is perversity, and it is the age of Antichrist, the age of the worst of men. The prophecy of Apocalypse xx. 7 is being fulfilled. The millennium has passed, and the hour is near:

Þusend geara and eac ma is nu agan syððan Crist wæs mid mannum on menniscan hiwe, and nu syndon Satanases bendas swyðe toslopene, and Antecristes tima is wel gehende, and ðy hit is on worulde a swa leng swa wacre.[28]

In the face of Antichrist, the archfiend (*þeodfeond*), the evil and deceitful thrive.

Although it begins with translations of Mark xiii.19, 17, the homily through line 52 is probably commentary on the abomination of desolation of Mark xiii.14 and follows in a general way the development of Ælfric's exegesis of Matthew xxiv.15–20. But it is typically independent in its allusion to II Timothy, in its hortatory impulses, and in its refusal to indulge in the obscurantism of the theme of abomination, which becomes (more topically) the signs of the times. The difficult sayings about those pregnant and giving suck (Mark xiii.17, Matthew xxiv.19) seem to be subsumed among the signs without direct explication. The vivid Wulfstanian expressions concerning the aging cosmos – 'hit is on worulde a swa leng swa wacre ...' and woruld is þe wyrse'[29] – effectively emphasize his sense of the nearness of the end.

At line 53, Wulfstan returned to Ælfric and the explication of Mark xiii.19 (Matthew xxiv.21).[30] He begins, however, not with a paraphrase of the text but with Ælfric's observation that the sufferings of the age of the martyrs were great but that those of the coming age will be many times worse. Following also Adso and the Preface to Catholic Homilies I he observes that the early Christians worked wonders which gave hope to the faithful in the time of persecution. But not so in the age of Antichrist, the age of pillage and madness. Antichrist, filled with the spirit of the devil, is the worker of wonders. Deceit is his tool. God suffers[31] the evil one in retribution for man's sins. Those who persevere in the maintenance of God's law suffer more greatly than ever; but if they do not weaken, they will quickly have their reward. Wulfstan turns next to a passage of Adso[32] which states that even Enoch and Elias, whom God had so long steadfastly preserved, will be martyred as good examples for those who want to resist Antichrist. In lines 97–8, the archbishop paraphrases Matthew xxiv.21 and quotes the saying about brothers turning on brothers from x.21 of the same Gospel to lead into a 'highly rhetorical and poetic passage,'[33] concerning the conflicts of the Last Times. He concludes by quoting the statement about God's merciful shortening of the age of Antichrist from the following verse.[34] Antichrist will be consigned to hell and God will judge mankind, rewarding those who love him and fulfilling his law.

In Secundum Marcum, Wulfstan followed the Matthaean portion of Ælfric's De Die Iudicii, selecting for commentary three parallel verses in Mark but so dividing his attention that the Marcan homily becomes a two-part sermon concentrating on the signs of the Last Times and their significance for his congregation. Thus the work, though derivative, is very much stamped with his own personality. It consummates the set of eschatological homilies in that it is the culmination of the process – apparently carried out in chronological sequence – of elaboration on the theme of the Last Times and the Age of Antichrist.

It is important to look back over these five homilies as a set, for it is clear that Wulfstan worked them over very carefully, keeping the earlier texts in mind as he worked on the later and, perhaps, even keeping track of the texts he was using and had used with the aid of a harmony of the Gospels. If one plots his citations from the Synoptic Apocalypse in a Gospel parallel, the results are quite interesting. Wulfstan seems to avoid treating difficult texts which were often the favourites of the exegetes because they required elaborate explanations, and there may have been some effort to avoid repetition of texts. But he returns in all the homilies except *Secundum Matheum* to treat some part of the passage Matthew xxiv.21–2: *Erit enim tunc tribulatio magna, qualis non fuit ab initio mundi usque modo, neque fiet. Et nisi breviati fuissent dies illi non fieret salva omnis caro: sed propter electos breviabuntur dies illi.* This must have seemed to him the *locus classicus* for description of the Age of Antichrist, and it always appears in homilies that specifically mention the Antichrist. As a framework for the material concerning the great adversary, it fits his purposes exactly, for he is inclined to avoid and suppress the exotic, the miraculous, and the narrative-historical in favour of straightforward descriptions of symptoms of the Last Times in the world in which he lived and preached. Although the five earlier eschatological homilies are not so radical in this respect as the *Sermo ad Anglos*, they share the same tendency to minimize the doctrinal or the intellectual and to emphasize the parenetic or hortatory and the topical. All five of these earlier homilies serve the same end; but each does it in a slightly different way, like a variation on a musical theme.

The Antichrist theme virtually dropped from Wulfstan's works after these five homilies and was replaced by more general references to the retributions of the Last Day. Several times, however, the theme was introduced again in less extended form. First, in Wulfstan's adaptation of a sermon of Ælfric, *De Septi-formi Spiritu*,[35] where a discussion of hypocrisy brought to mind the arch-hypocrite and his covert, deceitful work.[36] Second, in the famous *Sermo Lupi ad Anglos*, an impassioned indictment of the sins of the people, which was written about 1014 and survives in several versions,[37] Wulfstan opens with a reference to Antichrist:

Leofan men, gecnawað þæt soð is: ðeos worold is on ofste, and hit nealæcð þam ende, and þy hit is on worolde aa swa leng swa wyrse; and swa hit sceal nyde for folces synnan ær Antecristes tocyme yfelian swyþe, and huru hit wyrð þænne

egeslic and grimlic wide on worulde. Understandað eac georne þæt deofol þas
þeode nu fela geara dwelode to swyþe . . .[38]

An allusion at the end to the Judgment and the sentence to hell or to glory
serves to unify the sermon, which is otherwise a topical, legal indictment of the
sins of the age. Another reference to Antichrist occurs in a sermon that outlines
the history of the world, where it is said that his coming is imminent and that,
lest all perish, God will shorten his time of power.[39]

The dropping of reference to Antichrist in the later homilies raises again the
problem of millenarianism, for it is possible that Wulfstan was forced to alter his
eschatological expectations after 1000. Certainly the period of his London
episcopate was one in which he may well have thought he discerned the signs of
the end. There is in the eschatological homilies, however, no evidence of a
tendency to date the end save the single reference in Secundum Marcum to the
fact that the millennium had passed. Thus it is not advisable to restrict the
explanation of the virtual disappearance of Antichrist in these writings to this
single possibility. For one thing, Wulfstan was increasingly preoccupied after
his translation to York and Worcester with administration and with legal reform,
and the later homilies were more and more concerned with questions of liturgical
administration, the problem of paganism in the northern archdiocese and the
need for moral reformation in general.[40] It is possible that Wulfstan found his
earlier emphasis on Antichrist facile and not very useful when he came to deal
with the doctoral and pastoral demands of his new office.[41] Again – and this
seems to me the most likely explanation – the answer may rest somewhere
between these two extremes: Wulfstan as legislator and archbishop charged
with the maintenance of the social fabric did discover that he had to deal with
problems of an earthly present and future more seriously – or in a better framework than he had used before. Thus, perhaps, he tempered but did not entirely
abandon his proclamations that the social and political deterioration of his own
age, coupled with the external threat,[42] presaged the end of the world; he
returned occasionally to the earlier theme and often alluded to or described the
Day of Judgment, but Antichrist ceased to be the major motif of his writing.

One further problem has been raised in connection with Wulfstan's work. In
his preoccupation with the Last Times, he has very little to say about the soul
after death. The comment in one homily[43] that we must all return to the earth
from which we came prompted one early modern reader to write in the margin
of the manuscript, 'Hic Archiepiscopus Wulfstanus diserte negat tertium locum
post hanc vitam.'[44] One passage in the homily De Temporibus Anticristi, however,
casts doubt on this judgment. Wulfstan says that God allows Antichrist to reign
partly to allow quick purgation of the elect whom he will martyr:

Forðam nis nan man þæt ne sy synful, and ælc man sceal sar ðolian oðþon her oðþon elleshwær be ðam þe he þurh synna geearnað. And ðy bið seo ehtnes þonne godum mannum swa stið, forðam þe hy sculon beon raðe geclænsode and amerode ær se mycle dom cume. Ða ðe wæron forðferede for hund gearum oððon gyt firnor, wel þa magan beon nu geclænsode.[45]

Clearly the last sentence is dealing with post mortem expiation of sins. In view of Wulfstan's close association with Ælfric and of the general theological attitudes of the Early Middle Ages, it seems almost inconceivable that he should have denied the existence of an interim state for the soul. This would be so, even if there were no passage indicating he did accept the interim state. It is more likely that, as at so many points of theological discussion, he regarded the doctrine as a subtlety which could be left to the scholarly abbot while he in his moral exhortation concentrated on the ultimate struggle before the Judgment. Wulfstan frequently spoke in the manner of the Hebrew prophets of the sin of the nation as the cause of its woes.[46] In this spirit, concentration on the Last Judgment may have seemed appropriate to his preaching as bishop and archbishop since it tended to be more general than that of Ælfric and less concerned with individual transgressions of the divine law.[47]

Wulfstan describes the Last Judgment briefly and yet vividly, concentrating on the essential details of the separation of the evil from those who have followed God's law and teaching. Several allusions to the great Doom have already been mentioned. A typical reference brings a homily to a close:

And raðe syððan æfter þam, þæs ðe us bec secgaþ, gewyrð se micla dom, and ðeos woruld geendað. On þam dome witodlice sceal manna gehwylc habben swylc edlean swylc he on life ær geearnode: and ða þe Godes willan her wyrcað, þa sculan þonne habban ece blisse on heofona rice; and ða þe her nu deofle fyligað and his unlarum, þa sculon þonne mid deofle faran on ece forwyrd helle wites. Eala, leofan men, utan we don swa us mycel þearf is . . .[48]

There is a longer account in Wulfstan's exposition of the Creed,[49] which describes the assembling at the Doom of all the dwellers in heaven and earth and the fire of Judgment Day before describing the announcement of sentence and the joys of heaven and horrors of hell. In general, these passages are brief in comparison with those of Ælfric and the anonymous writers; as they avoid detail and narration to achieve directness, they add no new elements to the scenes depicted by Ælfric.

For all his differences from Ælfric, Wulfstan clearly belongs to the same reforming tradition. His alterations of the abbot's writings do not mean that he took issue theologically. The changes are functional, carefully devised to adapt the materials derived from Ælfric and the canonists to Wulfstan's own didactic, hortatory, and stylistic strategies. The preaching bishop had little need of the idea of reward and punishment meted out to the souls of the dead or of sophisticated allegorical distinctions between the rewards the Judge would give the several classes of men both lay and clerical. His concern was with the whole English nation. As statesman, legislator, and primate he was concerned with the fate of the whole body, political and ecclesiastical. Convinced that he lived in the last days, he exhorted priest and layman alike to resist the deceitful teachings of God's enemies and to present themselves as righteous followers of God's law and of true Christian teaching at the Last Day. Thus his preaching is even more clearly heroic in tone than that of the abbot of Eynsham: it is the great, final struggle that predominates in his understanding of the Last Things.

The result is a series of homilies which, though consciously loyal to the purified tradition of preaching introduced in the English vernacular by Ælfric, is also highly individual in tone and sophisticated in selection of material.

PART FOUR

ÆLFRIC AND WULFSTAN
IN HISTORICAL PERSPECTIVE

ÆLFRIC AND WULFSTAN
IN HISTORICAL PERSPECTIVE

The work of Ælfric and Wulfstan has always been admired by literary scholars; but there has been a tendency to examine it in rather narrow focus and to declare the writers successful in their endeavours because of their masterful prose styles and clarity of expression. The facts that their identity is known and that it has therefore been possible to study the personalities behind the homilies has doubtless influenced the general course of critical assessment. On the basis of these affirmative conclusions, there has been a tendency to assume that Ælfric and Wulfstan did indeed influence for the better the vernacular preachers of the eleventh century.

In this book two wider and major ramifications of the work of the abbot and the archbishop have been under scrutiny. The question of the uses for which their homilies were prepared has been raised; and, in the light of continental evidence concerning preaching, it has been suggested that Ælfric, in addition to such other uses as private devotional reading, intended his sermons to be read to the people in the liturgical context of the Prone – a vernacular office usually placed after the reading of the Gospel in the Mass. The patristic tradition of episcopal preaching having fallen into disuse long before, preaching was revived within the framework of the Prone. Often such preaching was catechetical or instructional. Such is the case of those of Wulfstan's homilies which were not entirely extra-liturgical and of those homilies of Ælfric which bear the rubric *quando volueris* or could be used at various times of the year. But the Gospel came also to be translated and explained in the Prone, and Ælfric's great contribution was to appropriate to this aspect of the Prone adaptations of the homilies of the Fathers which he found collected in homilies for the Office or for devotional reading. The second subject under examination in this book is the nature of the theological content of the homilies of the two masters. Against the background of the slightly earlier homilies of the Blickling and Vercelli collections, it has been shown that – largely as a result of the kinds of sources they used and in very different ways determined by their personalities and by the purposes for which their sermons were written – Ælfric and Wulfstan strove for greater clarity and consistency and stricter orthodoxy than their theological compatriots. Together, these aspects of the works of the two homilists indicate that they almost certainly hoped to achieve a reform of preaching practices and of the theological content of sermons.

The Old English homiletic corpus is fortunately extensive enough to betray the existence of two quite discontinuous traditions of Christian teaching, one of the anonymous homilies and the other of the sermons of Ælfric and Wulfstan. Both groups of writings combined the traditionalism common to early medieval theology with the characteristic early medieval emphasis on the dramatic or heroic moments in the history of salvation, but each was descended from a different body of source materials. One group of homilies was, by reason of its heritage, inconsistent in harmonizing details, closely related to the traditions of the apocryphal Christian writings, and not concerned to clarify or to systematize its teachings. The other derived from the English branch of the tenth-century revival and revitalization of monasticism. Ælfric attempted to present a complete or encyclopedic, clear, and internally consistent version of the teachings of the church which was based largely on the exegetical and canonistic writings of the most honoured fathers of the Latin West. Wulfstan, following Ælfric in many particulars but also ruthlessly excising details not necessary to his rhetorical and hortatory aims, sought a more limited application of this same tradition. As a result, there were in England at the millennium two schools of theological writing distinguishable in terms of content as well as of style and form. The only explanation of this dichotomy is that the reformed Carolingian heritage was appropriated by the English teachers of the monastic reform as opposed to the earlier, Gallican tradition. Thus the homilies of Ælfric and Wulfstan represent an important aspect of the intellectual achievement of tenth-century English monasticism.

Ælfric in the preface of the First Series of the *Sermones Catholici* attacked the propensity towards *gedwyld* in vernacular theology; but, aside from this and similar chance comments, the existence of the two schools of theological thought seems not to have attracted attention – let alone given rise to controversy – in England in the tenth and eleventh centuries. Indeed, throughout Europe in the ninth and tenth centuries there were few complaints of heresy, perhaps because in these years 'western Europe bore the brunt of the second barbarian invasions, [and] no town or village the length and breadth of the Continent was secure from ... attack.'[1] Nevertheless, there were clearly different channels of theological influence, and there must have been differences of opinion as to the nature of correct belief between those who lacked and those who shared with Ælfric and

Wulfstan a sense that one could and ought to discriminate among theological sources. The composers of the Blickling and Vercelli homilies drew at liberty from documents which, as Ælfric recognized, had been proscribed in the past as heterodox or pseudepigraphic.[2] Thus, in some degree, theological disagreement never completely disappeared, even in England where the absence of controversy has seemed characteristic of the Saxon period. One suspects that the strength of the monastic reform party and its ally the crown of Wessex was such that dissent could, in effect, be ignored by the last decade of the first millennium when Ælfric began to publish his work. Stories from a slightly earlier period, such as that of the unreformed monk of Winchester who won his way back to the monastery by reporting a vision of St Swithun in which the saint demanded to have his shrine rebuilt on a grander scale, may mask a greater degree of disagreement than has heretofore been imagined.[3]

The fate of the works of Ælfric as a coherent corpus, despite all his cares to avoid such an eventuality, and the fact that Ælfric and Wulfstan left no worthy successors may indicate that the reformers never completely succeeded in purifying the intellectual life of the church.[4] The evidence that Ælfric's effort to reform preaching never gained general acceptance and that, at such churches as Worcester, persons who used his work nonetheless ignored (or were ignorant of) his programmatic aims may signal a major failure. The fact that Ælfric and Wulfstan are without peers or even followers[5] may mean that, in terms of its educational if not its liturgical and political programs, the achievements of the monastic reform in England were superficial. On the other hand, these indicators may simply mean – as has been argued recently with respect to Cluny and the continental reform movement[6] – that the true moment of maturity and of the great achievements of the reformers came somewhat later. If this was the case, the new hierarchy imposed on the English church by the Normans got the credit for what the English monks had begun. But, if so, how does one account for the recopying in the eleventh century of items which also appear in the Blickling and Vercelli collections, for the writing or copying of numerous other anonymous homiletic pieces which seem to be related more to the theological milieu of the earlier anonymous works than to those of Ælfric and Wulfstan,[7] and for the occasional incorporation of Ælfrician material in alien settings?[8] It is true that Ælfric was regarded by eleventh-century writers of English as an authoritative figure, that his sermons were often the basis of new collections, and that his works became standard items for libraries. But at the same time as one must acknowledge his celebrity, he must also observe that his standards, his principles and his directives were not followed.[9]

These are issues for future students of eleventh-century literary and ecclesiastical culture in England to refine. Before the rest of the eleventh-century sermon texts have been edited, one can only say that it is not impossible that we will have to conclude that Ælfric failed in his efforts to reform the uses of preaching and to purify the content of sermons. Given the evidence of Worcester in the episcopate of Wulfstan II, it may even prove to have been the case that Archbishop Wulfstan contributed to the failure. All that can be done here is to make a few comments about the historical sources of the disparity between unreformed and reformed theology in England in the tenth and eleventh centuries and about the future of each of the traditions.

It would be rash to say that the anonymous homilies of the Blickling, Vercelli, and other codices represent in a later form the Mercian homiletic tradition,[10] although it has been thought that there are reasons for suggesting that this may actually have been the case.[11] The tradition that lies behind these works can, however, be likened without unfairness to the traditions that prevailed on the continent before the ecclesiastical reforms of Charlemagne and especially to the theological traditions of Gallician monasticism. The Gallican church was as confused in its structure and discipline as was the political order under the descendants of Clovis. It was marked in the Merovingian age by a strong, almost Eastern, ascetic bent which emanated from Lérins but was disseminated chiefly from Tours[12] and delighted in comparing its saints with the Egyptian anchorites. As in other areas the Gallican church was marked by the diversity of uses, so also in its monasticism it presented a bewildering array of customs and degrees of strictness. Among the chief doctors of Gallican Christianity were John Cassian for moral teaching and Caesarius of Arles, whose homilies were a favourite source of the anonymous Old English homilies, for doctrine and preaching.[13] But perhaps most influential was Gregory of Tours (ca. 540–94),[14] who as bishop of the See of St Martin became the spokesman for Gallican piety. Although he also wrote a commentary on the Psalter, Gregory fulfilled the teaching office chiefly in the form of the great *Historia Francorum* and a number of hagiographical works in which he continued the vivid tradition of the lives of the desert fathers and emphasized the role of miracles as evidences of the faith. Both before and after the great Viking disruptions of the eighth and ninth centuries, English Christians probably had contact with this tradition directly from its centres in the Loire valley, but they knew it as well through the Celtic church which had strong historic ties with the Gallican church of Merovingian times.[15]

This Gallican-Celtic tradition was in large measure displaced by the Carolingians with the assistance, among others, of English scholars in the eighth and ninth centuries.[16] The appointment of Alcuin to the abbacy at Tours symbolizes the eclipse of the Gallican tradition at its greatest centre, the shrine of its most important saint, Martin. The work of Alcuin and his associates was an attempt to reform the tradition of ecclesiastical life and teaching by standardizing uses and customs in accordance with the most authoritative sources from the Latin area of the Mediterranean. To take three examples, the liturgy was reformed on the lines of Roman use, though not without retention of some Gallican details; monasticism was standardized under the guidance of an exemplar of the *Regula Benedicti* obtained from Italy; and, as a guide for preaching, Paul the Deacon was commissioned to produce one homiliary to replace many. Paul probably performed this task at Monte Cassino, basing his collection on Augustine, Gregory, and other great Italian expositors and including only Bede – a strong follower of the Augustinian-Gregorian tradition – from the many homilists who had worked north of the Alps.[17] This tradition, through the homiliaries of Paul and others in the case of Ælfric and through Ælfric and the Carolingian canonists in the case of Wulfstan, was without any doubt the basis of the teaching of the Old English homilists; it has come to them by way of the monastic tradition of Benedict of Aniane in the ninth century and the reforms of Cluny and the upper Lorraine in the tenth.

If Gregory of Tours typifies the intellect of the church in Gaul, the traits of the southern tradition are epitomized in the works of his namesake and contemporary, Pope Gregory the Great (ca. 540–604).[18] Deeply ascetic, Gregory nevertheless devoted most of his literary efforts to exegetical exercises: the great lectures or *Moralia* on Job; commentaries on the *Cantica Canticorum*, Kings, and Ezechiel; homilies on the Gospel pericopes. In his letters and *Liber Regulae Pastoralis* he is an eminently practical ecclesiastical administrator. Only in the *Dialogues* does he devote himself exclusively to tales of the saints and their miracles. Derived in large measure from Augustine and later adopted by Bede, the stress of Gregory on explication strongly coloured the literature of monasticism in the tenth and eleventh centuries and gave it its great theme of impending Judgment. The balance of his work towards the practical implications of the Christian faith and away from overemphasis on the miraculous were also reflected in the work of the later monastic movement.

If one knew only the published works of the Old English homilists, he might assume that the reformed tradition of the late tenth century had succeeded in displacing the kind of teaching represented by the earlier, anonymous homilies; but the manuscripts testify that, despite the continuing popularity of their writing, Ælfric and Wulfstan did not succeed in suppressing the older tradition and that their work was not generally distinguished from that of the anonymous homilists by their contemporaries.

Indeed, Ælfric and Wulfstan stand out among late Anglo-Saxon churchmen for their ability to discriminate among sources – a fact I have been at pains to demonstrate throughout this study. But later adapters of the work of Ælfric in particular were not adverse to putting excerpts of his work into alien contexts. An example is the Ælfrician piece which Professor Pope calls 'Visions of Departing Souls' (xxvii), which was probably lifted from an unknown homiletic context by one of the pseudo-Wulfstan homilists and, by another editor, later inserted into a sermon from the Second Series.[19] Another is Ælfric's treatment of Jonah which was conflated with another version of the Jonah tale from a homily in the Vercelli and other manuscripts.[20] The history of some of the Old English poetic manuscripts also suggests the general failure to distinguish among sources and the traditions. Old English religious poetry is, on the whole, more closely related to the anonymous homilies in source and outlook; yet the poems were collected in the manuscripts from which we know them at about the same time as Ælfric's and Wulfstan's literary activity. The Vercelli codex combines poetry and prose apparently selected – and this is itself evidence of the relatedness of the religious poetry and the anonymous homilies – with certain thematic and didactic purposes in mind. The Exeter Book was exclusively poetic; and it has already been noted that there may be some collateral relationship between Ælfric's patrons, Æthelweard and Æthelmær, and the history of the Exeter Book before Leofric took it to his church in the mid-eleventh century.[21] At least some of the poetry was, therefore, preserved in circles influenced theologically by Ælfric; and there is no evidence that the diverse theological outlooks of the poets of the Exeter Book and Ælfric were distinguished by those who came into contact with the two traditions.

It must be pointed out once more that – despite Ælfric's injunctions against mixture of his homilies with those of other translators and his invective against the heterodoxy of English writings which, in his allusions, sound very like the anonymous homilies – a number of the later manuscripts contain items of the anathematized tradition interspersed among genuine Ælfrician pieces.[22] Evidently, then, both traditions were alive in the eleventh century, and the disparity between the two was not generally appreciated.[23]

Each tradition, moreover, had a subsequent history. That of the anonymous homilists influenced the popular religious literature of the later Middle Ages. The Apocalypse of Thomas continued to be known in a form similar to that appearing in the four Old English versions and probably lay behind the development of a more elaborate tradition of the fifteen signs before Doomsday which was popular in the later period.[24] The Body and Soul literature and the *Visio Pauli* materials were still considered didactically useful and were known in a variety of forms throughout the Middle Ages.[25] The apocalyptic motifs of the anonymous homilists – notably those associated with the Gospel of Nicodemus – can be traced collaterally, if not generically, in such literature of the later Middle Ages as the vernacular drama. On the other hand, the tradition of monastic teaching based on patristic sources which Ælfric represented and Wulfstan adapted has been shown to be the continuing tradition of monastic theology from which emerged such great preachers and teachers as St Bernard of Clairvaux[26] and which coexisted with scholastic theology.

But the Anglo-Saxon homilists wrote at the end of an era and on the threshold of the birth of modern Europe and had little, if any, direct influence on these later developments. The traditions they represented were subtly but importantly changed in subsequent years under the influence of a new intellectual tradition and a more individual or romantic approach to religious and other subjects. The case of the doctrine of purgatory is symptomatic of this fact because of its ultimate impact on the relations between Eastern and Western Christendom and on the upheaval of the sixteenth century. The idea of purgatory appears to have originated as an extension of the Doomsday fire, partly as a means of justifying intercessory prayer and, rather later, in connection with the concept that sins must be expiated.[27] The idea of a purgatorial interim after death is present in the anonymous homilies, but the texts are ambiguous and contradictory. They are based largely on visionary and apocalyptic materials, and rarely do they give even a brief expository account of the purgatorial state. In Ælfric's tradition the case is far clearer. Visions are recounted, but they come to the homilist from the patristic and homiletic tradition; there is an extended expository statement of the doctrine and an attempt to avoid inconsistency and heterodox sources. Only hints of the doctrine survive in the work of Wulfstan.

The striking fact is that the apocalyptic expectation in both types of tradition outweighs the purgatorial. In the anonymous works, Doomsday and purgatorial materials are inextricably confused; but very often it is the picture of the Judgment that predominates. Ælfric gave a clear account of the interim state of souls, but he had a lively expectation of the imminent advent of the Antichrist and of the Last Times which, even in the *Sermo ad Populum in octavis Pentecosten Dicendus* where the interim is only a prelude to the protracted and moving Last Judgment, was far more important in his theological scheme. This is borne out by the near-absence of purgatorial teaching in the vivid eschatological writing of his associate, Wulfstan of York. In the reformed homiletic tradition, more clearly than in the anonymous homilies, purgatorial teaching was a means to the end of justifying intercession for the dead. But its place in the penitential system had not been fixed, and it had not yet become so integral a part of the eschatological pattern that it had to be included in commentary on the destiny of man. This situation is, it seems to me, not at all surprising when the social values of the age are recalled: it is society with the Lord which is the aim of the religious life, and the community can only be fulfilled when, on the Last Day, the King will generously reward his faithful followers with their due reward. He will give them the treasure above all treasures, participation in the Kingdom which he has won in his struggle against the cosmic powers of evil. They will have earned a share of this booty by struggling heroically in their own wise against evil in the world in the service of their Lord.

Two forces worked for the transformation of this eschatological picture in the Later Middle Ages. First, there occurred a change of attitude which tended to transform the hero and to emphasize a more individualistic, romantic ideal. Professor Southern has impressively documented this change and concludes that from the eleventh century,

we find less talk of life as an exercise in endurance, and of death in a hopeless cause; and we hear more of life as a seeking and a journeying. Men begin to order experience more consciously in accordance with a plan: they think of themselves less as stationary objects of attack by spiritual foes, and more as pilgrims and seekers.[28]

The solitary quest of the Grail or the search for truth tends to displace the solitary struggle of the epic hero who, as monk or lay leader battling against cosmic forces, expresses the individual's quest for salvation. Even the Christ figure is fitted to this mould and loses his heroic stature. One no longer sings of 'the young Hero (that was God Almighty)':

> Dulcis Iesu memoria
> dans vera cordi gaudia:
> sed super mel et omnia
> eius dulcis praesentia.

Second, from the time of the reappropriation of the logical treatises and commentaries of Boethius by Gerbert (later Pope Sylvester II), theology became an analytic and not a descriptive discipline by means of which one sought to impose order upon an unruly body of materials and to remove from the sources – the traditions of the Fathers – all their ambiguities.

In later medieval teaching on eschatology, the analytic method coupled with the new individualism transformed the interim after death into a logical stage in the progression from generation to beatification. St Thomas Aquinas in the *Summa Contra Gentiles*, for example, turned in the fourth book to the subject of soteriology and, when he came to the Last Things, began by discussing (chs. lxxix–lxxxix) the same questions on the nature of the glorified body which occupied the attention of Ælfric. On the subject of the suffering of incorporeal substances in corporeal fire (ch. xc), he held that it is suitable to punish a spiritual substance with a bodily thing, for in human life this is exactly the punishment of the soul in the body. Thus he is led to assert (chs. xci–xcv) that, at the separation of body and soul, the soul must be consigned either to punishment or to glory. As a result, the Last Judgment is but a second phase of retribution which must logically be given men according to the deserts of their lives (ch. xcvi).[29] In this logical and more individual treatment of the destiny of men, the chronological order of events is upset; and the interim existence of the soul tends to displace in importance the resurrection and Judgment, which have become no more than logical extensions of or appendages to the prior state of the soul in purgatory or paradise. The earlier tendency to emphasize the Judgment scene in all its heroic splendour has been supplanted in favour of a scheme in which the individual's solitary seeking leads him logically, but only consequentially, to the Last Day.

The Old English homilies, then, are not one but two groups of documents expressing in different ways the traditionalist outlook of the Early Middle Ages. Although the traditions of each group continued to exercise a limited influence on future English writers and although their traditions continued, they were written at the end of an age and are, in a sense, among the last expressions of the theological outlook of the Early Middle Ages. At the same time, the work of Ælfric in particular, but also of Wulfstan, may legitimately be seen as a step in the direction of the more rigorous ordering of theological materials which was a necessary prolegomenon to the work of the twelfth-century theologians. Though they may have had no direct influence and though their achievements and ambitions may not have been recognized by their countrymen, they may be seen as symptomatic of the trend towards more orderly treatment of theological motifs.

It may be well, by way of conclusion, to enter a caveat about the relationship of tradition to individuality in the homilies of Ælfric and Wulfstan. Led by such works as the monumental study of Ernst Robert Curtius, *European Literature and the Latin Middle Ages*, critics of the last several decades have been preoccupied by the notion – which is absolutely correct – that most medieval writing is highly conventional. Thus the dictates of genre upon content in, for example, the saint's life and the homily, the reliance of authors upon authorities, the influence of recognized rhetorical figures upon style, and the employment of commonplace subject matters or topics suitable to given contexts or subjects – these concerns have been among the chief preoccupations of recent critics and editors of medieval texts. The contributions to our understanding of the texts and the methods of their authors have been very considerable, as ought to be evident to any one who knows the recent secondary literature on Anglo-Saxon prose writings or has followed the footnotes of this study. Indeed, one of the aims of the insistence upon the crucial importance of traditionalism and of the analysis of methodology in the foregoing chapters is to make the same kinds of points. Nevertheless, this trend is not without its perils. Carried to an extreme, it can submerge the personality of an author and the originality of his work. The authors of two important studies, in particular, have attempted to redress the imbalance created by overenthusiastic disciples of Curtius. Erich Auerbach's important study of the history of Latin prose style in the Early Middle Ages [30] stresses that the writing of the period is not simply debased but rather displays a new style, forged by writers with personalities in response to the stimuli of their historical situation. More recent is a collection of essays by Peter Dronke bearing the title (a bold one at the moment of its appearance) *Poetic Individuality in the Middle Ages: New Departures in Poetry 1000–1150*.[31] Dronke confesses that his work is a response to Curtius. Its initial essay is a trenchant criticism of single-minded pursuit of the methods of Curtius and a plea for correlative study which recognizes and explains the nature of literary individuality in medieval writings.

No student of Ælfric and Wulfstan can afford to ignore Dronke's caveat, for these writers are at the same time profoundly conservative, traditional, and (even) unoriginal, and yet *so* original that the knowledgeable reader can hardly mistake their authorship. Each worked differently with his source materials, each had distinct purposes in mind as he addressed his audience, yet neither intended to nor in fact did make original theological observations. Insofar as either is original, his contribution arises from the purposes for which he adopted materials of the tradition, his ability to select and shape materials to those purposes, and his sense of discrimination among sources. Ultimately both Ælfric and Wulfstan attain eminence not only for their skill as prose stylists with unusually refined senses of what their audience most needed to know and a sure ear for the rhythms and forms which would best communicate their messages but also for their conceptions of the role of the preacher and for their creative combinations of traditional materials which achieve coherency and even originality because of the selective intelligence which formed them. It is conceivable that there were other such figures in England in their age; but on the evidence available, the achievements of Ælfric and Wulfstan are without parallel.

APPENDIX

Ælfric's Excerpts from Julian of Toledo, *Prognosticon Futuri Saeculi**

There follows the first complete edition of the Excerpts, apparently compiled by Ælfric, from the *Prognosticon Futuri Saeculi* of Julian, Bishop of Toledo (680–90), from the unique copy in folios 1–10 of MS 63 of the Bibliothèque publique de Boulogne-sur-Mer (Pas-de-Calais), France. Although this text has been afforded considerable attention in recent years, it has never been printed in its entirety. The connections of the manuscript with Ælfric have long been known, and the pastoral materials contained therein were edited by Bernhard Fehr in *Die Hirtenbriefe Ælfrics*.[1] In 1957, Enid M. Raynes [now Enid M. Edwards] published an article of great importance in which she pointed to connections of other items in the manuscript with Ælfric's work.[2] In particular, Raynes posited the connection between the text here edited and the, then unpublished, *Sermo ad Populum in Octavis Pentecosten Dicendus* (Pope, ed., *Homilies of Ælfric*, No XI) and argued that Ælfric was the compiler of the Excerpts. In 1966, I published an article on the Boulogne Excerpts, pointing to the fact that they provided sources for several brief passages in the First Series of *Catholic Homilies* and suggesting also that the Excerpts must be the earliest datable work of Ælfric, perhaps produced before he left Winchester for Cerne Abbas in 987.[3] Professor John C. Pope in his *Homilies of Ælfric* (Vol. I, 1967) accepted these arguments and, in his edition of the *Sermo*, printed in the apparatus all the relevant passages of the Excerpts (using the siglum *BE*, which I adopt below). Professor Pope collated *BE* with the edition of the *Prognosticon (Prog.)* in *Patrologia Latina* 96, cols. 461–524. The passages which Pope does not find to have been taken over into the Old English *Sermo In Octavis Pentecosten* and therefore does not print in his apparatus amount to about 241 lines of the total of 522 lines of manuscript text. These passages – rather more than 45 per cent of *BE* – contain some of Ælfric's more

* (Boulogne-sur-Mer, Bibliothèque Publique, MS. 63, folios 1–10).

interesting divergences from *Prognosticon*. He seems to have intended the *Sermo* to be closer to the original than to the Excerpts, as Miss Raynes hinted in the discussion of her original discovery.

Unfortunately, the edition of *Prognosticon* in *Patrologia Latina* is not very reliable, especially for the student of *BE*, since Ælfric clearly relied on a manuscript of Julian's tract closer to that which was the basis of the *editio princeps* of Joannes Cochlaeus (Leipzig, 1536) than to the textual tradition underlying the version in the *Patrologia*, the quite unreliable edition of Andreas Resendius (Paris, 1554). Furthermore, its apparatus of references to Julian's sources is both incomplete and inaccurate. It is, therefore, a happy coincidence that a new edition of the *Prognosticon* is about to appear in volume 116 (*Iuliani Toletani Opera Omnia*) of *Corpus Christianorum, Series Latina*; and its editor, Professor J.N. Hillgarth, has most graciously made a copy of the proofsheets of this edition available for me to use in preparation of the apparatus collating *BE* with the *Prognosticon* of Julian. (Incidentally, the form *Prognosticon* has been retained here in lieu of *Prognosticum*, which Professor Hillgarth prefers, because it is closer to the form of the title, *Pronosticon*, Ælfric – or at least the scribe of the Boulogne MS – knew.)

That Ælfric would naturally have been attracted to Julian's treatise on eschatology as an authoritative study and that the work would have been readily available in English monasteries at the end of the tenth century is made clear by the evidence amassed by Professor Hillgarth in studies of the manuscript tradition of the *Prognosticon*.[4] The work, itself a compendium of patristic teaching on the Last Things, treated a favourite subject, but one which had not before or since the time of the Bishop of Toledo been given an encyclopaedist's attention. Drawing on Cyprian, Jerome, Isidore, Augustine, Gregory, Origen, Cassian, and Chrysostom,[5] the treatise worked in a genre – the *florilegium* – which was extraordinarily popular during the Early Middle Ages. Like the writings of his compatriot Isidore, Julian's work was enormously successful; and its early dissemination may largely have been the work of Irish and Anglo-Saxon monks. 'From the ninth to the twelfth century, it is found in almost all libraries.'[6] Enough record survives of its popularity in England among persons involved in the monastic revival and in the main centres of monastic literary activity to assure us that it would have been surprising had Ælfric *not* known the *Prognosticon*. Indeed, it is probable that Bishop Æthelwold of Winchester, to whose teaching and memory Ælfric was so devoted, presented a copy to Peterborough Abbey, ca. 984, as part of a donation of some twenty volumes.[7]

Most of the pertinent observations concerning the relation of the *Boulogne Excerpts* to Ælfric's Old English *Sermo ad Populum* have already been given above (pp. 96–7), but some further comment on the qualities of the Latin

Excerpts and their kinship to Julian may be added here. Ælfric is not the only early medieval writer who epitomized the *Prognosticon futuri saeculi*. Another condensation, entitled *Sententiae de libro prognosticorum*,[8] was made by Heric of Auxerre, an author some of whose work Ælfric probably knew.[9] Unlike Ælfric, Heric did not rearrange Julian's work or otherwise concern himself with the aesthetic effects of his abridgement. He simply excerpted three chapters of the first book and seventeen each of the second and third. Thus, he was apparently less interested than Ælfric in Julian's first topic ('De origine mortis humanae') and equally interested in the second ('De animabus defunctorum quo modo se habeant ante ultimam corporum resurrectionum') and the third ('De ultima corporum resurrectione'). Ælfric, as has already been noted, stressed the final section of Julian's tract. As reference to the apparatus collating *BE* and *Prog.* will document, he also abbreviated freely (on occasion a chapter heading serves his purposes), occasionally added new references to patristic literature and Scripture, and rearranged and dilated on Julian so that the *sermo* which he excerpted is in effect a new and coherent tract.

Stylistically, Ælfric was often content with Julian's expression or that of the Fathers quoted by Julian, but his restatements or revisions are usually intended to simplify the expression of the original by removing overly abstract (sometimes metaphysical) notions, especially concerning the nature of the soul, and by deleting a number of references to and quotations of the Fathers. No full study of Ælfric's Latin style has ever been written, but Michael Lapidge has recently observed that he stands apart from most of the Anglo-Saxon writers of Latin in the late tenth century. As in Old English, so also in Latin, he strove always for brevity, clarity, and simplicity, but without neglect of a spare but elegant rhetoric. Virtually all of his contemporaries, on the other hand, affected the 'hermeneutic style' – one 'whose most striking feature is the ostentatious parade of unusual, often very arcane and apparently learned vocabulary.'[10] Dr Lapidge regards the Preface of *Sermones Catholicae* I, as a vigorous reaction against hermeneutic principles, even though its subject is the stylistic principles of the vernacular sermons.[11] The other Winchester writers and such other users of Ælfric's writings as Æthelweard, Ælfric 'Bata,' and Byrhtferth are all stylistically in the camp eschewed by the abbot of Eynsham. It is to be hoped that the availability of this text and the forthcoming edition of another text in MS Boulogne 63 which may be from his pen,[12] will help to encourage a full study of the Latin style of Ælfric.

If there is no difficulty understanding Ælfric's knowledge of Julian's writing on eschatological matters, there is also little concerning the history of the manuscript of the *Boulogne Excerpts*. Miss Raynes observed that folios 1–34, the portion of the manuscript connected with Ælfric (and to which the rest of the present codex, approximately contemporary and probably also English, was evidently joined at an early date) seems to have been a copy of a collection of materials kept by Ælfric for his personal use. That it is a copy and not the original is inferred from the fact that it appears to have been written by a single scribe at one time.[13] There is a consensus that the date of the writing is the early part of the eleventh century – that is, late in Ælfric's lifetime or very shortly after his death. It cannot have been copied before 1005, the date assigned the first Latin letter to Wulfstan on folios 10–13.[14] It is also known that the manuscript belonged in the later Middle Ages to the monastery of St Bertin at St Omer (Pas-de-Calais),[15] and that it was transferred thence to the public library of Boulogne-sur-Mer at the time of the French Revolution.[16] Since St Bertin's was an important monastic centre in Flanders in Ælfric's time, there is a possibility that the mauscript crossed the Channel within a few years of its writing. One's suspicions in this regard are confirmed if he identifies the Boulogne manuscript with the 'Iuliani pronostica' of an early twelfth-century catalogue of the St Bertin's library.[17]

Whether or not one accepts this identification, the relations of the English with Flanders in general and St Bertin's in particular were such in the eleventh century that one might almost abandon the search for the book's exporter with the knowledge that there are too many candidates for selection to be made in the absence of some virtually unequivocal clue.[18] England had received refugees of St Bertin's from the reforms of Gerald of Brogne, but the English reform was strongly influenced by the work of Gerald and intercourse between the Anglo-Saxons and the clergy at St Omer seems to have been uninterrupted throughout the eleventh century. Cnut visited both St Bertin and St Omer en route to Rome, as also did at least one archbishop of Canterbury. Emma, the widow of Æthelred and Cnut, found her encomiast at St Bertin's; Edith, the widow of the Confessor, probably encouraged a monk of the same house to assume the role of panegyrist of her husband. Herman, bishop of Ramsbury, retired from his see to St Bertin's in 1055 and, when he returned to England, took with him Goscelin, a monk of St Bertin's and one of the most important eleventh-century hagiographers. The library of St Bertin is widely renowned as, among other things, a great repository of illuminated manuscripts of the Winchester School; and its scriptorium is known as a centre for the dissemination of the Winchester style.

Despite all these justifications for the strong probability that Boulogne MS 63 was taken to St Bertin's before 1100, however, the book itself bears no evidence that I can discover of its presence in Flanders before the thirteenth century, when a librarian of St Bertin's made an entry in red ink at the bottom of folio 2.[19] The weight of circumstantial consideration rests with the earlier date of transfer. in part because by 1200 the majority of the contents of the codex could have had only limited and antiquarian interest among English scholars; to those on the East of the Channel they would have had even less appeal. But the relationship of England with the area of Calais and Boulogne was even closer – at least economically – at the later date than at the earlier, and the possibility that the volume was transferred late in the medieval period cannot be ruled out with absolute certainty.

The quarto manuscript itself is vellum, and its folios measure approximately 25.2 by 18 cm.[20] The three exposed edges have been reddened. With the exception of a few small holes and some signs of wear on the recto of folio 1, the portion of the volume containing the Excerpts is in excellent condition. The writing areas have been carefully lined in dry point to provide for twenty-nine lines of text per page; and the scribe has generally observed the margins, except for a few unavoidable excursions to the right. The hand is a typical, and handsome, late-Saxon minuscule, and its scribe clearly took pains to render an accurate and legible copy. Were the earliest possible date for the manuscript not dictated by the date of the writing of the Latin letter for Wulfstan, one might be inclined after comparison with other English samples of the same period, to assign a rather earlier date to the writing and to associate it with Winchester.[21] Perhaps the volume was copied in Ælfric's scriptorium, which probably retained the standards of handwriting of Winchester in his own days as a student there.

In preparing this edition, I have retained the readings of the manuscript and proposed only a few emendations in Apparatus I. Only in the very few places where the manuscript is illegible have I inserted letters. Abbreviations (e.g., ampersand, hooked *e* and *o*, and others common to medieval scribes) are silently expanded; and no note is taken of scribal erasures or corrections (all of which are in the main hand) unless they relate to suggested emendations. Vocalic *u* is transcribed as *v*, and the punctuation has been modernized somewhat. Although there are no divisions in the manuscript text, I have divided the piece into three paragraphs to correspond with the three books of Julian's work.

There are three sections of the Apparatus which indicate, respectively, suggested emendations and collations of the *Excerpts* with the Ælfric *Sermo* and the Hillgarth edition of *Prognosticon*. The following abbreviations are used in the apparatus:

BE   Boulogne Excerpts
OP   Ælfric, *Sermo ad Populum in Octavis Pentecosten Dicendus* (Pope XI)
Prog.   Julian of Toledo, *Prognosticon futuri saeculi*, ed. J. Hillgarth (*CCL*, 116).

HVNC SERMONEM EX MVLTIS
EXCERPSIMVS, DE LIBRO QVI DICITVR
PRONOSTICON, ✠ IN CHRISTI NOMINE

Primus igitur homo ea naturae qualitate creatus est ut inmortalitatis ac
5 mortis admodum capax, nec sic inmortalis fuerit, ut etiamsi peccaret, mori
non posset, nec ita mortalis, ut si noluisset peccare, morti succumberet.
Arbitrii quoque libertati donatus est, ut iure aut beatus esset qui noluisset
peccare cum posset, aut miser cum potuisset vitare peccatum, non aliqua
necessitate sed propria voluntate peccasset. Tunc diabolus invidia plenus
10 suasione decoepit hominem, ut contra vetitum manducaret fieretque mortalis,
sicut scriptum est: *Invidia autem diaboli, mors introivit in orbem terrarum*
(*Sap.* ii.24). *Deus mortem non fecit, nec letatur,* inquit, *in perditione vivorum*
(*Sap.* i.13). Unde ait apostolus: *Per unum hominem peccatum intravit in mun-*
dum, et per peccatum mors, et ita in omnes homines mors pertransivit, in quo omnes
15 *peccaverunt* (*Rom.* v.12). Unde et eosdem primos peccatores ita fuisse morte
multatos, ut etiam quicquid eorum ex stirpe esset exortum eadem pena
teneretur obnoxium. Tria sunt genera mortis, id est acerba, inmatura, naturalis.
Acerba infantium, inmatura iuvenum, matura, id est naturalis, senum. Mortem
carnis omnis homo timet, et mortem anime pauci. Pro morte carnis, quae sine
20 dubio quandoque ventura est, curant omnes ne veniat; inde est quod laborant.
Laborat ne moriatur homo moriturus, et non laborat ne peccet homo in
eternum victurus. Mala mors putanda non est, quam bona vita precesserit;
nec enim facit malam mortem, ni⟨si⟩ qui sequitur mortem. Non itaque
multum curandum [folio 1ᵛ] est eis qui necessario morituri sunt. Quid acci-
25 daet ut moriantur? sed moriendo quo ire cogantur? Due namque sunt
mortes: una corporis et altera anime. Sed mortem corporis nemo evadit, anime
vero mortem omnes electi evadunt, sicut Dominus ait: *Se quis sermonem meum*
servaverit, mortem non videbit in eternum (*Ioan.* viii.51). Faciamus quod ait

---

7 libertati: *Prog. reads* libertate. 8 *before*
cum potuisset: *Prog. reads* qui. 15 *after*
peccatores: *some texts of Prog. add* videmus. 23 ni⟨si⟩: -si *worn and illegible in*
ms. 24–5 accidaet: *read* accidat.

4–9 = *OP* 94–102. 9–13 = *OP* 103–10 [with *BE* 13–17 cp. *OP* 106]. 17–28 = *OP*
111–38.

4–9 = *Prog.* I.iii.3–9. 9–13 not *Prog.* (which emphasizes myth of angelic fall).
13–15 = *Prog.* I.i.6–8. 15–17 = *Prog.* I.ii.9–11. 17–18 = *Prog.* I.v.2–4. 18–22 =
Prog. I.xi.2–6. 22–5 = *Prog.* I.xii.15–19. 25–8 not *Prog.* (but based in part on I.xii-
xiii, which alludes to *Ioan.* viii.51). 28–41 not *Prog.*

Salomon et non timebimus mortem: *Deum time et mandata eius observa, hoc*
30 *est omnis homo (Eccl.* xii.13), quia omnis homo hoc facere deberet. Et Micheas
propheta dixit, *Indicabo tibi, o homo, quid sit bonum, et quid Dominus quaerat a*
te: utique facere iudicium et diligere misericordiam et sollicitum ambulare cum Deo
tuo (Mic. vi.8). Et Psalmista: *Spera in Domino et fac bonitatem: inhabita terram*
et pasceris in divitiis eius (Psal. xxxvi.3). Item ipse ait: *Qui diligitis Dominum,*
35 *odite malum (Psal.* xcvi.10). Non est ergo fidelibus Christianis expavescendum
mortem subire temporalem, sed valde cavendum ne incurrant aeternam.
Multi tamen perverso ordine timentes amittere vitam presentem inciderunt in
illam mortem perpetuam: sicut apostatae qui in persecutionibus negaverunt
Christum, nolentes mori pro eo, ac tamen post modum mortui sunt et incide-
40 runt in eternam mortem, quam evadere feliciter potuissent, si temporalem
vitam infeliciter non amassent. Sed illi famosi tres pueri, missi in fornacem
ignis apud Chaldeos, nolentes apostatare, evaserunt mortem temporalem simul
et eternam *(Dan.* iii). Illis vero qui pro Christo contigit mori, implebitur pro-
missio eius, qua dicit: *Qui credit in me, etiamsi mortuus fuerit, vivet (Ioan.*
45 xi.25); id est, qui credit in me, etiamsi mortuus fuerit ad tempus in carne,
vivit in anima donec resurgat et caro numquam postea moritura. Sed et modo
nonnulli dicuntur [folio 2] Christiani, qui si persecutio talis adesset, qualis
temporibus martyrum exstitit, magis vellent fidem abnegare quam poenarum
genera percurrere. Aderit adhuc maior et acrior persecutio tempore Anti-
50 christi, contra quam sicut sanctus Ambrosius scribit: Mittentur fortissimi
milites Christi, qui in fatigabundis viribus confligendo martyrio coro⟨nen⟩tur.
Nulli enim fidelium optandum est in ista vita diu permanere, nisi forte vita
eius multis prosit ad salutem. Obsessa mens hominis, et undique diaboli
infestatione vallata, vix occurrit singulis, vix resistit. Si avaritia prostrata est,
55 exsurget libido. Si libido conpressa est, succendit ambitio. Si ambitio con-
tempta est, ira exsuperat. Inflat superbia, violentia invitat, invidia concordiae
rumpit amicitiam, zelus abscidit. Cogeris maledicere, quod divina lex pro-
hibet. Conpellis iurare quod non licet. Tot persecutiones animus cotidie
patitur, tot periculis pectus urguetur, et delectat hic inter diaboli gladios diu
60 stare, cum magis concupiscendum et optandum sit ad Christum subveniente

51 coro⟨nen⟩tur: *erasure and wear; there*
is not enough room for the reading
coro⟨nabun⟩tur *to parallel* Mittentur.
56 exsuperat: *Prog. reads* exasperat.

56–7 *Prog. reads* invidia concordiam
rumpit, amicitiam zelus abscidit. 58
Conpellis: *Prog. reads* conpelleris.

52–3 = *OP* 160–2.   53–4 and 58–61 = *OP* 157–9.

41–3 not *Prog.* (but I.xiii has ref. to *Dan.* iii.5).   43–6 = *Prog.* I.xiii.33–6 (new
intro. clause).   46–53 not *Prog.*   53–61 = *Prog.* I.xv.17–26, 30.

velocius morte properare. Quis non ad letitiam venire festinet? Sicut Paulus
exemplum proposuit nobis dicens, *Cupio dissolvi, et esse cum Christo* (*Phil.* i.23).
Porro cum mundus oderit Christianum, quid amas eum qui te odit, et non
magis sequeris Christum qui te et redemit et diligit? Patriam nostram para-
65 disum computemus; parentes patriarchas habere cepimus. Quid non pro-
peramus et currimus, ut patriam nostram videre et parentes salutare possimus?
Magnus illic nos carorum numerus expectat, parentum, fratrum, filiorum
sequens nos [folio 2ᵛ] et copiosa turba desiderat, iam de sua incolomitate
secura, adhuc de nostra salute sollicita. Ad horum conspectum et complexum
70 venire, quanta et illis et nobis in commune letitia est. Cuidam namque epi-
scopo, infirmitate defesso cum de adpropinquante morte sollicitus inducias sibi
precaretur, adstitit angelus Domini et cum magna indignatione infremuit, et
dixit, Pati timetis exire non vultis. Quid faciam vobis? Nititur namque diabolus extrema vite hominis suis laqueis innectere, sed necesse habet Christianus
75 in ipso exitu sibi adesse frequens fratrum oratio; quia quosdam legimus in
hora transitus sui, ab adsistente et insidiante diabolo, fraternis precibus et
psalmoedie frequentia liberatos. Unde non est dubium, quia cum pii fideles et
verissimi Christiani ex hoc seculo transeunt, si sedula et frequens fratrum
adiuverit oratio, non eos audeat contingere malignorum spirituum cruenta
80 incursio. Cum in evvangelio mentio divitis et Lazari pauperis ageretur, sic
scriptum est: *Contigit mori inopem illum, et ferri ab angelis in sinum Abrahe*
(*Luc.* xvi.22). Qua sententia verissime confirmatur, quod in separatione
sanctarum animarum et egressu a corpore, angelorum semper habeantur
excubiae, et quod ab eisdem angelis animae eorum excipiantur perducendae
85 ad Deum quem coluerunt. Contigit etiam plerumque, ut per asperam mortem
carnis liberetur anima a peccatis. Nam vir Dei contra Samariam missus, quia
per inobedientiam in itinere comedit, hunc leo in eodem itinere occidit. Sed
statim illic scriptum est, *quia stetit leo iuxta asinum, et non* [folio 3] *comedit de
cadavere* (III *Reg.* xiii.28). Ex qua re ostenditur quod peccatum inobedeientiae
90 in ipsa fuerit morte laxatum, quia isdem leo qui eum occidendi ausum habuit,
de cadavere occisi comedendi licentiam non accepit. Unde et ita esse credendum est, quod plerumque de culpis minimis ipse solus pavor egredientes

68 sequens: *Prog. reads* frequens.

66–70 = *OP* 153–6.   73–7 = *OP* 163–76.   80–5 = *OP* 181–3.   85–6 and 91–4 =
OP 200–7.

61–2 not *Prog.*   63–70 = *Prog.* I.xv.76–8, 103–10.   70–3 = *Prog.* I.xvi.24–31(alt.).
73–80 = *Prog.* I.viii.16–17 and (after expansion) 21–7.   80–4 = *Prog.* I.x.7–12.
84–5 = *Prog.* I.x.19–27 (restated).   85–6 = *Prog.* I.vii.1–2.   86–94 = *Prog.* I.vii.15–29
(shortened).

iustorum animas purget. Quidam vero in ipso suo fine hilarescunt aeternorum contemplatione bonorum. Quamvis exequie funerum magis sint solacia vivo-
95 rum quam subsidia mortuorum; tamen antiquorum iustorum funera officiosa pietate curata sunt, et exsequiae celebrate, et sepultura previsa. Denique creditur non esse illorum fidem vacuam, qui pie viventes suorum cadavera in memoriis martyrum precipiunt tumulanda: licet multis aliis rationibus et maiorum didicerimus exemplis, quod illi dampnabiliter in ecclesia tumulentur,
00 qui usque in finem suum sceleratissime vivunt. Cum enim Deo sacrificia pro spiritibus defunctorum offeruntur, pro valde bonis gratiarum actiones sunt, pro non valde malis propitiationes sunt, pro valde malis, etiamsi nulla sint adiumenta mortuorum qualescumque tamen sunt consolationes viventium. Quibus tamen prosunt, aut ad hoc prosunt, ut sit plena remissio, aut certe ut
05 tolerabilior fiat ipsa dampnatio.

Unus est enim terrenus paradysus ubi primorum hominum corporaliter vita exstitit; alter celestis ubi anime beatorum statim ut a corpore exeunt transferuntur, atque digna felicitate letantes expectant receptionem corporum suorum. De qua loquitur Dominus ad latronem: *Hodie mecum eris in paradyso*
10 (*Luc.* xxiii.43). De discretione infernorum in beati Agustini tractatibus me legisse memini: ubi duos [folio 3ᵛ] esse infernos manifestius dicit, ut unus infernus superior terra, alter vero infernus inferior sub terra esse accipiatur, secundum vocem Psalmista Deo confitentis: *Eruisti animam meam ex inferno inferiore* (*Psal.* lxxxv.13). Nam propter ista duo inferna missus est filius Dei,
15 utique liberans. Ad hoc infernum missus est nascendo, ad illum moriendo. Tempus quod inter hominis mortem et ultimam resurrectionem interpositum est, anime abditis receptaculis continentur, sicut unaquaeque digna est, vel requie, vel erumna, pro eo quod sortita est in carne cum viveret. Purgatorias autem penas nullus futuras opinetur nisi ante illud ultimum tremendumque
20 iudicium. Unus quidem est gehenne ignis, sed non uno modo omnes cruciat peccatores. Uniuscuiusque etenim quantum exigit culpa, tantum illic sentietur et poena; sicut in hoc mundo sub uno sole multi consistunt, nec tamen eiusdem solis ardorem aequaliter sentiunt. Si viventis hominis incorporeus spiritus teneatur in corpore, cur non post mortem, cum incorporeus sit spiritus, etiam
25 corporeo igne teneatur? Dum ergo peccatorem divitem dampnatum veritas in

100–2 and 104–5 = *OP* 211, 212[?]. 100–3 = *OP* 223. 116–18 = *OP* 185–94 [rather remotely and in part].

94–6 = *Prog.* I.xix.1–5 (paraphr.), 21–3. 96–100 = *Prog.* I.xxi.25–30. 100–5 = *Prog.* I.xxii.8–14. 106–10 = *Prog.* II.i.5–8, 16. 110–15 = *Prog.*II.iv. 2–8. 116–8 = *Prog.* II.ix.3–6. 118–20 = *Prog.* II.xxi.17–18. 120–3 = *Prog.* II.xviii.3–7. 123–6 = *Prog.* II.xvii.3–5, 17–19.

ignibus perhibet, quisnam sapiens reproborum animas teneri ignibus neget
Anima denique quae semel in infernum proiecta fuerit, ibidem erit perpetu
permansura. Et exaltata ad gloriam semel, numquam perveniet ad suppliciurr
Anima namque, a corpore separata, sensibus suis non erit privata. Anim
130 autem similitudinem corporis habet, et in eadem corporali similitudin
requiem sentit perfertque tormenta. Constat namque quasdam culpas in ho
seculo, quasdam vero in futuro posse relaxari, quia Dominus ait in evvangelio
Si quis in Spiritum sanctum blasphemiam dixerit, neque in hoc seculo re- [folio 4
mittetur ei, neque in futuro (*Matth.* xii.32). Leviores quidem culpe ut stipul
135 ligna purgatorio igne consumentur; graviora vero crimina eterno supplici
dampnentur. Et ipse ignis purgatorius multo gravior erit quam quicquid hom
potest pati in hac vita. Non est ergo dubitandum quod se defunctorum spiritu
in illa regione pariter recognoscant. Possunt enim et boni bonos et mali malo
cognoscere. Fit autem in electis quiddam mirabilius, quia non solum ec
140 cognoscunt quos in hoc mundo noverant, sed velut visos ac cognitos recog
noscunt bonos quos numquam viderunt, quos in operibus semper noverun
Orant pro inimicis suis anime beatorum eo tempore, ut ait sanctus Gregoriu
quo possunt ad fructuosam penitentiam eorum corda convertere, atque ips
conversione salvare. Et quomodo pro illis tunc orabitur qui iam nullatenu
145 possunt ad iustitie opera ab iniquitate commutari? Eadem itaque causa es
cur non oretur tunc pro hominibus eterno igne dampnatis, quae nunc etiar
causa est ut non oretur pro diabolo angelisque eius eterno supplicio deputati
Si autem corpus corruptibile viventis hominis adgravat animam eius, erg
anima, corpore soluta, liberior efficitur. Est igitur anime post mortem e
150 sensus integer et memoria plena et recordans quos amavit in seculo com
mendare eos potest precibus Christo. Est quoque cura defunctis de suis cari
vivis, sicut de divite legitur qui rogabat Abraham mittere Lazarum ut monere
fratres suos, ne et ipsi devenirent in locum tormentorum (*Luc.* xvi.27, 28
Quomodo ergo piorum anime et maxime in requie constitute carorum super
155 stitum creduntur sollicitundinem amisisse? Orare ergo possunt pro salut
viventium, quantum a Domino permittuntur. [folio 4ᵛ] Possunt etiam spiritu
mortuorum aliqua – quae hic aguntur, quae necessarium est eos nosse, non solur
presentia vel preterita verum etiam futura, spiritu Dei revelante – cognoscere

127-37 = *OP* 214-28. 137-47 and 149-51 = *OP* 232-42. 151-3 = *OP* 271, 272.

127-8 = *Prog.* ii.xiv.1-2, 8-9 (restated). 129 = *Prog.* ii.xv.1-2 (restated). 129-31 =
Prog. ii.xvi.1-3. 131-4 = *Prog.* ii.xix.13-16 (rearranged, some restatement). 134-7 =
Prog. ii.xix.3-10 (restated). 137-41 = *Prog.* ii.xxiv (paraphr.). 142-7 = *Prog*
ii.xxv.3-5, 9-13. 148-51 = *Prog.* ii.xxvi.12-18 (some restatement). 151-3 = *Prog*
ii.xxvii (paraphr.). 154-6 = *Prog.* ii.xxvi.5-8. 156-8 = *Prog.* ii.xxix.13-16 (alt.
158-61 = *Prog.* ii.xxx.3-5, 13-14.

Mittuntur etiam ad vivos aliqui ex mortuis, sicut e contrario Paulus ex vivis
160 raptus est in paradysum, divina scriptura testante. Nam et Moyses in Deute-
ronomio mortuus legitur apparuisse viventibus. Et beatus Augustinus scripsit
aparuisse quendam defunctum filio suo superstiti in somnis, et indicasse ei de
quodam debito quod non dixerit moriens, ut ipse a magna molestia libe-
raretur. Anime denique beatorum, exute corporibus, sola iocunditate spiritus
165 perfruuntur, quae prima stola quietis atque felicitatis est. Secunda vero stola
erit cum receptis corporibus de anime et carnis inmortalitate letabuntur, tam
ineffabili facilitate ut sit eis corpus gloria, quod ante sarcina fuit. Et cotidie
desiderant sancti resurrectionem corporum suorum et dupplicationem beatitudinis sue, sed tamen expectant donec impleatur numerus fratrum et con-
170 servorum suorum. Cum igitur sancti regnantes in celo Creatoris sui claritatem
semper videant, nichil in creatura agitur quod videre non possint. Et quod
reproborum tormenta conspiciunt non potest minuere letitiam ipsorum; sed
tanto maiores ereptori suo gratias referunt quanto vident in aliis quod ipsi
perpeti potuissent, si ab illo relicti fuissent. Non enim impiorum sed sancto-
175 rum tantum anime norunt quid possit a viventibus agi in seculo. Sicut enim
credimus animas sanctorum esse in caelo, adtestatione sacri eloquii, sic oportet
ut et iniquorum animas in inferno per omnia esse credamus.

Iudicii enim tempus vel diem nullus hominum neque [folio 5] angelorum
novit (cf. *Marc.* xiii.32). Iohel propheta de loco iudicii sic ait: *In diebus illis et*
180 *in tempore illo, cum convertero captivitatem Iuda et Hierusalem, congregabo omnes*
gentes et deducam eos in valle Iosaphath, et disceptabo cum eis ibi (*Ioel.* iii.1–2).
Sed beatus Hieronimus dicit quod Iosaphath interpretatur Domini iudicium.
In valle enim Iosaphath: hoc est in valle iudicii quia sicut idem doctor tractat,
aut incredulae nationes, aut demones non iudicabuntur in montibus, non in
185 campestribus, sed in profundo et deorsum, ut statim iudicii locus ipse pro
pena sit. De hoc iudicio Paulus apostolus ait: *Quoniam ipse Dominus in iussu et*
in voce archangeli et in tuba Dei descendet de celo, et mortui, qui in Christo sunt,
resugent primi. Deinde nos qui vivimus, qui relinquimur, simul rapiemur cum illis
in nubibus obviam Christo in aera, et sic semper cum Domino erimus. Itaque

184 incredulae: *Prog. reads* incredulas.

164–75 = *OP* 243–70.   175–7 = *OP* 185–94 [in part; cp *BE* 116ff and Pope's appara-
tus].   178–9 = *OP* 273–5.

161–4 = Prog. II.xxvii (paraphr.).   164–7 = *Prog.* II.xxxv (restated).   167–70 = *Prog.*
II.xxxvii.21–8 (restated).   170–1 = *Prog.* II.xxxi (restated).   171–4 = *Prog.*II.xxxii.23–30
(restated).   174–5 = *Prog.* II.xxxi.1–2 (alt.).   175–7 = *Prog.* II.xiii (restated).   178–9 =
Prog. III.i (alt.).   179–86 = *Prog.* III.ii.6–23 (abbreviated).   186–90 = *Prog.* III.iv.12–24
(which quotes only part of I *Thess.* iv.16).

190 *consolamini invicem in verbis istis* (I *Thess.* iv.16–18). Et ipse Dominus in
evvangelio dixit, *Sicut enim fulgor exiit ab oriente et paret usque in occidentem,*
ita erit adventus Filii hominis. Ubicumque fuerit corpus, illuc congregabuntur
aquile. Statim autem post tribulationem dierum illorum sol obscurabitur, et luna
non dabit lumen suum, et stelle cadent de caelo, et virtutes caelorum commove-
195 *buntur. Et tunc apparebit signum Filii hominis in celo, et tunc plangent omnes*
tribus terre, et videbunt filium hominis venientem in nubibus celi cum virtute multa
et magestate. Et mittet angelos suos cum tuba et voce magna, et congregabunt
electos eius a quattuor ventis, a summis caelorum usque ad terminos eorum (*Matth.*
xxiv.27–31). De hoc adventu dixit Iohannes Crisostomus: Tunc, inquit,
200 quando venturus erit Christus, *sol obscurabitur, et luna non dabit lumen suum.*
Tanta enim erit [folio 5ᵛ] eminentia splendoris in Christo, ut etiam clarissima
celi luminaria pre fulgore divini luminis abscondantur. Exercitus denique
angelorum et archangelorum precedent eum, illud triumphale vexillum miro
fulgore coruscans preferentes. *Tunc plangent omnes tribus terre,* videntes ipsam
205 crucem, cognoscentesque peccatum suum. Quid autem miraris si crucem
adferens veniat, ubi et ipsa vulnera ostendet tunc ? Quoniam *videbunt,* inquit,
in quem compunxerunt (*Ioan.* xix.37). Hoc enim fuit voluntas eius, ut primus
adventus latenter fieret, et quereret quod perierat. De secundo vero eius
adventu Psalmista loquitur dicens: *Deus manifeste veniet, Deus noster, et non*
210 *silebit. Ignis in conspectu eius ardebit, et in circuitu eius tempestas valida* (*Psal.*
xlix.3). Tempestas namque examinat, quos ignis exurit. *Deus,* inquit, *noster*
manifeste veniet: qui venit occultus, veniet manifestus. Venit occultus iudi-
candus, veniet manifestus iudicaturus. *Es non silebit:* silet modo, et non silet.
Non silet ammonendo, silet iudicando. Tunc autem non silebit, quia de
215 iudicibus iuste iudicet qui, occultus ante iudicem stans iniuste, iudicatus est.
Ignis in conspectu eius exardescet: Timeamus ? Mutemur, et non timebimus.
Stipulam ad te congeris, veniet ignis. Non erit iste ignis ut focus tuus, sed
sicut precedens iudicium in diebus Noe per diluvium factum est sic erit
subsequens iudicium per ignem in adventu Christi. *Et in circuitu eius tempestas*
220 *valida:* Hac tempestate erit illa ventilatio qua separabitur frumentum a paleis,

195 plangent: l *crossed in ms.*

201–7 = *OP* 285–95.   216 and 217–9 = *OP* 296[?].

190–9 = *Prog.* III.iv.7–12 (which quotes only *Matth.* xxiv.29–31).   199–208 = *Prog.*
III.v.25–9, 35–41, 48–53, 15–16 (some restatement at beginning).   208–22 not *Prog.*
(*Prog.* III.iv.15–16 quotes *Psal.* xlix [1].3b. *BE* 212–14 may expand *Prog.* III.iv, which
paraphrases Augustine, *Ennar. in Psal.* xlix.6–8 [vs. 3], but *BE* quotes *Ennar.* more
accurately than does *Prog.* The ultimate source of most of the passage is *Ennar.,* but
BE's references to the Flood in 218, the threshing image of 220–1, and the last sentence
seem to be independent of Augustine and may point to an intermediate source).

omne inmundum a fidelibus. Ergo quot diebus iudicium illud extendatur incertum est. Beatus Hieronimus de novissima tuba sic scripsit: Queritur cur de novissima tuba mortuos scripserit Apostolus resurrecturos (I *Cor.* xv.52). Quando enim novissima dicitur, utique aliae precesserunt. In Apocalipsi
25 Iohannis (xi) septem angeli [folio 6] describuntur cum tubis, et unoquoque clangente, primo videlicet, secundo, et tertio, quarto, et quinto, et sexto, et septimo, quid per singulos actum sit, indicatur. Novissime autem, id est septime, claro tube strepitu personante mortui suscitantur, corpora, quae prius habuerunt corruptibilia, incorrupta recipientes. Et tanta fiet celeritate
30 resurrectio mortuorum, ut vivi, quos in corporibus suis consummationis tempus invenerit, mortuos de inferis resurgentes prevenire non valeant, sicut ait Apostolus, *in momento, in ictu oculi* (I *Cor.* xv.52). Item ait Apostolus: *Omnes quidem resurgemus, sed non omnis immutabimur* (I *Cor.* xv.51), quia resurrectio communis omnibus erit, bonis et malis. Inmutatio autem solis
35 data est iustis, que utique glorificationem insinuat aeterne beatitudinis. Una erit resurrectio omnium hominum; et omnes simul resurrecturi credendi sunt, sed sancti homines ad gloriam, et impii ad supplicium. Resurgent ergo omnes homines tam magni corpore et in illa statura in qua erant viventes, vel futuri erant si vixissent: *in mensura* vero *etatis plentitudinis Christi* (*Ephes.*
40 iv.13), hoc est in illa etate et in illo robore ad quam Christus pervenit in mundo. Quia si maiores Christo in statura deberent redigi ad eius staturam, plurimum periret de multorum corporibus, cum ipse nec capillum periturum esse promiserit. Sicut enim Christus resurgens ex mortuis palpabilem se prebuit discipulis suis, sic etiam corpus nostrum inmortalitatis gloria subli-
45 matum subtile erit per effectum spiritalis potentiae, sed palpabile per veritatem nature. Resurgent itaque omnium sanctorum corpora omni felicitate et gloria inmortalitatis conspicua, sine ulla corruptione, sine difficultate, vel onere, aut deformitate: [folio 6ᵛ] in quibus, ut ait sanctus Agustinus, tanta facilitas quanta felicitas erit. De reprobis vero quid dicendum est, nisi quod ubi erit
50 dentium stridor, aeternus et incessabilis fletus, inaniter quaeritur corporum decus? Dominus dixit in evvangelio: *In resurrectione enim nec femine nubent,*

227 Novissime: *Prog. reads* novissimo.   229 habuerunt: *Prog. reads* habuerant.
228 septime: *Prog. reads* septimo.

227-32 = *OP* 297-301.   237-41 = *OP* 305-11 [some rearrangement].   244-6 = *OP* 325.   246-8 = *OP* 320-4 [cp *BE* 280-2].   249-51 = *OP* 326-31.   251-6 = *OP* 312-19.

222-9 = *Prog.* III.xv.3-13 (some restatement).   229-32 = *Prog.* III.xv.15-19 (alt.). 232-7 = *Prog.* III.xix.7-15 (restated).   237-46 = *Prog.* III.xx-xxi (restated).   246-9 = *Prog.* III.xxii.3-6.   249-51 = *Prog.* III.xxiii.8-9 (minor alt.).   251-6 = *Prog.* III.xxiv.13-20 (some restatement).

nec viri uxores accipient (*Matth.* xxii.30). Ex quibus sacratissimis verb
apertissime patet quod ibi non sexus, sed concubitus desit; nec carnis s
natura mutanda, sed eius concupiscentia finienda., Sicut enim omnipoter
255 Deus utrumque sexum condidit, instituit, ac redemit, sic etiam utrumque i
resurrectione restituet. Pater igitur non iudicat quemquam sed omne iudiciur
dedit Filio, qui manifestabitur homo iudicaturus, sicut est homo iudicatu
Nec ipse Pater videbitur in iudicio, sed videbunt in quem pupugerunt. Form
illa erit iudex, quae stetit sub iudice; illa iudicabit quae iudicata est. Iudica
260 est enim inique, iudicabit iuste. Redemptor humani generis, cum apparueri
et mitis iustis et terribilis erit iniustis. Sed ideo hunc electri terribilem no
videbunt, quia modo terrorem illius considerare non desinunt; et ideo reprot
terribilem illum conspicient, quia modo ultimi iudicii postponunt terroren
et, quod peius est, quasi securi in suis fecibus iacent. Humanitatem namqu
265 eius et iusti et iniusti visuri sunt; divinitatem vero eius non videbunt nisi sc
iusti, sicut Isaias dicit: *Tollatur impius, ne videat magestatem Domini* (*Isc*
xxvi.10). Hoc quod dicitur – quod ipse iudicaturus est vivos ac mortuos – no
pertinet ad viventes in carne inventos, sed vivos iustos intelligimus, et mortuo
peccatores qui merito mortui apellantur. [folio 7] Quidam tamen volur
270 habere viventes qui in carne inveniendi sunt, et mortuos iam defunctos. Ip
vero qui viventes repperiuntur in die iudicii, sicut docet pater Agustinus, i
ipso raptu nubium (I *Thess.* iv.17) momentaneam mortem gustabunt, et sic i
terram ibunt quia corpus exanime terra est, et iterum statim in ipsis nubibu
spiritum vite accipient. Agustinus dicit de abortivis fetibus: Ex quo eni
275 incipit homo vivere, ex illo utique mori potest. Mortuus vero, ubicumque il
mors potuit evenire, quomodo ad resurrectionem non pertineat mortuorun
repperire non possumus. De monstris vero et de bimembribus dicit Augus
tinus: Absit enim, ut illum bimembrem qui nuper natus est in oriente; absi
inquam, ut unum hominem dupplicem ac non potius duos quod futurur
280 fuerat si gemini nascerentur resurrecturos existimemus. Sic et cetera qua
amplius vel minus aliquid habuerunt, vel debiles vel ceci fuerunt, cum integr
numero membrorum corporis sine deformitate resurgent. Etsi a bestiis devo
rentur, sive igne concremantur et in auras aspergantur, potens est tamen eo

260–1 = *OP* 348–9.   264–6 = *OP* 350–3.   270–4 = *OP* 302–4.   280–2 = *OP* 320–
[? cp *BE* 246–8].   282–5 = *OP* 332–42.

256–60 = *Prog.* III.ix.3–9 (alt. at beginning).   260–4 = *Prog.* III.vii.3–4, 6–10.   264–6 =
Prog. III.viii.3–8 (alt.).   266–70 = *Prog.* III.x (restated).   270–4 not *Prog.*   274–7 =
Prog. III.xxviii.9–12 (alt. at beginning).   277–82 = *Prog.* III.xxviii.9–10, 12–14 (plu
restatement).   282–4 = *Prog.* III.xxix (restated).

in puncto temporis reformare, qui de nichilo mundum creavit. Etsi indumenta
35 fuerint, spiritalium corporum spiritalia erunt. Solent namque quidam homines
dicere: Carnem hominis lupus comedit, lupum leo devoravit, leo moriens ad
pulverem rediit; cum pulvis ille suscitatur, quomodo caro hominis a lupi et
leonis carne dividitur? Quibus sic respondit sanctus Gregorius: Certe tu
ȟomo qui loqueris, aliquando in matris utero spuma sanguinis fuisti; ibi
90 quippe ex patris semine et matris sanguine parvus ac liquidus [folio 7ᵛ] globus
eras. Dic, rogo, si nosti, qualiter ille humor seminis in ossibus duravit, qualiter
in medullis liquidus remansit, qualiter in nervis solidatus est, qualiter in
carnibus crevit, qualiter in cute extensus est, qualiter in capillis atque unguibus
distinctus, ita ut capilli molliores carnibus, et ungues essent teneriores ossibus,
95 carnibus duriores? Si igitur tot et tanta ex uno semine et per species distincta
sunt, et tamen in forma remanent coniuncta, quid mirum si possit omnipotens
Deus in illa resurrectione mortuorum carnem hominis distinguere a carne
bestiarum, ut unus idemque pulvis, et non resurgat in quantum pulvis lupi et
leonis est, et tamen resurgat in quantum pulvis est hominis? Sedes igitur
00 habebunt apostoli in quibus Christo iudicante sessuri sunt, iuxta illud quod
ipsa Veritas ait: *Vos qui secuti estis me, in regeneratione cum sederit Filius hominis
in sede magestatis sue, sedebitis et vos super sedes duodecim; iudicantes duodecim
tribus Israel* (*Matth.* xix.28) – et non solum duodecim apostoli, sed consenti-
entibus catholicis doctoribus luce clarius constat, quod omnes sancti qui
05 perfecte mundum reliquerunt cum Domino residentes ceteros iudicabunt.
Tunc quoque implebitur illud quod in divinis litteris legitur: *Nobilis in portis
vir eius, quando sederit cum senatoribus terre* (*Prov.* xxxi.23). Igitur perfectorum
sanctorum primus ordo erit, qui cum Domino iudicat, et non iudicatur, sed
regnat. Alius quoque est ordo electorum quibus dicitur, *Esurivi et decistis mihi
10 manducare* (*Matth.* xxv.35). Hi iudicantur et regnant. Item reproborum
ordines duo sunt. Unus eorum, qui Dei cognitionem habuerunt, sed fidem
dignis operibus non exercuerunt, isti iudicabuntur et peribunt, quibus dicetur
a Domino: *Esurivi et non dedistis mihi manducare; ite, maledicti, in ignem
aeternum* (*Matth.* xxv.41, 42). Alter quoque ordo reproborum [folio 8] est
15 paganorum videlicet, qui Dei cognitionem non habuerunt, qui sine lege
peccaverunt, et sine lege peribunt. Separatis igitur per angelica ministeria
bonis a malis, et electis quidem a dextris, reprobis vero a sinistris adstantibus,

299–305 = *OP* 354–9 [some omissions].   307–16 = *OP* 361–90.   316–17 = *OP* 345–6.
317–21 and 325–9 = *OP* 391–404 [independently developed].

284–5 = *Prog.* III.xxvi (restated).   285–99 = *Prog.* III.xxix.13–33 (some alt.).
299–305 = *Prog.* III.xi (restated and expanded).   305–7 = *Prog.* III.xii.4–6.   307–16 =
Prog. III.xxxiii.6–15 (alt. and rearranged).   316–39 = *Prog.* III.xxxvi (some alt. and
rearrangement).

tunc libri aperti erunt, id est, conscientie singulorum manifestabuntur
Iohannes enim apostolus dicit: *Vidi mortuos magnos et pusillos; et aperti sun*
320 *libri; et alius liber apertus est, qui est vite uniuscuiusque. Et iudicati sunt mortui e.*
his scripturis librorum secundum facta sua (*Apoc.* xx.12). Isti libri si carnalite
intelliguntur, quis eorum multitudinem sive magnitudinem valeat estimare
Aut quanto tempore legi potuerint? Sed libros apertos voluit intelligi sancto
omnes Novi et Veteris Testamenti, in quorum vita velut in libris cognoscimu
325 quid facere debeamus. In isto autem libro de quo dicit, *alius liber apertus est*
qui est vitae uniuscuiusque, quaedam vis est intellegenda divina qua fiet u
cuique opera sua vel bona vel mala cuncta in memoriam revocentur, et menti
intuitu ita celeritate cernantur, ut accuset vel excuset scientia conscientiam
atque simul et omnes et singuli iudicentur. Quae nimirum vis divina libr
330 nomen accepit. In ea quippe quodammodo legitur quicquid a faciente recoli
tur. Tunc dicet Christus his qui a dextris eius erunt: *Venite, benedicti Patri*
mei, possidete paratum vobis regnum ac constitutione mundi. Esurivi enim, e
dedistis mihi manducare. Hospes eram, et collegistis me. Nudus, et operuistis me
Infirmus, et visitastis me. In carcere eram, et venistis ad me; etcetera (*Matth*
335 xxv. 34–36). A sinistra quoque parte adstantibus reprobis inputaturus es
quod ea non fecissent, quae in dextera parte adstantes fecisse commemorat
His duobus sermonibus Domini nostri Ihesum Christi finitis, [folio 8ᵛ] *Ibun*
impii, ut ipsa Veritas dicit, *in supplicium aeternum, iusti autem in vitan*
aeternam (*Matth.* xxv. 46). Hinc Danihel propheta scripsit: *Multi,* inquit, *qu*
340 *dormiunt in terre pulvere evigilabunt: alii in vitam aeternam, alii in obprobrium*
Qui autem docti fuerint, fulgebunt, quasi splendor firmamenti; et qui ad iustitian
erudiunt multos, quasi stelle in perpetuas aeternitates (*Dan.* xii.2–3). Sanctu
Iohannes scripsit in Apocalipsi (xx.15) ut, qui non fuerint inventi in libr
vitae scripti, mittantur in stagnum ignis. Et Agustinus dicit quod liber ill
345 predestinationem significat eorum quibus aeterna vita dabitur, quia Deu
oblivionem non patitur, ut libri recitatione indigeat. Sequitur Iohannes ii
Apocalipsi dicens: *Et iudicati sunt singuli secundum opera sua, et mors et infernu*
missi sunt in stagnum ignis (*Apoc.* xx.13, 14). Mors et infernus diabolus intelli-
gitur, quia ipse est auctor mortis omniumque poenarum. Unus quippe ignis
350 erit utrisque, et demonibus et impiis hominibus, sicut ipsa Veritas dicit: *It*

331–5 = *OP* 405–29 [where quotation of *Matth.* xxv extended and modified]. 337–9 =
OP 451–4 [after greatly expanded ref. to *Matth.* xxv]. 342–6 = *OP* 466–72. 346–9 =
OP 459–65. 349–50 and 352–4 = *OP* 473–7.

339–42 not *Prog.* 342–6 = *Prog.* III.xxxix (restated). 346–9 = *Prog.* III.xxxviii.4–8
(alt.). 349–58 = *Prog.* III.xl (much restatement; ref. to *Matth.* xxv added).

in ignem eternum, qui preparatus est diabolo et angelis eius (Matth. xxv.41).
Ergo sempiterno igne ardebunt et mori omnino non poterunt, quia eterna
erunt corpora omnium bonorum scilicet et malorum post communem resurrectionem. Anima namque, cuius presentia corpus vivit et se movet
355 ambulando et operando, patitur dolorem in corpore, nec tamen mori potest.
Hoc igitur erit tunc etiam in corporibus dampnatorum, quod nunc esse
scimus in animabus hominum. Ardebunt enim tunc sine detrimento, et
dolebunt sine interitu. Sanctus itaque Augustinus de poena demoniorum sic
ait: Cur enim non dicamus, quamvis miris, tamen veris modis etiam demones
360 incorporeos posse poena corporalis ignis affligi, [folio 9] si animas hominum
nunc possint includi corporalibus membris in quibus patiuntur dolores ? Et
nos dicimus quod omnipotens Deus, qui sanctos angelos in caelesti regno
remunerat et letificat, potest etiam dampnatos angelos eterni ignis cruciatibus
afligere. Tanto igitur quisque hominum ibi tolerabiliorem habebit dampna-
365 tionem, quanto hic minorem habuit iniquitatem, quia ipse ignis pro diversi-
tate meritorum, aliis erit levior, aliis gravior. Mitissima omnium poena erit
eorum qui, preter peccatum quod originale traxerunt, nullum insuper addi-
derunt. Credendum vero est quod ante retributionem extremi iudicii iniusti in
poenis quosdam iustos in requie conspiciunt, ut eos videntes in gaudio, non
370 solum de suo supplicio sed etiam de illorum bono crucientur. Post iudicium
autem nesciunt quid agatur in gaudio beatorum; boni tamen sciunt quid
agatur in suppliciis miserorum. Precurrit ergo impiorum dampnatio, et post
sequitur electorum remuneratio, dicente Christo: *Ibunt* impii *in supplicium
eternum, iusti autem in vitam eternam (Matth.* xxv.46). Et Iohannes in Apoca-
375 lipsi eundem ordinem servans: *Mors,* inquid, *et infernus missus est in stagnum
ignis. Et omnis qui non est inventus scriptus in libro vite, missus est in stagnum
ignis (Apoc.* xx.14, 15). Et ilico adiecit: *Et vidi celum novum et terram novam
(Apoc.* xxi.1). Quibus verbis datur intellegi quod iusto Dei iudicio prius
peccatoribus inrogetur supplicium, et postea sanctis eternorum tribuantur
380 munera premiorum. Et hoc quod dicit, *celum novum et terram novam,* non alia
creanda sunt, sed hec ipsa renovantur per ignem. Et in celo novo et terra
nova, omnino non erunt nisi electi. Iam vero post iudicium pergit hinc

360 animas: *read* anime.

358–71 = *OP* 478–507.   371–4 = *OP* 455–8.   377–8 and 380–2 = *OP* 508–18.
382–91 = *OP* 519–41.

358–61 = *Prog.* III.xli (restated).   361–4 not *Prog.*   364–8 = *Prog.* III.xlii (rearranged
and alt.).   368–70 = *Prog.* II.xxxii.24–7 (alt.).   370–2 = *Prog.* III.li.1–3.   372–80 =
Prog. III.xliv.5–15 (restatement; quotation of *Apoc.* added).   380–2 = *Prog.* III.xlvi,
xlvii (restated).   382–4 = *Prog.* III.xlv.14–15.

Christus rex noster, et ducet secum ad celum corpus cui caput est, et offert
regnum Deo [folio 9ᵛ] *et Patri* (I *Cor.* xv.24). Sicut ipse in mundo promisit
385 suis sequacibus dicens ad Patrem: *Volo ut ubi ego sum et ipsi sint mecum, ut
videant claritatem meam* (*Ioan.* xvii.24). Si enim capitis membra sumus et
unus in se et in nobis est Christus, utique ubi ipse ascendit et nos ascensuri
sumus. Similes ergo tunc angelis erimus, quia sicut illi nunc vident, ita et nos
Deum post resurrectionem videbimus. Sicut Paulus ait: *Videmus nunc per
390 speculum in enigmate, tunc autem facie ad faciem* (I *Cor.* xiii.12). Et Iohannes
apostolus dixit, *Quoniam videbimus eum sicuti est* (*Ioan.* iii.2). Gradus honorum
atque gloriarum qui in illa vita futuri sunt, ut ait sanctus Agustinus, quis est
idoneus cogitare? Quanto magis dicere? Hinc Paulus apostolus ait: *Stella
autem ab stella differt in claritate; sic et resurrectio mortuorum* (I *Cor.* xv.41, 42).
395 Et nullus inferior invidebit superiori, sicut modo angeli non invident archange-
lis, nec aliquis ordo vult esse quod non accepit, sicut nec in corpore nostro
vult digitus esse oculus nec pes manus, sed unumquodque membrum totius
corporis, pacata compagine, hoc quod accepit possidet. Sic habitabitur tunc
illa superna civitas Hierusalem summa concordia et caritate quae numquam
400 cadit, in qua valde magnus civis habebitur qui minimus estimabitur. Finis
igitur desideriorum nostrorum Christus tunc erit, qui sine fine videbitur,
sine fastidio amabitur, sine fatigatione laudabitur, iuxta quod propheta ait:
Non laborabunt nec fatigabuntur (*Isa.* xi.31?). Patebunt etiam cogitationes
nostrae invicem nobis, et non egemus sustentari cibis aut poculis, quia non
405 erit ibi esuries aut sitis ubi erit *Deus omnia in omnibus* (I *Cor.* xv.28). Ipse
denique regnum, ipse possessio erit electorum suorum, ipse promisit se ipsum
nobis in premium daturum, quo nichil est aliud [folio 10] melius, in quo nobis
est vita et salus, et copia, et gloria, et honor, et pax, et omnia bona. Ibi erit
nobis dies eterna; ibi dupplicia, id est binas stolas, possidemus, et letitia
410 sempiterna erit nobis; et fulgebimus sicut sol in regno Patris nostri, qui vivit
et regnat sine fine. AMEN.

404 egemus: *read* agemus.

391–411 = *OP* 548–74 [with minor omissions].

384–8 = *Prog.* III.lii.8–11 (alt.).   388–91 = *Prog.* III.lv.7–11 (some alt.).   391–3 =
Prog. III.lviii.3–5.   393–4 not *Prog.*   395–8 = *Prog.* III.lviii.7–12 (some restatement).
398–400 not *Prog.*   400–3 = *Prog.* III.lx.2–6.   403–5 not *Prog.* (except quotation of
I *Cor.* = *Prog.* III.lxi.9–10).   405–11 = *Prog.* III.lxi–lxii (largely restated).

Bibliography

NOTE Editions are listed under editors, but cross-reference is provided for major sources (Ælfric, Anonymous Sermons, Wulfstan). For abbreviations, see the list at pp. xi–xii above. No effort is made to list here the many Latin texts cited in passing from *PL*, *CCL*, *MGH*, etc. References to medieval authors and manuscripts are to be found in the Index.

Ackerman, Robert W. '*The Debate of the Body and the Soul* and Parochial Christianity.' *Speculum*, 37 (1962), 541–65

Adams, Eleanor N. *Old English Scholarship in England from 1566–1800*. New Haven: Yale Studies in English, 55, 1917

Ælfric, Abbot of Eynsham. For major editions, see under Bateson, Crawford, Fehr, Needham, Pope, Skeat, Thorpe, Winterbottom

Albert, F.R. *Die Geschichte der Predigt in Deutschland bis Luther*. 3 vols. Gütersloh, 1892–96

Alger, William Rounesville. *The Destiny of the Soul: A Critical History of the Doctrine of a Future Life*. 10th ed., rev. Boston, 1880

Altaner, Berthold. *Patrologie*. 5th ed. Freiburg, 1958

Anderson, G.K. *The Literature of the Anglo-Saxons*. Rev. ed. Princeton, 1966

Andrieu, Michel, ed. *Les* Ordines Romani *du Haut Moyen Age*. 5 vols. Spicilegium Sacrum Lovaniense, Études et Documents, fasc. 11, 23, 24, 28, 29. Louvain, 1931–61

An Anglo-Saxon Dictionary. Comp. Joseph Bosworth. Supplement by T.N. Toller. 2 vols. 1882–1921; rpt. Oxford, 1954

Anglo-Saxon England, 1– . Ed. Peter Clemoes. Cambridge, 1972, sqq.

Anonymous Old English Sermons. For editions, see under Assmann, Belfour, Fada, Förster (*Vercelli*), Healey, Morris (*Blickling*), Warner

Ariès, Philippe. *Western Attitudes toward Death: From the Middle Ages to the Present.* Trans. Patricia M. Ranum. Baltimore, 1974

Assmann, Bruno, ed. *Angelsächsische Homilien und Heiligenleben.* Bibliothek der angelsächsischen Prosa, 3. 1889; rpt. with a Supplementary Introduction by Peter Clemoes. Darmstadt, 1964

Auerbach, Erich. *Literary Language and Its Public in Late Latin Antiquity and in the Middle Ages.* Trans. Ralph Manheim. Bollingen Series, 74. New York, 1965

Bäumer, Suitbert. *Histoire du Bréviaire.* Trans. Réginald Viron. 2 vols. Paris, 1905

Baker, Derek. '*Vir Dei*: Secular Sanctity in the Early Tenth Century.' *Popular Belief and Practice: Papers Read at the Ninth Summer and the Tenth Winter Meeting of the Ecclesiastical History Society.* Ed. G.D. Cuming and Derek Baker. Cambridge, 1972, pp. 41–53

Baldwin, Charles Sears. *Medieval Rhetoric and Poetic (to 1400).* 1928; rpt. Gloucester, Mass., 1959

Barlow, Frank. *Edward the Confessor.* London, 1970

– *The English Church, 1000–1066: A Constitutional History.* London, 1963

– et al. *Leofric of Exeter: Essays in Commemoration of the Foundation of Exeter Cathedral Library in A.D. 1072.* Exeter, 1972

– ed. *Vita Ædwardi Regis qui apud Westmonasterium requiescit: The Life of King Edward who Rests at Westminster, Attributed to a Monk of St Bertin.* Medieval Texts. London, 1962

Barré, Henri. 'L'Homiliaire Carolingien de Mondsee.' *RB*, 71 (1961), 71–107

– *Les Homéliaires Carolingiens de l'École d'Auxerre: Authenticité – Inventaire – Tableaux Comparatifs – Initia.* Studi e Testi, 255. Vatican, 1962

Bateson, Mary, ed. *Excerpta ex Institutionibus Monasticis Aethelwoldi Episcopi Wintoniensis compilata in Usum Fratrum Egneshamnensium per Aelfricum Abbatem.* Appendix VII in *Compotus Rolls of the Obedientiaries of St Swithun's Priory, Winchester.* Ed. G.W. Kitchin. London: Hampshire Record Society, 1892, pp. 173–98

– 'Rules for Monks and Secular Canons after the Revival under King Edgar.' *EHR*, 9 (1894), 690–708

– 'A Worcester Cathedral Book of Ecclesiastical Collections, Made ca. 1000 A.D.' *EHR*, 10 (1895), 712–31

Batiffol, Pierre. *Histoire du Bréviaire Romain.* 3rd ed. Bibliothèque d'Histoire religieuse. Paris, 1911

Beck, G.J. *The Pastoral Care of Souls During the Sixth Century.* Analecta Gregoriana, 51. Rome, 1950

Becker, Ernest J. *A Contribution to the Comparative Study of Medieval Visions of Heaven and Hell ...* Diss. Baltimore: Johns Hopkins, 1899

Becker, Gustavus. *Catalogi Bibliothecarum Antiqui*. Bonn, 1885

Belfour, A.O., ed. *Twelfth-Century Homilies in MS Bodley 343*. Part I, Text and Translation. E.E.T.S., O.S., 137. London, 1909

Bennett, J.A.W., and G.V. Smithers, eds. *Early Middle English Verse and Prose*. Oxford, 1966

Berlière, U. 'Le Prône dans la Liturgie.' *RB*, 7 (1890), 97–104, 145–51, 241–6

Bethurum, Dorothy. 'Archbishop Wulfstan's Commonplace Book.' *PMLA*, 57 (1942), 916–29

– 'The Connection of the Katherine Group with Old English Prose.' *JEGP*, 34 (1935), 553–64

– 'Episcopal Magnificence in the Eleventh Century.' *Studies in Old English Literature in Honour of Arthur G. Brodeur*. Ed. Stanley B. Greenfield. Eugene, Oregon, 1963, pp. 162–70

– 'The Form of Ælfric's *Lives of Saints*.' *SP*, 29 (1932), 515–33

– ed. *The Homilies of Wulfstan*. Oxford, 1952

– [Loomis]. '*Regnum* and *Sacerdotium* in the Eleventh Century.' *England before the Conquest: Studies ... Presented to Dorothy Whitelock*. Ed. Peter Clemoes and Kathleen Hughes. Cambridge, 1971, pp. 129–45

– [Loomis]. Review of *Wulfstan's Canons of Edgar*, ed. Roger Fowler. *MÆ*, 43 (1974), 151–5

– 'Wulfstan.' *Continuations and Beginnings*. Ed. Eric Gerald Stanley. London, 1966, pp. 210–46

Biddle, Martin. '*Felix urbs Winthonia*: Winchester in the Age of Monastic Reform.' *Tenth-Century Studies: Essays in Commemoration of the Council of Winchester and Regularis Concordia*. Ed. David Parsons. Chichester, 1975, pp. 123–40

Bischoff, Bernhard. 'Wendepunkte in der Geschichte der lateinischen Exegese im Frühmittelalter.' *Sacris Erudiri*, 6 (1954), 189–281

Bishop, Edmund. *Liturgica Historica: Papers on the Liturgy and Religious Life of the Western Church*. Oxford, 1918

Bishop, T.A.M. *English Caroline Minuscule*. Oxford Palaeographical Handbooks. Oxford, 1971

Blake, E.O., ed. *Liber Eliensis*. Royal Historical Society, Camden, 3rd Series, 93. London, 1962

Blake, N.F., ed. *The Phoenix*. Old and Middle English Texts. Manchester, 1964

Boase, T.S.R. *Death in the Middle Ages: Mortality, Judgment, and Remembrance*. New York, 1972

Bologna, Centro di Documentazione, Istituto per le Scienze Religiose, ed. *Conciliorum Oecumenicorum Decreta*. Comp. Joseph Albergio et al. Basel, 1962

Bolton, W.F. *A History of Anglo-Latin Literature*, 597–1066. Vol. 1. Princeton, 1967

Bossuet, W. *The Antichrist Legend: A Chapter in Christian and Jewish Folklore*. Trans. A.H. Keane. London, 1896

Braekmann, W. 'Ælfric's Old English Homily "De Doctrina Apostolica": An Edition.' *Studia Germanica Gandensia*, 5 (1963), 141–73

Brilioth, Yngve. *A Brief History of Preaching*. Trans. Karl E. Mattson, 1945. Philadelphia, 1965

Brown, Peter. *Augustine of Hippo: A Biography*. Berkeley, 1967

Burlin, Robert B., and Edward B. Irving, Jr., eds. *Old English Studies in Honour of John C. Pope*. Toronto, 1974

Burr, G.L. 'The Year 1000 and the Antecedents of the Crusades.' *American Historical Review*, 6 (1901), 429–31

Campbell, Alistair, ed. *Chronicon Æthelweardi: The Chronicle of Æthelweard*. Medieval Texts. London, 1962

– ed. *Encomium Emmae Reginae*. Royal Historical Society, Camden, 3rd Series, 72. London, 1949

Cameron, Angus F. 'Middle English in Old English Manuscripts.' *Chaucer and Middle English Studies in Honour of Rossell Hope Robbins*. Ed. Beryl Rowland. London, 1974, pp. 218–29

Chadwick, Nora K. *Celt and Saxon: Studies in the Early British Border*. Cambridge, 1963

Chambers, R.W. 'On the Continuity of English Prose from Alfred to More and His School.' *Nicholas Harpsfield's Life of Sir Thomas More*. Ed. E.V. Hitchcock and R.W. Chambers, E.E.T.S., O.S., 191. London, 1932. [rpt. separately as E.E.T.S., O.S., 191ᴬ; London 1966]

– See *Exeter Book*

Charland, Th.-M. *Artes Praedicandi: Contribution à l'Histoire de la Rhétorique au Moyen Age*. Publications de l'Institut d'Études Médiévales d'Ottawa, 7. Paris and Ottawa, 1936

Chickering, Howell D., Jr. 'Some Contexts of Bede's *Death-Song*.' *PMLA*, 91 (1976), 91–100

Clemoes, Peter A.M. 'Ælfric.' *Continuations and Beginnings*. Ed. Eric Gerald Stanley. London, 1966, pp. 176–209

– 'The Chronology of Ælfric's Works.' *The Anglo-Saxons: Studies in Some Aspects of Their History and Culture Presented to Bruce Dickins*. Ed. Clemoes. London, 1959, pp. 212–47

– 'Late Old English Literature.' *Tenth-Century Studies: Essays in Commemoration of the Millennium of the Council of Winchester and Regularis Concordia*. Ed. David Parsons. Chichester, 1975, pp. 102–14

– *Liturgical Influence on Punctuation in Late Old English and Early Middle English Manuscripts.* University of Cambridge, Department of Anglo-Saxon, Occasional Papers, 1. Cambridge, 1957

– '*Mens absentia cogitans* in *The Seafarer* and *The Wanderer.*' *Medieval Literature and Civilization: Studies in Memory of G.N. Garmonsway.* Ed. D.A. Pearsall and R.A. Waldron. London, 1969, pp. 62–77

– 'The Old English Benedictine Office, Corpus Christi College, Cambridge, MS 190, and the Relations between Ælfric and Wulfstan: A Reconsideration.' *Anglia,* 78 (1960), 265–83

– Review of *The Homilies of Wulfstan,* ed. Dorothy Bethurum. *MLR,* 54 (1959), 81–2

– *Rhythm and Cosmic Order in Old English Christian Literature.* An Inaugural Lecture. Cambridge, 1970

Clemoes, Peter A.M., and Rowland L. Collins. 'The Common Origin of Ælfric Fragments at New Haven, Oxford, Cambridge, and Bloomington.' *Old English Studies in Honour of John C. Pope.* Ed. Robert B. Burlin and Edward B. Irving, Jr. Toronto, 1974, pp. 285–326

Clemoes, Peter A.M., and Kathleen Hughes, eds. *England Before the Conquest: Studies in Primary Sources Presented to Dorothy Whitelock.* Cambridge, 1971

– See also *Anglo-Saxon England,* Assmann, Eliason, Dodwell, Fehr.

Clark, Cecily. 'Ælfric and Abbo.' *ES,* 49 (1968), 30–6

Clercq, Carlo de. *La Législation religieuse franque de Clovis à Charlemagne: Études sur les Actes des Conciles et les Capitulaires, les Statuts diocésains et les Règles monastiques.* 2 vols. I, Université de Louvain, Receuil de Travaux publiés par les Membres des Conférences d'Histoire et de Philologie, 2nd Ser., 38, Paris, 1936; II, Anvers, 1958

Colgrave, Bertram, and R.A.B. Mynors, eds. *Bede's Ecclesiastical History of the English People.* Oxford Medieval Texts. Oxford, 1969

Collins, Rowland L. See Clemoes.

Cook, Paul Mary, SND. 'Ælfric's *Catholic Homilies* Considered in Relation to the Rhetorical Theory Enunciated in St Augustine's *De Doctrina Christiana.*' Diss. Oxford, 1967

Cowdrey, H.E.J. *The Cluniacs and the Gregorian Reform.* Oxford, 1970

Crawford, S.J., ed. *Byrhtferth's Manual.* E.E.T.S., O.S., 177. 1929; rpt. London, 1966

– ed. *The Old English Version of the Heptateuch, Ælfric's Treatise on the Old and New Testament and His Preface to Genesis* ... E.E.T.S., O.S., 160. 1922; rpt. with two additional texts ed. by N.R. Ker. London, 1969

Cross, J.E. 'Ælfric and the Mediaeval Homiliary – Objection and Contribution.' Regiae Societatis Humaniorum Litterarum Lundensis, *Scripta Minora,* No. 4 (1961–62)

Cross, J.E. 'Ælfric – Mainly on Memory and Creative Method in Two *Catholic Homilies.' SN*, 41 (1969), 135–55
– 'Aspects of Microcosm and Macrocosm in Old English Literature.' *Comparative Literature*, 14 (1962), 1–22
– 'The Conception of the Old English *Phoenix.' Old English Poetry: Fifteen Essays*. Ed. Robert P. Creed. Providence, 1967, pp. 129–52
– 'Gregory, *Blickling Homily* x, and Ælfric's *Passio S. Mauricii* on the World's Youth and Age.' *NM*, 66 (1965), 327–30
– 'The Literate Anglo-Saxon – on Sources and Disseminations.' Gollancz Lecture. *PBA*, 58 (1972), 67–100
– 'More Sources for Two of Ælfric's *Catholic Homilies,' Anglia*, 86 (1968), 59–78
– 'On the Blickling Homily for Ascension Day (No. xi).' *NM*, 70 (1969), 228–40
– 'Source and Analysis of Some Ælfrician Passages.' *NM*, 72 (1971), 446–53
– '"Ubi Sunt" Passages in Old English.' Vetenskaps-Societetens i Lund, Årsbok (1956), pp. 23–44
Cross, J.E., and S.I. Tucker. 'Allegorical Tradition and the Old English *Exodus.' Neophilologus*, 44 (1960), 112–17
Cruel, R. *Geschichte der deutschen Predigt im Mittelalter*. Detmold, 1897
Curtius, Ernst R. *European Literature and the Latin Middle Ages*. Trans. Willard R. Trask. Bollingen Series, 36. New York, 1953
Dalbey, Marcia A. 'Hortatory Tone in the Blickling Homilies: Two Adaptations of Caesarius.' *NM*, 70 (1969), 641–58
Darlington, Reginald R. 'Ecclesiastical Reform in the Late Old English Period.' *EHR*, 51 (1936), 385–428
– ed. *The Vita Wulfstani of William of Malmesbury*. Royal Historical Society, Camden, 3rd Series, 40. London, 1928
Dauphin, H. 'Le Renouveau Monastique en Angleterre au xe Siècle et ses Rapports avec la Réforme de Saint Gérard de Brogne' [with a response by Eric John]. *RB*, 70 (1960), 177–203
Day, Virginia. 'The Influence of Catechetical *narratio* on Old English and Some Other Medieval Literature.' *ASE*, 3 (1974), 51–61
Deanesly, Margaret. *The Pre-Conquest Church in England*. An Ecclesiastical History of England, ed. J.C. Dickinson, 1. New York, 1961
– *Sidelights on the Anglo-Saxon Church*. London, 1962
Deering, Waller. *The Anglo-Saxon Poets on the Judgment Day*. Diss. Leipzig. Halle, 1890
Delage, Marie-José, ed. *Césaire d'Arles, Sermons au Peuple*. Sources Chrétiennes, 175. Paris, 1971
Devailly, Guy. 'La Pastorale en Gaule au ixe Siècle.' *Revue d'Histoire de l'Église de France*, 59 (1973), 23–54

Dickins, Bruce. See Fox

Dictionnaire d'Archéologie chrétienne et de Liturgie. Comp. Ferand Cabrol and Henri Leclercq. 15 vols. in 30 parts. Paris, 1924–53

Dictionnaire de Théologie catholique. Comp. A. Vacant and E. Mangenot. 15 vols. Paris, 1909–50

Dietrich, Eduard. 'Abt Aelfrik zur Literatur-Geschichte der angelsächsischen Kirche.' *ZHT*, 25 (1885), 487–594; 26 (1856), 163–256

Dix, Gregory. 'The Ministry in the Early Church.' *The Apostolic Ministry: Essays on the History and the Doctrine of Episcopacy.* Ed. Kenneth E. Kirk. London, 1946

– *The Shape of the Liturgy.* 2nd ed. London, 1945

Dodwell, C.R., and Peter Clemoes, eds. *The Old English Illustrated Hexateuch: British Museum Cotton Claudius B. iv.* E.E.M.F., 18. Copenhagen, 1974

Dronke, Peter. *Poetic Individuality in the Middle Ages: New Departures in Poetry 1000–1150.* Oxford, 1970

Dubois, Marguerite-Marie. *Ælfric: Sermonnaire, Docteur et Grammarien: Contribution à l'Étude de la Vie et de l'Action bénédictine en Angleterre au Xe Siècle.* Paris, 1943

Duchesne, L. *Christian Worship, Its Origins and Evolution: A Study of the Latin Liturgy to the Time of Charlemagne.* Trans. M.L. McClure. 5th ed. London, 1920

Duckett, Eleanor Shipley. *Alcuin, Friend of Charlemagne: His World and His Work.* New York, 1951

– *Carolingian Portraits: A Study in the Ninth Century.* Ann Arbor, 1962

– *Saint Dunstan of Canterbury: A Study of Monastic Reform in the Tenth Century.* London, 1955

Dudden, F. Homes. *Gregory the Great: His Place in History and Thought.* 2 vols. London, 1905

Dudley, Louise. 'An Early Homily on the "Body and Soul" Theme.' *JEGP*, 8 (1909), 225–53

Dumville, D.N. 'Biblical Apocrypha and the Early Irish: A Preliminary Investigation.' *Proceedings of the Royal Irish Academy*, 73C (1973), 299–338

Dunning, T.P., and Bliss, A.J., eds. *The Wanderer.* Methuen's Old English Library. London, 1969

Eisenhofer, Ludwig. *Handbuch der katholischen Liturgik.* 2 vols. [A revision of Valentin Thalhofer's earlier work.] Freiburg, 1933

Eliason, Norman, and Peter Clemoes, eds. *Ælfric's First Series of Catholic Homilies: British Museum MS Royal 7. C. xii.* E.E.M.F., 13. Copenhagen, 1966

Ellard, Gerald. *Master Alcuin, Liturgist: A Partner of Our Piety.* Chicago, 1956

Erb, Ewald. *Geschichte der deutschen Literatur von den Anfängen bis 1160.* Vol. i.1 of *Geschichte der deutschen Literature.* Ed. Klaus Gysi et al. Berlin, 1965

Ericson, Jon L. 'The Readings of Folios 77 and 86 of the Vercelli Codex.' *Manuscripta,* 16 (1972), 14–23

Étaix, Raymond. 'Le Prologue du Sermonnaire d'Alain de Farfa.' *Scriptorium,* 18 (1964), 3–10

Exeter Book of Old English Poetry, The [Facsimile]. Introductory chapters by R.W. Chambers, Max Förster, and Robin Flower. London, 1933

Fadda, Anna Maria Luiselli, ed. '"De descensu Christi ad inferos": una inedita Omelia anglosassone.' *Studi Medievali,* 3rd Ser., 13.2 (1972), 989–1011

Fehr, Bernhard, ed. *Die Hirtenbriefe Ælfrics* ... Bibliothek der angelsächsischen Prosa, 9. 1914; rpt. with supplement to introduction by Peter Clemoes. Darmstadt, 1966

Flower, Robin. See *Exeter Book*

Förster, Max. 'Altenglische Predigtquellen, i.' *Archiv,* 116 (1906), 308–10

– 'Der Inhalt der altenglischen Handschrift Vespasianus D. xiv.' *Englische Studien,* 54 (1920), 46–68

– ed. *Il Codice Vercellese con Omelie e Poesie in Lingua Anglosassone* [Facsimile]. Rome, 1913

– 'Die liturgische Bedeutung von ae. *traht.*' *Beiblatt zur Anglia,* 53 (1942), 180–4

– 'Der Vercelli-Codex cxvii nebst Abdruck einiger altenglischer Homilien der Handschrift.' *Studien zur Englischen Philologie,* 50 (1913), 20–179

– ed. *Die Vercelli-Homilien zum ersten Male Herausgegeben,* i. Hälfte. Bibliothek der angelsächsischen Prosa, 12. 1932; rpt. Darmstadt, 1964

– 'Die Weltzeitalter bei den Angelsächsen.' *Neusprachliche Studien: Festgabe Karl Luick. Die neueren Sprachen,* Beiheft 6 (1925), 183–203

– Über die Quellen von Ælfrics exegetischen *Homiliae Catholicae.*' *Anglia,* 16 (1894), 1–61

– '*Über die Quellen von Ælfrics Homiliae Catholicae: 1 Legenden.* Inaugural Diss. Berlin, 1892

– *Zur Geschichte der Reliquienkultus in Altengland.* Sitzungsberichte der Bayerischen Akademie der Wissenschaften, Philosophische-Historische Abteilung, 1943, Heft 8. Munich, 1943

– See also *Exeter Book*

Fowler, Roger. 'Some Stylistic Features of the *Sermo Lupi.*' *JEGP,* 65 (1966), 1–18

– ed. *Wulfstan's Canons of Edgar.* E.E.T.S., 266. London, 1972

Fox, Cyril, and Bruce Dickins, eds. *The Early Cultures of North-West Europe (H.M. Chadwick Memorial Studies).* Cambridge, 1950

Frere, W.H., ed. *The Leofric Collectar Compared with the Collectar of St Wulfstan* ... 2 vols. Henry Bradshaw Society, 45, 56. London, 1914–21

Froom, Leroy Edwin. *The Prophetic Faith of Our Fathers: The Historical Development of Prophetic Interpretation.* Vol. 1. Washington, 1946

Funke, Otto. 'Some Remarks on Wulfstan's Prose Rhythm.' *ES*, 43 (1962), 311–18

– 'Studien zur alliterierenden und rhythmisierenden Prosa in der ältern altenglischen Homiletik.' *Anglia*, 80 (1962), 9–36

Gaiffier, B. de. 'L'Homiliaire-Légendier de Valère (Sion, Suisse).' *Analecta Bollandiana*, 73 (1955), 119–39

Gamber, Klaus. 'Die fränkische Anhang zum Gregorianum im Licht eines Fragments aus dem Anfang des 9. Jh.' *Sacris Erudiri*, 21 (1972–73), 267–89

Gatch, Milton McC. *Death: Meaning and Mortality in Christian Thought and Contemporary Culture.* New York, 1969

– 'Eschatology in the Anonymous Old English Homilies.' *Traditio*, 21 (1965), 117–65

– 'The Fourth Dialogue of Gregory the Great: Some Problems of Interpretation.' *Studia Patristica*, 10 (*Texte und Untersuchungen zur Geschichte der altchristlichen Literatur*, 107; 1970), 77–83

– 'MS Boulogne-sur-Mer 63 and Ælfric's First Series of *Catholic Homilies*,' *JEGP*, 65 (1966), 482–90

– 'Noah's Raven in *Genesis A* and the Illustrated Old English Hexateuch.' *Gesta*, 14 (1975), 3–15

– 'Some Theological Reflections on Death from the Early Church Through the Reformation.' *Perspectives on Death.* Ed. Liston O. Mills. New York, 1969, pp. 99–136

– 'Two Uses of Apocrypha in Old English Homilies.' *Church History*, 33 (1964), 379–91

Gaudemet, Jean. 'La Paroise au Moyen Age: État des Questions.' *Revue d'Histoire de l'Église de France*, 59 (1973), 5–21

Gee, Henry, and William John Hardy, trans. *Documents Illustrative of English Church History.* London, 1896

Gem, Harvey S. *An Anglo-Saxon Abbot: Ælfric of Eynsham.* Edinburgh, 1912

Gerould, Gordon Hall. 'Abbot Ælfric's Rhythmic Prose.' *MP*, 22 (1925), 353–66

Gilson, Étienne. *Les Idées et les Lettres.* 2nd ed. Paris, 1955

Glossarium Mediae et Infimae Latinitatis. Comp. C.D. Du Cange; rev. G.A.L. Henschel. 7 vols. Paris, 1840–50

Gneuss, Helmut. 'Englands Bibliotheken im Mittelalter und ihr Untergang.' *Festschrift für Walter Hübner.* Ed. Dieter Riesner and Helmut Gneuss. Berlin, 1964, pp. 91–121

Gneuss, Helmut. 'The Origin of Standard Old English and Æthelwold's School at Winchester.' *ASE*, 1 (1972), 63–83

– Review of *Three Lives of English Saints*, ed. Michael Winterbottom. *N&Q*, 218 (1973), 479–80

– See also Zupitza

Göbl, Peter. *Geschichte der Katechese im Abendlande vom Verfalle des Katechumenats bis zum Ende des Mittelalters*. Kempten, 1880

Godden, M.R. 'The Development of Ælfric's Second Series of *Catholic Homilies*.' *ES*, 54 (1973), 209–16

– 'Old English Composite Homilies from Winchester.' *ASE*, 4 (1975), 57–65

– 'An Old English Penitential Motif.' *ASE*, 2 (1973), 221–39

– 'The Sources for Ælfric's Homily on St Gregory.' *Anglia*, 86 (1968), 79–98

– See also White

Godfrey, John. *The Church in Anglo-Saxon England*. Cambridge, 1962

Gordon, I.L., ed. *The Seafarer*. Methuen's Old English Library. London, 1960

Grau, Gustav. *Quellen und Verwandtschaften der älteren germanischen Darstellungen der Jüngsten Gerichtes*. Studien zur Englischen Philologie, 31. Halle, 1908

Greenfield, Stanley B. *A Critical History of Old English Literature*. New York, 1965

Grégoire, Réginald. *Les Homéliaires du Moyen Age: Inventaire et Analyse des Manuscrits*. Rerum Ecclesiasticarum Documenta, Series Maior: Fontes, 6. Rome, 1966

Gretsch, Mechthild. 'Æthelwold's Translation of the *Regula Sancti Benedicti* and Its Latin Exemplar.' *ASE*, 3 (1974), 125–51

– *Die Regula Sancti Benedicti in England*. Münchener Universitäts-Schriften, Texte und Untersuchungen zur englischen Philologie, 2. Munich, 1973

Grierson, Philip. 'The Relations between England and Flanders before the Norman Conquest.' *TRHS*, 4th Ser., 23 (1941), 71–112

Haddan, Arthur West, and William Stubbs, eds. *Councils and Ecclesiastical Documents Relating to Great Britain and Ireland*. Vol. 3. Oxford, 1871.

Hallinger, Kassius. *Gorze-Kluny: Studien zu den monastischen Lebensformen und Gegensätzen im Hochmittelalter*. 2 vols. Studia Anselmiana: Philosophica, Theologica, 22, 25. Rome, 1951–52

Halvorson, Nelius O. *Doctrinal Terms in Ælfric's Homilies*. University of Iowa, Humanistic Studies, 5.1. Iowa City, 1932

Handley, Rima. 'British Museum MS Cotton Vespasian D. xiv.' *N&Q*, 219 (1974), 243–50

Hanssens, Ioanne Michaele, ed. *Amalarii Episcopi Opera Liturgica Omnia*. 3 vols. Studi e Testi, 138–40. Vatican, 1948–50

Harlow, C.G. 'Punctuation in Some Manuscripts of Ælfric.' *RES*, N.S. 10 (1959), 1–19

Hart, Cyril. 'Byrhtferth and His Manual.' *MÆ*, 41 (1972), 95–109

Healey, Antonette di Paolo. 'The Vision of St Paul.' Diss. Toronto, 1973

Heist, William W. *The Fifteen Signs before Doomsday*. East Lansing, Mich., 1952

Hill, Thomas D. 'Notes on the Imagery and Structure of the Old English "Christ I."' *N&Q*, 217 (1972), 84–9

Hillgarth, J.N. 'El *Prognosticum Futuri Saeculi* de San Julián de Toledo.' *Analecta Sacra Tarraconensia*, 30 (1957), 5–61

– 'St Julian of Toledo in the Middle Ages.' *Journal of the Warburg and Courtauld Institutes*, 21 (1958), 7–26

Hosp, Eduardo. 'Il Sermonario di Alano di Farfa.' *Ephemerides Liturgicae*, 50 (1936), 375–83; 51 (1937), 210–41

Huber, M. *Die Wanderlegende von den Siebenschläfern: Eine literargeschichtliche Untersuchung*. Leipzig, 1910

Hughes, Anselm, ed. *The Portiforium of Saint Wulstan* (*Corpus Christi College, Cambridge, MS 391*). 2 vols. Henry Bradshaw Society, 89 (1956), 90 (1957). Leighton-Buzzard, 1958–60

Hughes, Kathleen. 'The Changing Theory and Practice of Irish Pilgrimage.' *Journal of Ecclesiastical History*, 11 (1960), 143–51

– *Early Christian Ireland: Introduction to the Sources*. The Sources of History: Studies in the Uses of Historical Evidence. London, 1972

– 'Evidence for Contacts between the Churches of the Irish and English from the Synod of Whitby to the Viking Age.' *England Before the Conquest: Studies ... Presented to Dorothy Whitelock*. Ed. Peter Clemoes and Kathleen Hughes. Cambridge, 1971, pp. 49–67

– See also Clemoes

Hunt, Noreen. *Cluny under St Hugh, 1049–1109*. London, 1967

Hurt, James. *Ælfric*. Twayne's English Authors Series, 131. New York, 1972

Irving, Edward B., Jr. See Burlin

Jalland, T.G. 'The Doctrine of the Parity of Ministers.' *The Apostolic Ministry: Essays on the History and the Doctrine of Episcopacy*. Ed. Kenneth E. Kirk. London, 1946, pp. 305–49

James, Montague Rhodes. *A Descriptive Catalogue of the Manuscripts in the Library of Corpus Christi College, Cambridge*. 2 vols. Cambridge, 1909–11

– Lists of Books formerly in Peterborough Abbey Library.' *Supplement to the Bibliographical Society Transactions*, No. 5 (1926)

– *The Western Manuscripts in the Library of Trinity College, Cambridge: A Descriptive Catalogue*. 4 vols. Cambridge, 1900–4

Jedin, Hubert, and John Dolan. *Handbook of Church History*. Trans. Anselm Biggs. Vol. 3. London, 1969

Jenkins, Claude. 'Bede as Exegete and Theologian.' *Bede: His Life, Times, and Writings*. Ed. A. Hamilton Thompson. Oxford, 1935, pp. 152–200

John, Eric. *Orbis Britanniae and Other Studies*. Studies in Early English History, 4. Leicester, 1966

– See also Dauphin

Jones, Charles W. 'Some Introductory Remarks on Bede's Commentary on Genesis.' *Sacris Erudiri*, 19 (1969–70), 115–98

Jørgensen, Ellen. *Catalogus Codicum Latinorum Medii Aevi Bibliothecae Regiae Hafniensis*. Copenhagen, 1926

Jost, Karl. 'Einige Wulfstantexte und ihre Quellen.' *Anglia*, 56 (1932), 265–315

– ed. *Die 'Institutes of Polity, Civil and Ecclesiastical'*: *ein Werk Erzbischof Wulfstans von York*. Swiss Studies in English, 47. Bern, 1959

– 'Unechte Aelfrictexte.' *Anglia*, 51 (1927), 81–103, 177–219

– *Wulfstanstudien*. Swiss Studies in English, 23. Bern, 1950

Jungmann, Joseph A. *The Mass of the Roman Rite: Its Origins and Development*. Trans. Francis A. Brunner. 2 vols. New York, 1951–55

Kantrowitz, Joanne. 'The Anglo-Saxon *Phoenix* and Tradition.' *PQ*, 43 (1964), 1–13

Kelly, J.N.D. *Early Christian Creeds*. 2nd ed. London, 1960

Kemble, J.M., ed. *Codex Diplomaticus Aevi Saxonici*, III. London, 1845

Kenney, James F. *The Sources for the Early History of Ireland: Ecclesiastical: An Introduction and a Guide*. Rpt. with revisions by Ludwig Bieler. New York, 1966

Ker, N.R. *Catalogue of Manuscripts Containing Anglo-Saxon*. Oxford, 1957

– 'Hemming's Cartulary.' *Studies in Medieval History Presented to Frederick Maurice Powicke*. Ed. R.W. Hunt et al. Oxford, 1948, pp. 49–75

– *Medieval Libraries of Great Britain: A List of Surviving Books*. 2nd ed. Royal Historical Society Guides and Handbooks, 3. London, 1964

– 'Old English Notes Signed "Coleman."' *MÆ*, 18 (1949), 29–31

– 'The Handwriting of Archbishop Wulfstan.' *England Before the Conquest: Studies ... Presented to Dorothy Whitelock*. Ed. Peter Clemoes and Kathleen Hughes. Cambridge, 1971, pp. 315–31

– See also Crawford

Kirby, D.P. *The Making of Early England*. New York, 1968

Klauser, Theodor. *A Short History of the Western Liturgy: An Account and Some Reflections*. Trans. John Halliburton. London, 1969

Kleinclausz, Arthur. *Alcuin*. Annales de l'Université de Lyon, 3rd Ser., 15. Paris, 1948

Knowles, David. *The Monastic Order in England: A History of Its Development from the Times of St Dunstan to the Fourth Lateran Council: 940–1216.* 2nd ed. Cambridge, 1963

Konrad, Robert. *De Ortu et Tempore Antichristi: Antichristvorstellung und Geschichtsbild des Abtes Adso von Montier-en-Der.* Münchener historische Studien, Abteilung mittelalterliche Geschichte, 1. Kallmünz, 1964

Krapp, George Philip, and Elliott van Kirk Dobbie, eds. *The Exeter Book.* The Anglo-Saxon Poetic Records, vol. 3. New York, 1936

Kuhn, Sherman M. 'Cursus in Old English: Rhetorical Ornament or Linguistic Phenomenon?' *Speculum*, 47 (1972), 188–206

– 'Was Ælfric a Poet?' *PQ*, 52 (1973), 643–62

Labriolle, Pierre de. *Histoire de la Littérature Latine Chrétienne.* 2 vols. 3rd ed. rev. G. Bardy. Paris, 1947

Labriolle, Pierre de, et al., eds. *De la Mort de Théodose à l'Élection de Grégoire le Grand. Histoire de l'Église depuis les Origines jusqu'à nos Jours.* Ed. Augustin Fliche and Victor Martin, vol. 4. Paris, 1948

Laistner, M.L.W. *Thought and Letters in Western Europe, A.D. 500 to 900.* 2nd ed. Ithaca, N.Y., 1957

Lampe, G.W.H., ed. *The Cambridge History of the Bible.* Vol. 2 [The West from the Fathers to the Reformation]. Cambridge, 1969

Lapidge, Michael. 'The Hermeneutic Style in Tenth-Century Anglo-Latin Literature.' *ASE*, 4 (1975), 67–111

– 'Three Latin Poems from Æthelwold's School at Winchester.' *ASE*, 1 (1972), 85–137

Leclercq, Jean. *L'Amour des Lettres et le Désir de Dieu: Initiation aux Auteurs Monastiques du Moyen Age.* Paris, 1957 [*The Love of Learning and the Desire for God.* Trans. Catharine Misrahi. New York, 1962]

– 'Le Florilège d'Abbon de Saint-Germain.' *Revue du Moyen Age Latin*, 3 (1947), 113–40

– 'Les Méditations d'un Moine au XIIᵉ Siècle.' *Revue Mabillon*, 34 (1944), 1–19

– 'Prédicateurs bénédictins aux XIᵉ et XIIᵉ Siècles.' *Revue Mabillon*, 33 (1943), 48–73

– 'Recherches sur d'anciens Sermons monastiques.' *Revue Mabillon*, 36 (1946), 1–14

Levison, Wilhelm. *England and the Continent in the Eighth Century.* The Ford Lectures, 1943. Oxford, 1956

Lingard, John. *The History and Antiquities of the Anglo-Saxon Church.* 2 vols. London, 1845

Linsenmayer, Anton. *Geschichte der Predigt in Deutschland von Karl dem Grossen bis zum Ausgange des vierzehnten Jahrhunderts.* 1886; rpt. Frankfurt, 1969

Lipp, Frances Randall. 'Ælfric's Old English Prose Style.' *SP*, 66 (1969), 689–718

Lopez, Robert Sabatino. *The Tenth Century: How Dark the Dark Ages?* Source Problems in World Civilization. New York, 1959

– 'The Trade of Medieval Europe: The South.' *The Cambridge Economic History of Europe*. Ed. M. Postan and E.E. Rich. Vol. 2. Cambridge, 1952, pp. 257–354

Loomis, Dorothy Bethurum. See Bethurum

Loomis, Grant. 'Further Sources of Ælfric's Saints' Lives.' *Harvard Studies and Notes in Philology and Literature*, 13 (1931), 1–8

Loyn, Henry R., ed. *A Wulfstan Manuscript Containing Institutes, Laws and Homilies: British Museum Cotton Nero A. I.* E.E.M.F., 17. Copenhagen, 1971

MacCulloch, J.A. *The Harrowing of Hell*. Edinburgh, 1930

McIntosh, Angus. 'Wulfstan's Prose.' Gollancz Lecture. *PBA*, 35 (1949), 109–42

MacLean, George Edwin, ed. 'Ælfric's Version of *Alcuini Interrogationes Sigewulfi in Genesin*.' *Anglia*, 6 (1883), 425–73, and 7 (1884), 1–59

McNally, Robert E. *The Bible in the Early Middle Ages*. Woodstock Papers, 4. Westminster, Maryland, 1959

Manitius, Max. *Geschichte der lateinischen Literatur des Mittelalters*. 2 vols. Munich, 1911–23

Mayr-Harting, Henry. *The Coming of Christianity to Anglo-Saxon England*. London, 1972

Mediae Latinitas Lexicon Minus. Comp. J.F. Niermeyer. Leiden, 1960–

Meyvaert, Paul. 'Diversity within Unity, a Gregorian Theme.' *Heythrop Journal*, 4 (1963), 141–62

Ministre de l'Instruction Publique. *Catalogue Général des Manuscrits des Bibliothèques Publiques des Départements*. Vol. 4. Paris, 1872

Mohrmann, Christine. 'Praedicare-Tractare-Sermo: Essai sur la Terminologie de la Prédication Paléochrétienne.' *Maison-Dieu*, 39 (1954), 97–107

Morin, Germain. 'L'Homéliaire d'Alcuin retrouvé.' *RB*, 9 (1892), 491–7

Morris, R., ed. *The Blickling Homilies*. E.E.T.S., O.S. 58, 63, 73. 1874–80; rpt. as one vol. London, 1967

Müller, L.C., ed. *Colectanea Anglo-Saxonica*. Copenhagen, 1835

Murphy, James J., comp. *Medieval Rhetoric: A Select Bibliography*. Toronto Medieval Bibliographies, 3. Toronto, 1971

– *Rhetoric in the Middle Ages: A History of Rhetorical Theory from Saint Augustine to the Renaissance*. Berkeley, 1974

Mynors, R.A.B. See Colgrave

Napier, Arthur S. 'Nachträge zu Cook's *Biblical Quotations in Old English Prose Writers*.' *Archiv*, 101 (1898), 309–24; 102 (1899), 29–42; 207 (1901), 105

– ed. *The Old English Version of the Enlarged Rule of Chrodegang* ... ; *An Old English Rendering of the Capitula of Theodulf: An Interlinear Old English Rendering of Epitome of Benedict of Aniane*. E.E.T.S., O.S., 150. London, 1916

– ed. *Wulfstan: Sammlung der ihm zugeschreibenen Homilien* ... Sammlung englischer Denkmäler in kritischen Ausgaben, 4. 1883; rpt. with a bibliographical supplement by Klaus Ostheeren. Dublin and Zurich, 1967

Napier, Arthur S., and W.H. Stevenson, eds. *The Crawford Collection of Early Charters and Documents Now in the Bodleian Library*. Anecdota Oxoniensa. Oxford, 1895

Needham, G.I., ed. *Ælfric: Lives of Three English Saints*. Methuen's Old English Library. London, 1966

Nichols, Ann Eljenholm. 'Ælfric and the Brief Style.' *JEGP*, 70 (1971), 1–12

– 'Ælfric's Prefaces: Rhetoric and Genre.' *ES*, 49 (1968), 215–23

– '*Awendan*: A Note on Ælfric's Vocabulary.' *JEGP*, 63 (1964), 7–13

Niebergall, Alfred. 'Die Geschichte der christlichen Predigt.' *Leiturgia: Handbuch des evangelischen Gottesdienstes*. Ed. Karl Ferdinand Müller and Walter Blankenburg. Vol. 2. Kassel, 1955, pp. 181–353

Ogilvy, J.D.A. *Books Known to the English, 597–1066*. Mediaeval Academy of America, Publication No. 76. Cambridge, Mass., 1967

Os, Arnold Barel van. *Religious Visions: The Development of the Eschatological Elements in Medieval English Religious Literature*. Amsterdam, 1932

Ostheeren, Klaus. See Napier

Ott, J.H. *Über die Quellen der Heiligenleben in Ælfrics Lives of Saints I*. Inaugural Diss. Halle, 1892

Parsons, David, ed. *Tenth-Century Studies: Essays in Commemoration of the Millennium of the Council of Winchester and Regularis Concordia*. Chichester, 1975

Patch, Howard Rollin. *The Other World: According to the Descriptions in Medieval Literature*. Smith College Studies in Modern Languages, N.S. 1. Cambridge, Mass., 1950

Pearsall, D.A., and R.A. Waldron, eds. *Medieval Literature and Civilization: Studies in Memory of G.N. Garmonsway*. London, 1969

Pelikan, Jaroslav. *The Christian Tradition: A History of the Development of Doctrine*. Vol. 1. Chicago, 1971

Petry, Ray C. *Christian Eschatology and Social Thought: A Historical Essay on the Social Implications of Some Selected Aspects in Christian Eschatology to A.D. 1500*. New York, 1956

Pickrel, Paul Murphy. 'Religious Allegory in Medieval England: An Introductory Study Based on the Sermon Before 1250.' Diss. Yale, 1944

Pope, John C. 'Ælfric and the Old English Version of the Ely Privilege.' *England*

Before the Conquest: Studies ... Presented to Dorothy Whitelock. Ed. Peter Clemoes and Kathleen Hughes. Cambridge, 1971, pp. 85–113

- ed. *Homilies of Ælfric: A Supplementary Collection* ... 2 vols. E.E.T.S., 259 and 260. London, 1967–68

- Review of *Ælfric* by James Hurt. *Speculum,* 49 (1974), 344–7

- Review of *The Homilies of Wulfstan,* ed. Dorothy Bethurum. *MLN,* 74 (1959), 338–9

Quadri, Riccardo, ed. *I Collectaneo di Erico di Auxerre.* Spicilegium Friburgense, 2. Freiburg, Switzerland, 1966

Quirk, R.N. 'Winchester Cathedral in the Tenth Century.' *Archaeological Journal,* 114 (1957), 28–68

- 'Winchester New Minster and Its Tenth-Century Tower.' *Journal of the British Archaeological Association,* 3rd Ser., 24 (1961), 16–54

Raine, James, ed. *The Historians of the Church of York and its Archbishops,* I. Rolls Series, 71.1. London, 1879

Rangheri, Maurizio. 'La "Epistola ad Gerbergam reginam de ortu et tempori Antichristi" di Adsone di Montier-en-Der e le sue Fonti.' *Studi Medievali,* 3rd Ser., 14 (1973), 677–732

Rauh, Horst Dieter. *Das Bild des Antichrist im Mittelalter: von Tyconus zum deutschen Symbolismus.* Beiträge zur Geschichte der Philosophie und Theologie des Mittelalters, N.F. 9. Münster, 1973

Raynes, Enid M. 'MS Boulogne-sur-Mer 63 and Ælfric.' *MÆ,* 26 (1957), 65–73

Religion in Geschichte und Gegenwart, Der. Comp. Hans Frhr. von Campenhausen et al. 3rd ed. 7 vols. Tübingen, 1957–65

Rivière, Jean. *Le Dogme de la Rédemption au Début du Moyen Age.* Bibliothèque Thomiste, 19. Paris, 1934

Robertson, J.G. *A History of German Literature.* 4th ed.; rev. by Edna Purdie et al. London, 1962

Rosenthal, Constance L. *The* Vitae Patrum *in Old and Middle English Literature.* Diss. Pennsylvania. Philadelphia, 1936

Rosier, James L., ed. *Philological Essays: Studies in Old and Middle English Language and Literature in Honour of Herbert Dean Meritt.* The Hague, 1970

Roth, Dorothea. *Die mittelalterliche Predigttheorie und das Manuale curatorum des Johann Ulrich Surgant.* Basler Beiträge zur Geschichtswissenschaft, 58. Basel, 1956

Russell, Jeffrey Burton. *Dissent and Reform in the Early Middle Ages.* Berkeley, 1965

Sackur, Ernst, ed. *Sibyllinische Texte und Forschungen.* Halle, 1898

Salmon, Pierre. *L'Office Divin: Histoire de la Formation du Bréviaire.* Lex Orandi, 27. Paris, 1959

Salter, H.E., ed. *The Cartulary of the Abbey of Eynsham*. Vol. 1. Oxford Historical Society, 49. Oxford, 1907

Scheifer, Theodor. *Winfrid-Bonifatius und die christliche Grundlegung Europas*. Freiburg, 1954

Schelp, Hanspeter. 'Die Deutungstradition in Ælfrics *Homiliae Catholicae*.' *Archiv*, 196 (1959–60), 274–95

Schmidt, Roderich. '*Aetates mundi*: Die Weltalter als Gleiderprinzip der Geschichte.' *Zeitschrift für Kirchengeschichte*, 67 (1955–56), 288–317

Schneyer, Johann Baptist. *Geschichte der katholischen Predigt*. Freiburg, 1969

Schubert, Hans von. *Geschichte der christlichen Kirche im Frühmittelalter: Ein Handbuch*. Tübingen, 1921

Scragg, D.G. 'The Compilation of the Vercelli Book.' *ASE*, 2 (1973), 189–207

Seymour, St John D. *Irish Visions of the Other-World: A Contribution to the Study of Medieval Visions*. London, 1930

Seeburg, Reinhold. *Textbook of the History of Doctrines*. Trans. Charles E. Hay. Rpt. Grand Rapids, Mich., 1958

Shepherd, Massey Hamilton, Jr. *The Oxford American Prayer Book Commentary*. New York, 1950

Silverstein, Theodore. *Visio Sancti Pauli: The History of the Apocalypse in Latin together with Nine Texts*. Studies and Documents, 4. Ed. Kirsopp Lake and Silva Lake. London, 1935

Sisam, Kenneth. *Studies in the History of Old English Literature*. Oxford, 1953

Sitwell, Gerald, ed. and trans. *St Odo of Cluny: Being the Life of St Odo of Cluny by John of Salerno and the Life of St Gerald of Aurillac by St Odo*. London, 1958

Skeat, Walter W., ed. *Ælfric's* Lives of Saints, *Being a Set of Sermons on Saints' Days Formerly Observed by the English Church*. 2 vols. E.E.T.S., O.S., 76, 82, 94, 114. 1881–1900; rpt. London, 1966

Smalley, Beryl. *The Study of the Bible in the Middle Ages*. 2nd ed. Indiana: Notre Dame, 1964

Smetana, Cyril L. 'Ælfric and the Early Medieval Homiliary,' *Traditio*, 15 (1959), 163–204

– 'Ælfric and the Homiliary of Haymo of Halberstadt.' *Traditio*, 17 (1961), 457–69

Smithers, G.V. 'The Meaning of *The Seafarer* and *The Wanderer*.' *MÆ*, 26 (1957), 137–53; 28 (1959), 1–22, 99–104

– See also Bennett

Southern, R.W. *The Making of the Middle Ages*. London, 1953.

Stanley, Eric Gerald, ed. *Continuations and Beginnings: Studies in Old English Literature*. London, 1966

Stanley, Eric Gerald. *The Search for Anglo-Saxon Paganism.* Cambridge, 1975

Stenton, F.M. *Anglo-Saxon England.* 2nd ed. The Oxford History of England, 2. Oxford, 1955

Stephens, George, ed. *Tvende Old Engelske Digte.* Copenhagen, 1853

Stephenson, J., ed. *Chronicon Monasterii de Abingdon.* Vol. 2. Rolls Series, 102. London, 1858

Stevenson, W.H. See Napier

Stuart, C.I.J.M. 'Wulfstan's Use of "Leofan Men."' *ES,* 45 (1964), 39–42

Stubbs, William, ed. *Memorials of Saint Dunstan.* Rolls Series, 63. London, 1874
- See also Haddan

Symons, Thomas, ed. *Regularis Concordia Anglicae Nationis Monachorum Sanctimonialumque: The Monastic Agreement of the Monks and Nuns of the English Nation.* Nelson's Medieval Classics. London, 1953
- 'Sources of the *Regularis Concordia.*' *Downside Review,* 59 (1941), 14–36, 143–70, 264–89

Szarmach, Paul E. 'Caesarius of Arles and the Vercelli Homilies.' *Traditio,* 26 (1970), 315–23
- 'Three Versions of the Jonah Story: An Investigation of Narrative Technique in Old English Homilies.' *ASE,* 1 (1972), 183–92
- ed. 'Vercelli Homily xx.' *Mediæval Studies,* 35 (1973), 1–26

Temple, Winifred. 'The Song of the Angelic Hosts.' *Annuale Mediaevale,* 2 (1961), 5–14

Thalhofer, Valentin. See Eisenhofer

Thorpe, Benjamin, ed. *Ancient Laws and Institutes of England* . . . 2 vols. London, 1840
- ed. *The Homilies of the Anglo-Saxon Church: The First Part, Containing the Sermones Catholici or Homilies of Ælfric.* 2 vols. London, 1844–46

Tixéront, J. *L'Ordre et les Ordinations: Étude de Théologie Historique.* 2nd ed. Paris, 1925

Tolhurst, J.B.L. *The Monastic Breviary of Hyde Abbey, Winchester.* Vol. 6 ('Introduction to the English Monastic Breviaries'). Henry Bradshaw Society, 80. London, 1942

Trahern, Joseph B., Jr. 'Amalarius *Be Becnum*: A Fragment of the *Liber Officialis* in Old English,' *Anglia,* 91 (1973), 475–8
- 'Caesarius of Arles and Old English Literature: Some Contributions and a Recapitulation.' *ASE,* 5 (forthcoming, 1976)

Tristram, Hildegard L.C. *Vier altenglische Predigten aus der heterodoxen Tradition.* Diss. Freiburg, 1970

Tucker, S.I. See Cross

Turner, Ralph V. '*Descendit ad Inferos*: Medieval Views on Christ's Descent into

Hell and the Salvation of the Ancient Just.' *Journal of the History of Ideas*, 27 (1966), 173–94

Turville-Petre, Joan. 'Translations of a Lost Penitential Homily.' *Traditio*, 19 (1963), 51–78

Ure, James M., ed. *The Benedictine Office: An Old English Text.* Edinburgh University Publications, Language & Literature, No. 11. Edinburgh, 1957

Vasiliev, A. 'Medieval Ideas of the End of the World: East and West.' *Byzantion*, 16 (1942–43), 462–502

Vleeskruyer, Rudolf, ed. *The Life of St Chad: An Old English Homily.* Amsterdam, 1953

Vogel, Cyrille, and Reinhard Elze, eds. *Le Pontifical Romano-Germanique du dixième Siècle.* Studi e Testi, 226, 227, 269. Vatican, 1963–72

Wadstein, Ernst. *Die eschatologische Ideengruppe: Antichrist – Weltsabbat – Weltende und Weltgericht, in den Hauptmomenten ihrer christlich-mittelalterlichen Gesamtentwicklung.* Leipzig, 1896

Wallace-Hadrill, J.M. *The Long-Haired Kings and Other Studies in Frankish History.* London, 1962

Wanley, Humphrey. *Librorum Vett. Septentrionalium, qui in Anglicae Bibliothecis extant ... Catalogus Historico-Criticus ...* Vol. 2 of George Hickes, *Linguarum Vett. Septentrionalium Thesaurus Grammatico-Criticus et Archaeologicus.* 1705; rpt. Hildesheim, 1970

Warner, Rubie D-N., ed. *Early English Homilies from the Twelfth-Century MS Vespasian D. xiv.* E.E.T.S., O.S., 152. London, 1917

Warren, F.E., ed. *The Leofric Missal as Used in the Cathedral of Exeter ... A.D. 1050–1072 ...* Oxford, 1883

Wasserschleben, F.W.H. *Die Bussordnungen der abendländischen Kirche ...* Halle, 1851

Watkins, Oscar D. *A History of Penance ...* 2 vols. 1920; rpt. New York, 1961

Weismann, Eberhard. 'Die Predigtgottesdienst und die verwandten Formen.' *Leiturgia: Handbuch des evangelischen Gottesdienstes.* Ed. Karl Ferdinand Müller and Walter Blankenburg. Vol. 3. Kassel, 1956, pp. 2–96

West, Phillip J. 'Liturgical Style and Structure in Bede's Homily for the Easter Vigil.' *American Benedictine Review*, 23 (1972), 1–8

Whitbread, L. 'The Old English Poems of the *Benedictine Office* and Some Related Questions.' *Anglia*, 80 (1962), 37–49

White, Caroline L. *Ælfric: A New Study of His Life and Writings.* Yale Studies in English, 2. 1898; rpt. with supplementary bibliography by Malcom Godden. Hamden, Conn., 1974

Whitelock, Dorothy. 'Archbishop Wulfstan, Statesman and Homilist.' *TRHS*, Ser. IV, 24 (1942), 24–45

Whitelock, Dorothy. 'The Authorship of the Account of King Edgar's Establishment of Monasteries.' *Philological Essays: Studies in Old and Middle English Language and Literature in Honour of Herbert Dean Meritt.* Ed. James L. Rosier. The Hague, 1970, pp. 125–36

– *Changing Currents in Anglo-Saxon Studies.* An Inaugural Lecture. Cambridge, 1958

– ed. and trans. *English Historical Documents.* Ed. David C. Douglas. Vol. 1 London, 1955

– 'The Interpretation of *The Seafarer.*' *The Early Cultures of North-West Europe (H.M. Chadwick Memorial Studies).* Ed. Cyril Fox and Bruce Dickins. Cambridge, 1950, pp. 261–72

– ed. *Sermo Lupi ad Anglos.* 3rd ed. Methuen's Old English Library. London, 1963

– ed. *Sweet's Anglo-Saxon Reader in Prose and Verse.* 15th ed. Oxford, 1967

– 'Two Notes on Ælfric and Wulfstan.' *MLR*, 38 (1943), 122–6

– 'Wulfstan and the Laws of Cnut.' *EHR*, 63 (1948), 443–52

– 'Wulfstan at York.' *Franciplegius: Medieval and Linguistic Studies in Honour of Francis Peabody Magoun, Jr.* Ed. Jess B. Bessinger, Jr. and Robert P. Creed. New York, 1965, pp. 214–31

– 'Wulfstan's Authorship of Cnut's Laws.' *EHR*, 70 (1955), 72–85

Wiegand, F. *Das Homiliarium Karls des grossen auf seine ursprünglische Gestalt hin untersucht.* Studien zur Geschichte der Theologie und der Kirche, I.2. Leipzig, 1897

Willard, Rudolph, ed. *The Blickling Homilies.* E.E.M.F., 10. Copenhagen, 1960

– 'The Blickling-Junius Tithing Homily and Caesarius of Arles.' *Philologica: The Malone Anniversary Studies.* Eds. Thomas A. Kirby and Henry Bosley Woolf. Baltimore, 1949, pp. 65–78

– *Two Apocrypha in Old English Homilies.* Beiträge zur englischen Philologie, 30. Leipzig, 1935

Winterbottom, Michael, ed. *Three Lives of English Saints.* Toronto Medieval Latin Texts. Toronto, 1972

– 'Three Lives of Saint Ethelwold.' *MÆ*, 41 (1972), 191–201

Wrenn, C.L. *A Study of Old English Literature.* London, 1967

– 'Some Aspects of Anglo-Saxon Theology.' *Studies in Language, Literature, and Culture of the Middle Ages and Later* [in honour of Rudolph Willard]. Ed. E. Bagby Atwood and Archibald A. Hill. Austin, 1969, pp. 182–9

Wulfstan, Archbishop of York. For major editions, see under Bethurum, Fowler, Jost, Napier, Whitelock.

Zupitza, Julius, ed. *Ælfrics Grammatik und Glossar: Text und Varianten.* Sammlung englischen Denkmäler in kritischen Ausgaben, 1. 1880; rpt. with foreword by Helmut Gneuss. Berlin, 1966

Notes

PART ONE

Chapter 1

1 The standard surveys are M.L.W. Laistner, *Thought and Letters in Western Europe, A.D. 500 to 900*, 2nd ed. (Ithaca, N.Y., 1957), and Max Manitius, *Geschichte der lateinischen Literatur des Mittelalters*, 2 vols. (Munich, 1911–23).

2 Vincent of Lérins, *Commonitorium* II.3. J.D.A. Ogilvy, *Books Known to the English, 597–1066*, Mediaeval Academy of America, Publication No. 76 (Cambridge, Mass., 1967), pp. 257–8, treats the problem of Anglo-Saxon knowledge of Vincent.

3 Beryl Smalley, *The Study of the Bible in the Middle Ages*, 2nd ed. (Notre Dame, Indiana, 1964), pp. 37–8. See also R.W. Southern, *The Making of the Middle Ages* (London, 1953), pp. 170ff.

4 In the case of Ælfric, J.E. Cross has recently drawn attention to a further, complicating factor: retention by memory ('Ælfric – Mainly on Memory and Creative Method in Two *Catholic Homilies*,' *SN*, 41 [1969], pp. 135–55; 'The Literate Anglo-Saxon – on Sources and Disseminations' [Gollancz Lecture], *PBA*, 58 [1972], 67–100).

5 Henri Barré, *Les Homéliaires Carolingiens de l'École d'Auxerre*, Studi e Testi, 225 (Vatican, 1962), p. 6.

6 See J.N.D. Kelly, *Early Christian Creeds*, 2nd ed. (London, 1960), pp. 378–83; J.A. MacCulloch, *The Harrowing of Hell* (Edinburgh, 1930).

7 For an amusing but sympathetic review of the character of the tenth century, see Robert Sabatino Lopez, *The Tenth Century: How Dark the Dark Ages?* Source Problems in World Civilization (New York, 1959).

8 'Some Aspects of Anglo-Saxon Theology,' in *Studies in Language, Literature, and Culture of the Middle Ages and Later* (in honor of Rudolph

Willard), ed. E. Bagby Atwood and Archibald A. Hill (Austin, 1969), pp. 182–9 at 182.

9 For the early history of Anglo-Saxon studies, see Eleanor N. Adams, *Old English Scholarship in England from 1566–1800*, Yale Studies in English, 55 (New Haven, 1917). Later scholarship did not suffer from exactly the same polemical biases, but that it had special axes to grind is apparent from a reading of E.G. Stanley's *The Search for Anglo-Saxon Paganism* (rpt. from *N&Q* 209 [1964] and 210 [1965], Cambridge, 1975). The history of Ælfrician scholarship is summarized by Peter Clemoes, 'Ælfric,' in *Continuations and Beginnings: Studies in Old English Literature*, ed. Eric Gerald Stanley (London, 1966), pp. 179–80.

10 James F. Kenney, *The Sources for the Early History of Ireland: Ecclesiastical: An Introduction and a Guide* (1929; rpt. with revisions by Ludwig Bieler, New York, 1966), p. 733. Kathleen Hughes, *Early Christian Ireland: Introduction to the Sources*, The Sources of History: Studies in the Uses of Historical Evidence (London, 1972), does not consider the homily a prominent early-Irish genre.

11 Often where there is apparent contact between Irish and Old English writings, the English may draw on the same sources rather than descend directly from the Irish. See the comment of J.E. Cross on the relation of *Catéchèses celtiques* and Vercelli Homily ix in *PBA*, 58 (1972), p. 95.

12 J.G. Robertson, *A History of German Literature* (4th ed. rev. by Edna Purdie et al.; London, 1962), pp. 20, 36; Ewald Erb, *Geschichte der deutschen Literatur von den Anfängen bis 1160*, vol. I.1 of *Geschichte der deutschen Literatur*, ed. Klaus Gysi et al. (Berlin, 1965), pp. 240, 242, 396–402.

13 R. Morris, ed., *The Blickling Homilies*, E.E.T.S., O.S., 58, 63, 73 (1874–80; rpt. as one vol., London, 1967); Rudolph Willard, ed., *The Blickling Homilies . . .* , E.E.M.F., 10 (Copenhagen, 1960). The Vercelli Homilies have not all been printed, although Max Förster published an edition of about half of the homiletic items in the ms (*Die Vercelli-Homilien zum ersten Male herausgegeben*, I. Hälfte, Bibliothek der Angelsächsischen Prosa, 12 [1932; rpt. Darmstadt, 1964]), and a facsimile of the ms (*Il Codice Vercellese con Omelie e Poesie in Lingua Anglosassone . . .* [Rome, 1913]). A number of other Vercelli homilies have been published (for information, see Gatch, 'Eschatology in the Anonymous Old English Homilies,' *Traditio*, 21 [1965], 117–65 at 136n and 138–42; a more recent addition is Paul E. Szarmach's ed. of Vercelli Homily xx, *Mediæval Studies*, 35 [1973], 1–26). A new edition of Blickling and a complete edition of Vercelli are in progress.

14 As a guide to the complete scope of homiletic material in Old English, see N.R. Ker, *Catalogue of Manuscripts Containing Anglo-Saxon* [hereafter, Ker, *Catalogue*] (Oxford, 1957), Index, s.v. 'Homiliaries,' 'Homilies.' Many of these pieces are in late mss, but a number seem to derive from collections antedating Blickling and Vercelli. For an example, see Paul E. Szarmach, 'Three Versions of the Jonah Story: An Investigation of Narrative Technique in Old English Homilies,' *ASE*, 1 (1972), 183–92. A number of the unpublished anonymous homilies are now being edited; e.g., Hildegard L.C. Tristram, *Vier altenglische Predigten aus der heterodoxen Tradition* ... , Diss. Freiburg 1970. Comparative study of the homilies will doubtless yield useful observations on forebears - of the surviving mss; see M.R. Godden, 'An Old English Penitential Motif,' *ASE*, 2 (1973), 221–39.

15 'Two Uses of Apocrypha in Old English Homilies,' *Church History*, 33 (1964), 379–91, and the article in *Traditio*, 21, cited in note 13 above. Those articles were originally joined with Part III of this study in a dissertation and should still be read in conjunction with it. It seems undesirable, however, to reprint the articles here, especially as I remain basically satisfied with their argument. Recent studies do, however, make substantial contributions. J.E. Cross, 'On the Blickling Homily for Ascension Day (No. XI),' *NM*, 70 (1969), 228–40 at 233, corrects a misreading on pp. 130–1 of the *Traditio* article; and Marcia A. Dalbey, 'Hortatory Tone in the Blickling Homilies: Two Adaptations of Caesarius,' ibid., pp. 641–58, demonstrates that the hortatory tone of the homilies is generally benevolent and that there was 'a deliberate attempt by the unknown collector to compile a homiliary consistent at all times with his doctrinal beliefs and parenetic [i.e. hortatory] techniques' (p. 642). These articles, had they been available when I wrote, would have led me to closer attention to rhetorical technique and to a rather more careful statement of my conclusion (which I believe still stands) that the anonymous homiletic collections are often self-contradictory. Paul E. Szarmach, 'Caesarius of Arles and the Vercelli Homilies,' *Traditio*, 26 (1970), 315–23, enlarges the contribution of Caesarius to the sources of Vercelli and, in conjunction with Dalbey's paper, may raise questions as to Caesarius' role in the source traditions behind the anonymous homilies. In 'The Compilation of the Vercelli Book,' *ASE*, 2 (1973), 189–207, D.G. Scragg contributes substantially to knowledge of the exemplars of the ms and its provenance. D.N. Dumville's 'Biblical Apocrypha and the Early Irish: A Preliminary Investigation,' *Proceedings of the Royal Irish Academy*, 73C

(1973), 299–338, provides a surer guide to this ancillary topic than has been available. The study of penitential motifs cited in note 14 also makes significant contributions to the study of the anonymous homilies.

16 The two collections differ in tone, style, and purpose. Blickling is a reasonably complete homiliary and is benevolent in tone, as Professor Dalbey has argued. Vercelli is a miscellany of verse and prose, penitential and, sometimes, harsh in tone (see Kenneth Sisam, 'Marginalia in the Vercelli Book,' *Studies in the History of Old English Literature* [Oxford, 1953], pp. 109–18). I hope that my general remarks do not blur these important distinctions, for they are meant to apply only to theological method and content, in which respects the similarities of the two books are striking.

17 Ker, *Catalogue*, 382 and 394. See also Blickling, Willard's introduction to E.E.M.F., 10. Scragg, *ASE*, 2 [1973], 189, without discussing his reasons, asserts that Vercelli is 'the earliest surviving collection of homilies in the vernacular.'

18 Morris, ed., *Blickling Homilies*, p. 119.

19 According to Scragg, *ASE*, 2 [1973], 205–7, Vercelli is a Kentish compilation, the contents of which were 'not planned in ... entirety before execution began.' The scribe used collections in south-eastern, Mercian, and West-Saxon dialect, and he had a fairly extensive collection of vernacular materials available for his work.

20 See the introduction to Rudolf Vleeskruyer, ed., *The Life of St Chad: An Old English Homily* (Amsterdam, 1953), pp. 38ff. On the relations of Vercelli to Mercian tradition, see also Joan Turville-Petre, 'Translations of a Lost Penitential Homily,' *Traditio*, 19 (1963), 51–78 at p. 75.

21 'Because I have seen and heard of much error in many English books, which unlearned men, through their simplicity, have esteemed as great wisdom ...' Benjamin Thorpe, ed., *The Homilies of the Anglo-Saxon Church: The First Part, Containing the* Sermones Catholici *or Homilies of Ælfric*, 2 vols. (London, 1844–46), I, 2/19–22 [hereafter, Thorpe, I or II; translations are Thorpe's from the facing (odd-numbered) pages].

22 For a general outline of the English movement, see F.M. Stenton, *Anglo-Saxon England*, 2nd ed., The Oxford History of England, 2 (Oxford, 1955), pp. 427–62. Margaret Deanesly, *The Pre-Conquest Church in England*, An Ecclesiastical History of England, ed., J.C. Dickinson, 1 (New York, 1961), pp. 276–327, deals with the canonical and continental backgrounds of the movement; see also her *Sidelights on the Anglo-Saxon Church* (London, 1962). Thomas Symons summarizes the many articles he has published in the *Downside Review* in the introduction to his edition of

Regularis Concordia Anglicae Nationis Monachorum Sanctimonialumque (*The Monastic Agreement of the Monks and Nuns of the English Nation*), Nelson's Medieval Classics (London, 1953). The classic account is that of David Knowles, *The Monastic Order in England: A History of Its Development from the Times of St Dunstan to the Fourth Lateran Council: 940–1216*, 2nd ed. (Cambridge, 1963), esp. at pp. 31–82. Also of interest but subject to criticism are two essays, 'The King and the Monks in the Tenth Century Reformation' and 'The Beginning of the Benedictine Reform in England,' in Eric John, *Orbis Britanniae and Other Studies*, Studies in Early English History, 4 (Leicester, 1966), at pp. 154–80 and 249–64, respectively. Important papers on a number of aspects of the reform are collected in *Tenth-Century Studies: Essays in Commemoration of the Millennium of the Council of Winchester and Regularis Concordia*, ed. David Parsons (Chichester, 1975). On continental connections, see the essays of D.A. Bullough and Abbot Symons, ibid., 20–59; also H. Dauphin, 'Le Renouveau Monastique en Angleterre au xᵉ Siècle et ses Rapports avec la Réforme de Saint Gérard de Brogne' and response by Eric John, *RB*, 70 (1960), 177–203. On the continuity of the movement in the following century, see R.R. Darlington, 'Ecclesiastical Reform in the Late Old English Period,' *EHR*, 51 (1936), 385–428. For warnings against too great or too exclusive emphasis on monasticism in late Anglo-Saxon church history, see D.P. Kirby, *The Making of Early England* (New York, 1968), pp. 92–114, esp. 103–4, and Frank Barlow, *The English Church, 1000–1066: A Constitutional History* (London, 1963), esp. p. vii.

23 'Synodale concilium': *Regularis Concordia*, Pref. 4 (ed. Symons, p. 2).

24 '... accitis Florensis beati Benedicti necnon praecipui coenobii quod celebri Gent nuncupatur uocabulo monachis, quaeque ex dignis eorum moribus honesta colligentes, uti apes fauum nectaris diuersis pratorum floribus in uno alueario, ita has morum consuetudines ad uitae honestatem et regularis obseruantiae dulcedinem, ut ab his qui uiam regiam mandatorum Domini absque iactantiae uitio lactei adhuc humiliter incedunt, depulso nausiae taedio, sine querela legitime haustu degustari libentissimo ac auidi amabili possent impleri deuotione, temperate cum magna ac subtili rationis discretione, Christi mundi Saluatoris opitulante gratia, hoc exiguo apposuerunt codicello' (ibid. 5 [Symons, pp. 3–4]).

25 For a comparison of the two movements, see Kassius Hallinger, *Gorze-Kluny: Studien zu den monastischen Lebensformen und Gegensätzen im Hochmittelalter*, 2 vols., *Studia Anselmiana: Philosophica*

Theologica, 22, 25 (Rome, 1951, 1952), pp. 54–8. See also the papers of Bullough, Symons, and Dauphin cited above, note 22.

26 Knowles, *Monastic Order in England*, p. 29.

27 *Regularis Concordia*, Pref. 5 (ed. Symons, p. 3).

28 British Museum MS. Cotton Tiberius A.3, f.2ᵛ, reproduced in Symons ed., facing p. ix.

29 The literary evidence for tenth-century architectural activity in Winchester was discussed by R.N. Quirk in two articles: 'Winchester Cathedral in the Tenth Century,' *Archaeological Journal*, 114 (1957), 28–68, and 'Winchester New Minster and Its Tenth-Century Tower,' *Journal of the British Archaeological Association*, 3rd ser., 24 (1961), 16–54. Reports by Martin Biddle on the excavations (1961–1970) are printed in *Archaeological Journal*, 119 (1962), and thereafter in *The Antiquaries Journal*, 44 (1964), sqq., and a summary report, *'Felix urbs Winthonia'* appears in *Tenth Century Studies*, ed. Parsons, pp. 123–40.

30 'The Origin of Standard Old English and Æthelwold's School at Winchester,' *ASE*, 1 (1972), 63–83, quotation at pp. 81–82.

31 A recent edition of three poems with a valuable survey of the Latin poetry of Winchester and extensive bibliography is to be found in Michael Lapidge, 'Three Latin Poems from Æthelwold's School at Winchester,' *ASE*, 1 (1972), 85–137.

32 Joseph A. Jungmann, *The Mass of the Roman Rite: Its Origins and Development*, trans. Francis A. Brunner, 2 vols. (New York, 1951–55), I, 87–92, has a useful account of the work of the most important of these liturgical scholars, Amalarius of Metz.

33 Smalley, *Study of the Bible*, p. 44. See also Robert E. McNally, *The Bible in the Early Middle Ages*, Woodstock Papers, 4 (Westminster, Maryland, 1959), for a survey and index of early medieval biblical commentaries; and G.W.H. Lampe, ed. *The Cambridge History of the Bible*, vol. 2 [The West from the Fathers to the Reformation) (Cambridge, 1969)].

Chapter 2

1 The basic treatment of Ælfric's life is Eduard Dietrich, 'Abt Aelfrik zur Literatur-Geschichte der angelsächsischen Kirche,' *ZHT*, 25 (1885), 487–594 and 26 (1856), 163–256. Earlier, much useful information on Alfric's writing had been printed by Humphrey Wanley, *Librorum Vett. Septentrionalium ... Catologus*, vol. 2 of George Hickes, *Linguarum Vett. Septentrionalium Thesaurus* (Oxford, 1705). Caroline L. White, *Ælfric: A new Study of His Life and Writings*, Yale Studies in English, 2 (1898; rpt. with supplementary biblio-

graphy by Malcom Godden, Hamden, Conn., 1974), depends on Dietrich but adds some new material. S. Harvey Gem, *An Anglo-Saxon Abbot: Ælfric of Eynsham* (Edinburgh, 1912) is popular. More ambitious is Marguerite-Marie Dubois, *Ælfric: Sermonnaire, Docteur et Grammarien: Contribution à l'étude de la vie et de l'action Bénédictine en Angleterre au Xᵉ Siècle* (Paris, 1943). The three later works must still be considered as secondary in authority to Dietrich, whose conclusions are, however, substantially revised by the studies of Sisam, Pope, and Clemoes (all cited in note 2) on the chronology and canon of Ælfric's writings. There is an expert summary article, dealing especially with Ælfric's literary technique, by Peter A.M. Clemoes: 'Ælfric,' in *Continuations and Beginnings: Studies in Old English Literature*, ed. Eric Gerald Stanley (London, 1966), 176–209. The latest general study, James Hurt, *Ælfric*, Twayne's English Authors Series, 131 (New York, 1972), suffers from failure to integrate the results of the work of Pope and Clemoes.

2 On the problems of chronology, see P.A.M. Clemoes, 'The Chronology of Ælfric's Works,' in *The Anglo-Saxons: Studies in Some Aspects of Their History and Culture Presented to Bruce Dickins*, ed. Clemoes (London, 1959) [hereafter, Clemoes,

'Chronology'], pp. 212–47, esp. at pp. 244–5; canon listed at pp. 214–19. Equally important are the relevant portions of the Introduction to John C. Pope, ed., *Homilies of Ælfric: A Supplementary Collection* ... , 2 vols. [consecutive pagination], E.E.T.S., 259 and 260 (London, 1967, 1968) [hereafter, Pope; references to texts by roman numeral for item number and arabics for lines; references to editorial material by page]. Pope holds that, rather than publishing successive editions, or even new series of homilies for the Temporale (per Clemoes), Ælfric constantly emended and expanded his homiletic works, producing new pieces as occasion demanded. Final decision between these positions (which will not materially alter the arguments of this book) must await the full-dress presentation of Clemoes's argument in his forthcoming edition of the First Series of *Catholic Homilies* for E.E.T.S. Also important is the article of Kenneth Sisam, 'MSS. Bodley 340 and 342: Ælfric's *Catholic Homilies*,' rpt. in *Studies in the History of Old English Literature* (Oxford, 1953), pp. 148–98. On the extent of Ælfric's contribution to the Old English Hexateuch (compiled by Byrhtferth of Ramsey ?) see Clemoes in *The Old English Illustrated Hexateuch: British Museum Cotton Claudius B.iv*, ed. C.R. Dodwell and Peter Clemoes,

E.E.M.F., 18 (Copenhagen, 1974), 42–53.

3 It was once argued that he may have returned to Winchester for a time (Dietrich, *ZHT*, 26 [1856], 245). In view of the fact that the writing of the earliest ms of *Catholic Homilies*, I (B.M. Royal 7 C. xii, ff. 4–218) is now quite confidently assigned to Cerne Abbas, where it came under Ælfric's close scrutiny, the notion of a return to Winchester's larger scriptorium to oversee the dissemination of his writing has been abandoned. On the Royal MS, see Clemoes in the introduction to the facsimile, *Ælfric's First Series of Catholic Homilies*, ed. Norman Eliason and Peter Clemoes, E.E.M.F., 13 (Copenhagen, 1966), pp. 28–35.

4 '... and ic me sylfe wylle mid ðære geferrædne gemænelice libban, and ðære áre mid him notian ða hwile ðe mín lif bið' (Eynsham Charter, printed in J.M. Kemble, ed., *Codex Diplomaticus Aevi Saxonici*, III [London, 1845], 339–46 at 344). The document was once ascribed to Ælfric (Dietrich, *ZHT*, 26 [1856], 240; White, *Ælfric*, 60–1); it is not now included in the canon (but for a charter text which may be by Ælfric, see J.C. Pope, 'Ælfric and the Old English Version of the Ely Privilege,' in *England Before the Conquest: Studies ... Presented to Dorothy Whitelock*, ed. Peter Clemoes and Kathleen Hughes [Cambridge, 1971], pp. 85–113).

The Eynsham charter clearly shows the reform ideology in the donation not to the abbot but 'Góde and sancta Marian, and eallon his hálgan, and sancte Benedicte intó Egnesham ... ðam ðe Benedictus regol æfre rihtlíce healdað.' Further, Æthelmær promises not to inhibit abbatial elections and invokes King Æthelred's royal patronage.

5 The date traditionally assigned was ca. 1020, but reasons for advancing the date to ca. 1014 have been put forth by Dorothy Whitelock, 'Two Notes on Ælfric and Wulfstan,' *MLR*, 38 (1943), 122–4. See, too, Clemoes, 'Chronology,' 245.

6 Clemoes, 'Chronology,' 245–6.

7 On Ælfric's use of the 'credentials formula,' which 'includes name and title (*intitulatio*) and some claim of authority to speak or write,' and on the related 'modesty formula,' see Ann Eljenholm Nichols, 'Ælfric's Prefaces: Rhetoric and Genre,' *ES*, 49 (1968), 215–23, esp. 217ff. Nichols relies heavily on Ernst R. Curtius, *European Literature and the Latin Middle Ages*, trans. Willard R. Trask, Bollingen Series, 36 (New York, 1953), esp. pp. 83–5, 407–13, and appears to believe that rhetorical *topoi* do not necessarily reflect 'biographical fact.' One must, however, keep in mind that *topoi* are often vehicles for fact or for the author's sentiments; see chaps. 1 and 2 of Erich Auerbach, *Literary Language and Its Public in Late Latin*

Antiquity and in the Middle Ages, trans. Ralph Manheim, Bollingen Series, 74 (New York, 1965).

8 Lat. Pref., Thorpe, I, 1; opening epistle of *Vita S. Æthelwoldi* (The edition by Michael Winterbottom, *Three Lives of English Saints,* Toronto Medieval Latin Texts [Toronto, 1972] replaces that by J. Stephenson in *Chronicon Monasterii de Abingdon,* 2, Rolls Series, 102 [London, 1858], 255). The preface to the *Grammar* (Julius Zupitza, ed., *Ælfrics Grammatik und Glossar: Text und Varianten,* Sammlung Englischen Denkmäler in kritischen Ausgaben, 1 [1880, rpt. with foreword by Helmut Gneuss; Berlin, 1966], 1–2) alludes to Æthelwold while stressing the importance of Latin for the maintenance of religion and the role of that language in the reform.

9 Thorpe, I, 2/12 ('munuc and mæssepreost'); II, 2/5 ('munuc'); 'Preface to Genesis,' ed., S.J. Crawford, *The Old English Version of the Heptateuch, Ælfric's Treatise on the Old and New Testament and his Preface to Genesis* ... , E.E.T.S., O.S., 160 (London, 1922) [hereafter, Crawford, *Heptateuch*], 76 ('munuc'). In the preface to *LS* (Walter W. Skeat, ed., *Ælfric's Lives of Saints, being a Set of Sermons on Saints' Days formerly Observed by the English Church* ... , 2 vols., E.E.T.S., O.S. 76, 82, 94, 114 [1881–1900; rpt. London, 1966] I, 2–6), he addresses himself to Æthelweard and Æthelmær, to

whom he is well known, and uses no title; perhaps the monastic passional was self-authenticating. The Genesis preface, also addressed to Æthelweard, contains an identification of Ælfric as 'munuc.'

10 In works after 1005; prefaces collected in White, *Ælfric,* pp. 175, 177, 181.

11 Where he has no such authority, he is careful to avoid the subject; see *Pastoral for Wulfsige* in which he says he has no right to speak on the nature of the episcopate (Bernhard Fehr, *Die Hirtenbriefe Ælfrics* ... , Bibliothek der angelsächsischen Prosa, 9 [1914; rpt. with supplement to introduction by Peter Clemoes; Darmstadt, 1966], 1).

12 *LS,* I, 2–6. Nichols also deals with the issue of translation in the article cited in note 7, suggesting again (p. 219) that the 'motive' is 'rhetorical rather than biographical.' Her argument is in many ways valid, but it is perhaps worth noting that Ælfric may have had some scruples about making the monastic passional available to his lay patrons. See also Nichols, 'Awendan: A Note on Ælfric's Vocabulary,' *JEGP,* 63 (1964), 7–13.

13 Crawford, *Heptateuch,* 76 ('... I fear, if an ignorant man reads this book or hears it read, that he will think that he can live now in the new law as the ancient fathers lived in the time before the old law was established or as men lived under Moses' law').

14 Ibid., 80 ('I say now that I dare not and want not to translate any book from Latin to English; and I pray you, beloved ealdorman, that you no longer ask me this lest I should be disobedient to you, or lest I do it. May God be eternally merciful to you'). A similar note appears in the prayer at Thorpe, II, 520, where Ælfric claims that he will never again translate 'godspel oþþe godspel-trahtas' from Latin to English. But much of the rest of his career was spent filling out the homilies of the Temporale. Perhaps (contra Clemoes) he meant he would never again publish a formal series – although even this he violated in some sense. Had Nichols known the work of Pope and Clemoes, she could not have advanced the arguments made in ES, 49 (1968), 222–3.

15 See Pope, pp. 109–12. Nichols, 'Ælfric and the Brief Style,' JEGP, 70 (1971), 1–12, argues that the homilist, using the method of abbreviation, was aiming at something like the 'brief style' of the rhetoricians.

16 The best, most detailed, and most authoritative analysis of Ælfric's style is that of Pope, at pp. 105–36 of his Homilies of Ælfric; see also his essay in England before the Conquest, ed. Clemoes and Hughes, pp. 85–115. The famous argument on Ælfric's influence on Middle English prose is presented in R.W. Chambers, 'On the Continuity of English Prose from Alfred to More and His School,' in Nicholas Harpsfield's Life of Sir Thomas More, ed. E.V. Hitchcock and R.W. Chambers, E.E.T.S., O.S., 191 (1932; rpt. separately as E.E.T.S., O.S. 191A, London, 1966), but the best study of Ælfric's stylistic influence on early Middle English prose is that of Dorothy Bethurum, 'The Connection of the Katherine Group with Old English Prose,' JEGP, 34 (1935), 553–64. The influence is now sometimes questioned, however; see Pope, p. 106n, and J.A.W. Bennett and G.V. Smithers, eds., Early Middle English Verse and Prose (Oxford, 1966), p. 224. For a recent study of knowledge of Old English in the later Middle Ages with full bibliography, see Angus Cameron, 'Middle English in Old English Manuscripts,' Chaucer and Middle English Studies in Honour of Rossell Hope Robbins, ed. Beryl Rowland (London, 1974), pp. 218–29.

17 Gordon Hall Gerould, 'Abbot Ælfric's Rhythmic Prose,' MP, 22 (1925), 353–66 first posited that Ælfric adapted elements of Latin cursus. Gerould's position was questioned by Bethurum (see note 18) and has been refuted by Pope and by Frances Randall Lipp ('Ælfric's Old English Prose Style,' SP, 66 [1969], 689–718), who shows that the basic 'alliterative and rhythmical framework' of Ælfric's prose does not derive from imitation of Latin models, although the abbot

'superimposed' a number of 'Latinate effects' on his basic prose structure. The issue was most recently discussed by Sherman M. Kuhn, 'Cursus in Old English: Rhetorical Ornament or Linguistic Phenomenon?' *Speculum*, 47 (1972), 188–206.

18 Dorothy Bethurum, 'The Form of Ælfric's *Lives of Saints*,' *SP*, 29 (1932), 582. Professor Bethurum notes that the earlier, anonymous prose bears traces of alliteration and rhythm which show closer relation to Old English poetic tradition. More recently, Otto Funke ('Studien zur alliterierenden und rhythmisierenden Prosa in der ältern altenglischen Homiletik,' *Anglia*, 80 [1962], 9–36) has argued that Ælfric developed stylistic traits which are already discernible in older English prose.

19 Sherman M. Kuhn has reopened the possibility that Ælfric was writing verse, claiming that his rhythmical style is not prose but alliterative verse anticipatory of Laȝamon ('Was Ælfric a Poet?' *PQ* 52 (1973), 643–62).

20 *Rhythm and Cosmic Order in Old English Christian Literature: An Inaugural Lecture* (Cambridge, 1970), p. 21.

21 Thorpe, I, 1/14–18 ('Hos namque auctores in hac explanatione sumus sequuti, videlicet Augustinum Hipponensem, Hieronimum, Bedam, Gregorium, Smaragdum, et aliquando Haymonem; horum denique auctoritas ab omnibus catholicis libentissime suscipitur').

22 See the comments on Alcuin in the adaptations of the *Interrogationes Sigewulfi* (George Edwin MacLean, 'Ælfric's Version of Alcuini Interrogationes Sigewulfi in Genesin [Fortsetzung],' *Anglia*, 7 [1884], 2, lines 1–18) and, more briefly, on the Latin grammarians (Zupitza, ed., *Ælfrics Grammatik*, pp. 1–2).

23 The treatise *De vetere testamento et de novo* (Letter to Sigeweard; Crawford, *Heptateuch*, pp. 15–75), for example, combines two patristic genres: the summary of faith history and the outline of biblical content (on these, see Bethurum, *Wulfstan*, p. 293). It is probably not so closely related to Augustine's *De doctrina Christiana* as Dubois (*Ælfric*, 91) and others imply, but its indebtedness to some such document and to the genre of catechetical *narratio* is evident enough (see Virginia Day, 'The Influence of Catechetical *narratio* on Old English and Some Other Medieval Literature,' *ASE*, 3 [1974], 51–61).

24 Thorpe, I, 3/4–8 ('Precor modo obnixe almitatem tuam ... ut digneris corrigere per tuam industriam, si aliquos nevos malignae haeresis, aut nebulosae fallaciae in nostra interpretatione repperies ...'.

25 Thorpe, II, 332/22–24 ('Humeta rædað sume men ða leasan gesetnysse, ðe hí hatað Paulus gesihðe, nu hé sylfe sæde þæt hé ða digelan word gehyrde, þe nán eorðlic mann

sprecan ne mót?'). He delayed translating the Passion of St Thomas, heeding Augustine's criticism of it (Thorpe, II, 520), but finally translated an expurgated version for Æthelweard (LS, II, xxxvi). Critical of speculation on the Immaculate Conception of the Virgin, he at first refused to discuss the birth of Mary (Thorpe, II, 466/15–18 ['Hwæt wylle we secgan ymbe Marian gebyrd-tíde, buton þæt heo wæs gestyrned þurh fæder and ðurh moder swa swa oðre men, and wæs on ðam dæge acenned þe we cweðað sexta idus Septembris?']). Later he provided a sermon for the occasion which avoided the subject by dwelling on virginity (Assmann, III). He also rejected fanciful accounts of St George (LS, I, 306–8). Ælfric probably knew from the portion of the Gelasian decretal preserved in MS Boulogne-sur-Mer 63 (see Enid M. Raynes, 'MS. Boulogne-sur-Mer 63 and Ælfric,' MÆ, 26 [1957], 65–73 at 71) that the Visio [Revelatio] Pauli and the transitus, id est Assumptio sanctae Mariae, were condemned (PL, 59, 164), but he seems to base his objections to the Thomas tradition on Augustine rather than Gelasius.

26 On the OE translation, see Antonette di Paolo Healey, The Vision of St Paul, Diss. Toronto 1973. The ms in question is Oxford, Bodleian Junius 85+86 (mid-eleventh century).

27 Thorpe, II, 332–48 (Fursey), 348–54 (Dryhthelm).

28 Thorpe, I, 8/9–16; II, 2/22–6; LS, I, Pref./74–6 ('Ic bidde nu on godes naman gif hwa þas bóc awritan wille. þæt he hí wél gerihte be þære bysne. and þǽr namare betwux ne sette þonne we awendon'); On the Old and New Testament (Crawford, Heptateuch, 75); 'Preface to Genesis' (ibid., 80).

29 For example, Oxford, MS Bodleian, Bodley 340+342 and Cambridge, Corpus Christi College MS 198 (items 309, 48 in Ker, Catalogue), both of the eleventh century. Both are based on CH, but the Bodleian MS contains three items also in the Vercelli book, and the Corpus MS has the same homilies and two which are also in Blickling. Scribes, in other words, sometimes constructed new homiliaries about an Ælfrician core, exactly as the homilist feared they might. See Pope, pp. 20–2; Sisam, Studies, pp. 148–98.

30 Thorpe, I, 218/30–1 ('Circlice ðeawas forbeodað to secgenne ænig spel on þam þrym swig-dagum'); II, 262/16 ('Ne mot nán man secgan spell on þam ðrim swig-dagum'). Blickling is silent on these days, but not so the mss discussed in the preceding note. Both have homilies for all three occasions (arts. 24–6 of both mss), and in both the Good Friday homily is the same as Vercelli Homily I (ed. Förster, pp. 1–43). Ælfric may refer to the fact that the Martyrology was not read on these days (T.S. Symons, 'Sources of the Regularis Concordia,' Downside Re-

view, 59 [1941], 279), but, if so, he seems to be confused. On Coleman's objections to this Ælfrician dictum, see Part II.

31 Seventeen instances of repetition of texts are listed by Clemoes, 'Chronology,' pp. 246–7. For a discussion of an example of cross reference, see J.E. Cross, *SN*, 41 (1969), 135–55 at 148.

32 Pope first showed in 1931 (see Pope, p. 7) that MS Royal 7 C. xii contains several alterations in Ælfric's hand. The most interesting of these is the cancellation of a passage in *CH*, I, 186 after line 18, which alludes to the history of Moses. According to the marginal note, it was deleted 'lest it should seem tiresome if it were in both books' (i.e., in Thorpe, II, 188–224). See Sisam, *Studies*, p. 173n; Clemoes's introduction to E.E.M.F., 13, p. 35, and the facsimile of fol. 64^{r-v} (text of the note reconstructed in the introduction by Eliason, p. 18n).

33 See Peter Clemoes, *Liturgical Influence on Punctuation in Late Old English and Early Middle English Manuscripts*, University of Cambridge, Department of Anglo-Saxon, Occasional Papers, 1 (Cambridge, 1957); C.G. Harlow, 'Punctuation in Some Manuscripts of Ælfric,' *RES*, N.S. 10 (1959), 1–19; and Clemoes in the introduction to E.E.M.F., 13, pp. 24–5.

34 See Clemoes's discussion of the early history of MS Royal 7 C. xii, E.E.M.F., 13, pp. 28–35.

35 Clemoes, 'Chronology,' p. 224, dates the composition of I in 989 and its publication in 991; he gives 992 as the year of publication for II. See also Sisam, *Studies*, pp. 156–60; Pope, pp. 7–8, and Clemoes in introduction to facsimile of Royal MS.

36 Clemoes, 'Chronology,' p. 234n; Sisam, *Studies*, p. 160n.

37 Clemoes, E.E.M.F., 13, pp. 28–9.

38 See the Latin Prefaces; Sisam, *Studies*, pp. 156–65.

39 Sisam, *Studies*, pp. 164–5, addressed the problem that forty sermons were promised (Thorpe, I, 8/17; II, 2/14) and more than forty were given in the Second Series. M.R. Godden, 'The Development of Ælfric's Second Series of *Catholic Homilies*,' *ES*, 54 (1973), 209–16, makes important corrections of details in Sisam's argument.

40 Thorpe, II, 2/11–13.

41 The basic study of the sources of the hagiographical homilies is Max Förster, *Über die Quellen von Ælfrics Homiliae Catholicae: 1. Legenden*. Inaugural Diss., University of Berlin (Berlin, 1892).

42 Epistle of Charlemagne, reprinted *inter alia* in F. Wiegand, *Das Homiliarium Karls des grossem auf seine ursprüngliche Gestalt hin untersucht*, Studien zur Geschichte der Theologie und der Kirche, I.2 (Leipzig, 1897), 15–16. See further Part II.

43 Cyril L. Smetana, 'Ælfric and the Early Medieval Homiliary,' *Traditio*,

15 (1959), 163–204, made this identification. The suggestion had been entertained but rejected by Förster in 'Über die Quellen von Ælfrics Exegetischen *Homiliae Catholicae*,' *Anglia*, 16 (1894), 1–61. In addition to Smetana's evidence, note that Ælfric refers to the work as the translation of a single book (Thorpe, I, 3/17–18: 'Þa bearn me on mode, ic truwige þurh Godes gife, þæt ic ðas boc [*acc. sg.*] of Ledenum gereorde to Engliscre spræce awende ...').

44 Smetana, 'Ælfric and the Homiliary of Haymo of Halberstadt,' *Traditio*, 17 (1961), 457–69. Although Ælfric listed Haymo as a source, the extent of his borrowing had not been recognized before the publication of this article. Since the publication of Smetana's article, however, Haymo – traditionally identified as a bishop of Halberstadt – has been conclusively shown to have been a monk of the abbey of St Germain at Auxerre. See Henri Barré, *Les Homéliaires Carolingiens de l'École d'Auxerre*, and (for further bibliography) Pope, pp. 157–8.

45 This conclusion has been developed – and the phenomenon that occasioned it labelled 'retentive memory' – in a series of recent articles by J.E. Cross, of which the most important is the item in *SN*, 41 (1969), 135–55, already cited in note 30.

46 One instance, Homily xx of Thorpe, I, is discussed by Professor Clemoes in E.E.M.F., 13, pp. 31–2: the ms text of the homily contains four cross signs, Ælfric's characteristic marks for insertions at points where, as J.E. Cross had shown ('Ælfric and the Mediaeval Homiliary – Objection and Contribution,' Regiae Societatis Humaniorum Litterarum Lundensis, *Scripta Minora*, 1961–62, no. 4, at pp. 24–34), he later added material to the text. Thus, Clemoes concludes, it is probable 'that Ælfric had not marshalled all his supplementary, illustrative material for this homily in a single operation at the outset but that he had added suitable passages as he had come across them or called them to mind.' For further perceptive comment on Ælfric's use of his sources, see Pope, pp. 150ff.

47 Godden, *ES*, 54 (1973), 215.

48 The evidence of further development is discussed by Clemoes, 'Chronology,' and introduction to E.E.M.F., 13; by Pope, pp. 1–85 and 136–50; and by Sisam, *Studies*, pp. 148–98. Full discussion of the history of the text of *CH*, I, awaits publication of Professor Clemoes's edition for E.E.T.S., and for that of II, an edition by M.R. Godden. For discussion of the chronology of the later Temporale homilies, see Pope, pp. 136–50, and Clemoes, 'Chronology.' Pope and Clemoes (the former arguing contra) disagree as to whether one can legitimately speak of one or two series of homilies for the Temporale.

49 Clemoes, 'Chronology,' pp. 224 and

219–27. The work as we have it does contain also more general homilies for new occasions, some of which supplement *CH* (*LS*, Nos. I, X, XII, XIII, XV, XVIII, XXXI, XXXVI). Clemoes (p. 220) feels that Ælfric included all the material he had at hand at the time of publication, since two independent ms traditions agree in a general way on content. For purposes of discussion here, however, I assume that the purer version implied by the prefaces existed at least in the author's imagination.

50 *LS*, Pref./37 ('þære halgena þrowunga'). The chief source studies are J.H. Ott, *Über die Quellen der Heiligenleben in Ælfrics Lives of Saints I*, Inaugural diss. (Halle, 1892); Grant Loomis, 'Further Sources of Ælfric's Saints' Lives,' *Harvard Studies and Notes in Philology and Literature*, 13 (1931), 1–8; G.H. Gerould, 'Ælfric's Lives of St Martin of Tours,' *JEGP*, 24(1925), 206–10; M.R. Godden, 'The Sources for Ælfric's Homily on St Gregory,' *Anglia*, 86 (1968), 79–98; Cecily Clark, 'Ælfric and Abbo,' *ES*, 49 (1968), 30–6.

51 *Regularis Concordia*, chap. 21 (ed. Symons, p. 17: before the homily, 'tunc residentibus cunctis legatur martyrologium ...').

52 So Clemoes, 'Chronology,' p. 220n. But the rubrics printed in *LS* date the saints' days.

53 On the possibility that this expression is conventional, see Nichols in *ES*, 49 (1968), 220n.

54 *LS*, Pref./12–13. If by *Vitae Patrum*, Ælfric means the 'general body of literature concerning the Christian ascetics in Egyptian deserts' usually attributed to Jerome (Constance L. Rosenthal, *The* Vitae Patrum *in Old and Middle English Literature*, Diss. Pennsylvania [Philadelphia, 1936], p. 11), he probably means that he regards their treatment of visions as suspect unless carefully interpreted and, therefore, to be withheld from the uninitiated. He did, however, use materials from the *Vitae Patrum* in *LS* (Rosenthal, pp. 59–62; but *LS* XXIII and XXXIII are by general consent not Ælfrician) and in Pope, VIII, 139–52 (V *after Easter*); XIX, 62–5 (*De Doctrina Apostolica*); and XXVII (addition to Thorpe, II, XVI *after Pentecost*); and twice refers specifically to the collection in *CH* (Thorpe, I, 544–6; II, 272/13).

55 *LS*, Pref./43–8 ('Nu ge-wearð us þæt we þas bóc be þæra halgena ðrowungum and life. gedihton þe mynster-menn mid heora þenungum betwux him wurðiað./ Ne secge we nán þincg niwes on þissere gesetnysse./ forþan ðe hit stod gefyrn awriten/ on ledenbocum þeah þe þa læwedan men þæt nyston').

Chapter 3

1 Dorothy Whitelock in her *Changing Currents in Anglo-Saxon Studies: An Inaugural Lecture* (Cambridge, 1958), 11–12, gives a short outline of this reevaluation, to which she has herself made important

contributions. The major studies are listed in her notes and in my documentation below. More recent bibliographies are to be found in Dorothy Bethurum's survey article, 'Wulfstan,' in *Continuations and Beginnings*, ed. E.G. Stanley at 210–46; Whitelock, ed., *Sermo Lupi ad Anglos*, 3rd ed., Methuen's Old English Library (London, 1963), pp. 70–2; and (carrying on from 1963) Klaus Ostheeren's bibliographical supplement to the rpt. of Arthur Napier, ed., *Wulfstan: Sammlung der ihm zugeschriebenen Homilien* ... , Sammlung englischer Denkmäler in kritischen Ausgaben, 4 (1883; rpt. Dublin and Zürich, 1967), pp. 319–67. Briefly, however, the monuments of the movement are Karl Jost's works on the canon, especially 'Einige Wulfstantexte und ihre Quellen,' *Anglia*, 56 (1932), 265–315, the *Wulfstanstudien*, Swiss Studies in English, 23 (Bern, 1950), and his edition of the *Institutes of Polity, Civil and Ecclesiastical*, Swiss Studies in English, 47 (Bern, 1959); Whitelock's studies of Wulfstan as legislator for Æthelred II and Cnut and of the historical context of his work in a series of articles, all of which are cited in the bibliographies aforementioned and in the Preface to the *Sermo*; Angus McIntosh's 1948 Gollancz Lecture ('Wulfstan's Prose,' *PBA*, 35 [1949], 109–42) which established Wulfstan as a very important prose stylist; and Dorothy Bethurum's edition of the genuine homilies (*The Homilies of Wulfstan* [Oxford, 1952]) with an introduction which synthesizes the results of these labours, giving the first complete and balanced re-evaluation of the genius of the archbishop. A number of ms notes by Wulfstan have been analysed by N.R. Ker, 'The Handwriting of Archbishop Wulfstan,' in *England Before the Conquest*, ed. Clemoes and Hughes, pp. 315–31, and Henry R. Loyn, *A Wulfstan Manuscript containing Institutes, Laws and Homilies: British Museum Cotton Nero A.I*, E.E.M.F., 17 (Copenhagen, 1971), p. 31 and appended facsimiles. *Wulfstan's Canons of Edgar* have recently been expertly edited by Roger Fowler, E.E.T.S., 266 (London, 1972). There remains now the task of assimilating the results into more general historical studies – a challenge which recent historians of the Anglo-Saxon period have failed to meet or, in the main, to recognize (see, for example, the references to Wulfstan in D.P. Kirby, *The Making of Early England*).

2 Bethurum in *Continuations and Beginnings*, ed. Stanley, p. 210. The homilies of Wulfstan are cited below from the ed. of Bethurum by number and line (editorial material by page); Napier's ed. is similarly cited. Cross reference to Napier's edition is made in Bethurum's table of contents, and Ostheern provides a comparative table at pp. 366–7 of the rpt. of Napier.

3 I rely on Bethurum's introduction, pp. 54–87; Whitelock's introduction to her ed. of *Sermo Lupi ad Anglos*, pp. 7–37, and her 'Archbishop Wulfstan, Statesman and Homilist,' *TRHS*, Series IV.24 (1942), 24–45. On Wulfstan's reputation at Ely, see *Liber Eliensis* II.87 (ed. E.O. Blake, Royal Historical Society, Camden Third Series, 93 [London, 1962]).

4 See Bethurum, Appendix II.3, 15 ('Lupus Lundoniensis episcopus').

5 The plurality was not new and was probably established because the richer see's endowments were needed to support the archiepiscopate in the north where the church had never recovered from the invasions. On the effect of this plurality on Wulfstan's reputation at Worcester after the Conquest, see Bethurum, pp. 65–8; Whitelock, *Sermo Lupi*, pp. 8–9.

6 Jost (*Wulfstanstudien*, pp. 94–103) is the sole dissenter from Whitelock's demonstration of Wulfstan's authorship of Cnut's legislation ('Wulfstan and the Laws of Cnut,' *EHR*, 63 [1948], 433–52; 'Wulfstan's Authorship of Cnut's Laws,' ibid., 70 [1955], 72–85). Other aspects of Wulfstan's archiepiscopal career are treated in Whitelock, 'Wulfstan at York,' *Franciplegius: Medieval and Linguistic Studies in Honor of Francis Peabody Magoun, Jr.*, ed. Jess B. Bessinger, Jr. and Robert P. Creed (New York, 1965), pp. 214–31; Bethurum, 'Episcopal Magnificence in the Eleventh Century,' *Studies in Old English Literature in Honor of Arthur G. Brodeur*, ed. Stanley B. Greenfield (Eugene, Oregon, 1963), pp. 162–70.

7 Bethurum, p. 86. See also Dorothy Bethurum Loomis. '*Regnum* and *Sacerdotium* in the Eleventh Century,' in *England Before the Conquest*, ed. Clemoes and Hughes, pp. 129–45.

8 Bethurum XIV, XV are associated with Lenten penance, specifically with those who must atone for mortal sin (XIV deals with the beginning of their discipline on Ash Wednesday and XV with their reconciliation on Maundy Thursday); neither refers to the pericope. XVII and XVIII are for an episcopal consecration and the dedication of a church. The former opens with reference to Luke xxiv. 49ff., but only lines 9–14 are explicatory. The latter, based on Ælfric's *In Dedicatione Ecclesiae* (Thorpe, II, 574–94), and replete with references to the dedication of Solomon's Temple (II Chronicles vi, etc.), is not in the standard form of exegetical sermons. A number of the catechetical homilies (Bethurum VII–X, in particular) have to do with more-or-less liturgical texts.

9 See Jost, *Wulfstanstudien*, pp. 45–62. Added instances of reliance on Abbo, discovered but not yet published by Alan K. Brown, are discussed below.

10 See Bethurum, pp. 299–354, for sources.

11 Bethurum XI, XVIa, XVIb, and notes.

12 Bethurum Ia, VIIIa, xb, XVIa. The Ælfrician epitome of Julian of Toledo (edited in the appendix of this volume) was unknown to Professor Bethurum, so her comment on p. 305 denying his use of such documents, except perhaps in the case of Napier VIII, must be revised. Raynes also showed that the Boulogne ms contained a Latin sermon which Ælfric may have written and which served as his source for a Nativity homily, LS, I, I (MÆ, 25 [1957], 67–8).

13 In addition, he may also have paid fairly close attention to the reproduction and revision of his mss. See Neil R. Ker, 'Hemming's Cartulary,' *Studies in Medieval History Presented to Frederick Maurice Powicke*, ed. R.W. Hunt et al. (Oxford, 1948), pp. 49–75 at 70f.; the study of Wulfstan's handwriting cited in n.1; and Bethurum, p. 6.

14 McIntosh, *PBA*, 35 (1949), 114. See also Bethurum, pp. 92–4, and, for the grouping of these rhythmical units in larger units of two and three, pp. 292–3. Also important are Otto Funke, 'Some Remarks on Wulfstan's Prose Rhythm,' *ES*, 43 (1962), 311–18, and Roger Fowler, 'Some Stylistic Features of the *Sermo Lupi*,' *JEGP*, 65 (1966), 1–18. In an earlier article . . . ,' *Anglia*, 80 (1962), 33–5, Funke discussed the Old English and Latin antecedents of Wulfstan's style.

15 See the analysis of style in Bethurum, pp. 87–98.

16 The only exemplum possibly written by Wulfstan (Napier XVI, pp. 98.5–101.5) was omitted in Bethurum IV, after line 70, because its uniqueness and style made it seem to the editor unlikely to be genuine; this editorial decision has been criticized in a review by Pope, *MLN*, 74 [1959], 338–9.

17 Bethurum V. 27–32 ('That is in English,/ because evil waxes/ all too widely,/ true love is cooled./ Neither does one love God/ as he should/nor do men's pledges/ stand for anything,/ but evil reigns/ far and wide,/ and uncertain covenants/ are among men,/ and that is evident/ in many ways,/ let him understand who is able'). I have made the line arrangement and marked the stresses to emphasize the contrast with Ælfric. Translations of Wulfstan mine except as noted. The nota (7) is silently expanded to *and*.

18 Pope XVIII.328–37 ('He meant not the winter which customarily comes in the year's circuit, but as he said in another place, *Quia abundabit iniquitas, refrigescet caritas multorum*. That is in the English language, that in the evil time injustice will arise and greatly multiply, and true love will greatly cool, not of all men, but of very many, so that they love not at all the living God, nor their neighbors, nor therefore themselves; because he who loves not God loves not himself'). Pope points out the relation between these texts in his introduction and notes (pp. 585, 611).

19 Bethurum XVIII.66, 68, 92, 112. This piece is atypical enough, however, for some doubt to persist as to its genuineness (Bethurum, p. 35); its source is Ælfric, *In Dedicatione Ecclesiae*, Thorpe, II, 574–94.

20 On his theology, see Jost, *Wulfstan-studien*, pp. 168–72.

21 For comment on their literary relationship, in which the line of dependence seems almost invariably to run from Ælfric to Wulfstan, see Peter Clemoes, 'The Old English Benedictine Office, Corpus Christi College, Cambridge, MS 190, and the Relations between Ælfric and Wulfstan: A Reconsideration,' *Anglia*, 78 (1960), 265–83 at 281–3. Clemoes's article is a response to James M. Ure, *The Benedictine Office: An Old English Text*, Edinburgh University Publications, Language & Literature No. 11 (Edinburgh, 1957), on which see also L. Whitbread, 'The Old English Poems of the *Benedictine Office* and some Related Questions,' *Anglia*, 80 (1962), 37–49.

PART TWO

1 Many comments which state or imply such a conclusion are to be found in general surveys: e.g., C.L. Wrenn, *A Study of Old English Literature* (London, 1967), pp. 238, 224, 226 (speaking of Ælfric and making a distinction between his homilies and those of Wulfstan): John Godfrey, *The Church in Anglo-Saxon England* (Cambridge, 1962), pp. 333–4, 341 (Ælfric's sermons were 'for the parish clergy and their people'); John Lingard, *The History and Antiquities of the Anglo-Saxon Church*, 2 vols. (London, 1845), II, 312 (similar to Godfrey). Marguerite-Marie Dubois, *Ælfric: Sermonnaire, Docteur et Grammarien*, pp. 79–80, speaks of Ælfric's 'vocation mission-aire' and 'l'apostolat bénédictin.' Peter Clemoes avoids discussion of liturgical setting but stresses the fact that many of the *Catholic Homilies* (as opposed to the *Lives of Saints*, which are 'reading pieces') are based on the Gospel pericopes appointed for reading at Mass ('Ælfric' in *Continuations and Beginnings:* ed. E.G. Stanley, p. 181).

2 E.g., G.K. Anderson, *The Literature of the Anglo-Saxons* (rev. ed.; Princeton, 1966), chaps. 9–10; Stanley B. Greenfield, *A Critical History of Old English Literature* (New York, 1965), pp. 48–61. Dorothy Bethurum Loomis (review of Roger Fowler, ed., *Wulfstan's Canons of Edgar*, *MÆ*, 43 [1974], 151–5) remarks that the issue is basically unstudied.

3 See Trent, Sessio v.ii ('super lectione et praedicatione'), and Sessio XXIV: De reformatione, canon iv (Bologna, Centro di Documentazione, Instituto per le Scienze

Religiose, ed. *Conciliorum Oecumeni-corum Decreta*, comp. Joseph Albergio et al. [Basel, 1962], pp. 643–6, 739).

4 E.g., Theodor Klauser, *A Short History of the Western Liturgy: An Account and Some Reflections*, trans. John Halliburton (London, 1969), pp. 64, 69; Joseph A. Jungmann, *The Mass of the Roman Rite: Its Origins and Development*, I, 71. (See also pp. 456–61 where Jungmann correctly stresses the importance of the Gallican–Carolingian contribution to the history of preaching.) See below for further references, especially to the work of Amalarius.

5 See notes 6, 7 below.

Chapter 4

6 Notably Réginald Grégoire, *Les Homéliaires du Moyen Age: Invent-aire et Analyse des Manuscrits*, Rerum Ecclesiasticarum Documenta, Series Maior: Fontes, 6 (Rome, 1966); Henri Barré, *Les Homéliaires Carolingiens de l'École d'Auxerre*. Both volumes contain helpful bibliographical notes. Grégoire's contains an illuminating preface by Jean Leclercq, who has actively stimulated the study of homiliaries.

7 'Ælfric and the Early Medieval Homiliary,' *Traditio*, 15 (1959), 163–204, and 'Ælfric and the Homiliary of Haymo of Halberstadt' [*recte*: Haymo of Auxerre], ibid., 17 (1961), 457–69. Another important essay by Smetana, 'Paul the Deacon's Patristic Anthology,' forthcoming in

a collection of papers edited by Paul Szarmach, has a useful discussion of the nature of Paul's homiliary, the ms tradition in England, and Paul's use of the terms *homilia* and *sermo*.

8 Barré, p. 1; Grégoire, p. 2. I rely on both of these volumes for the reconstruction of the early history of the homiliary which follows.

9 Barré, p. 2, quoting *Reg. Ben.* from Hanslik's ed. ('expositions [of the lections] which were made by the renowned and orthodox catholic Fathers').

10 Barré, p. 2; Grégoire, pp. 2, 6. Caesarius is both one of the most important and the most difficult to assess of the figures in the history of medieval preaching and homiliary-making. Major consideration of his work is reserved for the following section.

11 Grégoire, p. 6, lists the works of Caesarius, Fulgentius of Ruspe, and Maximus of Turin as early homiliaries for the Office. On the widening of the obligation to participate in the Office, see Pierre Salmon, *L'Office Divin: Histoire de la Formation du Bréviaire*, Lex Orandi, 27 (Paris, 1959), pp. 18–34, 69–97.

12 Salmon, pp. 140–2. I use the term 'Night Office' to reflect the monastic use of terms at this stage. The early medieval Nocturnal Office came later to be called Matins, a term applied in the early period to the second office of the horarium. For an outline of the contents of the Night Office, see J.B.L. Tolhurst,

The Monastic Breviary of Hyde Abbey, vol. 6 (Introduction to the English Monastic Breviaries), Henry Bradshaw Society, 80 (London, 1942), pp. 179–80, and p. 187: 'On Sundays and on many feasts, [the lessons] of the third nocturn were of the Gospel and the homily upon it. In such cases, the first sentence of the Gospel followed by the words *et reliquae* were read before the ninth lesson. That and the remaining three were taken from the homily. An exception to this occurred at Christmas, when all four lessons of the third nocturn were from homilies on different Gospels; in this case the appropriate verse of the Gospel was read before each of these lessons.'

13 On Alan, see Barré, pp. 2–3; Grégoire, pp. 2, 6–7, 17ff.; Eduardo Hosp, 'Il Sermonario di Alano di Farfa,' *Ephemerides Liturgicae*, 50 (1936), 375–83 and 51 (1937), 210–41. On the date of the Roman Office homiliary, see also Salmon, p. 145, and the studies there cited.

14 Ed. Barré, pp. 23–6, following Raymond Étaix, 'Le prologue du sermonnaire d'Alain de Farfa,' *Scriptorium*, 18 (1964), 3–10. (Note also the comments of Étaix on the limitations of Hosp, at p. 3.)

15 Étaix, *Scriptorium*, 18 (1964), 9–10.

16 See Grégoire, pp. 6–11, 18.

17 I omit Alcuin, who is reputed also to have assembled a homiliary ('Collegit multis de patrum operibus omeliarum duo volumine,' *Vita Alcuni*, ed. in *MGH, Scriptores* xv.1, p. 195; on the qualities of this early *vita*, see Arthur Kleinclausz, *Alcuin*, Annales de l'Université de Lyon, 3rd Ser., 15 [Paris, 1948], pp. 8–9 ['originale et sincère mais insuffisante']). Germain Morin believed at one time he had rediscovered Alcuin's homiliary ('L'Homéliaire d'Alcuin retrouvé,' *RB*, 9 [1892], 491–7), but, according to Eleanor Shipley Duckett (*Alcuin, Friend of Charlemagne: His World and His Work* [New York, 1951], p. 199n; see also Gerald Ellard, *Master Alcuin, Liturgist: A Partner of Our Piety* [Chicago, 1956], pp. 87–90), Morin later confessed doubts as to the correctness of his argument. It is now generally held that Alcuin's homiliary is unknown; and Morin's ms has recently been identified as an abridged copy of the Homiliary of Heric of Auxerre (Barré, pp. 78–9). But it is usually stated with some confidence that Alcuin did assemble a homiliary and that it was designed for use by the secular clergy (e.g., Kleinclausz, p. 107 [not 'destiné aux lecteurs de l'office divin ... mais à l'usage des prédicateurs']). The latter point is supported by reference to Alcuin's *Epistle* 136 (*MGH, Epp.* 4, 205–10), in which he stresses the importance of preaching by all orders of clergy; but the letter is addressed to the two-sword theory of polity and is concerned only, in this context, with the issue whether the preaching office is reserved to the episcopate. There is no internal

indication that Alcuin completed a homiliary or intended it for use in the secular church; if it existed and was for secular churches, it was still probably for the Offices, not the Mass. One suspects greater scepticism is in order. Perhaps the author of the *Vita* was somehow confused and attributed the 'official' homiliary of Paul to Alcuin, whom he knew both as a student of patristic exegesis and as an agent of Charlemagne's program of liturgical reform and uniformity. Certainly the relevant sentence of the Epistle could describe Paul's two volumes of patristic selections. Grégoire (p. 10), without reviewing the internal evidence, concludes, 'on peut se demander si l'homéliaire d'Alcuin a jamais existé.' It may also be noted that it is now doubted that Alcuin was responsible for the Supplement to the *Gregorianum* (see, inter alios, Klaus Gamber, 'Die fränkische Anhang zum Gregorianum im Licht eines Fragments aus dem Anfang des 9.Jh.,' *Sacris Erudiri*, 21 [1972–73], 267–89).

18 'Epistola Generalis,' *MGH*, *Leges* II, *Capitula* I, pp. 80–1 (trans. Ellard, *Master Alcuin*, p. 89: 'Lastly [among his liturgical projects], because we find the Lessons for the night Office compiled with scant if well-intentioned effort of certain people, to be nonetheless quite ill suited, as set out without the words of the authors, and bristling with countless mistakes, we have not tolerated that in these our days such solecisms should resound in the Lessons at the public [*sic*] Offices, and we have charted our course for a reform of the same. This task of improvement we assigned to our client, Paul the Deacon, so that, carefully paging the writings of the Catholic fathers, he might gather together selected blossoms from those vast meadows, and (as it were) arrange into one wreath whatever is found useful.') See also Paul's dedicatory verses, rpt. Grégoire, p. 75, from *MGH*, *Poetae* I, pp. 68–9. The latest and most reliable printed inventory of Paul's Homiliary is Grégoire's at pp. 77ff.

19 It may be noted that as late as the episcopate of Gregory I there was wide tolerance of liturgical diversity. Uniformity was first exploited as a tool for reform by the Carolingians. See Paul Meyvaert, 'Diversity within Unity, a Gregorian Theme,' *Heythrop Journal*, 4 (1963), 141–62, esp. 162.

20 Not that it was not tampered with by later hands. Owing to additions, reconstruction of Paul's original work remains difficult. See Barré, pp. 3–4.

21 On this point and the distinction in some later homiliaries between *sermones* for the second Nocturn and the *homiliae in Evangelium* for the third Nocturn, see B. de Gaiffier, 'L'Homiliaire-Légendier de Valère (Sion, Suisse),' *Analecta Bollandiana*, 73 (1955), 119–39 at 119–22.

22 Barré, p. 4. The following remarks on the 'Carolingian homiliaries' are based on Barré and citations are given only for points of special interest and quotations; see especially Barré's 'conclusion,' pp. 139–42.

23 Barré, p. 6: 'Liturgiques par leur ordonnance et leur objet, leurs Homéliaires ne sont plus par leur destination; au lieu de fournir des *lectiones* pour l'Office divin, ils servent à la lecture méditée ou bien à la prédication, "ad legendum vel ad praedicandum," précise Raban (*PL*, 110, 10).' The case of Rabanus is especially interesting, for he produced two homiliaries, one (*PL*, 110, 9ff.), dedicated to Archbishop Haistulf, as a preachers' handbook which could also be read for meditation; the other (the only surviving portion of which is printed in *PL*, 110, 135ff.) was dedicated to the emperor Lothair, treated the Gospels and Epistles, and was for devotional use. Barré, pp. 13–14, remarks that the contents of the former are *sermones*, those of the latter *homiliae*. Whereas the former draws heavily on Caesarius, the latter does not.

24 On early preaching terms, see Christine Mohrmann, 'Praedicare-Tractare-Sermo: Essai sur la terminologie de la prédication paléochrétienne,' *Le Maison-Dieu*, 39 (1954), 97–107. On aspects of English use, see also Max Förster, 'Die liturgische Bedeutung von ae. traht,' *Beiblatt zur Anglia*, 53 (1942), 180–4.

25 Barré, p. 141. See also his elaborate comparative tables of the contents of these and related collections, pp. 211ff.

26 Preface to Grégoire, p. vi.

27 See Suitbert Bäumer, *Histoire du Bréviaire*, trans. Réginald Viron, 2 vols. (Paris, 1905), I, 410–13; Pierre Batiffol, *Histoire du Bréviaire Romain*, 3rd ed., Bibliothèque d'Histoire religieuse (Paris, 1911), esp. pp. 124–46; Salmon, *L'Office Divin*, pp. 154, 230–4; W.H. Frere, ed., *The Leofric Collectar Compared with the Collectar of St Wulfstan . . .*, vol. 2; Henry Bradshaw Society, 51 (for 1918; London 1921); Anselm Hughes, ed., *The Portiforium of Saint Wulstan (Corpus Christi College, Cambridge, MS 391)*, 2 vols; Henry Bradshaw Society, 89 (for 1956) and 90 (for 1957) (Leighton Buzzard, 1958–60), esp. the Introduction, which appears in vol. 2; J.B.L. Tolhurst, ed., *The Monastic Breviary of Hyde Abbey, Winchester*, vol. 6.

28 Rabanus says his first homiliary is 'ad praedicandum populo' (*PL*, 110, 9; Barré p. 13; see also note 23, above); the Chartres homiliary is said to be intended 'fournir aux prêtres des modèles et des suggestions pour leurs allocutions au peuple chrétien' (ibid., p. 24). The majority of the contents of both are to be characterized as 'sermons' rather than 'homilies.' One may also mention the homiliary of Lantperthus, abbot of Mondsee in Bavaria,

'destiné à un évêque parlant à son clergé et son peuple' (ibid., p. 25). Occasional homiliaries for the Mass also existed: e.g., the late seventh-century Toledo homiliary inventoried by Grégoire, pp. 161–85. Gregory the Great's *XL Homiliarum in Evangelia* (*PL*, 76, 1075ff.) was used by many for preaching to the people. Rabanus may follow Gregory in devoting the first forty of the homilies dedicated to Archbishop Haistulf to feasts of the calendar (1–8 for Advent through Epiphany, 9–23 for Quadragesima through Pentecost, 24–40 for saints' and common days) before appending thirty more pieces on general, usually moral subjects.

29 F.R. Albert, *Die Geschichte der Predigt in Deutschland bis Luther*, 3 vols. (Gütersloh, 1892–96); R. Cruel, *Geschichte der deutschen Predigt im Mittelalter* (Detmold, 1897); Anton Linsenmayer, *Geschichte der Predigt in Deutschland von Karl dem Grossen bis zum Ausgange des vierzehnten Jahrhunderts* (1886; rpt. Frankfurt, 1969). Cruel's work is the more frequently cited; but I have found Linsenmayer's the more useful, for he perceives what seem to me to be the basic issues. Also useful are Hans von Schubert, *Geschichte der christlichen Kirche im Frühmittelalter: Ein Handbuch* (Tübingen, 1921), pp. 652–4; and Ludwig Eisenhofer, *Handbuch der katholischen Liturgik*, 2 vols. (revising the earlier work of

Valentin Thalhofer; Freiburg, 1933), II, 114–26.

30 Yngve Brilioth, *A Brief History of Preaching*, trans. Karl E. Mattson (1945; Philadelphia, 1965) is a perceptive, brief survey and the latest in English. See also Alfred Niebergall, 'Die Geschichte der christlichen Predigt,' in *Leiturgia: Handbuch des evangelischen Gottesdienstes*, ed. Karl Ferdinand Müller and Walter Blankenburg, vol. 2 (Kassel, 1955), 181–353; Eberhard Weismann, 'Die Predigtgottesdienst und die verwandten Formen,' ibid., 3 (1956), 2–96; and Johann Baptist Schneyer, *Geschichte der katholischen Predigt* (Freiburg, 1969), pp. 99–109. Useful guides to documentary evidence related to pastoral preaching are Guy Devailly, 'La Pastorale en Gaule au IXe Siècle,' *Revue d'Histoire de l'Église de France*, 59 (1973), 23–54, and Jean Gaudemet, 'La Paroise au Moyen Âge: État des Questions,' ibid., 5–21. The documents are studied by Carlo de Clercq, *La Législation religieuse franque de Clovis à Charlemagne: Études sur les Actes des Conciles et les Capitulaires, les Statuts diocésains et les Règles monastiques*, 2 vols.: I (507–814), Université de Louvain, Receuil de Travaux publiés par les Membres des Conférences d'Histoire et de Philologie, 2nd ser., 38 (Paris, 1936); II (814–900) (Anvers, 1958). The documents for the years 511–695 have been edited by de Clercq in *CCL*, 162^A, though I cite earlier editions below.

31 Notable apparent exceptions to the rule that preaching remained an episcopal function are Jerome, whose homilies on the Psalter are transcriptions of exegetical addresses delivered in the Jerusalem monastery, and Gregory I, whose *Moralia in Job* was delivered before his election to the pontificate in similar circumstances at Constantinople. Bede's homilies, largely derivative of the Fathers, should be considered under the rubric of monastic homilies. He refers frequently in his address to the *fratres* to the previous reading of the Gospel (e.g. *Sermo* I.1 in *CCL*, 122, 1); the setting is, thus, more likely to have been the Night Office than the Mass (see note 12, above). (See, on Jerome, Berthold Altaner, *Patrologie*, 5th ed. [Freiburg, 1958], pp. 361–2; and on Bede, W.F. Bolton, *A History of Anglo-Latin Literature, 597–1066*, vol. 1 [Princeton, 1967], 166–7). Cruel divides the first part of his study into three periods: 'Die Zeit der Missionpredigt' (600–900); 'Die Zeit der bischöflischen Predigt' (900–1100); and 'Die Zeit der Parochialpredigt' (1100–1200). Such monks as Rabanus (*PL*, 110, 9), Abbo of St-Germain-des-Près (*PL*, 132, 761–64), and Ælfric (Prefaces to *CH*, I and II) who wrote sermons to be read to lay congregations tended to address their collections to bishops for dissemination. On problems associated with the preaching of monks to the laity, see further, p. 47.

32 The best survey of this issue, despite its polemicism, is T.G. Jalland, 'The Doctrine of the Parity of Ministers,' in *The Apostolic Ministry: Essays on the History and the Doctrine of Episcopacy*, ed. Kenneth E. Kirk (London, 1946), pp. 305–49. A slightly different view is implied by Gregory Dix, 'The Ministry in the Early Church,' at 220 of the same volume. On Jerome's role in this development, see Altaner, *Patrologie*, pp. 364–5.

33 From the time of Gregory onwards most missionaries were monks.

34 See J. Tixéront, *L'Ordre et les Ordinations: Étude de Théologie Historique* (2nd ed.; Paris, 1925), pp. 53–4.

35 This development is reflected in Ælfric's Pastoral Letters: I.29–45; 2.115–31; II.99–116; see also the fragment *De Septem Gradibus aecclesiasticis* and the excerpt from Jerome (Anhang v) in Fehr, *Hirtenbriefe*. See Dubois, *Ælfric*, pp. 136–7. Alfric's main source is Isidore, the chief mediator (in his *De Ecclesiasticis Officiis* [*PL*, 931) of the views of Jerome. The older position, however, also continued to be maintained in some quarters (see Jalland in *Apostolic Ministry*, p. 340).

36 Confusion sometimes arises because of this situation in the meaning of the term *sacerdos*, which was originally applied only to bishops. Carolingian writers sometimes failed to understand distinctions implied by their sources, and we may

likewise miss the intention of authors who wished to restrict the term's reference to bishops. See the entry *s.v. sacerdos* in J.F. Niermeyer, *Mediae Latinitas Lexicon Minus* (Leiden, 1960–   ).

37 von Schubert, *Geschichte*, p. 652.

38 The *Admonitio* is Sermo I in the ed. of Germain Morin (*CCL*, 103–4); the canons of Vaison are printed in *MGH, Leges* III, *Concilia* I, pp. 54–8. The best recent survey of Caesarius' career is the introduction by Marie-José Delage to *Césaire d'Arles, Sermons au Peuple*, 1, Sources Chrétiennes, 175 (Paris, 1971). See also Henry G.J. Beck, *The Pastoral Care of Souls During the Sixth Century*, Analecta Gregoriana, 51 (Rome, 1950); G. de Plinval in *Histoire de l'Église depuis les Origines jusqu'à nos Jours*, ed. Augustin Fliche and Victor Martin, vol. 4 (De la Mort de Théodose à l'Élection de Grégoire le Grand, ed. P. de Labriolle, et al.) (Paris, 1948), pp. 406–12; Altaner, *Patrologie*, 439–40.

39 Plinval (*Histoire*, 412). See *Sermo* I.12 ('Ista enim omnia et his similia non solum sacerdotes domini in civitatibus, sed etiam in parrochiis presbyteri et diaconi et possunt et debent frequentius praedicare.'); I.15 ('Vere dico, quia etiamsi omnes presbyteri desint qui hoc facere possint, non est incongruum vel indignum, si homilias sanctorum patrum publice in ecclesia praecipiatur etiam diacono recitare: quia si dignus est diaconus quisque ut legat quod locutus est Christus, non debet iudicare indignus ut recitet quod praedicavet sanctus Elarius, sanctus Ambrosius, sanctus Augustinus, vel reliqui patres.'); and *Sermo* II, the preface to a collection of *sermones* of Caesarius which are recommended for public readings by presbyters or deacons. In *Sermo* I.15, Caesarius seems aware that his program is innovative and invokes the customs of the East as precedent.

40 This fact would be explained were it true (as I noted above some scholars believe) that Caesarius' collections were for the Office and his injunctions somehow connected with wider imposition on the clergy of the duty to say the Offices. The sermon was clearly part of the episcopal Mass at Arles (see Delage, p. 159). But it also was featured in the Offices, which Caesarius made an attempt to bring into general use and to make available to the people (ibid., pp. 150–3). See also Beck, *Pastoral Care*, pp. 108–21, 135–42.

41 Caesarius was not included in Paul the Deacon's Homiliary except for Homily I.28 (see Grégoire, p. 81), which was admitted under the name of Maximus of Turin; but he is represented in Alan of Farfa and a number of the Carolingian collections. Paul may have excluded Caesarius because his sermons were more suited to pastoral than to monastic use, for it is inconceivable that Caesarius was not available in some form to Paul.

42 Concilium Latunense (673–75), canon xviii (*MGH*, *Leges* II, Concilia I, 219 'that he may warm the flock committed to him with spiritual foods').

43 Theodor Scheifer, *Winfrid-Bonifatius und die Christliche Grundlegung Europas* (Freiburg, 1954), pp. 244–5. The canons of Clovesho are printed in Arthur West Haddan and William Stubbs, eds., *Councils and Ecclesiastical Documents Relating to Great Britain and Ireland*, vol. 3 (Oxford, 1871), 360–76; trans. in Henry Gee and William John Hardy, *Documents Illustrative of English Church History* (London, 1896), pp. 15–32.

44 One is reminded of William of Malmesbury's report of Aldhelm (*De Gestis Pontificum Anglorum* v.190, ed. N.E.S.A. Hamilton, Rolls Series, 52 [London, 1870], p. 336) and of Bede's account of Cuthbert's missionary preaching before he became a bishop (*Historia Ecclesiastica* IV.27).

45 'Preach sound faith to others, or give a knowledge of the word' (trans. Gee and Hardy). Canon vi of the Legatine Synod of 787 (Haddan and Stubbs, III, 447–62) does not mention preaching; perhaps the legates of Rome are deliberate in this.

46 Canon xi defines sacerdotal ministry as 'baptizando, et docendo, et judicando,' and stresses the necessity of right belief if one is to fulfil his catechetical duties.

47 'Let them by preaching instruct the servants subject to them from the declarations of sacred Scripture. It is also decreed that on Sunday and the major festivals, the people, often invited by the priests of God, should assemble for hearing the word of God and frequently be present at the sacraments of Masses and at sermons of doctrine.'

48 If this reading were sustained, one would have a catechetical or moral sermon, not a homily. Such a situation might accord with the strong romanizing tendency of Clovesho (see canons xiii, xv, xviii), since the homily or sermon was almost certainly not a feature of the Mass of the Roman rite at this time.

49 *Brief History*, p. 70.

50 Printed in *MGH*, *Leges* III, Concilia II, pp. 245–306. The councils of Arles, Rheims, Mainz, Chalon-sur-Saône, Tours, and the summary *Concordia Episcoporum* are cited parenthetically below by canon numbers. Also extremely important is Charlemagne's *Admonitio generalis* of 789, esp. section 82 (*MGH*, *Leges* II, *Capitularia* I, 52–62), which I read as a clarion call to general or catechetical (but not to expository) preaching.

51 'How bishops ought to be diligent to preach the sermons and homilies of the holy fathers in accordance with the proper signification of language so that all can understand.'

52 'It is our unanimous opinion that each bishop should have homilies containing needful admonitions by

which his subjects may be taught, that is concerning the catholic faith, in order that they may be able to embrace it, concerning the perpetual retribution of the good and the eternal damnation of the evil, concerning the coming general resurrection and last judgment and by what works one may merit eternal life and by what works be excluded from it. And that each should be diligent to translate clearly the same homilies into the rustic Romance language or German, in which all may the more easily be able to understand the things which are said.

53 See Barré, p. 25, and his 'L'Homiliaire Carolingien de Mondsee,' RB, 71 (1961), 71–107.

54 'That not only in cities but also in the [rural] parishes, presbyters should make addresses to the people.' The issue of deacons as preachers or readers of homilies was not raised.

55 'Concerning the presbyters stationed [in parishes] and their preaching and possession of homilies of the Fathers and according to the Fathers' teaching for preaching, as it is set out in the capitulary by the Lord [Charlemagne] and in the community of Tours, everyone was pleased.'

56 The homilies of Abbo of St-Germain-des Près, when edited completely, may provide important new material, for Abbo seems to have written them in something approaching Romance dialect (Jean Leclercq, 'Le Florilège d'Abbon de

Saint-Germain,' Revue du Moyen Âge Latin, 3 [1947], 113–40 at 115). Professor Alan K. Brown of the Ohio State University reported to the Modern Language Association's Old English Group in 1973 that he had discovered new evidence of Wulfstan's reliance on Abbo of St-Germain, whose homiliary abbreviates that of Haymo of Auxerre.

57 For a catalogue of preachers' materials, see Schneyer, Gesch. der katholischen Predigt, pp. 104–7. On the ordines, see Ordo x in Michel Andrieu, Les Ordines Romani du Haut Moyen Âge, 5 vols., Spicilegium Sacrum Lovaniense, Études et Documents, fasc. 11, 23, 24, 28, 29 (Louvain, 1931–61), vol. II at 357 (= Ordo VI in PL, 78, 992; see also item 98 of Cyrille Vogel and Reinhard Elze, ed., Le Pontifical Romano-Germanique du dixième Siècle, Studi e Testi, 226, 227, 269 [Vatican, 1963–72], II, 353). This ordo, the only one in Andrieu's collection which refers to preaching, was Rhenish in origin and was known in England in a ms associated with Bishop Wulfstan II of Worcester and the priest Coleman (on whom see below) which also contained canonical and liturgical materials connected with Ælfric and Wulfstan of York (Cambridge, Corpus Christi College 265; see also Ker 53; Montague Rhodes James, A Descriptive Catalogue of the Manuscripts in the Library of Corpus Christi College, Cambridge, II.1 [Cambridge, 1911],

21; and Mary Bateson, 'A Worcester Cathedral Book of Ecclesiastical Collections, Made c. 1000 A.D.,' *EHR*, 10 [1895], 712–31. The text, at p. 324, is incomplete and breaks before the passage quoted below). The passage simply indicates that, after the reading of the Gospel, the bishop, having been censed and having kissed the Gospel-book, 'ad predicationem per manus presbiteri et archidiaconi perducendus est.' While he preaches 'ad populum,' the subdeacon carries the book among the brothers to be kissed; but if 'episcopus predicare noluit,' he begins to intone the Creed (secs. 30–3).

58 *MGH*, *Leges* II, *Capitularia*, I–II (e.g., Mainz, 847, canon ii at II.176; 'Capitularia de Presbyteris Admonendis,' cap. i at I.237; Edictum Pistense, 864, at II.311, etc.).

59 Ibid. (e.g., Haitonis [d.823], cap. vi at I, 363; 'Brevum Exempla,' 810, cap. v at I.251).

60 Theodulf ed. in *PL* 105, 191–206; OE trans. in Oxford MS. Bodley 865 ed. Arthur S. Napier, *The Old English Version of the Enlarged Rule of Chrodegang ...*; *An Old English rendering of the Capitula of Theodulf; An Interlinear Old English rendering of Epitome of Benedict of Aniane*, E.E.T.S., O.S., 150 (London, 1916); the later OE vers. of MS. Corpus Christi College, Cambridge, 201, ed. Benjamin Thorpe, *Ancient Laws and Institutes of England ...* , 2 vols (London, 1840), II, 400.

61 Caps. 22, 28, 46. The last of these mentions Mass and sermon in a manner similar to that of the Clovesho canons.

62 On this development and on Chrodegang, see von Schubert, *Geschichte*, pp. 576–7; Salmon, *L'Office Divin*, pp. 27–34.

63 Cap. xliv (*PL* 89, 1076): the people need baptism, confirmation, confession, and preaching, 'Unde constituimus ut bis in mense per totum annum, de quinto decimo, in quinto decimo, verbum salutis ei praedicetur, qualiter ad vitam aeternam, Deo auxiliante, perveniat. Et si omnibus festis et Dominicis diebus assidua fuerit praedicatio, utilior est, et juxta quod intelligere vulgus possit, ita praedicandum est.' (Compare the OE version, cap. xlii [ed. Napier, p. 50]: 'For þi þonne we gesettað þæt tuwa on monþe, þæt is ymbe feowertine niht, man æfre þam folce bodige mid larspelle, hu hi þurh Godes fultum magon to þam ecean life becuman. and þeah hit man ælce Sunnandæge singallice and freolsdæge dyde, þæt wære betere. and do ma þa larbodunge be þam þe þæt folc understandan mage.')

64 See *Missae expositionis geminus codex* I.8; *Eclogae de ordine romano* 9; *Ordinis totius missae expositio prior* I.9 (all in *Amalarii Episcopi Opera Liturgica Omnia*, ed. Ioanne Michaele Hanssens, Studi e Testi, 138–40 [Vatican, 1948–50] at I, 261–2; III, 248; III, 305, respectively).

Some of this material is in MS. CCCC 265 (see note 53, above).

65 *Liber Officialis* III.i (Hanssens, ed., II, 257–60). This passage was translated into Old English, perhaps from an abridgement of Amalarius, in the front matter of an eleventh-century pontifical (Joseph B. Trahern, Jr., 'Amalarius *Be Becnum*: A Fragment of the *Liber Officialis* in Old English,' *Anglia*, 91 [1973], 475–8).

66 L. Duchesne, *Christian Worship, Its Origins and Evolution: A Study of the Latin Liturgy to the Time of Charlemagne*, trans. M.L. McClure (5th ed.; London, 1920), pp. 170–1; Klauser, *Short History*, p. 64.

67 Duchesne, *Christian Worship*, p. 196; Beck, *Pastoral Care*, pp. 135–42.

68 On medieval catechesis, see H.W. Surkau, *s.v.* 'Katechetik,' 'Kathechismus,' *Der Religion in Geschichte und Gegenwart* (3rd ed.; Tübingen, 1954): Peter Göbl, *Geschichte der Katechese im Abendlande vom Verfalle des Katechumenats bis zum Ende des Mittelalters* (Kempten, 1880).

69 Although the existence of the Prone is well attested, the critical literature is sparse. See, in general, H. Leclercq in *DACL*, *s.v. prône*; U. Berlière, 'Le Prône dans la Liturgie,' *RB*, 7 (1890), 97–104, 145–51, 241–6; Jungmann, *Mass of the Roman Rite*, I, 456–94; Weismann, 'Die Predigtgottesdienst und die verwandten Formen,' *Leiturgia*, III, 18–21; von Schubert, *Gesch. der chr.*

Kirche im Frühmittelalter, pp. 652–3; Devailly, *Revue d'Histoire de l'Église de France*, 59 (1973), 32–4. The etymological comments of Leclercq and Berlière (p. 98) are of some interest, although they are perhaps somewhat fanciful. The *pronaos* may be the forecourt or narthex where, in earlier centuries, catechumens and penitents received instruction; after the disappearance of the catechumenate, the term may have come to be applied to the nave. Alternatively, *pronaos* may simply refer to the area before the *naos* (i.e., the presbytery and sanctuary). In any case, the term comes to refer to allocutions, devotions, and announcements delivered among the people rather than from the choir or sanctuary and also to the place from which they were delivered (Du Cange, *Glossarium Medie et Infimae Latinitatis* [Paris, 1845], *s.v. pronus*).

70 *Gesch. der Predigt*, p. 29; see also Weismann in *Leiturgia*, III, 19.

71 *Mass of the Roman Rite*, I, 458.

72 E.g., Caesarius, *Sermo* I; Alcuin, Epistle 136. Jungmann, *Mass of the Roman Rite*, I, 459n, notes that confusion is sometimes caused by the fact that *praedicare* can also mean 'to read solemnly.'

73 See, in addition to the histories of preaching already cited, Th.-M. Charland, *Artes Praedicandi: Contribution à l'Histoire de la Rhétorique au Moyen Age*, Publications de l'Institut d'Études Médiévales d'Ottawa, 7 (Paris and Ottawa, 1936); Dorothea

Roth, *Die mittelalterliche Predigt-theorie und das Manuale Curatorum des Johann Ulrich Surgant*, Basler Beiträge zur Geschichtswissenschaft 58 (Basel, 1956). For bibliography of later preaching theory, see James J. Murphy, *Medieval Rhetoric: A Select Bibliography*, Toronto Medieval Bibliographies, 3 (Toronto, 1971), pp. 71–81, and *Rhetoric in the Middle Ages: A History of Rhetorical Theory from Saint Augustine to the Renaissance* (Berkeley, Calif., 1974), pp. 269–355.

Chapter 5

1 *MGH, Leges* II, *Capitularia Regum Francorum* I, 343–9.

2 See Noreen Hunt, *Cluny under Saint Hugh, 1049–1109* (London, 1967), pp. 99–117; Jean Leclercq, *The Love of Learning and the Desire for God*, trans. Catherine Misrahi (1961; New York, 1962), pp. 168–70. On specific sources of *Regularis Concordia*, see the ed. of Thomas Symons.

3 Tolhurst, *Breviary of Hyde Abbey*, VI, pp. 50–5. The earliest English mss that collect the *capitula* or lections of the Offices rarely include extra-biblical materials (W.H. Frere, ed., *The Leofric Collectar*, II, xvii).

4 *The Love of Learning and the Desire for God*, pp. 168ff.; 'Recherches sur d'anciens Sermons monastiques,' *Revue Mabillon*, 36 (1946), 1–14. In another article, 'Prédicateurs béné-dictins aux XIᵉ et XIIᵉ Siècles,' ibid., 33 (1943), 48–73, Leclercq notes

that the problem of monastic preaching to the laity merits special study. Another topic which invites further attention and impinges on the use of homiletic matter for *lectio divina* is *ruminatio* (see Leclercq, *Love*, pp. 78–9, and 'Les Médita-tions d'un Moine au XIIᵉ Siècle,' *Revue Mabillon*, 34 [1944], 1–19; Philip J. West, 'Liturgical Style and Structure in Bede's Homily for the Easter Vigil,' *American Benedictine Review*, 23 [1972], 1–8; and a very suggestive paper by Thomas D. Hill, 'Notes on the Imagery and Structure of the Old English "Christ I,"' *N&Q*, 217 [1972], 84–9).

5 Ed. Symons, cap. 21 at p. 17 ('the Rule or, on feast days, the Gospel of the day, shall be read and the prior shall explain what has been read as the Lord shall inspire him'). Note that some consuetudinaries read *omelia* for *euangelium* and then require a 'sermonem de presenti lectione.'

6 One should also mention the *collatio*, a reading on which there may have been commentary. See *Reg. Conc.*, caps. 26–7, and Leclercq as cited in note 4.

7 This system, perhaps introduced to Ramsey from Fleury by Abbo, seems to be presupposed in some passages of Byrhtferth's *Manual* (ed. S.J. Crawford, E.E.T.S., 177 [1929]) according to Cyril Hart, 'Byrhtferth and his Manual,' *MÆ*, 41 (1972), 95–109, at 96–7. If monasteries more or less regularly served as diocesan

seminaries, instructing clerks in the vernacular, the Offices or parts of them may have been read in the vernacular. Such a background provides an interesting setting for Ælfric's earlier exegetical work and for his Letter for Wulfsige.

8 I offer this suggestion, here and elsewhere, with great hesitancy and against the advice of Father Smetana.

9 Ed. Fehr, *Hirtenbriefe*, hereafter cited parenthetically, using Fehr's arabic numbering for the Latin letters and Roman for the English.

10 I is headed 'epistola de canonibus'; II, in the version revised by Wulfstan, 'To gehadedum mannum'; 2, 'Sermo Episcopi ad Cleros'; and 3, 'Sermo ad Sacerdotes.' III, 'Quando Dividis crisma,' is largely liturgical instructions; its latter portions stress the teaching office but not liturgical preaching.

11 On dates, see Clemoes in Fehr, pp. cxxvii ff., and 'Chronology' at 244–5.

12 II.106 and 2.121 mention instead the deacon's role as gospeller. The stance of Ælfric in Fehr I may be compared with the argument in Alcuin, Epistle 136, that the reading of the Gospel and the Fathers' homilies is in fact preaching.

13 '61. The priest is to relate the meaning of the Gospel in English to the people on Sundays and Mass-days. 62. And also concerning the *Pater Noster* and the Creed, as often as he can, for their inspiration, that they know the faith and keep their religion. 63. Let the teacher warn against what the prophet says: *Canes ... latrare*. Dumb hounds cannot bark. 64. We ought to bark and preach to the laity lest for lack of instruction they be lost.'

14 'To preach the true faith to men and recite a discourse to them' (II.175); for the latter phrase, the Latin reads 'the meaning of the Gospel in their own language.' 'It is seemly for us bishops that we open for you priests the bookish lore which our canon teaches us and also the Gospel in English' (II.2). For II, I quote the version of MS 0 (Corpus Christi College, Cambridge, 190).

15 Parenthetical numbers suggest associations among the lists; indications of abbreviation omitted. I have ignored many tantalizing problems, going into detail only insofar as necessary to consider the issue of homiliaries. In treating I, however, I read *passionalem* with Fehr's MSS Gg (Cambridge, University Library, Gg.3.28) and X (Oxford, Bodleian, Junius 121) in preference to the *pastoralem* of 0. The latter is almost surely scribal error, perhaps (as Professor Whitelock has suggested to me) by confusion with the *Cura Pastoralis*. 0 also reads *sangboc* for *-bec* in Gg and X. Gg is the closest to Ælfric of these MSS; 0 and X are from Worcester.

16 Prologue to *Poenitentiale Egberti*, quoted in Fehr's apparatus at pp. 51–2 as Ælfric's source. See also

ed. in F.W.H. Wasserschleben, *Die Bussordnungen der abendländischen Kirche* ... (Halle, 1851), p. 232. Fehr also quotes a Carolingian canonist, Haito of Basel (d. 823), who lists necessary books: liber sacramentorum (4), lectionarius (2), antiphonarius (5), baptisterium (6), computus (7), canon poenitentialis (9), psalterium (1), homiliae per circulum anni dominicis diebus et singulis festibitatibus aptae.

Pseudo-Egbert, like Ælfric, refers to the liturgical books as the *arma* of the clergy.

17 Ed. Max Förster in *The Exeter Book of Old English Poetry*, with Introductory Chapters by R.W. Chambers, Max Förster, and Robin Flower(London, 1933), at pp. 10–32, text and important notes at pp. 18–30; books cited listed at pp. 21, 25–8. I have omitted the Benedictionals and/or Pontificals (p. 26), the Boethius and 'micel Englisc boc' (p. 28) and the Latin volumes (pp. 28–9). When he came to Exeter, Leofric is said to have found 'boca na ma buton .i. capitularie 7 .i. for-ealdod niht-sang 7 .i. pistel-boc 7 .ii. for-ealdode rædingbec swiðe wake 7 [departing from books to add other necessities of mass-priests] .i. wac mæssereaf' (p. 28). For a recent study of the career of Bishop Leofric, see Frank Barlow in Barlow et al., *Leofric of Exeter: Essays in Commemoration of the Foundation of Exeter Cathedral Library in A.D. 1072* (Exeter, 1972), pp. 1–16.

The Leofric Inventory, later and for a better-equipped, episcopal church than Ælfric's list, has the value of providing a comparison for Ælfric's English vocabulary. Unfortunately, the twelfth century list of books given by Æthelwold of Winchester to Peterborough (M.R. James, 'Lists of Books formerly in Peterborough Abbey Library,' *Supplement to the Bibliographical Society Transactions*, No. 5 [1926], p. 19) contains no liturgical items.

18 See also introduction, p. lxxxvi ff.

19 See esp. v *post Pascha* (Pope VIII.1–11).

20 Leofric's *Cristes-boc* is Cambridge University Library MS. ii.2.11 (Ker 20), which has rubrics indicating when a passage is to be read and giving the Latin incipit.

21 For *Cristes-boc*, see Pope's glossary; examples of the two uses of *godspell* are Pope I.2, II.2, 59, III.46, 120, etc. (pericope) and I.17, II.84, 16, etc. (whole book).

22 Given the uses of *spell* cited in Pope's glossary, Ælfric, too, would have used the word. See Förster's important notes 89 and 94 at pp. 26–8 of *Exeter Book* on *ræding-boc* and *spel-boc*.

23 Clemoes in the rpt. of Fehr, p. cxxxiv. Professor Whitelock drew my attention to the matters discussed in this paragraph.

24 'Be gehadedum mannum' printed as XXIII in the Anhang to Karl Jost, ed., *Die 'Institutes of Polity Civil and Ecclesiastical,' ein Werk Erzbischof*

Wulfstans von York, Swiss Studies in English, 47, pp. 217–22. Only the sections from 6 or 7 on are by Wulfstan; of these 11–16 have to do with educational prerequisites to ordination. See Jost, pp. 25–28.

25 Dorothy Bethurum Loomis, review of Fowler, *MÆ*, 43 (1974), 153, notes Wulfstan's mitigations of Ælfric's requirement that the clergy be present at or recite the Daily Offices. On similar situations in continental churches, see Devailly, *Revue d'Histoire de l'Église de France*, 59 (1973), 29–34.

26 Ed. Jost, cited parenthetically ('both to teach well and to instruct well by example'; 'to teach and to guide'). On parallels to the expressions mentioned here, see Roger Fowler, ed., *Wulfstan's Canons of Edgar*, E.E.T.S., 226 (London, 1972), p. xxxii.

27 For example, Eugenii II Concilium Romanum, cap. iii (*MGH, Leges* II, *Capitulae Regum Francorum*, I, 372). Such warnings are also patristic and prophetic commonplaces.

28 *The Homilies of Wulfstan*, p. 348.

29 Fowler, ed., p. xxviii ('And we teach that priests ought both to preach to the people every Sunday and always teach them well by example').

30 *Excerptiones pseudo-Ecgberti*, III, quoted by Fowler, p. 37 ('That on all feasts and Dominical days every priest should preach the Gospel of Christ to the people'). See Fowler, p. lii, for further comment on canon 52.

31 Ibid., p. 36. Neither Ælfric nor Wulfstan says that the people are to attend the Offices.

32 See Mary Bateson, 'Rules for Monks and Secular Canons after the Revival under King Edgar,' *EHR*, 9 (1894), 690–708.

33 Frank Barlow, *The English Church, 1000–1066*, p. 90.

34 In the two earlier lives of Æthelwold, the only references I find to preaching are general and commonplace (Ælfric's *Vita Æthelwoldi*, cap. 18; the *vita* attributed to Wulfstan the Cantor, caps. 25–7; both ed. Michael Winterbottom, *Three Lives of English Saints*. Despite Winterbottom's argument to the contrary ('Three Lives of Saint Ethelwold,' *MÆ*, 41 [1972], 191–201), Ælfric's *vita* is almost certainly the older (review of Winterbottom by Helmut Gneuss, *N&Q*, 218 [1973], 479–80). Both the Ælfric and the 'Wulfstan' lives quote Isaiah lviii.1 when speaking of Æthelwold's preaching; the same biblical reference occurs in the English Preface to *CH*, I (Thorpe, I, 6/31). I find no passages relevant to this discussion of preaching in the *Vita S. Oswoldi* by Byrhtferth (ed. James Raine, *The Historians of the Church of York and Its Archbishops*, I, Rolls Series 71.1 [London, 1879], 399–475; on authorship, see Michael Lapidge, 'The Hermeneutic Style in Tenth-Century Anglo-Latin Literature,' *ASE*, 4 [1975], 67–111 at 90–94).

35 Ed. in William Stubbs, *Memorials of Saint Dunstan*, Rolls Series, 63

(London, 1874), pp. 3–52. The same volume also contains the lives by Adelard, Osbern, Eadmer, and William of Malmesbury, to which reference is made below by chapters. For brief, recent assessment of the comparative values of these *vitae*, see Eleanor Shipley Duckett, *Saint Dunstan of Canterbury: A Study of Monastic Reform in the Tenth Century* (London, 1955), pp. 233–5. On the identity of B, see Lapidge, *ASE*, 4 (1975), 81–2.

36 Cap. 38 ('By these addresses and other wholesome declarations – three on a single day at his celebration [of the Mass] – he adequately admonished the hearts of his subjects: first so that the ecclesiastical rite taught the Gospel after the lection [reading *lectionem*]; second after the free benediction of the power conferred on him; and third after the conferring of the holy peace when we have sung together the song, 'O Lamb of God ... ,' the pious pastor committed himself and the little sheep entrusted to him to be preserved without blemish in the safekeeping of peace, having already been lightened from their heavy sins by the Lamb, namely by Jesus Christ who, being compassionate, comes to take away the offenses of the world.') See also Adelard, lectio xi; Osbern, cap. xlii; Malmesbury, cap. xxxi; Eadmer, caps xxxviii–xl. On the episcopal blessing and *Agnus Dei*, see Jungmann, *Mass of the Roman Rite*, II, 294–7, and I, 84–5.

37 It is not unlike the kind of summary Ælfric used at the beginning of a Sermon for the *Octave of Pentecost* (Pope XI) and separately (Pope XIa). There may also be some connection between the Ascension sermons of Dunstan and the preceding Rogation Days which seem to receive peculiar emphasis in England as preaching days.

38 Ed. Reginald R. Darlington, Royal Historical Society, Camden 3rd Series, 40 (London 1908).

39 Cap. 8 ('Every Sunday and on major feasts in church he imparted to them admonitions of salvation ... from a high station.')

40 Cap. 20 of the Wulfstan *vita* states that the bishop by the force of his Sunday preaching was able to stop traffic in slaves with Ireland. Professor Bethurum cites the Winric incident in connection with the role of bishops as preachers in the eleventh century (*Homilies of Wulfstan*, p. 85).

41 See N.R. Ker, 'Old English Notes Signed "Coleman,"' *MÆ*, 18 (1949), 29–31; *Catalogue*, p. lvi. The MSS in which the notes occur are Cambridge, University Library Kk. 3.18 (Ker 23) at Bede, *History*, v. 13 on the vision of Drihthelm; CCCC 265, p. 41 (Ker 53) translating the title of a passage of the penitential of Egbert; CCCC 178 (Ker 41A) at articles 8 and 27; and Bodleian, Hatton 113, ff. 70^v, 78^v, 108^v, 128^v (Ker 331). Coleman objected to the note at Thorpe, I, 218/30–1 (as

reproduced in CCCC 178, p. 229, as a pendant to *Palm Sunday* [Pope, p. 66]) that preaching was indeed done on the what Ælfric called the 'still days' in connection with the penitential rites and the blessing of chrism. See further below.

42 Barlow in *Leofric of Exeter*, p. 9 note 1, quotes a service note in a twelfth-century Exeter calendar (British Museum, MS Harley 863 [Ker 232], f. 3ᵛ) which is the earliest reference I have found: Pope Leo IX is to be commemorated, 'de quo totum vigiliae servicium preter pronum et missam (*with* pronum et *crossed out*).'

43 Ker, *Catalogue*, p. 13 ('A book of catholic [i.e., general, orthodox] English sermons to be recited in church during the year'). Gg.3.28 is Ker's 15. See also 'Table of Ælfric's *Sermones Catholici*,' Ker, pp. 511–15. The incipit for *CH* II in MS Gg.3.28 (Ker 15, art. 44) is 'Incipit liber sermonum catholicorum anglice in anno secundo. Catholicus sermo de natale domini ...' Variation of the incipit occurs in British Museum MS Royal 7C.xii, f. 4 (Ker 257, art. 1, reading 'anglice in anno primo'). Oxford, Bodleian MS Bodley 340–2 (Ker 309, art. 33) has the Royal incipit; Corpus Christi College, Cambridge, MS 188 (Ker 43) may well have had an incipit before the Hexaemeral homily which replaces *De Initio Creaturae*.

44 'For the edification of simple persons ... whether reading or hearing [in language] which can more easily reach the heart of readers or auditors to the benefit of their souls.' 'For reading by men who do not know Latin.' At lines 11–12 it is explained that the two-book arrangement for alternate years makes the pieces less tedious 'to gehyrenne.' The expression 'legentium vel audientium' may be a commonplace of homiliary prefaces which indicates that one is dealing with a Carolingian homiliary of the sort which can be used for private devotions or as a preacher's manual. Compare Rabanus (*PL*, 110, 10) and Abbo of St-Germain-des-Près (*PL*, 132, 761–4: 'vel legendo vel audiendo'), and contrast Paul the Deacon (Grégoire, p. 76: 'legendi per totius anni circulum'), where only public reading at the office seems to be in mind.

45 See above, note 34, on a comparable passage in the *Vita S. Æthelwoldi*.

46 See Ker's 'Table,' pp. 512–13.

47 On this note, see Kenneth Sisam, *Studies in the History of Old English Literature*, pp. 160–1.

48 The chief point of the note, as Sisam shows, is that a table of contents is not necessary since it should be clear from the Preface that the volume contains forty items. I know of no discussion of why Ælfric settled on forty as the appropriate number of sermons. I suspect he knew this was the number of homilies on the Gospels by Gregory the Great and was influenced by this fact. The

number may in this way have become a conventional one for homilies to be preached to the laity. Rabanus has forty homilies assigned to the calendar in his collection, but adds to these thirty more general pieces.

49 See the ed. by A. Campbell for Medieval Texts (London, 1962).

50 *Exeter Book*, ed. Chambers et al., pp. 85–90.

51 Peter Clemoes, 'Ælfric,' in *Continuations and Beginnings*, ed. E.G. Stanley, p. 182.

52 See 'Preface to Genesis,' pp. 76–80 of Crawford, *Heptateuch ... ,* E.E.T.S., O.S., 160 (1922; rpt. with two additional texts ed. by N.R. Ker, London, 1969).

53 I cannot offer a full argument here, but I would like to suggest tentatively that Ælfric's Old Testament translations and paraphrases (as listed by Clemoes, 'Chronology,' p. 218, and Pope, p. 143, but adding the Job sermon in *CH* II [*Dominica* I *in Mense Septembri*] and the Midlent Homilies of *CH* II [both pieces] and *De Populo Israhel* [Pope xx]) are intimately connected with the monastic calendar's cycle of Old Testament readings. (See the important but neglected section of the *Letter to the Monks of Eynsham* at pp. 194–6 of the ed. by Mary Bateson in Appendix VII of *Compotus Rolls of the Obedientiaries of St Swithun's Priory, Winchester*, ed. G.W. Kitchin [Hampshire Record Society, London, 1892], pp. 173–98, of

which I am preparing a study.) The Pentateuch plus Joshua and Judges (in Roman tradition; in the later breviaries only Genesis and Exodus were prescribed) were read in pre-Lent and Lent; Kings from I post Pentecosten to 1 August; Job in the first half of September; Judith and Esther later in September; Maccabees in October (compare the Eynsham letter with the several variants detailed by Salmon, *L'Office Divin*, pp. 135–8; see also Bäumer, *Histoire du Bréviaire*, I, 394–6; and Frere, ed. *Leofric Collectar*, II, xxv–xxvi). Ælfric seems to have selected for translation (or, in the case of the 'summer histories,' for compression into short homilies or reading-pieces) elements suitable for lay instruction. A good deal of work with mss and lectionaries must be done, however, to establish this point firmly and to assess its implications.

54 *Liturgica Historica: Papers on the Liturgy and Religious Life of the Western Church* (Oxford, 1918), p. 213.

55 W.H. Stevenson, ed., in *The Cartulary of the Abbey of Eynsham*, ed. H.E. Salter, vol. I (Oxford Historical Society, 49 [1907]), 19–28 at 24 (an earlier ed. by Kemble is cited above, p. 174, note 4) ('and I intend myself to live in common with the congregation and to enjoy the benefit [or, perhaps, "the property" or "the revenues"] with them so long as I live').

56 On Gerald, see Gerald Sitwell, ed. and trans., *St Odo of Cluny: Being the Life of St Odo of Cluny by John of Salerno and the Life of St Gerald of Aurillac by St Odo* (London, 1958). Derek Baker, '*Vir Dei:* Secular Sanctity in the Early Tenth Century,' in *Popular Belief and Practice: Papers Read at the Ninth Summer Meeting and the Tenth Winter Meeting of the Ecclesiastical History Society*, ed. G.D. Cuming and Derek Baker (Cambridge, 1972), pp. 41–53, takes a more measured view of Gerald's actual piety; but for our purposes what Odo (whose work, since he was the reformer of Fleury, was very likely to have been known in England or, at least, to the advisers who came from Fleury) thought of Gerald and of the *vir Dei* ideal is all that matters.

57 The will, to which my attention was drawn by Professor Whitelock, is printed in A.S. Napier and W.H. Stevenson, eds., *The Crawford Collection of Early Charters and Documents Now in the Bodleian Library*, Anecdota Oxoniensa (Oxford, 1895), no. x, lines 9–10, at p. 23. The 'Hrabanus' may have been one of the homiliaries.

58 Thorpe, I, 1/23–2/1; italics mine ('And we have another book in hand just now for writing out, which contains those tracts and passions which the present one omitted; and yet we do not touch all the Gospels for the year's cycle, but those only by which we hope to be able to suffice for the emendation of the souls of simple persons . . .').

59 It must be stressed that these generalizations apply only to this ms, for no two mss of *CH* are exactly alike and many, as I shall try to demonstrate below, display markedly different principles of selection and arrangement. On Cambridge University Library MS Gg.3.28, see, in addition to Ker's *Catalogue*, Sisam, *Studies*, pp. 165–71; Pope, pp. 34–5; Clemoes in the facsimile of MS Royal 7C.xii, E.E.M.F., 13, p. 29.

60 Note that in *CH* I the sermon is on the pericope for the first Mass; in II it is based on prophetic passages read in the Office during Advent (and is thus analogous to the Job piece of *CH* II in its choice of material); only in Pope I does Ælfric deal with the pericope of the Principal Mass of Christmas. On the readings of the Office at Christmas, see p. 187, note 12.

61 M.R. Godden, 'The Development of Ælfric's Second Series of Catholic Homilies,' *ES*, 54 (1973), 210. I had reached approximately this conclusion before Godden's article appeared.

62 Thorpe, II, 288/6–8 ('We ween that ye will not all be present here on the day when we shall read that Gospel'). Note also Thorpe, II, 282/30–1, on the rationale for adding the exegetical pieces for Easter.

63 'Twice each month, that is fortnightly.'

64 See note 40 above. Thorpe prints the explicit of II at p. 594; the end of *CH* I is imperfect in MS Gg.3.28 and, as Sisam (*Studies*, p. 166n) and Ker suggest, an explicit for the first series has probably been lost.

65 See Cruel's definitions in *Gesch. der deutschen Predigt*, pp. 2–4.

66 Oxford MS Bodley 343 (Ker 310, arts. 13, 47; see also Pope pp. 14–18; *CH* items in the ms 'derive from the earliest ascertainable state of the text' though the ms is late twelfth century): CCCC 162 (Ker 38, arts. 1–3); CCCC 178 + 162 (Ker 41A, art. 5): Oxford Bodleian MS Hatton 115 (Ker 332, arts. 2–3) are examples. Ker 41A, art. 19 is a note explaining the division of the book into homilies *quando volueris* and for the Temporale. See below for further comment on the *quando volueris* materials. Godden (*ES*, 54 [1973], 212) believes the second and third items for Rogation Tuesday in *CH* II are in fact a general homily put here 'not because [Ælfric] wanted two homilies for Tuesday in Rogationtide but because this composite homily [Thorpe's XXIII, XXIV] was not adapted for any particular occasion and had the same subject as XXII. Then XXIV would be an *exemplum* of part of the argument of XXIII.'

67 See the tables in Barré, *Homéliaires Carolingiens*, and Grégoire, *Homéliaires du Moyen Âge*. A study of materials associated with the Rogation Days in Old English is in progress (Cross, *PBA*, 58 [1972], 85). For discussion of special characteristics of Anglo-Saxon observance of these days, see Max Förster, *Zur Geschichte der Reliquienkultus in Altengland*, Sitzungsberichte der Bayerischen Akademie der Wissenschaften, Philosophische-Historische Abteilung, 1943, Heft 8 (Munich, 1943), 4–6. Like Ælfric, Rabanus expounds on the Lord's Prayer at Rogationtide.

68 Unfortunately, the translated pericopes are omitted by Thorpe. The omitted translations were first printed by A.S. Napier, 'Nachträge zu Cook's, *Biblical Quotations in Old English Prose Writers*,' *Archiv für das Studium der neueren Sprachen*, 101 (1898), 309–24; 102 (1899), 29–42; 107 (1901). 105.

69 For example, the ending of the first *St Stephen* piece (Thorpe, I, 56) and the conclusion of Quinquagesima (Thorpe, I, 164).

70 'Über die Quellen von Ælfrics Exegetischen *Homiliae Catholicae*,' *Anglia*, 16 (1894), 40–1. On Smaragdus, see Barré, pp. 12–13, 211. The sources of the *CH* I homily for *I in Advent* require further study.

71 The rubric of which (see Ker 15, art. 93) tends to stress the fact that we are dealing with non-homiletic materials: it 'nis to spelle geteald.'

72 *Studies*, pp. 166–8. Sisam translates the heading of *De Temporibus*, which states that the piece is not a homily but useful reading.

73 This is the opinion of Clemoes as

communicated to J.E. Cross and reported by the latter in 'More Sources for Two of Ælfric's *Catholic Homilies*,' *Anglia*, 86 (1968), 59–78, at 78.

74 Indeed, it concludes (Thorpe II, 606/22ff.) with an expanded paraphrase of the second article of the Creeds.

75 ('The teacher shall say to the laymen the sense of the Pater noster and of the Creed, that they may know what to pray for to God, and how they shall believe in God.') Through this point, the material in this item was repeated in Skeat's *LS* XII (*Ash Wednesday*). The subsequent material should probably be regarded as a separate item with quite different subject matter. See Clemoes, 'Chronology,' 246 and 221, note 2.

76 The title *de canonibus* doubtless refers to canon law, for the nominal form was usually reserved for the law (even though, according to Niermeyer's *Lexicon*, it can refer to rules of life for Christians, 'especially clerks and monks') and the adjectival *canonicus* for the canonical clergy. Given the contents of the letter and its sources, however, it is not inappropriate to connect it with the *Regulae canonicorum*. The effort of Eduard Dietrich ('Abt Ælfric zur Literatur-Geschichte der angelsächsischen Kirche,' *ZHT*, 26 [1856], 234) to associate the letter with Wulfsige's introduction of regulars in Sherborne in 998 is without force.

The failure of the reform represented by *Brief* I may, however, have led to the regularization of 998. (See also Caroline Louisa White, *Ælfric*, pp. 58, 135–59; Fehr, *Hirtenbriefe*, pp. xxxv–xxxviii.)

77 Professor Whitelock reminds me that, considering materials like those appended to MS Gg.3.28 which were provided by Ælfric for catechetical teaching or preaching, one might also refer to the passages on the Decalogue and the Deadly Sins in Fehr III.121–76. These sections are omitted in the Latin version (Fehr 3), which survives only in Wulfstan mss, perhaps because they were thought unnecessary for priests who had a command of Latin.

78 *ES*, 54 (1973), 209–16; quotation at p. 215.

79 The *Commune Sanctorum*, an integral part of the Homiliary of Paul the Deacon, was similarly provided for by a group of pieces at the end of *CH* II. There is some admixture of Temporale and Sanctorale in Paul, especially for the summer season. Paul begins the year at Advent; others (e.g., Alan of Farfa) begin at Christmas.

80 Bosworth and Toller's collection of citations in *An Anglo-Saxon Dictionary* (rpt. Oxford, 1954) suggests to me a far more general meaning (simply 'priest') than some commentators on 'Ic Ælfric munuc and mæssepreost' imply. For a new instance of use of the term in connection with preaching, see

Trahern, *Anglia*, 91 (1973), 475–8, text line 30.

81 See note 7, above, on the two schools of Ramsey. I suggest the Winchester connection because *CH* I and II presuppose a larger library than would have existed at Cernel or the diocesan see at Sherborne in the 990s. In at least the instance of the epitome of Julian's *Prognosticon* it is very likely that Ælfric was using material prepared at Winchester before he went to Cernel.

82 Similarly, *seculares* (1.2/1) may refer to secular clergy (canons). Abbo of St-Germain-des-Près speaks of *simplicium clericorum* who will be enabled to preach by use of his work in rustic idiom (*PL*, 132, 761–4).

83 I am indebted to Professor Pope for a number of these references. For introductory comments on the Gospels in the other homilies of Pope's edition, see the references in note 21, above. The fact that there are so few references in *CH* II is curious; perhaps it is to be explained in the light of the greater freedom given users of II.

84 See Clemoes, 'Chronology'; Pope, introduction. Both of these studies are rich in observations which remain to be integrated in our assessment of all aspects of Ælfric's achievement.

85 Pope, pp. 226–7; Clemoes, 'Chronology,' p. 227. The set appeared as an appendix in B.M. MS Cotton Vitellius C.V (Ker 220, arts. 63–6), though Assmann v and a sixth

(unrelated) homily are now lost from this ms and Pope VI ends imperfectly. Interspersed among the Lenten Sunday pieces, the set also appears in MS CCCC 162 (Ker 38, arts. 17, 20, 22, 24, 26); the fourth and fifth items also occur in other mss.

86 Pope, p. 160.

87 See Barré's 'Tableaux Comparatifs,' *Homéliaires Carolingiens*, pp. 214ff.

88 On the likelihood of the absence of the laity on weekdays in Easter week, see Thorpe, II, 288/6–8. Clemoes, 'Chronology,' p. 220 note 3, argues that a distinction is made by Ælfric between narrative liturgical pieces and narrative, non-liturgical reading-pieces by the inclusion in the former of 'a reference to the anniversary *today*.' But references to 'þam halg(a)n godspelle (þe ge gehyrdon nu ræd)on' (Pope II.2) may not bear such a significance in the exegetical *sermones*. The sentence just quoted, incidentally, is not in MS CCCC 162, which begins at Pope's line 5; but the formula also appears in Pope VI.1 and Assmann v.1. As we have already seen in the case of *CH*, both private and public reading seem to have been contemplated for some exegetical pieces.

89 See Clemoes, 'Chronology,' pp. 230–3, and Pope [MS U], pp. 77–80, in addition to Ker's description.

90 It is without incipit but has a frontispiece which (despite Archbishop Parker's tampering) indicates

that the beginning of the text must be complete. The frontispiece is reproduced in Montague Rhodes James, *The Western Manuscripts in the Library of Trinity College Cambridge: A Descriptive Catalogue*, IV (Cambridge, 1904), plate xi, and as the frontispiece to this book.

91 Easter has arts. 1, 2, and 3 for Feria IV[a]; arts. 14–16 are for *Pentecost*; 17–18 for *I post Pent*. All other Sundays, the Rogation Days, and Ascension have one piece.

92 Allusion must be made to yet another mutation of the Ælfric canon, which Clemoes calls *Temporale Homilies I* (B.15.34 being a witness to *TH* II) and which ran from Christmas through Pentecost and was framed by the kind of summary of the events of the seasons therein contained which are found in Pope XI and XIa. If Clemoes 'Chronology,' (pp. 227–30) is correct that Ælfric himself conceived of and issued such a grouping (Pope, pp. 47–8, 79 has doubted that the evidence proves his involvement in the assembling of *TH* I or II), this collection is as boldly original as I have argued are *CH* I and II.

93 As *Ælfric* has Wulfstan say in Fehr, *Hirtenbriefe*, II.2, it is not expected that all clergy will be fluent in Latin, and, therefore, bishops have to provide them in English with explanations of 'þa bóclican lare þe ure canon us tæcð and eac seo Cristes bóc.'

94 Clemoes, 'Chronology,' p. 221:

'Evidently Ælfric considered homilies directly dependent on the liturgy unsuitable for inclusion in his non-liturgical reading-book, but those on general themes suitable.' But Clemoes, pp. 226–7, also suggests (expanding on Sisam, *Studies*, p. 163 note 1) that *LS* XXXII (*St. Edmund*) and other early *LS* items may have been in Æthelweard's augmented *CH* I.

95 'Chronology,' p. 235; see also 235–8. The possible exception – 'so remote that it does not deserve consideration' – is Gloucester Cathedral MS 35 (Ker 117).

96 The term would surely be more appropriate than 'Homiliary for the Sanctorale,' since lesser feasts did not have their own propers. It will be remembered that in *Regularis Concordia*, cap. xxi, reading of the martyrology and commentary on the Gospel (the latter as a substitute for the commentary on the *Rule*) are associated with the capitular office. The martyrology, originally a calendar of saints' days, had only brief narratives; longer lessons for use in the offices were collected in the passional (see the lists of liturgical books, pp. 42–3).

97 'The Common Origin of Ælfric Fragments at New Haven, Oxford, Cambridge, and Bloomington' in *Old English Studies in Honour of John C. Pope*, ed. Robert B. Burlin and Edward B. Irving, Jr. (Toronto, 1974), pp. 285–326.

98 Ibid., p. 300.

99 *The Study of the Bible in the Middle Ages*, pp. 44–5: the late tenth and eleventh centuries saw 'a dramatic pause in the history of Bible studies and we should miss its significance if we explained it away as the demoralizing effect of war and Viking invasion. They certainly made scholarship difficult, but the real reason was a shift of interest. The Cluniac and other tenth-century religious reformers emphasized the liturgy at the expense of study. As the offices multiplied, *lectio divina* moved out of the cloister into the choir.'

100 See above, n. 48.

101 The following are mss associated by Ker and Pope with Worcester:

Cambridge, Corpus Christi College 178 (Ker 41A, dated XI^1; Pope's siglum R, pp. 62–7): a double collection of homilies for general occasions (i.e., catechetical) and for major feasts, mostly by Ælfric; a note (art 19, ed. Ker, *Catalogue*, p. 62) explains the organization and states that originally there were twelve items in each part (expansion has taken place, including the introduction of the *Palm Sunday* homily of *CH* I with its note on the still days, to which Coleman objected [see notes 41, 105]);

Oxford, Bodleian Junius 121 and Hatton 113, 114 (Ker 338 and 331, dated XI [3rd quarter]; Pope's T, pp. 70–7): perhaps not originally a single volume but clearly a set comprised of writings by Ælfric, Wulfstan, and others and associated with St Wulfstan; Junius 121 contains canonical and added homiletic material; Hatton 113, 114, arts. 1–30 is largely Wulfstan homiletic material to be used *quando volueris*; arts. 31 sqq. are largely Ælfric and – after two initial items *quando volueris* – covers the main events of the Temporale from Christmas-Annunciation and Quinquagesima-Pentecost; there follows a Sanctorale; probably copied in part from CCCC 178;

Oxford, Bodleian Hatton 115 (Ker 332, dated XI^2; Pope's P, pp. 53–9): the original 32 arts. are all by Ælfric, and 'the principle of selection appears to be simply that no piece shall be limited to a specific occasion' (Pope, p. 53); the presence of the ms at Worcester before the thirteenth century is uncertain, and it is unlikely that it was written at Worcester;

Oxford, Bodleian Hatton 116 (Ker 333, dated XII^1; Pope's S, pp. 67–70): a largely Ælfrician miscellany similar to Ker 332 and 41A, without calendrical designations for its articles; if not written at Worcester, certainly from the neighbourhood;

Ker 412 (a lost Worcester MS, described by Young so as to suggest similarity to the *quando volueris* collections).

102 See above, p. 47.

103 See Pope, pp. 74–5; Dorothy Whitelock, *Sermo Lupi ad Anglos*, p. 22.

104 It should be remembered that, as Clemoes has pointed out ('Late Old English Literature,' *Tenth Century Studies*, ed. Parsons, 106), Canterbury and Exeter collections containing sermons of Ælfric also have a special character. One might also work out a picture of the local peculiarities of homiletic liturgical practice there. See also M.R. Godden, 'Old English Composite Homilies from Winchester,' *ASE*, 4 (1975), 57–65.

105 Ed. Ker, *MÆ*, 18 (1949), 29: 'ac þis ne þynceð no us well gesæd. forðy on ælcne timan mon ah to læranne and to tihtanne folc to bereowsunge. and to wirceanne ures drihtnes willan and allra swiðost folce is to reowsienne on ðissum ðrim dagum. þonne hi gehyrað hu ure drihten hælend crist ðrowade for us. Eac biscepas æt heora bisceopstole sæcgað larspel þonne he lædað in penitentes. and hi doð absolutionem, and sume sæcgað spell of þære crismhalgunge and of þæm balsome.' Coleman's comments call to mind the directives of the 'Romano-Lotharingian offices for Holy Week' of the Leofric Missal. The only sermons stipulated in this document are catechetical addresses between the blessing of palms and procession on Palm Sunday ('*Tunc episcopus siue presbiter faciat sermonem de sancta cruce*') and at the blessing of chrism ('*His ista statutis, conuertat se episcopus, aut cui ille precepit, tam ad clerum quam ad populum, et faciat sermonem de consecratione crysmatis congruentem*'). (F.E. Warren, ed., *The Leofric Missal as Used in the Cathedral of Exeter ... A.D. 1050–1072 ...* [Oxford, 1883], pp. lvii, 256, 259.) I believe that Coleman had in mind when he wrote this note the sermons on reconciliation of penitents in Holy Week of Abbo St-Germain-des-Près which were probably available to him in a ms that contains notes by Archbishop Wulfstan: Copenhagen, Kongelike Bibliothek, GL. KGL. SAM. 1595 (4°) (Ker 99; described by Ellen Jørgensen, *Catalogus Codicum Latinorum Medii Aevi Bibliothecae Regiae Hafniensis* [Copenhagen, 1926], pp. 43–6).

106 Ed. Anna Maria Luiselli Fadda, '"De descensu Christi ad inferos": una inedita Omelia anglosassone,' *Studi Medievali*, 3rd Ser., 13.2 (1972), 989–1011 at 998 ('Now we have related to you simply the Gospel which the Deacon just now read before us all, how Christ on this day arose from the dead. Now we intend further to relate how he descended to hell and bound the devil and led thence all those who were obedient and dear to him here in life'). A short portion of the homily is based on Ælfric. On its other sources, see Fadda, esp. p.

997, note 17; on the ms, see note 101 above.

107 *Studies*, p. 118.

108 Scragg, *ASE*, 2 (1973), 189–207.

109 Annunciation, which usually falls in Lent, appears before Quinquagesima; and a group of saints' day sermons (the first of which, Assumption, is out of order) follow Pentecost. Thus it looks as though fixed feasts of the Sanctorale are grouped appropriately in relation to variable and Dominical feasts and as though the original set was not divided into summer and winter *partes*. Joan Turville-Petre, 'Translations of a Lost Penitential Homily,' *Traditio*, 19 (1963), 51–78, at 74–5, has argued that the placement of Annunciation before Lent was customary in pre-Ælfrician homiletic collections.

110 Morris, ed., pp. 15, 27, 161, 229. None of these references is unambiguous; perhaps 'on þissum bocum and on þissum halgum gewrite' (p. 161) is the clearest, but the homily (on St John the Baptist) is not truly exegetical.

111 More detailed comments are to be found in the study of Wulfstan's eschatology in Part III.

112 The exceptions are Bethurum XIV and XV, both of which have to do with Lenten penance.

113 I owe my awareness of this possibility to the generosity of Alan K. Brown. Only a few items from Abbo's extensive collection are printed in *PL*, 123.

114 I plan to address this issue in a separate essay.

115 Æthelwold translated the Benedictine Rule for Edgar and his queen, Ælfthryth, presumably so they might more readily appreciate the constitution of the institution whose revival they were promoting. It may be that the desires of patrons were to some degree responsible for the translation of ecclesiastical texts in this as in other cases; but Æthelwold in his account of the monastic reform lays equal or even greater stress on the fact that the translation is needful for monolingual converts to monasticism lest they plead ignorance in breaking the Rule (trans. Dorothy Whitelock, *English Historical Documents*, ed. David C. Douglas, I [ca. 500–1042] [London, 1955], 846–9 at 848). Æthelwold's arguments for the use of the vernacular Rule are among the strongest indications that, at least in some circles, there may have been some tolerance for the liturgical or quasi-liturgical use of English texts. The survival of a number of copies of the translation of the *Rule*, often presented next to the Latin, indicates it was probably found useful within the monastic communities for just these purposes (see Mechthild Gretsch, 'Æthelwold's Translation of the *Regula Sancti Benedicti* and Its Latin Exemplar,' *ASE*, 3 [1974], 125–51, and *Die Regula Sancti Benedicti in England*, Münchener

Universitäts-Schriften, Texte und Untersuchungen zur englischen Philologie, 2 [Munich, 1973]). On the writings of Æthelwold, see Dorothy Whitelock, 'The Authorship of the Account of King Edgar's Establishment of Monasteries,' *Philological Essays: Studies in Old and Middle English Language and Literature in Honour of Herbert Dean Meritt*, ed. James L. Rosier (The Hague, 1970), pp. 125–36.

PART THREE

1 This expression is chosen deliberately to reflect the title of Ernst Wadstein's study, *Die Eschatologische Ideengruppe: Antichrist – Weltsabbat – Weltende und Weltgericht, in den Hauptmomenten ihrer christlich-mittelalterlichen Gesamtentwicklung* (Leipzig, 1896). In addition to the numerous useful entries in *Dictionnaire de Théologie Catholique* and *DACL*, a number of other studies (some of limited usefulness) touching on the history of eschatology in early medieval literature may be listed alphabetically: William Rounesville Alger, *The Destiny of the Soul: A Critical History of the Doctrine of a Future Life* (10th ed. rev.; Boston, 1880); Philippe Ariès, *Western Attitudes toward Death: From the Middle Ages to the Present*, trans. Patricia M. Ranum (Baltimore, 1974); Ernest J. Becker, *A Contribution to the Comparative Study of Medieval Visions of Heaven and Hell ...* , Diss. Johns Hopkins (Baltimore, 1899); T.S.R. Boase, *Death in the Middle Ages: Mortality, Judgment and Remembrance* (New York, 1972); W. Bossuet, *The Antichrist Legend: A Chapter in Christian and Jewish Folklore*, trans. A.H. Keane (London, 1896); Waller Deering, *The Anglo-Saxon Poets on the Judgment Day*, Diss. Leipzig (Halle, 1890); LeRoy Edwin Froom, *The Prophetic Faith of Our Fathers: The Historical Development of Prophetic Interpretation*, I (Washington, 1946); Gustav Grau, *Quellen und Verwandtschaften der älteren germanischen Darstellungen der Jüngsten Gerichtes*, Studien zur Englischen Philologie, 31 (Halle, 1908); William W. Heist, *The Fifteen Signs Before Doomsday* (East Lansing, Mich., 1952); Arnold Barel van Os, *Religious Visions: The Development of the Eschatological Elements in Medieval English Religious Literature* (Amsterdam, 1932); Howard Rollin Patch, *The Other World: According to the Descriptions in Medieval Literature*, Smith College Studies in Modern Languages, N.S.1 (Cambridge, Mass., 1950); Ray C. Petry, *Christian Eschatology and Social Thought: A Historical Essay ...* (New York, 1956); Paul Murphy Pickrel, 'Religious Allegory in

Medieval England: An Introductory Study Based on the Sermon before 1250,' Diss. Yale, 1944; Jean Rivière, *Le Dogme de la Rédemption au Début du Moyen Age*, Bibliothèque Thomiste, 19 (Paris, 1934); St John D. Seymour, *Irish Visions of the Other-World: A Contribution to the Study of Medieval Visions* (London, 1930); Oscar D. Watkins, *A History of Penance* ... (1920; rpt. New York, 1961); Rudolph Willard, *Two Apocrypha in Old English Homilies*, Beiträge zur Englischen Philologie, 30 (Leipzig, 1935).

2 The best guide to patristic theology is Berthold Altaner, *Patrologie*; also useful are the standard histories of doctrine, esp. Reinhold Seeburg, *Textbook of the History of Doctrines*, trans. Charles E. Hay (rpt. Grand Rapids, Mich., 1958), and Jaroslav Pelikan, *The Christian Tradition: A History of the Development of Doctrine*, I (Chicago, 1971). I have attempted to review some of the larger contexts of the history of eschatological thought in *Death: Meaning and Mortality* ... (New York, 1969), esp. Parts II–III, and 'Some Theological Reflections on Death from the Early Church through the Reformation,' in *Perspectives on Death*, ed. Liston O. Mills (New York, 1969), pp. 99–136. See further Part IV, below.

3 I have deliberately refrained from documenting the following paragraphs and have also tried to avoid a number of problems surrounding the interpretation of the poems in recent criticism, for these comments do not go beyond the observation that eschatology is frequently in the minds of the poets. For a sensitive essay on the interpretation of a poem dealing with death and its eschatological ramifications, see Howell D. Chickering, Jr., 'Some Contexts of Bede's *Death-Song*,' *PMLA*, 91 (1976), 91–100.

4 Peter Brown, *Augustine of Hippo: A Biography* (Berkeley, 1967), esp. pp. 340ff., 398ff.; for Gottschalk, consult Eleanor Shipley Duckett, *Carolingian Portraits: A Study in the Ninth Century* (Ann Arbor, 1962), esp. pp. 258–64.

5 See Hubert Jedin and John Dolan, *Handbook of Church History*, trans. Anselm Biggs, III (London, 1969), pp. 160–1.

6 *PBA*, 58 (1972), pp. 88–9.

Chapter 6

1 In addition to the sermons in Thorpe's *CH*, *LS*, and Pope, my survey has covered the other known homiletic writings of Ælfric, reserving only Pope XI and XVIII and an unpublished passage for consideration in chapter 8. Chief among the additional pieces are Assmann III–IV; and A.O. Belfour, ed. *Twelfth-Century Homilies in MS Bodley 343*, Part I, Text and Translation, E.E.T.S., O.S., 137 (London, 1909), I–IV, VIII, XIV. (A number of the Belfour texts are based on incomplete and late mss. Thus Pope

has re-edited them as follows: Belfour I = Pope XII; II = Pope VIII; XIV = Pope VI.) A homily for the *Third Sunday in Lent*, twice published on the basis of Grundtvig's transcript (by L.C. Müller, ed., *Collectanea Anglo-Saxonica* [Copenhagen, 1835], pp. 19–27, and George Stephens, ed., *Tvende Old Engelske Digte* [Copenhagen, 1853], pp. 81–99) should now be consulted in Pope's ed., no. IV. On the corpus of Ælfric's writings, see Pope's catalogue of the Ælfric canon, pp. 136–45; Clemoes, 'Chronology;' Pope, pp. 136–45; Sisam; and Karl Jost, 'Unechte Aelfrictexte,' *Anglia*, 51 (1927), 81–103 and 177–219.

2 See my article in *Traditio*, 21 (1965), 129, n.43.

3 *III in Lent*, Pope IV, 178–9 ('Godes rice is eac Godes gelaþung, þæt is eall Cristen folc þe on Crist gelyfð').

4 *II after Epiphany*, Thorpe, II, 66/28–9 (Babylon and Jerusalem 'wiðriað betwux him symle swa lange swa þes middaneard stent'). Ælfric also recognizes, of course, a spiritual interpretation of the church as the type (*getacnung*) of the heavenly Jerusalem.

5 *XXI after Pentecost*, Thorpe, I, 520/10–14 ('... gelomlice ic eow sæde, þæt gehwær on halgum godspelle þeos andwerde gelaðung is geháten heofenan rice. Witodlice rihtwisra manna gegaderung is gecweden heofonan rice'); *Septuagesima*, Thorpe, II, 72/24–6; *XXIII after Pentecost*, Belfour, IV, 32. For a

better edition of *Septuagesima*, including the translation of the pericope, see Dorothy Whitelock, ed., *Sweet's Anglo-Saxon Reader in Prose and Verse*, 15th ed. (Oxford, 1967), XIII.

6 *St Peter*, Thorpe, II, 384/21–8.

7 *XXI after Pentecost*, Thorpe, I, 536/6ff. In *Midlent*, Thorpe, I, 182/25ff. the Sea of Galilee is the present world to which Christ came and over which he passed.

8 *IV after Pentecost*, Thorpe, I, 344/11–14, reading *geþungenum* as 'virtuous' for Thorpe's 'religious.'

9 *Epiphany*, Thorpe, II, 42/8–11.

10 *Epiphany*, Thorpe, I, 118/27–30 ('Ac us is micel neod þæt we ðurh oðerne weg þone swicolan deofol forbugan, þæt we moton gesæliglice to urum eðele becuman, þe we to gesceapene wæron'). See also *Rogation Monday*, Thorpe, I, 248/14–16 ('He cwæð, "cuma," forðan ðe we ealle sind cuman on ðisum life, and ure eard nis na her; ac we sind her swilce wegferende menn ...'); *Assumption*, Thorpe, II, 442/13 ('On þissum wræcfullum life ...,' reading with Thorpe in the metaphoric sense of exile); *Common of Apostle*, Thorpe, II, 526/36 (friends await us at our homeland); *Vincent Homily*, Belfour, VIII, 76. For more complete citations of uses of *eðel* and *eard* as 'heaven' and of *neorxna-wang*, see Nelius O. Halvorson, *Doctrinal Terms in Ælfric's Homilies*, University of Iowa, Humanistic Studies, 5. 1 (Iowa City, 1932), 85–7.

11 *Midlent*, Thorpe, II, 214/28ff.; *Quin-*

quagesima, Thorpe, I, 154/25ff. Both passages are clearly based on the same (unidentified) source.

12 From the large and growing list of relevant studies, see in particular Dorothy Whitelock, 'The Interpretation of *The Seafarer,*' in Cyril Fox and Bruce Dickins, eds., *The Early Cultures of North-West Europe (H.M. Chadwick Memorial Studies)* (Cambridge, 1950), pp. 261–72; G.V. Smithers, 'The Meaning of *The Seafarer* and *The Wanderer,*' *MÆ,* 26 (1957), 137–53, and 28 (1959), 1–22, 99–104; and (both for their comments and their bibliographies) the editions for Methuen's Old English Library of *Seafarer* by I.L. Gordon (London, 1960) and of *Wanderer* by T.P. Dunning and A.J. Bliss (1969). Also suggestive on aspects of exilic wandering are Kathleen Hughes, 'The Changing Theory and Practice of Irish Pilgrimage,' *Journal of Ecclesiastical History,* 11 (1960), 143–51, and Peter Clemoes, '*Mens absentia cogitans* in the *Seafarer* and *The Wanderer,*' *Medieval Literature and Civilization: Studies in Memory of G.N. Garmonsway,* ed. D.A. Pearsall and R.A. Waldron (London, 1969), 62–77.

13 *Easter,* Thorpe, I, 224/16 (deadlic, undeadlic).

14 *St Cecilia, LS,* II, xxxiv.295–6 ('from death to glory, as if a man should give away loam and himself get gold').

15 *Friday in 4th Week of Lent,* Pope VI, 154–9.

16 *St Clement,* Thorpe, I, 576/9–12 ('Þeah se reða reafere ús æt æhtum bereafige, oððe feores benæme, hé ne mæg us ætbredan urne geleafan ne þæt ece líf, gif we us sylfe mid agenum willan ne forpærað.')

17 *Palm Sunday,* Thorpe, I, 218/18–23 ('The death of sinful men is evil and miserable, because they pass from this short life to everlasting torments: and the death of righteous men is precious, for when they end this life of tribulation they will be brought to the life eternal ...').

18 *Traditio,* 21 (1965), pp. 124, 146.

19 *De initio creaturae,* Thorpe, I. 20/12–20; *Christmas, LS,* I, I, pp, 18–20.

20 *Quinquagesima,* Thorpe, I, 160/4–5.

21 *Midlent,* Thorpe, II, 206/25–7 ('Ne beoð ða sawla nahwar ǽrðan wunigende, ac se Ælmihtiga Wyrhta hí gescypð ælce dæg, swa swa hé deð þa lichaman.') At least once in homilies related to the apocryphal *Visio Pauli,* there is a hint of the heretical doctrine of the pre-existence of the soul (Gatch, *Church History,* 33 [1964], 385).

22 *XVII after Pentecost,* Thorpe, I, 490ff.; *Friday in 4th Week of Lent,* Pope VI (lines 170–208, rearranged and modified somewhat, are Belfour XIV; for this discussion, I have treated the second, fuller version of the homily which adds lines 209–91 to the original text, based on Augustine's treatment of the pericope in *Tractates* on John [see Pope, pp. 303–10]).

23 Pope VI.111–36. Cp. Pope XXVb (addition to *Ascension Eve*, Thorpe, II, 368 after line 17) in which Ælfric declares that the work of sustaining and directing the world requires as much skill as creation *ex nihilo*.

24 Pope VI.139–42 ('when the soul rises from the death of sins; for whoever sins, his soul does not live unless through confession it revives, and through penance pleases its Lord' – a quite independent extension of the Augustinian source).

25 Ibid., 160–208.

26 *De initio creaturae*, Thorpe, I, 26/27–28/5 ('he came to us because he would suffer death for us, and so, by his own death, redeem all mankind who believe from hell's torment. He would not take us forcibly from the devil's power, unless he had forfeited it; but he forfeited it entirely when he whetted and instigated the hearts of the Jewish men to the slaying of Christ. Then Christ consented that the bloodthirsty ones should take him, and bind, and, hung on a cross, slay him. Verily then two believing men honourably buried him; and Christ, in that time, went to hell, and overcame the devil, and took from him Adam and Eve, and their offspring, that portion which had previously been most acceptable to him, and led them to their bodies, and arose from death with that great host on the third day of his passion'). Cf. *De Sancta Trinitate et de Festis Diebus per Annum*, Pope XIa. 44ff., and *III*

in *Lent*, Pope IV. 188–96, on the bondage of Adam and Eve, a motif necessary to the early medieval elaboration of the *descensus* as the locus of salvation. Also Pope IV.135, 140ff. (the last same as *In octavis Pentecosten dicendus*, Pope XI.38ff.). On the importance of the descent in early medieval theology, see J.N.D. Kelly, *Early Christian Creeds*, pp. 378–82; Ralph V. Turner, '*Descendit ad Inferos*: Medieval Views on Christ's Descent into Hell and the Salvation of the Ancient Just,' *Journal of the History of Ideas*, 27 (1966), 173–94.

27 *Traditio*, 21 (1965), 125–7 and 147–8. Note especially the statement in Vercelli Hom. V that those rescued must 'a second time taste of death' which conflicts with Vercelli Hom. I, the teaching of which is more like Ælfric's.

28 *Midlent*, Thorpe, I, 190/30–1 ('fram deofles anwealde, and fram hellewíte'); *Palm Sunday*, Thorpe, I, 214/34–5 ('mancynn alysan fram ðam ecan deaðe mid his hwilwendlicum deaðe').

29 *Christmas*, Thorpe, I, 36/25–6 ('forðan þe Cristes acennednys gegladode heofenwara, and eorðwara, and helwara').

30 *Epiphany*, Thorpe, I, 108/21–2 ('Hell oncneow, ðaða heo hire hæftlingas unðances forlet').

31 *Easter*, Thorpe, I, 224/31–3 ('manega halige menn, ðe wæron on ðære ealdan æ forðfarene, ... hí arison mid Criste').

32 More than in the anonymous homilies, perhaps because Ælfric's sources – and especially Gregory the Great whose works were prominent in the Homiliary of Paul the Deacon – commonly introduced an exemplum, often visionary, just before the conclusion of the homily. Visions were also prominent features of hagiographical and historical writing and are also introduced into Ælfric's work from this channel.

33 St Martin, LS, II, XXXI, pp. 232–4.

34 Forty Soldiers, LS, I, XI, p. 252; SS Alexander, Eventius, and Theodolus, Thorpe, II, 312. In XI after Pentecost, Thorpe, I, 412/34ff., a man is taken off by black spirits despite his prayers; thus, says the homilist, the vision was given as a warning to us and not to benefit the visionary.

35 Sexagesima, Thorpe, II, 98/1–13; St Cuthbert, Thorpe, II, 150/21ff.; Common of Martyrs, Thorpe, II, 546/26ff.; St Oswald, LS, II, XXVI, p. 142; St Martin, LS, II, XXXI. p. 306.

36 St Stephen, Thorpe, I, 56/32–3; St John the Evangelist, Thorpe, I, 76/13; Holy Innocents, Thorpe, I, 82/33ff.; St Bartholomew, Thorpe, I, 468/33–4; Septuagesima, Thorpe, II, 78/17ff. (the thief converted on the cross). Rogation Monday, Thorpe, II, 326/6ff., contains a reverse statement that Eli died, though righteous, because he was responsible for the sins of his children. (On the source of the last passage, see J.E. Cross, 'Source and Analysis of Some Ælfrician Passages,' NM, 72[1971], 446–53 at 447.

37 XI after Pentecost, Thorpe, I, 410/5–10 ('The devils show to the sinful soul its evil thoughts, and pernicious speeches, and wicked deeds, and with manifold reproaches afflict it, that on its departure it may know by what foes it is beset, and yet find no outlet whereby it may flee from the hostile spirits.') See also p. 408 (evil men are in peace on earth but not after death), and St Bartholomew, Thorpe, I, 470/31–4 (the purgation of the sinful sometimes begins in the world and continues after the soul's departure).

38 V in Lent, Thorpe, II, 232/24–9 ('Se lichama [of the good] awent to eorðan, and anbidað æristes, and on ðam fyrste nán ðing ne gefrét. Seo clæne sawul anbidað eac þæs ecan æristes, ac heo wunað on wuldre on ðære hwíle mid halgum. Þæs mánfullan mannes deað is, þæt his sawul færð fram ðissere scortan blisse to ðam ecum witum, on ðam heo sceal écelice cwylmian, and swa-ðeah næfre ne ateorað.')

39 Pope XXVII; Thorpe, II, 460–6. On the history of the text, see Pope, pp. 770–4.

40 Pope XXVII.70–80; see also Winifred Temple, 'The Song of the Angelic Hosts,' Annuale Mediaevale, 2 (1961), 5–14.

41 Line 102 ('seeing the sun is completely obscured for you'). The text of the second vision is badly damaged. Although it is only

possible to guess in what context Ælfric may originally have set these visions, it is perhaps pertinent to note that the author of the transitional non-rhythmical passages (lines 1–14, 107–23) draws on passages by Wulfstan and Ælfric relating penance to the judgment of Doomsday (see Pope, pp. 770–4). Thus the redactor relates the exempla to the Last Judgment rather than to the post-mortem condition of the soul.

42 Pope XIX (also ed. W. Braekmann, 'Ælfric's Old English Homily "De Doctrina Apostolica"': An Edition,' *Studia Germanica Gandensia*, 5 [1963], 141–73). The Bedan sources are *Historia Ecclesiastica* [hereafter *HE*] v.13–14 (i.e., immediately following the Drihthelm vision, treated below in the Ælfrician version). The homily is not assigned liturgically, but (as Pope notes, pp. 613–14) it would be appropriate to Lent or Rogationtide.

43 Pope XIX.138–207.

44 On the literary relation of the Bedan version to apocryphal traditions, see the ed. of *HE* by Bertram Colgrave and R.A.B. Mynors, Oxford Medieval Texts (Oxford, 1969), p. 500n, and the work of Rudolph Willard therein cited (*Two Apocrypha in Old English Homilies*).

45 Pope XIX.208–41.

46 Bede's expression ('Non est mihi modo tempus vitam mutandi, cum ipse viderim iudicium meum iam esse completum') is perhaps intentionally moderated by Ælfric's 'Hu mæg ic

nu gecyrran, þonne ic sylf geseah min setl on helle ?' (lines 223–4).

47 *St Eugenia, LS*, I, II, p. 48; *St Agnes, LS*, I, VII, p. 184. See also *St Lawrence*, Thorpe, I, 422/17ff. (Hippolytus at his baptism sees innocent souls rejoicing in God).

48 *II after Pentecost*, Thorpe, I, 330–4.

49 Bede, *HE*, III.19 (Fursey), v.12 (Drihthelm).

50 *Rogation Tuesday*, Thorpe, II, 332. The vision is on pp. 332–48. Ælfric's source for Fursey is not Bede but *Vita Fursei* (Förster, *Quellen von Aelfrics Homiliae Catholicae*: 1, *Legenden*, p. 39). The Fursey source is so close in many respects to the *Visio Pauli* that it must at some stage have come under its influence.

51 *Rogation Tuesday (Alia Visio)* Thorpe, II, 348. The vision is on pp. 348–54. Godden (*ES*, 54 [1973], 213) believes that Ælfric intended the three Rogation Tuesday pieces of *CH* II, which are related in subject matter, 'to be combined in some way to form only one or two homilies.'

52 Thorpe, II, 352/19–354/17 ('He answered me and said, The great burning valley which thou first sawest is the penal place, in which the souls of men are punished and cleansed, who would not correct their sins in life and health, but yet were penitent at their last day, and so departed from the world with repentance, and will on doom's day all come to the kingdom of heaven. Some of them also, through aid of friends and alms-deeds, and, above

all, through holy masses, will be delivered from those torments before the great doom. But the swart abyss that thou sawest with the boundless darkness and foul stench is the mouth of hell, and he who once falls therein will never to eternity be thence delivered. This winsome and this flower-bearing place is the dwelling of those souls that ended in good works, but yet were not so perfect that they might straightways enter into the kingdom of heaven, though they, nevertheless, will all come to sight of Christ and joy after the great doom. But those who are perfect in thought, in word, in work, as soon as they depart from the world they come into the kingdom of heaven; from that thou sawest the great light with the winsome fragrance, and thence thou heardest the sweet melody. But thou, now thou returnest to the body, if thou wilt amend thy deeds and morals, then wilt thou receive after death this winsome dwelling which thou now seest.')

53 *Be gehadedum mannum*, 1–5; ed. Jost, *Institutes of Polity*; See also pp. 44 and 199 n24, above.

54 See *Traditio*, 21 (1965), 124–5.

55 Added to *Rogation Tuesday*, Thorpe, II, 356–8. The source is Bede, *HE* IV.22. See note 51, above.

56 Thorpe, II, 358/15–17 ('If, therefore, I were now in the other world, then were my soul released from torments through the holy masses.')

57 *LS*, I, IX.24–9 ('amongst hosts of angels, splendidly adorned, and called to her thus, crying from above, "My sister Lucy, true virgin of God, why prayest thou of me which thou couldst thyself grant? Thy holy faith has helped thy mother, and lo! she is entirely healed by Christ ..."'').

58 *St Maur, LS*, I, VI.106–7 ('Þu ahreddest mine sawle/ fram fyrenum witum').

59 *Assumption*, Thorpe, I, 448/20–2. In *St Oswold, LS*, II, XXVI, pp. 140–2, the saint's relics aid a dying man who wants the saintly king's intercession; *XXI after Pentecost*, Thorpe, I, 532–6, tells of a monk saved by monks' prayers from a dragon which had come for his soul; and *St Martin*, Thorpe, II, 504, of an unbaptized proselyte rescued from death by the prayers of Martin.

60 For a reference to Gregory as an authority, see Thorpe, II, 358/28–31 (see, on the source, Cross, *NM*, 72 [1971], 449). I have studied the problem in Gregory's *Dialogues* in 'The Fourth Dialogue of Gregory the Great: Some Problems of Interpretation,' *Studia Patristica*, 10 (*Texte und Untersuchungen zur Geschichte der altchristlichen Literatur*, 107; 1970), 77–83, and in *Death*, pp. 142–8.

61 *St Swithun, LS*, I, XXI, 410–13 ('Those dreams are pleasant which come from God, and those are fearful which come from the devil; and God Himself forbade us to follow dreams, lest the devil have power to bewitch us.') Also ed. G.I. Needham, *Ælfric: Lives of Three English*

Saints, p. 78. Ælfric did not find this passage in the *vita* by Landferth which was his chief source.

62 Pope XXIX.4–35 (same as *LS*, I, XXI.464–95) and 36–128. On the history of these texts and their relation to *De Auguriis* (*LS*, I, XVII) see Pope, pp. 64, 786–9; Clemoes, 'Chronology,' p. 239.

63 Pope XXIX.26–128 comments on Saul and the Witch of Endor and has to do with the prediction of Saul's death. The devil, having been an angel, has correct foreknowledge of such matters. The point of the exemplum seems to be that Saul mistakes Satan for the spirit of Samuel.

64 *LS*, II, XXV.468–80 ('Judas then gathered a good deal of spoil, that amounted to twelve thousand shillings, all of white silver, and sent to Jerusalem to offer for their sins for the release of the souls of them that were there slain, understanding religiously, concerning the resurrection of us all. Excepting he believed that they, after long delay, would arise from death, they who there were slain, otherwise he offered in vain his offering. But he verily considered that they that with true religion in death shall decease, that they with the Lord shall have the happiest gift in the true life. It is a holy thought, and religious to pray for those who are departed, that they may be released from sins'). Editorial comments adapted from Vulg. of II Macc. xii. 43–6. A. Michel,

art. 'Purgatoire,' *Dictionnaire de Théologie Catholique,* XIII.1 (1936), 1166–7, discusses the importance of the text in the development of the doctrine of purgatory.

65 *Holy Innocents,* Thorpe, I, 89/34ff.; *St Lawrence,* Thorpe, I, 434/35ff.; *Assumption,* Thorpe, I, 452/33ff.; *St Stephen,* Thorpe, I, 50/33–4 (Stephen's prayer for his persecutors saved St Paul: 'Se árfæsta wæs gehyred, and se arleasa wearð gerihtwisod'). The example of Stephen is also cited as antithetic to that of the lax monk in Pope XIX, 231–5. To these citations might be appended the additions to *Rogation Wednesday* (Ascension Eve), Pope XXVa and c; both passages speak of the ascended Christ as the intercessor *par excellence,* and the former hints that monks achieve beatification before laymen.

66 See M.-M. Dubois, *Ælfric,* pp. 185–90, esp. the word study at p. 189; and Halvorson, *Doctrinal Terms in Ælfric's Homilies,* pp. 76–8. Ælfric adds one term, *pinung* ('torment,' as at Thorpe, I, 164/12 and 334/2, which are eternal and purgatorial, respectively, in their reference) to the terminology of the earlier homilists. The matter of OE vocabulary for terms related to the soul and its destiny needs further study.

Chapter 7

1 *Friday in the 3rd Week of Lent,* Pope v.247–78.

2 For Blickling on this subject, see my

article in *Traditio*, 21 (1965), 129–30; on the silence of Vercelli, ibid., 152. Note 44 at p. 130 of this article should be corrected in the light of J.E. Cross, 'On the Blickling Homily for Ascension Day (No. xi),' *NM*, 70 (1969), 233.

3 Smetana, *Traditio*, 15 (1959), 196; ibid., 17 (1961), 463–4. The Bede Homily is i.14, *CCL*, cxxii, 95–104.

4 *II after Epiphany*, Thorpe, ii, 58/9–10 ('extended with uncertain ending to the coming of Antichrist'). One further treatment of the six-ages tradition by Ælfric awaits publication by Professor Clemoes: the rhythmical *De Sex Etatibus Huius Seculi* (see Pope, pp. 86–7; Clemoes, 'Chronology,' 241–2, 245, entitles the piece *De Sex Ætatibus Mundi*), which is found only in MS Cotton Otho C.i; (Ker, *Catalogue*, 182, art. 6). It is closer to the Sigeweard letter than to the homily for *II after Epiphany*.

5 Thorpe, ii, 58/14–19 ('Witodlice mihte Drihten æmtige fatu mid wíne afyllan, seðe ealle ðing of nahte gesceop, ac hé wolde swiðor þæt wanne wæter to mærlicum wíne awendan, and mid þam geswutelian þæt hé ne com to ðy þæt hé wolde towurpan ða ealdan æ oððe wítegan, ac wolde hí æfter gastlicum andgite gefyllan').

6 Thorpe, ii, 70/8–12 ('Witodlice mid þyssere getácnunge us bið awend þæt sixte wæter-fæt to deorwurðum wíne, and we magon clypian soðlice

to Criste, þæt hé sparode þæt góde wín oð his ágenum to-cyme, þæt hé scencð nu geond his gelaðunge oð ende þises middaneardes').

7 'Die Weltzeitalter bei den Angel-sächsen,' *Neusprachliche Studien: Festgabe Karl Luick; Die Neueren Sprachen*, Beiheft 6 (1925), 183–203. For a general survey of the subject see Roderich Schmidt, '*Aetates mundi*: Die Weltalter als Gleider-prinzip der Geschichte,' *Zeitschrift für Kirchengeschichte*, 67 (1955–56), 288–317; Charles W. Jones, 'Some Introductory Remarks on Bede's Commentary on Genesis,' *Sacris Erudiri*, 19 (1969–70), 115–98 at 191–8.

8 I.e., *De Sancta Trinitate et de Festis Diebus*, Pope xia. 61; *Nativitas Sanctae Mariae Virginis et De Sancta Virginitate*, Assmann, iii.60–1; *De Veteri Testamenti et de Novo* (Letter to Sigeweard) in Crawford, ed., *Heptateuch*, line 892. On the relation of these, see Pope, pp. 453–62 and 465 (Apparatus iii). See also *De Falsis Diis*, Pope xxi.498–9.

9 *Septuagesima*, Thorpe, ii, 74/18–21, 76/14–23 (for a more authoritative edition, see Dorothy Whitelock, ed., *Sweet's Anglo-Saxon Reader*, xiii.61–4 and 92–101). On sources, see Whitelock's notes and J.E. Cross in *SN*, 41 (1969), 147–55. On the five-age tradition, see Förster in *Die Neueren Sprachen*, Beiheft 6, pp. 184–5.

10 See *De Veteri Testamenti*, Crawford, ed., *Heptateuch*, lines 166ff.

11 Förster, *Die Neueren Sprachen,* Beiheft 6, p. 185.

12 Crawford, ed., *Heptateuch,* lines 1185–94 (trans. William L'Isle [1623]: 'So the sixt age of this world reacheth from Christ vnto the day of doome, which no man knowes, but the Lord himselfe. A seuenth age [of men] is that which runneth on together with [all] these six, from the righteous Abel vnto the worlds end, not of men liuing here but of soules departed & in that other life; whence they reiocie still in expectation of eternall life after their resurrection; as rise againe from death we must all with whole & sound bodies to meet our Lord. The eighth age is that one euerlasting day after our resurrection, when we shall reigne with God in euerlasting happinesse both of soule and body: of that day there shall be no end; and then the Saints shal shine as the Sun doth now'). This section does not occur in the sources listed by Dubois, *Ælfric,* p. 91, but Förster cites a similar remark of Bede (*Die Neueren Sprachen,* Beiheft 6, p. 186n).

13 The evidence is surveyed by A. Vasiliev, 'Medieval Ideas of the End of the World: East and West,' *Byzantion,* 16 (1942–43), 462–502; G.L. Burr, 'The Year 1000 and the Antecedents of the Crusades,' *American Historical Review,* 6 (1901), 429–31; and, with special reference to England, Bethurum, pp. 278–82.

14 For example, *II in Advent,* Thorpe, I, 608/23 and esp. 614/1–22; *Roga-*tion Monday, Thorpe, II, 330/5–7; Ash Wednesday, *LS,* I, XII.279–83; Memory of Saints, *LS,* I, XVI.232–45; St Maurice, *LS,* II, XXVIII.165–73. See Cross, 'Aspects of Microcosm and Macrocosm,' *Comparative Literature,* 14 (1962), 1–22, and 'Gregory, *Blickling Homily X,* and Ælfric's *Passio S. Mauricii* on the World's Youth and Age,' *NM,* 66 (1965), 327–30.

15 *II in Advent,* Thorpe, I, 618/18–35 ('My brothers, set the remembrance of this day before your eyes, and whatsoever now appears to be trouble, it shall all be mitigated on comparison with it. Correct your lives, and change your conduct, punish your evil deeds with weeping, withstand the temptations of the devil; eschew evil and do good, and ye will be by so much the more secure at the advent of the eternal Judge, as ye now with terror anticipate his severity. The prophet said, that the great day of God is very near at hand and very swift. Though there were yet another thousand years to that day, it would not be long; for whatsoever ends is short and quick, and will be as it had never been, when it is ended. But though it were long to that day, as it is not, yet will our time not be long, and at our ending it will be adjudged to us, whether we in rest or in torment shall await the common doom. Let us, therefore, profit by the time which God has given us, and merit the everlasting life with him who

liveth and reigneth for ever and ever, Amen'); see also pp. 608–14. The renewed invasions were serious enough to hamper Ælfric's work (Lat. Pref, Thorpe, II, 1/14–15: 'multis injuriis infestium piratarum' delayed publication of the Second Series; see Sisam, *Studies*, pp. 158–60 on these raids), and may have influenced this thinking. The expansion on the Augustinian source material in *Common of Virgins* (Thorpe, II, 568/13ff.) is comparable; Pope XXVIII is inserted in line 19.

16 *Hom. in Evang.* I, *PL*, 76, 1081 ('Whence indeed it is necessary to consider [the approaching end] because these present tribulations are dissimilar from that last tribulation in the same degree as the role of the herald differs from the power of the judge. Therefore reflect upon that day, dearest brothers, with all your mind, correct your life, change your habits, conquer evil temptations by resisting, and avenge those perpetrated with tears. For you will see the coming of the eternal judge, whenever it is to be, so much the more securely as you now anticipate the punishment of the same event by being afraid').

17 As in the sermon which Ælfric quotes from Gregory of Tours, *Historia Francorum* X.1 in *St Gregory*, Thorpe, II, 124–6. According to M.R. Godden ('The Sources for Ælfric's Homily on St Gregory,' *Anglia*, 86 [1968], 79–98), Ælfric relied on Paul the Deacon's *Vita*

Gregorii, which in turn drew from the *Historia*.

18 *Rogation Wednesday* [Eve of Ascension], Thorpe, II, 370/13–17 ('Nu behófige ge, læwede men, micelre láre on ðisne timan, forðan ðe þeos woruld is micclum geswenct ðurh menigfealdum gedrefednyssum; and swa near ende þyssere worulde swa máre ehtnys þæs deofles, and bið unstrengre mennisc ðurh máran tyddernysse'). Among other passages related to the approach of the end, the following may be cited: *I in Advent*, Thorpe, I, 602/26ff.; *Sexagesima*, Thorpe, I, 98/7ff.; *Common of Virgins*, Thorpe, II, 568, 574; *Memory of Saints, LS*, I, XVI.219–31; *St Peter*, Thorpe, II, 388/6ff.

19 Thorpe, I, 2/27–30 ('and also because men have need of good instruction, especially at this time, which is the ending of this world, and there will be many calamities among mankind before the end cometh ...').

20 Verses 21, 5, 24, 22 are quoted in that order at pp. 2–4.

21 His source is sometimes (so Bethurum, p. 289) said to be the *Epistola Adsonis ad Gerbergam reginam de Ortu et Tempore Antichristi* (ed. Ernst Sackur in *Sibyllinische Texte und Forschungen* [Halle, 1898], 104–13; recent studies of Adso are Robert Konrad, *De Ortu et Tempore Antichristi: Antichristvorstellung und Geschichtsbild des Abtes Adso von Montier-en-Der*, Münchener Historische Studien, Abteilung Mittelalterliche Geschichte, 1 [Kallmünz,

1964]; Maurizio Rangheri, 'La "Epistola ad Gerbergam reginam de ortu et tempori Antichristi" di Adsone di Montier-en-Der e le sue Fonti,' *Studi Medievali*, 3rd Ser., 14 [1973], 677–732; Horst Dieter Rauh, *Das Bild des Antichrist im Mittelalter: von Tyconus zum deutschen Symbolismus*, Beiträge zur Geschichte der Philosophie und Theologie des Mittelalters, N.F. 9 (Münster, 1973]).

The dependence of Ælfric on Adso, if any, is very general and probably does not extend beyond the interpretation of Antichrist as 'ðwyrlic Crist' (Thorpe I, 4/22); for this and other details, however, Ælfric might have gone to the commentary of Haymo on II Thessalonians ii ('*Qui adversatur*, id est contrarius est Christo,' 'contrarius Christo,' *PL*, 117, 779–80). As Rangheri shows, Adso also used Haymo. Here and in Pope XVIII it seems to me impossible to identify Ælfric's sources, for all the details of his accounts are simply never found in one place (see also Pope, p. 588). Furthermore, Ælfric suppresses reference to a major motif of most literature on Antichrist: the connection of his advent with the end of Roman imperial history. It is the sort of detail Ælfric might well suppress as too obscure for his audience and irrelevant to the political situation of his times; but it is so integral to Haymo, Adso, and others that it seems remarkable it could be removed without trace.

Förster and Smetana are silent on the subject of the sources of the Preface, but Max Förster ('Altenglische Predigtquellen, I,' *Archiv*, 116 [1906], 308–10) argued for the reliance of Wulfstan on Adso. Adso, abbot of Montier-en-Der from 978 to 992, wrote the tract ca. 950; and it was known in England, at least in the Wulfstan circle (an OE translation in MSS Corpus Christi College, Cambridge, 419 and Oxford, Bodleian, Hatton 114 appears as no. XLII of Arthur Napier, ed., *Wulfstan*: Latin texts appear in MSS CCCC 190 and British Museum, Cotton Vespasian D ii).

22 Thorpe, I, 4/14–24 ('[he] is human man and true devil, as our Saviour is truly man and God in one person. And the visible devil shall then work innumerable miracles, and say that he himself is God, and will compel mankind to his heresy: but his time will not be long, for God's anger will destroy him, and this world will afterwards be ended. Christ our Lord healed the weak and diseased, and the devil, who is called Antichrist, which is interpreted, Opposition-Christ, weakens and enfeebles the hale, and heals no one from diseases, save those alone whom he himself had previously injured'). Ælfric used this text again in a later (unpublished) version of the *I in Advent* sermon of Thorpe I, (Clemoes, 'Chronology,' p. 246).

23 Thorpe, I, 6/23ff. Ælfric speaks of Antichrist elsewhere: in *I in Lent*,

Thorpe, II, 100/7–9, he refers to the tradition that Enoch and Elijah will return to overcome Antichrist; in *Common of Martyrs*, Thorpe, II, 540/31ff., and *SS Chrysanthus and Daria*, *LS*, II, xxxv.347–61, he remarks that the tribulations of the age of martyrs were nothing in comparison with those of the age of Antichrist; in *Job*, Thorpe, II, 452/1–3, he says again that Antichrist, like the devil in Job, will seem to bring down fire from heaven.

24 Thorpe, II, 568/19. The homily explicates the parable of the wise and foolish virgins (Matth. xxv.1–13), the bridegroom being Christ returned for the Judgment.

25 Pope xxviii.13 ('just as darkness disappears at the coming of the sun').

26 It is an overemphasis of this element of Ælfric's thought to exclaim, as does Dubois (*Ælfric*, p. 190) of his exhortations to be prepared for the end, 'Quel bel example de force morale et de résignation à la volonté de Dieu!'

27 *In Evang.* I, *PL*, 76, 1078 ('Nam gentem super gentem exsurgere, earumque pressuram terris insistere, plus jam in nostris temporibus cernimus quam in Codicibus legimus, quod terrae motus urbes innumeras subruat, ex aliis mundi partibus scitis quam frequenter audivimus. Pestilentias sine cessatione patimur. Signa vero in sole, et luna, et stellis, adhuc aperte minime videmus, sed quia et haec

non longe sint, ex ipsa jam aeris immutatione colligimus'). Ælfric's appeal to Matt. xxiv. 39 to clarify the astronomical signs is from Haymo (*PL*, 118, 17–25; see Smetana, *Traditio*, 17 [1961], 467).

28 *II in Advent*, Thorpe, I, 608–18; *Common of Martyrs*, Thorpe, II, 12–20; *Common of Virgins*, Thorpe, II, 568.

29 *II in Advent*, Thorpe, I, 618/9–17; *Christmas*, Thorpe, II, 12–22.

30 See Gatch, *Church History*, 33 (1964), 379–84.

31 *II in Advent*, Thorpe, I, 616/3–4.

32 Ibid., 616–18; *Common of Virgins*, Thorpe, II, 568–70; *Dedication of a Church*, Thorpe, II, 590/1–8.

33 *XVI after Pentecost*, Thorpe, II, 464/13ff.

34 *I after Easter*, Thorpe, I, 236/5–22 ('We will speak concerning the resurrection. Now there are some men who have doubt of the resurrection, and when they see the bones of dead men, they say, How can these bones be again quickened? as if they speak wisely! But we say against them, that God is Almighty, and can do all that he will. He wrought heaven and earth and all creatures without matter. Now it seems that it is somewhat easier to him to raise the dead from the dust, than it was to him to make all creatures from naught: but truly to him are all things alike easy, and nothing difficult. He wrought Adam of loam. Now we cannot investigate how of that loam he made flesh and

blood, bones and skin, hair and nails. Men often see that of one little kernel comes a great tree, but in the kernel we can see neither root, nor rind, nor boughs, nor leaves: but the same God who draws forth from the kernel tree, and fruits, and leaves, may from dust raise flesh and bones, sinews and hair, as he said in his gospel, "There shall not be lost to you one hair of your head"'). The image of the seed, derived from I Cor. xv. 35ff., was popular among exegetes as an explanation of resurrection as early as Origen (e.g., *Contra Celsum* v. 18ff.). See also John xii.24. The paragraph is translated almost literally from Gregory, *In Evang.* XXVI.12 (*PL*, 76, 1203–4), but Ælfric adds the following paragraphs on the resurrection of the body from his own epitome of the Julian text which is appended to this volume (see Gatch, 'MS Boulogne-sur-Mer 63 and Ælfric's First Series of *Catholic Homilies*,' *JEGP*, 65 [1966], 482–90 at 486–8).

35 *Seven Sleepers*, Thorpe, II, 426/9–19; *St Edmund, LS*, II, XXXII.250–54.

36 *St Paul*, Thorpe, I, 394/34–5 ('ure lichaman ge-edcennede to unbrosnigendlicum lichaman').

37 *Palm Sunday*, Thorpe, I, 218/23–6; *IV after Easter*, Pope VII, 158–62.

38 *I after Easter*, Thorpe, I, 236/23–8; *Common of Martyrs*, Thorpe, II, 544/1–4; *Rogation Wednesday* [*De Fide Catholica*], Thorpe, I, 294/1–3.

39 *II after Pentecost*, Thorpe, I, 532/4–8.

40 *Easter*, Thorpe, I, 224/5–8. See also *II after Epiphany*, Thorpe, II, 68–70, on the circumcision as a foretoken of resurrection. Ælfric usually distinguishes Christ's resurrection from the general (*gemænlic*) resurrection (Halvorson, *Doctrinal Terms in Ælfric's Homilies*, pp. 79–80).

41 *Friday in 1st Week of Lent*, Pope II.90–114.

42 *Friday in 4th Week of Lent*, Pope VI.126–36. The passage explains why, having raised Lazarus and others, Christ put off the resurrection of other men.

43 *De Falsis Diis*, Pope XXI.56–65.

44 *Letter to Wulfgeat*, Assmann I.76–84; the same material was incorporated (probably not by Ælfric) in *De Sancte Trinitate et de Festis Diebus per Annum*, Pope XIa.162–70 (on the relationship, see Pope, p. 459).

45 *St James*, Thorpe, II, 420/8–9; *St Stephen*, Thorpe, I, 48/28–33.

46 *Easter*, Thorpe, I, 222/33–224/1; *Easter*, Thorpe, II, 282/11–13.

47 *St Paul*, Thorpe, I, 394/22–5.

48 *Common of Confessors*, Thorpe, II, 558/11–17.

49 *Common of Virgins*, Thorpe, II, 570/32–572/4; *St Alban* [Ahitophel and Absalom], *LS*, I, XIX.175–6; *V after Pentecost*, Pope XIII.74–81 (but see also 91–2); *VII after Pentecost*, Pope XV.125–42; *X after Pentecost*, Pope XVI.94–8, 187–203.

50 *Rogation Monday*, Thorpe, II, 328/11–13.

51 *I in Lent*, Thorpe, II, 106/21–108/35.

52 *Rogation Tuesday* [Lord's Prayer], Thorpe, I, 262/32–264/15.
53 *St Peter*, Thorpe, II, 386/29–34.
54 See *Traditio*, 21 (1965), 155–6.
55 *Common of Virgins*, Thorpe, II, 572/16–18, 22–5 ('that the holy Mary, the mother of Christ, and some other saints, should, after the doom, harrow the sinful from the devil, each his part … Neither the blessed Mary nor any other saint will lead the foul, and the wicked, and the impious, who have ever continued in sins, and in sins have ended, into the pure house of the joy of heaven's kingdom; but they will be like unto devils …'). The sermon is based on Augustine, *Sermo* XVIII (*PL*, 38, 573–80) and Gregory, *In Evang.* XII (*PL*, 76, 1118–23), neither of which has this remark. Ælfric must, then, be referring to the Vercelli Hom. XV or to its source tradition, the Apocalypse of Thomas.
56 Thorpe, I, 396/16–32 ('There will be four assemblages at the great doom, two of chosen men, and two of rejected. The first assemblage will be of the apostles and their imitators, who forsook all worldly things for the name of God: they will be the judges, and to them shall no judgment be judged. The second class will be of faithful men of this world: on them will doom be set, so that they will be sundered from the fellowship of the rejected, the Lord thus saying, "Come to me, ye blessed …" One class will be of those rejected, who had knowledge of God, but did not cultivate their faith with God's commandments: these will be condemned. The other class is of those heathen men, who have had no knowledge of God: on these will be fulfilled the apostolic sentence, "Those who have sinned without God's law, shall perish also without any law." To these two classes the righteous Judge will then say, "Depart from me, ye accursed, into the everlasting fire …"'). The source is Ælfric's epitome of the *Prognosticon Futuri Saeculi* of Julian of Toledo (see my article in *JEGP*, 65 [1966], 484–5, and the discussion of the *Sermo ad Populum in Octavis Pentecosten Dicendus*, Pope XI, in the following chapter).
57 Thorpe, I, 396/34–398/19.
58 Thorpe, I, 400/31–3 ('and to imitate the apostles, that they, with them and with God, may have everlasting life').
59 *Quinquagesima*, Thorpe, I, 162/23–5.
60 *St Maurice*, *LS*, II, XXVIII.119–41; *Annunciation*, Thorpe, I, 204/1–12.
61 *Rogation Monday*, Thorpe, I, 250/28–30.
62 *Ascension*, Thorpe, I, 296/29–34; *Rogation Tuesday* [Lord's Prayer], Thorpe, I, 270/28–272/3.
63 *St Michael*, Thorpe, I, 512/29–30.
64 *Birth of the Virgin*, Assmann III.510–25
65 *I in Lent*, Thorpe, I, 174/1–3.
66 *St Agnes*, *LS*, I, VII.137–40.
67 *III after Epiphany*, Thorpe, I, 132/25–30 ('There shall be weeping

and gnashing of teeth; for their eyes shall be tormented in the great burning, and their teeth shall afterwards quake in the intense cold. If any one doubt of the universal resurrection, let him understand this divine saying, That there shall be a true resurrection, where there shall be weeping eyes and gnashing teeth').

Chapter 8

1 See Clemoes, 'Chronology,' pp. 244–5.

2 The ms term is *Quando volueris* (see Clemoes, p. 217; Pope, p. 141).

3 MSS Cambridge, Corpus Christi College, 188, pp. 170.20–173.5 (Q in the Pope-Clemoes system of sigla; Ker, *Catalogue*, 43, art. 17); 178, pp. 242.4–244.5 (R; Ker 41A, art. 29); Bodleian, Hatton 114, ff. 96ʳ.22–97ʳ.10 (T; Ker 331, art. 51); British Museum, Cotton Faustina A. IX, ff. 148ᵛ.12–150ʳ.12 (N; Ker 153, art. 29) are the basis of the quotations below. I have not collated two MSS: British Museum, Cotton Vitellius C.v, ff. 95ʳ.4–96ʳ.3 (H; Ker 220, art. 21), and Trinity College, Cambridge, B.15.34, pp. 40.2–50.1 (U; Ker 86, art. 5), although I have examined the latter. My reading, for which MS Q provides the basic text, was made from photographs supplied by Professor Pope, who also edited the passage in his 1931 Yale diss. The fragment will be published by Professor Clemoes in his forthcoming edition of *Catholic Homilies, I*, for E.E.T.S.

4 The passage occurs between lines 22 and 23 of Thorpe, I, 236; i.e., between the paragraph from Gregory, *In Evang.* XXVI (*PL*, 76, 1203–4) and the paragraph adapted from Julian of Toledo on the nature of the resurrection of the body (see above, p. 226 note 34.

5 *PL*, 76, 1204 ('Therefore all these things are hidden at the same time in the seed which nevertheless do not appear simultaneously from the seed. For from the seed is produced the root, from the root comes the shoot, from the shoot fruit grows, and in the fruit seed is produced. Therefore we may add also that the seed is hidden in the seed. What marvel, therefore, if He should bring back bones, sinews, flesh, and hair who daily rebuilds limbs, fruit, foliage from the little seed into the great structure of the tree').

6 On uses of the topos in Old English literature, see J.E. Cross, '"Ubi Sunt" Passages in Old English,' Vetenskaps-Societetens i Lund, *Årsbok* (1956), pp. 23–44. (The instances adduced by Étienne Gilson, *Les Idées et les Lettres* [2nd ed.; Paris, 1955], pp. 31–8, could now be multiplied.) Characteristically, the device is employed in discussions of the brevity of life ('Brevis est hujus mundi felicitas, modica est hujus saeculi gloria, caduca est et fragilis temporalis potentia. Dic ubi sunt reges? ubi principes? ubi imperatores? ...' – Isidore of Seville, *Synonyma* II.91 [*PL*, 88, 713–14]

quoted by Cross, p. 26). Ælfric's use of the rhetorical tag *ubi sunt ?*, however, is quite different here, for it presents examples which give one reason for hope of resurrection rather than despair over mortality. I know of no strict *ubi sunt ?* passage in Ælfric (though one might argue that Pope XIII.22 reflects the tradition); but it was known widely among Ælfric's contemporaries, probably including Wulfstan, and the present passage shows that he knew it well enough to adapt it with startling freedom.

7 Lines 1–7 ('Where are the plants' blossoms in winter ?/ Where are all the fruits of all the tree family ?/ Where are they visible in the wintry chill/ on any tree, which will all again be quickened/ on plants and trees through the eternal Maker/ who will raise the dead bones from the dust/ as easily as he formerly made them ?').

8 On the silkworm as a type of the resurrection in hexaemeral works and the OE *Phoenix*, see Joanne Kantrowitz, 'The Anglo-Saxon Phoenix and Tradition,' *PQ*, 43 (1964), 1–13.

9 Although Ælfric confuses eggs with dust, his description is very accurate and has led Professor Pope to wonder if he may not have observed silkworms in Italy where sericulture had been introduced from the East in the tenth century. The expression 'swa swa we oft gesawon' (line 23) in Ælfric's usage suggests to Pope personal observation. Certainly Ælfric knows more than Isidore of Seville (*Etymologiarum* XIII.5.8 [*PL*, 82, 499]: 'Bombyx, frondium vermis, ex cuius textura bombycinum conficitur. Appelatur autem hoc nomine ab eo quod evacuetur, dum fila generet, et aer solus in eo remanet'), or Rabanus Maurus who only quoted Isidore (*De Universo* VIII.14 [*PL*, 111, 235]). The only other reference to silkworms indexed in *PL*, 201, 556, is in [pseudo-] Hugh of St Victor and is also a quotation of Isidore. Sericulture, long a Byzantine state monopoly, was introduced in the West at the monastery of Santa Giulia in Brescia in the tenth century (see R.S. Lopez, 'The Trade of Medieval Europe: The South,' in *The Cambridge Economic History of Europe*, ed. M. Postan and E.E. Rich, vol. 2 [Cambridge, 1952], p. 265). Although there is no evidence Ælfric ever left England, he might easily have done so, and Brescia could not have been far off the usual route through the Alps (see Napier XXXI [by Ælfric]; Sisam, 'Marginalia in the Vercelli Book,' *Studies*, p. 118). It would be dangerous, however, to put too much stress on this possibility in the light of the fact that references to the silkworm as types of the resurrection are commonplace.

10 Lines 30–5 ('Now there is a very clear example in this silkworm/ which revives from dust: that our Lord can/ raise us from death, from

dust, to life;/ we will be eternal after our resurrection/ since he the weak worms which turn again to dust/ as easily revives to the same strength.')

11 The absence of the funeral pyre, not peculiar to Ælfric, may have to do with the Christian aversion to cremation. The pyre and also the worm are present in the OE *Phoenix* (George Philip Krapp and Elliott van Kirk Dobbie, eds., *The Exeter Book*, The Anglo-Saxon Poetic Records, vol. 3 [New York, 1936], 94–113).

12 It is tempting in the light of recent readings of the poem to see some connection with *The Phoenix*: see J.E. Cross, 'The Conception of the Old English *Phoenix*,' in *Old English Poetry: Fifteen Essays*, ed. Robert P. Creed (Providence, 1967), pp. 129–52; the edition by N.F. Blake, Old and Middle English Texts (Manchester, 1964); and the article by Kantrowitz cited in note 8. It is conceivable that lines 63–78 originally followed line 51, Ælfric having added the Seven Sleepers passage as an afterthought. If so, the conclusion sounds very like *Phoenix*, lines 474ff., as read by Cross; and it is easier to understand the rationale for Ælfric's quotation, 'In domo patris mei mansiones multe sunt' (line 69).

13 Thorpe, II, 424–6. The homily in *LS*, I, is not by Ælfric. In both of his treatments (the other is Thorpe, II, 424/56), Ælfric says the sleep lasted 372 years. Professor Pope

suggests that an Anglo-Saxon text counting 186 by half-years may have been misread and, thus, the period of sleep doubled. Error as to the extent of time exists, however, in the Latin tradition (M. Huber, *Die Wanderlegende von den Siebenschläfern: Eine literargeschichtliche Untersuchung* [Leipzig, 1910], p. 157).

14 Lines 63–5 ('Whether we will it or not, we will dwell forever quick/ after our resurrection, according to our deserts,/ either good or evil, which we formerly wrought.')

15 Lines 73–8, bracketed readings from MSS R, U ('and I am myself foolish if I do not want to make for myself/ the eternal dwellings while I can and must,/ since I do not want even to travel over land,/ or ride to a monastery, unless I have considered/ where I can dwell and have a certain lodging/ for the little time of the transitory journey.')

16 On the convention, see J.E. Cross and S.I. Tucker, 'Allegorical Tradition and the Old English *Exodus*,' *Neophilologus*, 44 (1960), 122–7, at 124. Compare with Ælfric Augustine, *Sermo* CXI.ii (*PL*, 37, 642–3): 'Suscipis hospitem, cujus et tu es comes in vita; quia omnes peregrini sumus. Ipse est christianus qui et in domo sua et patria sua peregrinum se esse cognoscit.' See also *Ennar. in Psal.* XXXIV.4 (*PL*, 36, 326): this life is 'stabulum viatori, non ... domus habitatori.' There is a sentence in Vercelli Homily XIV (fol. 77.16–23) which is remotely reminiscent of

Ælfric's (see Jon L. Ericson, 'The Readings of Folios 77 and 86 of the Vercelli Codex,' *Manuscripta*, 16 [1972], 14–23, and the facsimile ed. Max Förster, 1913).

17 See Cross, art. in *Old English Poetry*, ed. Creed, at pp. 138 and 150, n.38; Kantrowitz, *PQ*, 43 (1964), 1–13. A typical collection of natural analogies to the resurrection (the closest I have found to Ælfric's, but by no means his source) is Tertullian, *De Resurrectione Carnis* xii–xiii (*PL*, 2, 856–8). In *Phoenix*, lines 250–7, the seed image is added to the source; this metaphor was, of course, Ælfric's starting-point in the Gregory homily.

18 Homilies II (Förster, ed., *Die Vercelli-Homilien*, pp. 44–53), xv (Förster, 'Der Vercelli-Codex CXVII nebst Abdruck einiger altenglischer Homilien der Handschrift,' *Studien zur Englischen Philologie*, 50 (1913), 20–179 at pp. 117–28). Several other occurrences of the rubric are noted in Ker's *Catalogue*.

19 Pope's apparatus for the homily, his XVIII, shows that through line 221 there is a very general similarity to the exegesis of Luke xvii.21–30 in Bede's Commentary on Luke (CCL, 120). For the second half of the work, there seems to be some relation to the pseudo-Bedan Commentary on Matthew xxiv.15–30; Caesarius of Arles, Sermo CLIV; and, at one place, Gregory's *Moralia in Job* XXXII.24. See also Pope, pp. 584–9.

20 Pope, pp. 588–9. None of the texts on which Ælfric comments is a Sunday pericope, though Luke xvii.20–7 was the subject of a homily for Friday in the second week of Pentecost by Rabanus based on Bede (inventoried by Barré).

21 On Bede as exegete, see W.F. Bolton, *A History of Anglo-Latin Literature*, 1, pp. 105–33, and as homilist, pp. 166–7; Claude Jenkins, 'Bede as Exegete and Theologian,' in *Bede: His Life, Times, and Writings*, ed. E. Hamilton Thompson (Oxford, 1935), pp. 152–200; and especially Charles W. Jones, 'Some Introductory Remarks on Bede's Commentary on Genesis,' *Sacris Erudiri*, 19 (1969–70), 115–98.

22 See Clemoes, 'Ælfric,' in *Continuations and Beginnings*, ed. Stanley, pp. 191–2.

23 Pope XVIII.47–54 ('but we believe nonetheless, that it will not be left unfulfilled for us/ that he will truly come with his shining angels/ at this world's ending/ to judge us, each according to his deserts;/ and he will then give to those who were obedient to him,/ and to those who ever made him glad with good works,/ the eternal joys and the eternal fellowship/ with all his saints in the heavenly kingdom.') On aspects of interpretation of the Noah story, see Gatch, 'Noah's Raven in *Genesis A* and the Illustrated Old English Hexateuch,' *Gesta*, 14 (1975), 3–15.

24 Lines 83–5 ('and [the earth] will not

232 Notes pp. 90–93

at all be burned, but will be cleansed from/ all the impurities which from the beginning have befallen it/ and it thus will abide continuously in eternity, all shining.')

25 Lines 92–7 ('They will be in bed who are in silence,/ and devoid of all worldly cares,/ and perform God's service with good intentions;/ but they are not two units, but divided in two parts./ The one is called and acceptable to God,/ the other is discovered to be hypocritical in his service.')

26 Lines 119–22 ('Concerning these he says two women and does not intend to say two men,/ because they are truly not in such perfection/ that they themselves can instruct themselves,/ but they must live by their teachers' guidance . . . .')

27 In *St Paul*, Thorpe, I, 396/17–20, 398/6–15, and in *Octave of Pentecost*, Pope XI.356–9. There is some basis for this elaboration in Bede, *In Luc.* on xvii.34–5 (CCL, 120, 319–20) but Ælfric goes beyond his known sources.

28 See the textual note to lines 227–8, Pope, p. 600. Note also that this device prevents repetition of passages which Matthew has in common with Luke xvii (Pope, p. 586).

29 Lines 227–8 ('Interrogatus Iesus a discipulis de consummatione saeculi,/ dixit eis, Cum autem uideritis abhominationem desolationis, et reliqua.')

30 Line 323 ('who are filled with vices like sows in farrow').

31 Lines 383–7 ('Our Saviour Christ will not come to mankind/ openly manifested in this world/ before the great day when he will judge mankind;/ but the false Christs and the false prophets/ will come in Antichrist's time.')

32 *History of Anglo-Latin Literature*, I, 114.

33 Bernhard Bischoff, 'Wendepunkte in der Geschichte der lateinischen Exegese im Frühmittelalter,' *Sacris Erudiri*, 6 (1954), 189–281.

34 Ibid. The most common kind of exploitation of the literal was that in which the commentator remarked upon a point of grammatical nicety. An example is the distinction between *twegen* and *twa* in *De Die Iudicii* (see lines 95, 113, 143, 201–2, based on Bede) which opens the way to a 'spiritual' distinction between the masculine and feminine as cleric and lay.

35 Hanspeter Schelp, 'Die Deutungstradition in Ælfrics Homiliae Catholicae,' *Archiv*, 196 (1959–60), 274–95. But see also Clemoes in *Continuations and Beginnings*, ed. Stanley, pp. 188–9, and Paul Mary Cook, SND, 'Ælfric's *Catholic Homilies* Considered in Relation to the Rhetorical Theory Enunciated in St Augustine's *De Doctrina Christiana*,' Diss. Oxford, 1967.

36 Schelp, pp. 278–9. For the tropological formula, see *Epiphany*, Thorpe, I, 116/32–3; *II in Lent*, Thorpe, II, 110/26.

37 Schelp, pp. 277–8, cites *Quin-*

quagesima, Thorpe, I, 154; *Midlent*, Thorpe, I, 186. The Genesis preface (Crawford, ed., *Heptateuch*, pp. 77–80), of course, rests on the assumption that the literal meaning of Scripture is often misleading; paraphrase or translation for the laity is, therefore, a perilous undertaking in that it leaves no room for exposition of spiritual meaning.

38 Best consulted in Whitelock, ed., *Sweet's Reader*, pp. 61–8, to which parenthetical reference is made below. Thorpe does not print the translation of the pericope which, for Ælfric, may well have been a treatment of the literal sense. Whitelock's notes (pp. 249–51) outline the sources; see also Cross, *SN*, 41 (1969), 135–55.

39 See Cross, *SN*, 41 (1969), 148.

40 Lines 314–17 ('We must tell you so that you can understand,/ now simply in proportion to your own intelligence,/ again to open the inner mystery for you,/ for you might easily not understand it entirely.')

41 Pope XI. I have discussed the piece briefly in *Death*, pp. 87–93, 156–7, and 'Some Theological Reflections on Death ... ,' in *Perspectives on Death*, ed. L.O. Mills, pp. 113–19.

42 Pope, p. 410; Clemoes, 'Chronology,' pp. 229–34, 242, 245.

43 Clemoes, 'Chronology,' p. 229; in addition to the authority there cited (Dom Gregory Dix, *The Shape of the Liturgy*, 2nd ed. [London, 1945], pp. 358, 585) see Massey Hamilton Shepherd, Jr., *The Oxford American*

Prayer Book Commentary (New York, 1950), facing pp. 186–8.

44 Lines 73–5 ('and now today we are praising the Holy Trinity/ with our divine service, and this week/ until the eve of Sunday we will sing about that'). The reference may, however, be only to the Preface of the Mass for the octave in the Gelasian and Gregorian Sacramentaries which emphasizes the Trinity.

45 Pope XII (Belfour I). In addition to the introduction to XII, see Pope, pp. 333–7.

46 Pope, p. 410n. *De Die Iudicii* is also given this designation: although exegetical, it is not a homily on the pericope.

47 Notably in *De Fide Catholica: Rogation Wednesday*, Thorpe, I, 274–94. For other references, see N.O. Halvorson, *Doctrinal Terms in Ælfric's Homilies*, p. 14. *Letter to Wulfgeat*, Assmann I, had not yet been composed.

48 Lines 4–5 ('so that you may discern an interpretation therein/ of how the whole course of the year serves God Almighty'). See also Pope XIa.

49 The best study of Julian is J.N. Hillgarth, 'St Julian of Toledo in the Middle Ages,' *Journal of the Warburg and Courtauld Institutes*, 21 (1958), 7–26. (Pp. 22–3 discuss the Boulogne MS, Ælfric, and other Anglo-Saxon references to the work; one ms of *Prognosticum* [the form of the title Hillgarth prefers] was given by Ælfric's mentor, Bishop Æthelwold, to Peterborough in 984.) On

MSS of *Prognosticon,* see Hillgarth, 'El *Prognosticum Futuri Saeculi* de San Julián de Toledo,' *Analecta Sacra Tarraconensia,* 30 (1957), 5–61; J.D.A. Ogilvy, *Books Known to the English, 597–1066,* p. 188. Unfortunately the early mss in England cannot be traced to the libraries that originally owned them, to judge from N.R. Ker, *Medieval Libraries of Great Britain: A List of Surviving Books,* 2nd ed., Royal Historical Society Guides and Handbooks, 3 (London, 1964).

50 Enid M. Raynes, 'MS Boulogne-sur-Mer 63 and Ælfric,' *MÆ,* 26 (1957), 65–7, first pointed out this relationship and connected other items of the MS with Ælfric. See also Pope, pp. 407–9. The excerpts, with the rubric 'Hunc sermonem ex multis excerpsimus de libro qui dicitur Pronosticon. In Christi nomine,' are found on ff. 1ʳ–10ʳ of the MS. The text is edited as an appendix to this volume. Passages of the Boulogne excerpts (BE) which were used by Ælfric in the *Sermo* are printed in the apparatus of Pope's edition.

51 See my 'MS. Boulogne-sur-Mer 63 and Ælfric's First Series of *Catholic Homilies,*' *JEGP,* 65 (1966), 482–90, and Pope, pp. 409, 448, 450.

52 Lines 112–17 ('That is in English, the painful death,/ the premature death, and the natural./ That is called the bitter death which occurs to children,/ and the premature death, to young men,/ and the

natural which happens to the old'). On the use of 'classification,' see Clemoes, 'Ælfric,' in *Continuations and Beginnings,* ed. Stanley, p. 189.

53 Lines 134–5 ('and yet never dies in the torment of hell,/ but is ever renewed for the eternal punishments.')

54 Lines 147–9 ('both men and women, and the ignorant children,/ and all men in holy orders who protect their purity/ and daily fight against the devil's temptation.')

55 Ælfric adds to BE and *Prognosticon* I.xvii the exemplum of lines 163–76, retold from memory from one or more of the several versions of Gregory (Cross, *NM,* 72 [1971], 448–9).

56 Lines 181–4; BE, f. 2ᵛ ('... in separatione sanctarum animarum et egressu a corpore, angelorum semper habeantur excubiae.')

57 Lines 189b–90 ('until they become clean,/ and through intercession are released from thence.')

58 Lines 216–19 ('The soul has truly, as books tell us,/ the likeness of the body in all its members,/ and it feels comfort or pain,/ whichever it is in, as it earned before.')

59 Lines 356–9 ('and all the holy men who forsook the world,/ and entirely rejected worldly possessions,/ will truly sit on judgment-seats with them,/ and they will judge mankind with the Saviour.') As at Thorpe, I, 396–98, from BE, f. 7ᵛ ('Et non solum duodecim apostoli, sed ... omnes sancti qui perfecte mundum

reliquerunt cum Domino residentes ceteros iudicabunt.')

60 Lines 427–9, 449–50 ('Truly I say to you, that ye did to me/ these aforesaid things as often as ye did them/ to one of these little ones my brothers .../ Truly I say to you, ye denied it to me/ as often as ye denied one of these little ones.')

61 Lines 473–7 ('In one fire they will burn in the burning lake,/ the poor human men and the proud devils;/ that fire will then be eternal, and they will burn eternally,/ but their bodies can never be consumed/ because they will be eternal after the resurrection.')

62 BE, f. 8ᵛ–9ʳ, restating and expanding *Prognosticon* III.xli, which, in turn, cites Augustine.

63 Lines 487–92 ('Just as easily almighty God can/ confine the devils in the dark fire, so that therein they will suffer and be unable to come out;/ and he who makes glad the holy angels in the heavens,/ the same can also torment the devils in the fire,/ though they are spirits, entirely guilty.')

64 Lines 562–3 ('loving him without intermission,/ and praising him without weariness.')

65 Gatch, *JEGP*, 65 (1966), 488–9.

Chapter 9

1 Even the apparent conflict between the five- and six-ages traditions, discussed above in Chapter 7, is not an inconsistency. The use of the five-ages tradition in the *Septuagesima* homily of *CH* II is based on a well-established convention in explication of the parable of the vineyard; the six-ages tradition was used for other purposes.

2 See the tables in *Traditio*, 21 (1965), 119–22 and 138–42.

3 The pseudo-Augustinian homilies and the homilies *Ad Fratres in Eremo* of *PL*, 39–40 – both collections containing much Caesarian material. One reason for linking the homilies in English with a common tradition is the frequent reference to 'se æþela lareow' as the source, as though this were a common name for some authoritative teacher. (On this expression, see Rudolph Willard, 'The Blickling-Junius Tithing Homily and Caesarius of Arles,' *Philologica: The Malone Anniversary Studies*, ed. Thomas A. Kirby and Henry Bosley Woolf [Baltimore, 1949], pp. 65–78 at 66.

4 See Joseph B. Trahern, Jr., 'Caesarius of Arcles and Old English Literature: Some Contributions and a Recapitulation,' *ASE*, 5 (forthcoming 1976). Pope has identified several short passages from pseudo-Augustine and Caesarius (pp. 166, 168); Cross (*NM*, 72 [1971], 452) has pointed to other connections with pseudo-Augustine, Caesarius, and Alan of Farfa; there have been other identifications of this sort, and more are doubtless forthcoming. But (as in one instance first mentioned by Förster and refined by Smetana, *Traditio*, 15 [1959], 183)

sometimes Ælfric could have come across Caesarian materials under other names in his version of Paul the Deacon; and sometimes his Caesarian materials may have been amalgamated in composite homilies of the Carolingian sort. The exact nature of his relationship to pseudo-Augustinian materials, to Caesarius, and to Alan of Farfa remains, it seems to me, unsettled; the answers (if we ever have them) will arise from a better knowledge of Carolingian homiliaries to which Ælfric may have had access.

5 *Studies*, p. 118.

6 See Jean Leclercq, *The Love of Learning and the Desire for God*, p. 186.

7 Henri Barré, *Les Homéliaires Carolingiens*, p. 1, quoting an anonymous notice of the work of Honoratus, a late fifth-century bishop of Marseilles.

8 *Traditio*, 15 (1959), 163–204; 17 (1961), 457–69; see also J.E. Cross, 'Ælfric and the Mediæval Homiliary'; Pope, pp. 156–8. On the conception of the Homiliary of Paul, see Barré, *Homéliaires*, pp. 3–4, and that of Haymo, pp. 31ff.

Chapter 10

1 The chronology of Wulfstan's homilies is a difficult matter, and I have in general accepted the arrangement of Bethurum and her discussion of the matter at pp. 101–4 of *The Homilies of Wulfstan*. Peter Clemoes, in a review of Bethurum (*MLR*, 54

[1959], pp. 81–2), used Ælfrician evidence to argue for greater preciseness in dating in a few instances – namely 'that the first part of IX was not composed after 1005, but that V and XII were, and that IV was composed before V and XII' (p. 82) – thus vindicating in part the order in which the 'Eschatological Homilies' are presented by Bethurum.

2 Bethurum Ib.

3 Bethurum, p. 103, argues for the order II, III, Ia, Ib, IV, V. There is little reason to doubt this order, and I believe the discussion below strengthens the argument that II must be the earliest of the run.

4 Bethurum Ia ('Dear men, understand very well that you properly and scrupulously foster what you have greatest need to foster, namely true Christianity. For each of those who acts too greatly in opposition to it or teaches another what is opposed to what pertains to his Christianity – each of those is called Antichrist. Antichristus is in Latin *contrarius Cristo*, that is in English "God's adversary." He is God's adversary who abandons God's law and teaching, and through the devil's teaching acts at variance with that which pertains to his Christianity, and too greatly defiles himself in sins or leads another astray into sins. And although it should be that many men should never see Antichrist with their own eyes, yet there are very many of his limbs [members] whom one can now see far and

wide and know through their evil, just as it is read in the Gospel: *Surgent enim pseudocristi, et reliqua.* Far and wide it happens that false liars rise up and are plausibly deceitful; and those injure many and bring them to error. And very great hardship will yet happen in many ways far and wide in the world, as books tell, through the sons of the devil who will practice injustice such as never before has happened in the world; for the greatest evil will come to men when Antichrist himself shall come, which never before happened in the world. And it seems to us that it is extremely near to that time, because this world is continually from day to day the longer the worse.

'Now there is great need for all of God's preachers to warn God's people often against the terror which is approaching men, lest they be found unprepared and then too quickly be led astray by the devil. But let every priest so do in the district of his authority as confessor that men shall hear it often and frequently, lest it come to pass that the people should be lost of God by want of instruction; and although it should happen that any of you who now lives should not then be living, yet we need to warn now zealously the religious flocks how they can most scrupulously withstand the devil, Antichrist himself, when he most widely shall spread abroad his mad power. And let us now warn also against his bad teachings very zealously, and eagerly pray to God almighty that he shield us from that public enemy. May God guard us against that terror, and open the way for us to the eternal joy which is prepared for those who do his will. There is eternal bliss and ever will be in all ages, world without end. Amen').

5 He uses, according to Bethurum, pp. 282–6, Ælfric, Adso, Gregory and biblical texts, but in most cases the resemblances are very general. On Ælfric and Adso and Adso mss in England, see note 21 to chapter 7 above. Wulfstan almost certainly knew Adso, for the tract in Latin and in English is preserved in mss closely associated with him (Bethurum, 'Archbishop Wulfstan's Commonplace Book,' *PMLA*, 57 [1942], 925), but I think he need not have consulted him anew in preparing his sermons.

6 Bethurum, p. 283, citing Charles Sears Baldwin, *Medieval Rhetoric and Poetic (to 1400)* (1928; rpt. Gloucester, Mass.: Peter Smith, 1959), pp. 233–4. One may suppose that some English preachers continued to translate ex tempore from Latin texts, even after the introduction of written translations or adaptations of Latin sermons in English.

7 See C.I.J.M. Stuart, 'Wulfstan's Use of "Leofan Men",' *ES*, 45 (1964), 39–42.

8 Bethurum, p. 285.

9 Thorpe, I, 4/22 ('Opposition-Christ').

10 Bethurum Ia.6, reads *contrarius Cristi*. As Bethurum, p. 283, points out the form in the Old English version is probably based on Augustine but is also close to Adso.

11 See Bethurum, p. 283, for citations.

12 Bethurum II.

13 Bethurum, p. 286, states that this is the pericope for Thursday in the Third week of Lent; it is not, however, the pericope commented on in the Carolingian homiliaries under that day.

14 Pp. 20–1, above.

15 Bethurum III.

16 *II Advent*, Thorpe, I, 608–18. *Common of Martyrs*, Thorpe, II, 536–48, is based on Luke xxi.9–19.

17 Professor Alan K. Brown permits me to note this fact, which he has discovered. The Abbo homily, a transcription of which has been made available to me but from which I feel it improper to quote before Brown publishes his findings, is an adaptation of the second item in the homiliary of Haymo of Auxerre (*PL*, 118, 17–25), itself taken from Gregory and Bede. Ælfric, according to Smetana (*Traditio*, 17 [1961], 467) may have taken his reference to Matthew xxiv.29 in *II in Advent* (Thorpe, I, 610/6–10) from the sermon of Haymo. It might equally well have been suggested by Abbo; but, the collection being designed for use by bishops and these being no known

citations of Abbo by Ælfric, this seems unlikely. The Abbo sermon for II in Advent does not appear among the other Abbo materials in the Copenhagen MS which is so closely associated with Wulfstan. The chief witnesses to Abbo's collection are Paris, Bibliothèque Nationale MS 13203 fonds Latin, and Chartres, Bibliothèque Municipale MS 14, ff. 66ff. (The Chartres MS is earlier but largely illegible.) Brown will show that Bethurum III, lines 7–21, 27–36, 65–78 are Wulfstan's only major departures from Abbo. The first of these passages may to some degree be indebted to another Abbonian sermon, 'Sermo adversus raptores qui bona pauperum hominum diripiunt' (the 'Sermo ad raptores' at ff. 37–9 of Copenhagen, MS Gl. kgl. S. 1595 [4°] ?).

18 Bethurum III.7–9 ('And truly just as flood came before on account of sins, so will fire come over mankind also on account of sins, and for that purpose it will approach very eagerly'). Compare *De Die Iudicii*, Pope XVIII.60–85. The idea also occurs in Matthew xxiv.37, which Wulfstan had not treated in Bethurum II. I have already pointed out the reliance of Bethurum V on this sermon of Ælfric.

19 Bethurum III.51–3 ('that hypocrites and false Christians will quickly fall from right faith and bow eagerly to Antichrist and become his helpers with all their might'). J.E. Cross, 'Aspects of Microcosm ... ,'

Comparative Literature, 14 (1962), 21, remarks that this passage is 'merely an allegorical explanation,' by which he evidently means that neither Wulfstan nor other Anglo-Saxons believed that these signs had begun to appear.

20 Bethurum IV. Jost, *Wulfstanstudien*, pp. 188–94, discusses the difficulties at length, concluding finally that 'Die Untersuchung ergibt, dass sehr viel für und nur wenig gegen Wulfstans Verfasserschaft spricht. Ich nehme daher meinen anfänglichen Zweifel wieder zurück.' Bethurum at line 70 omits an exemplum from the Acts of Peter and Paul found in Napier XVI, 98.5–101.5 which Jost (pp. 191–2) and Pope (*MLN*, 74 [1959], 338–9) feel is so well integrated in the text as to belong to it. If so, it is the only real exemplum in Wulfstan's writing, and it seems to me to depart from the main course of the sermon. It tells of Peter and Paul's conflict with Simon Magus and illustrates the resistance of Christians to demonic temptation and deceit; in purpose, it is not unlike the additions (Pope XXIX) to Ælfric's *De Auguriis*, *LS*, I, XVII.

21 Lines 11–12, quoting Matthew xxiv.22, a verse not treated before by Wulfstan. Lines 1–2 reflect Matthew xxiv.21, quoted in Homily Ib; but despite this possible instance (I doubt Bethurum's reference to xxiv.14 as a source for lines 77ff.) one has the impression that Wulf-stan is not being guided by the Scriptural passages but by Ælfric and recollected sources.

22 Bethurum V.

23 Pope XVII.

24 Neither, however, follows the Vulgate exactly. In Matthew xxiv.15, Ælfric substitutes the *autem* of Mark xiii.14 for Matthew's *ergo*, and Wulfstan omits the conjunction altogether; Ælfric does not quote the rest of the Latin, but Wulfstan in vs. 17 omits the *autem* common to both Gospels and in vs. 19 *dies illi*, which brings him in some ways closer to Matthew's vs. 21. In the last instance, Ælfric may have led the way by conflating the Marcan text with Matthew or substituted it for Matthew. (I use for the Vulgate the Clementine ed., *Biblia Sacra Juxta Vulgatam Clementinam* [Paris, 1956]).

25 Bethurum Ia. 15ff.; Ib. 18ff.; IV.3ff. (a rather more remote allusion).

26 Bethurum Ia, Ib.

27 Bethurum V.14–16 ('La, nyde hit sceal eac on worulde for folces synnan yfelian swiðe, forðam nu is se tima þe Paulus se apostol gefyrn forsæde').

28 Bethurum V.44–7 ('A thousand years and more have now passed since Christ was with men in human likeness, and now Satan's bonds are extremely loose, and Antichrist's time near at hand, and therefore it is in the world the longer the weaker.')

29 Bethurum V.47–8 ('in the world things grow weaker the longer they

continue ... and the world is so much the worse'). See J.E. Cross, *Comparative Literature*, 14 (1964), 4–5. The topos also appears in *Sermo Lupi*, Bethurum xx.7ff., and in two of the other exegetical homilies: Ib.24 and III.14.

30 Pope xviii.345ff. and the note at p. 611. Pope and Bethurum agree that he is also using the Preface to *CH* I, and Pope suggests that Wulfstan's *scincræft* ('sorcery,' Bethurum v.71) may be influenced by Ælfric's use of the term at lines 257, 380, 390. See also the note at Pope, pp. 611–12 on the madness of Antichrist.

31 Bethurum v.77, suggested by Pope xviii.291.

32 See Bethurum, p. 292.

33 Bethurum, p. 292.

34 Mark xiii.20; Matthew xxiv.22 (also quoted in variant form in Bethurum iv.12ff.).

35 Napier viii is the Ælfric text. Wulfstan's adaptation is Bethurum ix.

36 Bethurum ix.107–51. The section is part of an addition to the Ælfrician material and probably to Wulfstan's original version.

37 Whitelock, ed., *Sermo Lupi ad Anglos*, pp. 7ff. sketches the historical background. Professor Whitelock has an excellent translation of the 'i' text (one of two used for the third version of Bethurum xx) in her vol. i of D.C. Douglas, ed., *English Historical Documents*, 855–9. It was the celebrity of the *Sermo ad Anglos*

coupled with its eloquent attack on the vices of the day which won Wulfstan alone among the English homilists a place in Ray C. Petry, *Christian Eschatology and Social Thought*, pp. 120–3. A.K. Brown believes the *Sermo ad Anglos* is based on Abbo of St-Germain-des-Près, *Sermo ad Milites*, which is to be found at ff.35–7 of the Wulfstan MS in Copenhagen.

38 Bethurum xx.7–12 [pp. 267ff.] ('Beloved men, realize what is true: this world is in haste and it approaches its end; and therefore in the world things go from bad to worse, and so it must of necessity deteriorate greatly on account of the people's sins before the coming of Antichrist, and indeed it will then be dreadful and terrible far and wide throughout the world. Understand well also that for many years now the devil has led astray this people too greatly.' – trans. Whitelock). The rubric reads, 'Sermo Lupi ad Anglos quando Dani maxime persecuti sunt eos, quod fuit anno millesimo .xiii. ab incarnatione Domini nostri Iesu Cristi,' and reflects the exile of Æthelred as well as the harassment suffered from the Danes.

39 Bethurum vi.199–207.

40 Bethurum vi, vii, ix instruct on the true faith, while viiia, b, c and ix are concerned with Baptism. Regularization of the secular clergy is dealt with in xa, b, c, and episcopal functions give rise to xiii–xviii. All contain hortatory elements based on

Wulfstan's legal studies, and paganism is a theme touched several times (as in xx).

41 This is a theme of the second half of Bethurum ib as well, however, for he says the clergy must prepare their people even though they might be dead by the time of Antichrist's reign.

42 None of the sermons, as I read Professors Bethurum and Whitelock, dates definitely from the reign of Cnut when the situation was somewhat improved.

43 Bethurum xiii.8–11.

44 In MS Corpus Christi College, Cambridge, 201 (Ker, *Catalogue* 49), quoted in Bethurum, p. 399. According to Ker, p. 83, some notes in this volume are by John Joscelyn, Archbishop Parker's secretary. The comment reflects the desire of the Parker circle to find doctrinal details in pre-Conquest documents closer to the teachings of the reformed English church than to those of the High Middle Ages.

45 Bethurum iv.24–30 ('Therefore there is no man who is not sinful, and every man must suffer sorely whether here or elsewhere according as he has earned through sins. And therefore is the persecution of good men so severe, for they must be quickly cleansed and purified before the great Doom comes. Those who have been dead for a hundred years or yet more may well not be cleansed'). Despite the issues discussed above in note 20, there is no

stylistic reason to question this passage.

46 See Bethurum x and xvia, b.

47 On the other hand, it has to be admitted that Wulfstan passes over opportunities to meet this subject. One striking example, albeit in a rather different vein, is his treatment of the communion of saints in Bethurum vii.90–3. In an early version Wulfstan had combined the two interpretations of this troublesome article of the Western Creed, but, as Bethurum notes (p. 308), he dropped the sacramental reference in a subsequent version: 'And we gelyfað þæt haligra gemana sy. Halige men habbað gemanan her on life on godum dædum, and hy habbað eac gemanan on þæm toweardan þurh ða edlean þe heom þonne God gyfð.' *Toweard* ('future') is ambiguous, but the reference is probably to fellowship after Doomsday.

48 Bethurum vi.207–17. ('And immediately thereafter, as books tell us, will come the great Doom, and this world will end. At that Doom, indeed, must each man have such recompense as he formerly earned in his life: and those who do God's will here, they shall then have eternal bliss in the heavenly kingdom; and those who now follow the devil here and his bad teaching, they will then go with the devil into the destruction of punishment in hell. Lo, beloved men, let us do as there is great need for us . . .').

49 Bethurum vii.104–58. See also

vIIa.33–41. The latter, incidentally, in lines 29–30 makes the Harrowing of Hell explicit in a paraphrase of the Western Creed: 'and we gelyfað þæt he to helle ferde and ðærof gehergode eal þæt he wolde.'

PART FOUR

1 Jeffrey Burton Russell, *Dissent and Reform in the Early Middle Ages* (Berkeley, 1965), p. 247. Russell, pp. 243–6, suggests that the exposure of England to outside attack throughout the Early Middle Ages may be responsible for its remarkable immunity from heretical controversy.
The evidence is summarized in *Traditio*, 21 (1965), 117–65.
The story is retold by Ælfric, *St Swithun, LS*, I, xxI.21–94; most recently ed. by G.I. Needham, *Ælfric, Lives of Three English Saints.* The recent excavations at Winchester conducted by Martin Biddle have vastly increased our appreciation of the importance of the shrine of Swithun at the Old Minster (see *Tenth-Century Studies*, ed. Parsons, pp. 136–8).

4 What Ælfric would have considered the contamination of his work by juxtaposition with materials that appear in Blickling and Vercelli is documented in the analyses of the mss by Ker and Pope. Further instances are mentioned below.

5 Instances in which Ælfric's works were adapted to different ends are cited below, notes 19, 20. The problem of imitators of Wulfstan is discussed by Jost, *Wulfstanstudien*, pp. 110ff., 271.

6 See H.E.J. Cowdrey, *The Cluniacs and the Gregorian Reform* (Oxford, 1970).

7 See, in addition to the homilies indexed in Ker's *Catalogue*, the dissertations of Tristram and Healy. British Museum, MS Cotton Vespasian D.xiv is an example of a late and mixed, but primarily Ælfrician, collection (ed. Rubie D-N. Warner, *Early English Homilies*, E.E.T.S., O.S., 152 [London, 1917]; see also Max Förster, 'Der Inhalt der altenglischen Handschrift Vespasianus D.xiv,' *Englische Studien*, 54 [1920], 46–68, and Rima Handley, 'British Museum MS Cotton Vespasian D.xiv,' *N&Q*, 219 [1974], 243–50.

8 See notes 19, 20, below.

9 Malcom Godden observes that Ælfric was treated as 'almost a learned authority' in the eleventh century by those who plundered his writings for their own ends (*ASE*, 4 [1975], 64). On Ælfric holdings in libraries, see Helmut Gneuss, 'Englands Bibliotheken im Mittelalter und ihr Untergang,' *Festschrift für Walter Hübner*, ed. Dieter Riesner and Gneuss (Berlin, 1964), pp. 91–121 at 97–9. The suggestion of Hurt (*Ælfric*, p. 11) that one might speak of an 'Age of Ælfric' is

rightly criticized by John C. Pope in a review, *Speculum*, 49 (1974), 344–7.

10 See Vleeskruyer, *Life of St Chad*, pp. 18–22.

11 Ibid.; see also Nora K. Chadwick in *Celt and Saxon: Studies in the Early British Border* (Cambridge, 1963), pp. 335–46, for suggestions on the relations of this largely hypothetical Mercian tradition to the Celtic church.

12 See Henry Mayr-Harting, *The Coming of Christianity to Anglo-Saxon England* (London, 1972), pp. 83–6.

13 Note the prominence of Caesarius and of the pseudo-Augustinian sermons, for example, in the Homiliary of Alan of Farfa and the relative lack of such items in Paul the Deacon.

14 See Altaner, *Patrologie*, pp. 440–2; J.M. Wallace-Hadrill, *The Long-Haired Kings and Other Studies in Frankish History* (London, 1962), pp. 49–70; Laistner, *Thought and Letters in Western Europe*, pp. 129–35; and Pierre de Labriolle, *Histoire de la Littérature Latine Chrétienne*, 2 vols. (3rd ed., rev. G. Bardy; Paris, 1947), II, 791–8.

15 Future study and editing of the Irish exegetical materials discussed by Bernhard Bischoff ('Wendepunkte in der Geschichte der lateinischen Exegese im Frühmittelalter,' *Sacris Erudiri*, 6 [1954], 189–281) may help to establish some connections in this regard.

See Mayr-Harting, cited above; Kathleen Hughes, 'Evidence for Contacts between the Churches of the Irish and English from the Synod of Whitby to the Viking Age,' in *England Before the Conquest*, ed. Clemoes and Hughes, pp. 49–67. A seminal article by David N. Dumville, 'Biblical Apocrypha and the Early Irish: a Preliminary Investigation,' (*Proceedings of the Royal Irish Academy*, 73C [1973], 299–338) suggests Spanish sources may also have been very important.

16 See Wilhelm Levison, *England and the Continent in the Eighth Century*, The Ford Lectures, 1943 (Oxford, 1956), pp. 148–72.

17 See note 13 above.

18 Altaner, *Patrologie*, pp. 430–6; Laistner, *Thought and Letters*, pp. 103–11; Labriolle, *Histoire*, II, 804–15; F. Homes Dudden, *Gregory the Great: His Place in History and Thought*, 2 vols. (London, 1905). On the problem of miracles and purgatory in *Dialogues*, see Gatch, *Studia Patristica*, 10 (1970), 77–83.

19 Pope, pp. 770–4.

20 Szarmach, *ASE*, 1 (1972), 183–92.

21 See the discussion of Robin Flower in *The Exeter Book*, pp. 85–90.

22 See Pope's analyses of the mss, in his Introduction.

23 An interesting and analogous case of conflict of traditions is noted by Kenneth Sisam in his discussion of the Old English *Seasons for Fasting* in *Studies*, pp. 48–50. The poem (ca. 990–1010) reflects a conflict

between the dating of the Ember Days as supposedly appointed by Gregory the Great and the more modern Roman dating used in the continental monasteries. A ms related to Ælfric notes the difference impartially, but the Wulfstanian code Æthelred VI settles in favour of the Gregorian use. The radical reformers probably favoured the continental practice, but the more native tradition evidently prevailed for a time.

24 See William W. Heist, *The Fifteen Signs before Doomsday.*

25 Derivation chart in Louise Dudley, 'An Early Homily on the "Body and Soul" Theme,' *JEGP*, 8 (1909), 225–53; see also Robert W. Ackerman, '*The Debate of the Body and the Soul* and Parochial Christianity,' *Speculum*, 37 (1962), 541–65. On the *Visio Pauli*, see Theodore Silverstein, *Visio Sancti Pauli: The History of the Apocalypse in Latin together with Nine Texts*, Studies and Documents, ed. Kirsopp Lake and Silva Lake, 4 (London, 1935); Healey diss.

26 See Jean Leclercq, *L'Amour des Lettres et le Désir de Dieu*. The point is well taken if one allows for the changes of outlook detailed by Southern, *The Making of the Middle Ages.*

27 See the arts. s.v. 'Feu' by A. Michel

in *Dictionnaire de Théologie Catholique* and my article in *Perspectives on Death*, ed. Mills, pp. 99–136. On this and other changing attitudes toward death in the Middle Ages, see the first two of the important lectures of Philippe Ariès, *Western Attitudes toward Death in the Middle Ages.*

28 *The Making of the Middle Ages*, p. 222. As allusion has been made to the *peregrinus* motif, it may be noted here that Southern distinguishes the exile of the *peregrini*, their 'removal from friends and homeland, rather than a search for new experiences and adventures,' from the 'movement' of later 'pilgrims and seekers.' The rest of this paragraph depends on Southern.

29 It is sometimes objected to this reading of Thomas that the point is belied by continuing interest in the Judgment in later medieval theology and in such seminal writings as the *Sentences* of Peter Lombard, but it seems to me almost preordained that dialectical scholastic thought would move in this direction; it did, although the picture of the ultimate Judgment was never abandoned.

30 '*Sermo Humilis*' and 'Latin Prose in the Early Middle Ages,' in *Literary Language and Its Public in Late Latin Antiquity and in the Middle Ages.*

31 Oxford, 1970.

APPENDIX

1 Bibliothek der angelsächsischen Prosa, 9 (1914; rpt. Darmstadt, 1966). The rpt. contains a supplement to the introduction by Peter

Clemoes which, at p. cxxvii, updates Fehr's comments on the ms. Further comments on the ms. by Clemoes are to be found in 'The Old English Benedictine Office, Corpus Christi College, Cambridge, MS 190, and the Relations between Ælfric and Wulfstan: A Reconsideration,' *Anglia*, 78 (1960), 265–83 at 273–75, 277–79, 280–82; and in pp. xxviii–xxix of the supplement to the introduction of Bruno Assmann, ed., *Angelsächsische Homilien und Heiligenleben*, Bibliothek der angelsächsischen Prosa, 3 (1889; rpt. 1964).

2 'MS Boulogne-sur-Mer 63 and Ælfric,' *MÆ*, 26, 65–73.

3 'MS Boulogne-sur-Mer 63 and Ælfric's First Series of *Catholic Homilies*,' *JEGP*, 65, 482–90.

4 'El Prognosticum Futuri Saeculi de San Julián de Toledo,' *Analecta Sacra Tarraconensia*, 30 (1957), 5–61 [pp. 19–39 contain a catalogue of mss. of *Prog.* of which No. 158 at p. 37 is *BE*; on pp. 44–57, there is a list of medieval catalogues which mention *Prog.*, including at No. 13, p. 45, the 12th-century catalogue of St Bertin – perhaps the ms. of *BE*]; 'St Julian of Toledo in the Middle Ages,' *Journal of the Warburg and Courtauld Institutes*, 21 (1958), 7–26.

5 The list is Hillgarth's, 'St Julian,' p. 17, and the subsequent discussion is based on the same article.

6 Ibid., p. 20.

7 Ibid., pp. 22–3. The list of books – from a twelfth-century cartulary – is printed by M.R. James, *List of Manuscripts formerly in Peterborough Abbey* (Oxford, 1926), p. 2, item 4 ('Proviso futurarum rerum'). Another Peterborough catalogue of the early twelfth century lists 'pronosticon futuri seculi,' and James (p. 28, item 40) suggests that the items may be identical.

8 Riccardo Quadri, ed., *I Collectaneo di Erico di Auxerre*, Spicilegium Friburgense, 2 (Freiburg, Switzerland, 1966), 65 and 140–57.

9 See Pope, p. 169.

10 Lapidge, 'The Hermeneutic Style,' *ASE*, 4 (1975), 67. See also A. Campbell, ed., *The Chronicle of Æthelweard*, Medieval Classics (London, 1962), pp. xlv ff.

11 Lapidge, p. 101.

12 The Latin version of *LS*, I (*Christmas*) in MS Boulogne 63, described by Enid Raynes (*MÆ*, 26 [1957], 65–73), who is preparing an edition.

13 Raynes, 73.

14 Fehr, *Hirtenbriefe*, pp. 34–57. On the date, see Clemoes, 'Chronology,' pp. 241ff.

15 At f. 1, there is the notation 'De Libraria Sancti Bertini' in a fourteenth- or fifteenth-century hand; at f. 2, in an earlier hand (thirteenth century?), there is an unusual form of the St Bertin library's anathema (on which see further note 19, below); on the last folio of the ms there are references to St Bertin's in scribbles. At the top of f. 1, there is a cataloguer's notation of the first word on f. 2; such marks were sometimes intended to distinguish

multiple copies of the same work in a given library. At the bottom of f. 1, an incomplete and inaccurate fourteenth- or fifteenth-century table of contents:

Quaedam excerpta de sanctis doctoribus.

Item Augustinus super Apocalipsim.

Item epistola Augustinus ad Paulinum de ratione animae.

Item eiusdem epistola ad Conscensium episcopum.

The only trace left by readers of the text of the Excerpts is on f. 6^v: lines 6–end are marginally marked, with special emphasis at lines 17–18 and lesser emphasis at 26–28.

16 Ministre de l'Instruction Publique, *Catalogue Général des Manuscrits des Bibliothèques Publiques des Départements*, IV (Paris, 1872), 565ff. The ms is described at p. 613.

17 Gustavus Becker, *Catalogi Bibliothecarum Antiqui* (Bonn, 1885), Catalogue 77, Item 128, at p. 183. The suggestion is Hillgarth's; but on the basis of his own evidence concerning the ubiquity of Julian's tract, one must wonder that so important a foundation as St Bertin did not own a complete copy.

18 The evidence outlined below is chiefly drawn from Philip Grierson, 'The Relations between England and Flanders before the Norman Conquest,' *TRHS*, 4th Ser., 23 (1941), 71–112. But see also Alistair Campbell, ed., *Encomium Emmae Reginae*, Royal Historical Society, Camden 3rd Ser., 72 (London, 1949), pp. xixff., 37 (*Enc. Em.* II.20–1); Frank Barlow, ed., *Vita Ædwardi Regis qui apud Westmonasterium requiescit*, Medieval Texts (London, 1962), pp. xlivff., 91–111; and Barlow, *The English Church, 1000–1066*, pp. 82, 220f., and *Edward the Confessor* (London, 1970), p. 246.

19 Fehr, *Hirtenbriefe*, p. x. This entry is now badly faded, and I must rely on Fehr's transcription of it save to confirm that the hand is clearly earlier than that of the medieval marginalia on f. 1.

20 Fehr, ibid., reports 25 by 17.5 cm. My figures are based on my own measurement.

21 I make this observation after comparing the script with the samples given by T.A.M. Bishop, *English Caroline Minuscule*, Oxford Palaeographical Handbooks (Oxford, 1971), esp. plate 6a.

INDICES

Ælfric: Citations

NOTE The works are listed and classified in the order of the Ælfric canon as printed by Pope, pp. 137–45, and Clemoes, 'Chronology,' pp. 214–19. As in my notes, I cite Thorpe by volume and first page for *CH* I–II. (P) indicates sermons on the pericope. Items in the canon to which there is no reference are omitted.

Wulfstan: Citations

General Index